Luminos is the Open Access monograph publishing program from UC Press. Luminos provides a framework for preserving and reinvigorating monograph publishing for the future and increases the reach and visibility of important scholarly work. Titles published in the UC Press Luminos model are published with the same high standards for selection, peer review, production, and marketing as those in our traditional program. www.luminosoa.org

AMERICAN CROSSROADS

Edited by Earl Lewis, George Lipsitz, George Sánchez, Dana Takagi,
Laura Briggs, and Nikhil Pal Singh

Louder and Faster

Louder and Faster

Pain, Joy, and the Body Politic in Asian American Taiko

Deborah Wong

UNIVERSITY OF CALIFORNIA PRESS

University of California Press, one of the most distinguished university
presses in the United States, enriches lives around the world by advancing
scholarship in the humanities, social sciences, and natural sciences. Its
activities are supported by the UC Press Foundation and by philanthropic
contributions from individuals and institutions. For more information, visit
www.ucpress.edu.

University of California Press
Oakland, California

Suggested citation: Wong, D. *Louder and Faster: Pain, Joy, and the Body
Politic in Asian American Taiko*. Oakland: University of California Press,
2019. DOI: https://doi.org/10.1525/luminos.71

Library of Congress Cataloging-in-Publication Data

Names: Wong, Deborah Anne, author.
Title: Louder and faster : pain, joy, and the body politic in Asian American
    taiko / Deborah Wong.
Description: Oakland, California : University of California Press, [2019] |
    Series: American crossroads ; 55 | Includes bibliographical references and
    index. | This work is licensed under a Creative Commons
    [CC-BY-NC-ND] license. To view a copy of the license, visit
    http://creativecommons.org/licenses |
Identifiers: LCCN 2018058632 (print) | LCCN 2019000209 (ebook) | ISBN
    9780520973152 () | ISBN 9780520304529 (pbk. : alk. paper)
Subjects: LCSH: Taiko (Drum ensemble)--United States--History. | Asian
    American musicians. | Japanese American musicians.
Classification: LCC ML1038.T35 (ebook) | LCC ML1038.T35 W66 2019
    (print) | DDC 786.9089/956073--dc23
LC record available at https://lccn.loc.gov/2018058632

27   26   25   24   23   22   21   20   19
10   9   8   7   6   5   4   3   2   1

For the first generation of North American taiko players and teachers, with gratitude for your vision and ki.

For Rev. Shuichi (Tom) Kurai (1947–2018).

For my mother, Jean Carol Huffman Wong (1933–2018), who was always ready to go to a taiko gig.

here right here
we found our voices
made our moves
body and spirit
we took a great leap

in this space
taiko claimed rhythms
on this floor
we passed a century
and the beat goes on

reaching high
with our fingertips
we feel
freedom
in limitless space—

we slide, we fall
in this place we fly
on this floor
our roots are deep
women hold up half the sky

—GENIE NAKANO, "WOMEN HOLD UP HALF THE SKY"

People cannot create what they cannot imagine. Expressive culture is often a realm where new social relations can be rehearsed culturally before they can be implemented socially.

—GEORGE LIPSITZ, "A NEW BEGINNING"

CONTENTS

FIGURES

Figures are hosted at http://wonglouderandfaster.com.

EXAMPLES

Examples are hosted at http://wonglouderandfaster.com.

Video

1. Montage of Gary St. Germain's photos
2. Montage of Gary St. Germain's photos of Satori Daiko
3. Montage of Obon and *bon-odori* at Gardena Buddhist Church, August 4, 2007
4. Beverly Murata showing the contents of her gear bag
5. Satori Daiko members packing the van for a performance at the John Anson Ford Theatre in Los Angeles, August 22, 2007
6. Closing circle
7. Stop-action of the author's T-shirt collection
8. *Bon-odori* in Tsubetsu, Hokkaido, 2003
9. Michelle Fujii, Walter Clarke, and Kris Bergstrom teaching "Korekara" at the Southeast Japanese School and Community Center in Norwalk, California, 2005
10. Michelle Fujii teaching the "Korekara" dance to taiko players at the Southeast Japanese School and Community Center in Norwalk, California, 2005
11. "Korekara" debut at the North American Taiko Conference in Los Angeles, July 15, 2005
12. Rev. Tom Kurai and members of Satori Daiko discussing and volunteering for upcoming performances, August 2007
13. Satori Daiko playing "Aranami" at the Manzanar Pilgrimage

Audio

Introduction

Taiko is an invented tradition that has traveled far beyond its originating communities. Many kinds of people play it, mostly as a First World amateur recreation activity. For some Asian Americans, however, taiko is an important alternative academy, a repository of collective memory, and a third space—a public sphere where potential forms of social justice are acted out in plain sight.[1]

As I write this in 2015, it is the day of the annual Obon at Senshin Buddhist Temple. Obon is a yearly Japanese / Japanese American Buddhist gathering to commemorate the ancestors. Six years have passed since I stopped playing taiko seriously, but I still await the summer Obon season with joy, and the gathering at Senshin is probably my favorite—if it is possible to choose among so many, each with a unique character. Going to Obon at Senshin feels to me like returning to the root of North American taiko. The constellation of performance practices—dance, taiko, gathering together—are all explicitly articulated as Buddhist through Rev. Masao (Mas) Kodani's teachings, and this temple is home to one of the first taiko groups in the US, Kinnara Taiko. I can't wait to dance, to light a lamp in the courtyard, to enter the temple and burn incense, and to see the many taiko friends who will surely be there.[2]

I love how Japanese American Obon gatherings emphasize profound togetherness and a negation of self. As Rev. Mas has said, when you dance *bon-odori*—the unison circle dances that are central to Obon—"you're fully involved in what you are doing but . . . you're not watching yourself do it."[3] I wrote this book in that spirit, though of course you can't write without watching yourself do it. Nonetheless, my intent is to carry my community consciousness learned through taiko and bon-odori into this writing, with humility. I deliberately move in and out of theoretical language in this book because I need critical concepts and vocabulary to talk about the issues closest to my concerns. I write decidedly in the first person not only because taiko has been an intensely personal experience for me but also because I aim to write about it in the grounded way it demands. While one could say this about any music anywhere, taiko is so explicitly about the body and bodily experience that I have known from the first that this was the way I wanted to write about it.

This book is about the pleasures of playing taiko, but it is also about Asian American anger. Playing taiko has been one of the most joyful and fulfilling experiences I've ever had, but it is also interlaced with anger—and more than one kind of anger at that. My most driving question is how and why taiko is a key means for Asian American communities to articulate, declare, and affirm self-determination. Oliver Wang (2015) has wistfully written, "I find myself wanting to know more about the making of 'Asian-American-ness,' i.e. the internal, intra-community ways we've defined out place, our worth, our identities and cultures." Other Asian Americans stood with Japanese Americans in their fight for reparations for the mass incarceration during World War II: taiko was a key means to formulate intra–Asian American alliances and solidarity.[4] This book is fundamentally informed by my belief that that moment has not passed and that the Asian American Movement is still alive and needed.

Although I do not address Japanese taiko to any great extent in this book, I am provoked in all the right ways by Yoshitaka Terada's (2011a) work on how diasporic Okinawans and Buraku (low-caste "untouchables") have, like Japanese Americans and other Asian Americans, turned to taiko in search of self-determination; they seek a way to speak differently despite the relentless power of the nationalist "Japanese gaze" (247). Similarly, the taiko scenes I know best are acted out under not one but two imperial gazes, those of the US and Japan, yet North American taiko emerged from encounters *between* communities: Japanese Americans and other Asian Americans (hereafter Japanese/Asian Americans), Japanese Americans and African Americans, Japanese/Asian Americans and Latin@s, and—inevitably—Asian Americans and White Americans. Some of these encounters took/take place in the checkered interethnic communities of greater Los Angeles; others were/are *encuentro*, that is, planned, intentional convenings meant to bring new communities into existence.[5]

Some of this book is written "as if it were a memory," in the words of the poet Garrett Hongo (2007). I will come back to that feeling and to Hongo's words in chapter 3, on the summertime Obon dances. While my research methodology has been profoundly ethnographic, my work on Asian American expressive culture has taught me that what we know about ourselves, what we think we know about ourselves, and what we have been told about ourselves are interconstitutive. Cultural and political self-determination does not stand outside the "deathly embrace" of orientalism (Ma 2000) but is in sustained, irrevocable, and creative conversation with it. Taiko is fatally part of that dialogue. Taiko is beautiful, flawed, powerful, and imperfect. It offers a set of potentialities and political promises and it is easily overrun, depending on whether you regard it as a room into which you are invited[6] or as an open field of opportunity.

*   *   *

It's 2005. We just played for a wedding at Yamashiro, the landmark restaurant high on a hill in Hollywood, built in 1911–14 to resemble a Japanese palace. It serves "CalAsian" cuisine and is exquisitely, over-the-top exotic, with dark green tile floors and heavy wooden doors. A koi pond and a jewel-like garden with bonsai and miniature maples glow in the inner courtyard, open to the sky. Any number of Hollywood films and television series have been shot here, including scenes in *Sayonara* (1957) and *Memoirs of a Geisha* (2005). Tables line two of the courtyard's walls, and in front of the third is a small area under an overhang that serves as a stage. We have played in this courtyard many times. Today it holds us—a few members of the Satori Daiko group—a string trio, and a wedding party. The bride is Japanese American and the groom is Jewish, both in their forties. Part of the bride's family is South Asian, so the restaurant is full of happy, multiethnic, beautifully dressed people, including small children of all stripes, who poke around the garden and get wet when the sprinklers suddenly come on. I am unexpectedly and deeply moved when the huppah—the Jewish wedding canopy—is carried out by four friends, men and women, who hold it up through the entire ceremony. The rabbi sings the Song of Songs; the bride's parents escort her to the huppah; the groom can't stop smiling. We play them all in. The string trio plays Pachelbel. The bride's South Asian relatives come up and sing a Karnatak wedding song—I hear the name Sita in the lyrics, bride of brides. The rabbi places a wine glass under the groom's foot, he stomps on it, I shout *Mazel tov!* with everyone else, and we immediately start playing "Oni" (Demon) as the wedding party begins their exit procession, crossing in front of us only inches from my *chudaiko*. Several of them look at us, catch our eyes, and smile. I think, This is why I play taiko, and this is why I love playing taiko in California. This is how it works, in a restaurant built to provide orientalist splendor for Hollywood stars, now a backdrop for this wedding of genuine feeling between two communities—Jewish Americans and Japanese Americans—that struggle with out-marriage (Shinagawa and Pang 1996), for these people who have created new ways to draw together the dissimilar elements of their lives and their families.

Whenever we perform, audience members come up afterward, and someone inevitably says, "You must get rid of a lot of stress by hitting those drums!" *Yes*, we say agreeably, *yes, we do.* Among ourselves, however, we rarely talk about taiko as a stress reliever: we are much more likely to touch on the joy of performance and the things that went hilariously wrong. We don't discuss anger. I sought out taiko with a deep desire to put my joy and my rage together. As I have written elsewhere (Wong 2008), I saw San Jose Taiko perform in the 1990s and was instantly consumed by the desire to be Asian American in the strong, graceful, loud, joyful ways that they exemplify.

Much of this book reflects on my experiences as a member of an ensemble called Satori Daiko. I began studying taiko in 1997 with Rev. Shuichi Thomas Kurai, a Japanese American Zen Buddhist priest and taiko teacher (see fig. 1, Rev. Tom Kurai, at *http://wonglouderandfaster.com*). Since then I have spent time with taiko ensembles in Chicago, North Carolina, and Southern California. Rev. Tom—as he was known to his students, and as I refer to him throughout this book—was the founder and director of the Taiko Center of Los Angeles. The TCLA was the sum of Rev. Tom's many activities, including his taiko classes in several locations and a constant stream of performances. In 1999 Rev. Tom created a performing group drawn from students in his various classes, which he named Satori Daiko, or "Enlightenment Taiko." Satori is the flash of understanding posited in Zen Buddhism as an ephemeral moment of comprehension. It is attainable through meditation (zazen), and Zen Buddhist teachings suggest that training and practice can result in satori, though the discipline required is substantial. The name Satori Daiko thus signals a Zen Buddhist orientation.

At that time, Southern California had about twenty taiko groups, so Satori Daiko became part of a dynamic local community of taiko practitioners. I was a founding member and was immersed in the group until 2009: I attended weekly rehearsals and performed constantly, sometimes several times a week. I wish I had kept a diary of all our performances; my conservative estimate is that I performed more than two hundred times in those ten years. Some performances were full-length proscenium stage events (e.g., at Pomona College and in the Aratani Theatre in Little Tokyo, Los Angeles), but most were shorter, usually with only several Satori members, at cultural festivals, private events such as weddings and parties, school assemblies, Asian supermarket openings, and the like. I went to Japan four times on study tours led by Rev. Tom for the members of Satori and the TCLA, each time in August during Obon season (in 2001, 2003, 2005, and 2006). On each trip, Rev. Tom led us through two intense weeks of taiko-related experiences. We participated in Obon in Tsubetsu, Hokkaido; attended the Earth Celebration organized by Kodo on Sado Island; had workshops with renowned taiko teachers, including Kiyonari Tosha (one of the founders of Sukeroku Daiko); met Rev. Tom's *minyo* (folk music) teacher Sudo-sensei in Morioka, Iwate Prefecture, and participated in a Kurokawa Sansa Odori rehearsal with her; attended many *matsuri* (festivals); performed at a theme park (Shima Spain Village Parque España) in Mie Prefecture; toured the Asano taiko factory and showroom in Hakusan, Ishikawa Prefecture; visited the famous Buraku neighborhood and TaikoMasa factory in Naniwa Ward, Osaka, and saw the Buraku ensemble Ikari Taiko perform in their annual matsuri; and shopped in the Miyamoto taiko showroom in Asakusa, Tokyo, every time. In sum, I had extraordinary experiences thanks to Rev. Tom.

WHAT TAIKO IS AND WHAT IT COULD BECOME

Taiko is a decidedly contemporary form of ensemble drumming that is built on the bones of Japanese festival drumming. This "new tradition" is called *kumi-daiko*, "group taiko," because taiko ensembles usually feature numerous drums of at least three different sizes, often played in a fast, loud, virtuosic, athletic style that is quite unlike the dignified, minimalist solo drumming that continues to accompany Shinto and Buddhist ritual. In some ways taiko is very old, but in most of the ways that matter, it is a transnational, globalized, dynamic tradition that changes by the day. In Japan it is part of nationalist folklore movements. In the Americas it is a means by which communities of Japanese descent explore heritage and assert new diasporic sensibilities. More broadly, taiko has attracted multiethnic interest but is strongly and self-consciously Asian American . . . for now, though I suspect that moment is passing even as I write. It exemplifies the performative: it is a loud, physical platform for the emergence of newly racialized and gendered identities in the environment of post-1960s US and Canadian multicultural politics. Taiko does things for the people involved in its praxis—complicated identity work is always part of any performance activity, anywhere. This is the performative function of performance: performance changes accepted social realities and can either maintain or transform how people think about themselves and their relationships to others. Twenty-first-century kumi-daiko is particularly embroiled in performative identity work, regardless of location. The North American anthropologists Millie Creighton (2004, 2008) and Shawn Bender (2005) have considered its role in postwar Japanese definitions of "tradition" and *furusato* (home village, rural roots). Yoshitaka Terada (2001, 2005, 2008, 2010, 2011a, 2011b) has done long-term research on taiko in three minority communities: Okinawans and Buraku in Osaka, and Asian Americans in North America. The US ethnomusicologist Mark Tusler (2003) has charted the history of three formative Japanese American taiko groups in California. Kumi-daiko emerged in the 1950s and 1960s as a "new" tradition in a way that outlined a peculiarly (un)acknowledged discursive relationship between old and new, "tradition" and the innovative (Fujie 2001). Ideas about race, ethnicity, and gender are played out through taiko in a transpacific flow of performative exchange.

I used the word *tradition* repeatedly in the last paragraph, fully aware that this term, like *authenticity,* can only ever have quotation marks around it, thanks to almost fifty years of poststructural scholarship focused on culture in motion through representational play (Bendix 1997). I don't regard kumi-daiko as traditional, though some of its practitioners very much want it to be, and some of its elements are rooted in identifiable heritage practices; in my view, kumi-daiko combines, moves between, and exceeds the traditional and the popular. It reveals how First World locations allow kumi-daiko practitioners to play with and across those ideologies. As Tim Taylor (2016, 90) writes, in First World "neoliberal capitalist culture, authenticity has become a kind of floating ideology that is used to animate a variety of other ideologies/discourses." Kumi-daiko is constituted through a far-flung community of practice, and that, for me, is the point, and why I think it appropriate to refer to it as a tradition (which is not so traditional). Despite the range of styles and the dynamism of contemporary experimentation in taiko, its practitioners often share practices, ideas, and values. What's more, those shared things are often quite important to its practitioners. I thus argue that taiko, or twenty-first-century kumi-daiko, is a tradition, though one that constantly changes. My decision to use the term is no retrograde return to hardened categories of music but rather an acknowledgment that these thousands of practitioners mostly see themselves as connected. They believe themselves—mostly—to be a community of practice, though across vast geocultural spaces.

Taiko is now a hugely popular music that has mushroomed into a world phenomenon. In 2000, there were perhaps 150 taiko groups in North America; by 2005, there were perhaps 200; at the time of this writing, there are approximately 300.[7] By way of contrast, Chie Otsuka (1997, 17) estimated that Japan had perhaps 5,000 taiko groups in 1997. Japan has more kumi-daiko groups than North America, Latin America, Europe, and Australia combined, but interest in taiko outside Japan is clearly on the upswing.

An accurate count of taiko groups doesn't exist, though more information is available with each passing year. All attempts to create taiko databases have relied on self-registration, leading to incomplete data. Three well-known websites for taiko enthusiasts offer fascinating (though conflicting) information. The Rolling Thunder website, active from 1996 to 2010 (and no longer available), was long authoritative and included the first attempt at a directory of taiko groups worldwide. In August 2014, the Discover Nikkei site listed 151 groups in the US, 22 in Canada, 11 in Germany, 10 in England, 4 in Belgium, 3 in Brazil, 2 in Australia, 2 in New Zealand, 1 in Argentina, 1 in the Netherlands, and 1 in Peru, for a total of 208.[8] At that time, TaikoSource (*https://taikosource.com/*) listed 61 groups in the US, 26 in Germany, 22 in England, 20 in Japan, 16 in Canada, 7 in Switzerland, 4 in Australia, 4 in Belgium, 4 in Brazil, 4 in France, 4 in New Zealand, 2 in Hungary, 2 in Italy, 2 in Scotland, 1 in Argentina, 1 in Hong Kong, 1 in Ireland, 1 in Singapore, 1 in South Africa, 1 in Spain, 1 in Sweden, and 1 in Ukraine. In February 2019, TaikoSource listed 487 taiko groups worldwide (including only 20 in Japan, which is obviously much too low and the result of self-reporting). In 2013 and 2016 the Taiko Community Alliance conducted an online census for groups outside Japan, and the 2016 results showed that the US—and California in particular—contains the most taiko groups (of those that participated), that the UK dominates the scene beyond North America, that two-thirds of taiko players are women, and that the "Asian American" versus "White" participant ratio is about 4:3.[9] The rapidly rising number of White/Anglo taiko players in North America and Europe is part of the scene's explosive expansion.

The US west coast has a critical mass of taiko groups, and Southern California has a particularly large number. Taiko groups in Southern California receive constant invitations to play in public. City fairs and festivals require a steady stream of colorful ethnic music and dance. Corporations often contract taiko groups to play for parties and receptions. The vibrant Asian communities of Southern California—of which there are many, from East to Southeast to South Asian—not only support their own unique traditions but often emphasize intra-Asian connections, so it isn't unusual during the Lunar New Year season, for example, for taiko performers to run from one celebration to another, some hosted by the Vietnamese communities in Orange County and others organized by the huge, diverse Chinese communities of the San Gabriel Valley. We are accustomed to sharing green rooms with everyone from community-based martial arts schools to Korean *p'ungmul* musicians to Hawaiian hula groups.

The memory and trauma of the Japanese American incarceration camps is quite real and immediate. The last generation of internees is passing, but the annual community pilgrimages to the incarceration camp sites of Manzanar and Tule Lake continue, and taiko plays an essential role in them. One of the most important driving impulses for the earliest taiko groups in the 1970s was the anger that the Sansei (third-generation Japanese Americans) felt toward the incarceration. Many California taiko groups are based in Japanese Buddhist temples and are explicitly conceived as part of Buddhist practice, inextricably bound up with the deepest community-based practices. The annual explosion of summer Obon festivals at Japanese American Buddhist temples is vivid evidence that some of the oldest ritual contexts for taiko are alive and well . . . and changing in all the ways that point to cultural vitality: there is new as well old repertoire, accepted as well as emergent lines of teaching and transmission, and so on.

In sum, taiko is a casebook example of a heritage music that is anything but endangered. Its Japanese American community base is both deep and broad; a young generation of Japanese American practitioners and teachers is much in evidence; informed pan–Asian American participation is widespread. This is the stuff of which folklorists dream: a traditional practice that has been sustained by its own communities for real reasons, shepherded by any number of thoughtful teachers. Taiko is owned by its communities in all the ways that point to cultural sustainability (Schippers and Grant 2016). It has strong and explicit systems for teaching and learning; its musicians have a diverse range of positions within the far-flung community; and its practitioners have shared core values as well as flexible approaches to recontextualization and cross-cultural influences.

(PRE)HISTORIES

Taiko is a postwar tradition of Japanese drumming that is also Japanese American and Asian American. It is loud, physical, and powerfully expressive. It is a deeply mediated world music; it is both very old and quite contemporary; it is a fusion of different musical influences; it is folkloricized; and it is a global phenomenon, with approximately three hundred groups in North America and perhaps five thousand in Japan. I played taiko for twelve years and have spent more than a decade writing about it (Wong 2004, 2005, 2006, 2008). This book mostly addresses taiko in Southern California, particularly in greater Los Angeles. It focuses on how and why Asian Americans drum in environments defined by pervasive, banal multiculturalism and still somehow, sometimes, manage to open principled spaces of Japanese/Asian American self-awareness. This sonic and corporeal social justice work may or may not be intentional or explicit. The words available to describe this work are many, each powerful in different ways. Such critical work done by academics and activists has been characterized as antisubordination, antisubjugation, anticaste, antiracist. From a legal perspective, the point is equal citizenship. Critical race theory first emerged from civil rights legal scholarship for good reason. As Balkin and Siegel (2003, 1) write, "Antisubordination theorists contend that guarantees of equal citizenship cannot be realized under conditions of pervasive social stratification and argue that law should reform institutions and practices that enforce the secondary social status of historically oppressed groups." Several of the first Japanese American taiko groups (especially Kinnara and San Jose Taiko) were driven by postincarceration sensibilities and were directed toward exactly such questions. As Joe Schloss puts it, ethnomusicologists study "the way people use art—especially music—to develop new perspectives on social, cultural and political issues."[10]

 Here is one brief example of how the sound of taiko is part of broader cultural and political social aesthetics. Taiko players use the onomatopoetic syllable *don* to indicate the strike of a drumstick (*bachi*) on a drumhead, especially and specifically a deep, loud strike (the syllable *ten* is used for an identical strike on a smaller, higher-pitched drum like the *shime*). *Don* is not confined to drums or music, however. It is part of the compound word *pikadon*, inextricably related to the atomic bombs dropped on Hiroshima and Nagasaki: *pika* means "a brilliant flash of light," and *don* is "a thunderous clap or boom." Those closest to the point of detonation experienced only pika and were no longer present to hear or feel the don. Pika preceded don on those days in 1945. Put together, these words onomatopoetically enact the need for new vocabulary to address the magnitude of the bombs' impact on Japanese society. Nobuko Miyamoto starts her 2015 song "Sembazuru," commemorating the seventieth anniversary of those atomic bombs, with a chorus of children repeating the phrase "PIKA-don, PIKA-don, PIKA-don-don."[11] Taiko doesn't refer to the bombs, nor did the bombs refer to taiko: rather, the noise of taiko is part of a broader sphere of powerful sound that is felt and heard. The syllable *don* indicates a place beyond translation but within sensate experience and knowledge.[12]

Taiko has centuries-old roots in Japanese Buddhism, as ritual practice and as festival music; in the 1950s and 1960s, young Japanese from the postwar generation reworked it into a folkloricized tradition featuring large ensembles of massed drums.[13] Simultaneously, these musicians infused the performance practice with the principles and choreographies of martial arts and transformed taiko—by then called kumi-daiko—into a presentational music for the proscenium stage. Kumi-daiko was brought to the United States in 1968 by Seiichi Tanaka, who founded San Francisco Taiko Dojo; his extended circle of students continues to form the pedagogical core of the North American taiko scene. Although bon-odori and certain kinds of matsuri drumming were already part of the Japanese American immigrant community, kumi-daiko appealed to Sansei in particular: its strength and presence spoke assertively against regimes of racist representation that young Asian Americans were then just beginning to address. At the time of this writing, North American taiko groups are mostly amateur, and they address the range of possible identifications (Buddhist, Japanese American, Asian American, non-Asian, non-Japanese, etc.) in different ways. In sum, the postwar Japanese tradition of taiko drumming was transported to North America fifty years ago and has become an important stage for Asian American identity work. The transpacific movement of taiko and taiko performers between Here and There remains central to its development and its problematics.

Most North American participants in this tradition use the term *taiko* in everyday conversation, though they are aware that the more proper term is *kumi-daiko,* for "group of drums." Kumi-daiko was specifically invented by Daihachi Oguchi in 1951, as explored in depth by Shawn Bender (2012, 48–52, 174–76). Some argue that the most accurate term is *wadaiko* (e.g., Pachter 2013), but the North American practitioners I know seldom use it. The uses and histories of these interrelated terms reflect the dynamism of the performance practices based on such drums. The drums themselves are unquestionably very old in Japan and directly linked to Buddhist and Shinto ritual practice, including sutra chanting and marking the ritual times of day (Malm 2000, 56–58, 72; De Ferranti 2000, 40–47). Percussion is intrinsic to matsuri traditions but, although regarded as traditional, has changed in response to local and national needs (Schnell 1999). For English-speaking North Americans, *taiko* is a Japanese word whose meaning is now widely known, along with *sushi, karate, teriyaki,* and *geisha*—all now phantasmatically familiar through uneven historical processes of exoticization and appropriation.

Only three English-language books have been published on taiko.[14] Heidi Varian's *The Way of Taiko* (2013) is an excellent introduction and is imbued with Tanaka-sensei's teachings. Shawn Bender's extraordinary monograph *Taiko Boom* (2012) is to date the most comprehensive English-language ethnographic study of taiko in Japan. Angela Ahlgren's *Drumming Asian America* (2018) is very close to my own questions and commitments, and I have learned much from our conversations over the years. A number of English-language dissertations and MA theses have addressed kumi-daiko in the US, Canada, and Latin America.[15] My work is indebted to Varian's and Bender's publications, but my thinking (and Ahlgren's) is located in twenty-first-century Asian American studies, and I emphasize intra–Asian and Asian American culture flows. As Kandice Chuh (2002, 292) argues, the Asian American transnation is "both *of* and *not of*" America, and it tells a story about Asian American "*difference* and *mutability* rather than *identity* and *fixity*," though audiences *and* taiko players often prefer the latter and deny the former. Japanese ≠ Japanese American ≠ Asian American, yet the points of contact, both real and imagined, are significant for both audiences and taiko players. Happily, I have learned much from the lively circle of other scholars who also do research on taiko, including Ahlgren, Susan Asai, Lei Ouyang Bryant, Linda Fujie, Masumi Izumi, Henry Johnson, Wynn Kiyama, Kim Noriko Kobayashi, Jennifer Milioto Matsue, Pachter, Kimberly Powell, Yoshitaka Terada, Tusler, Minako Waseda, and Paul Yoon. Virtually nothing I write about here is new or terra incognita, though I hope my critical lens is useful. The spectacular performativity of taiko has drawn all of us to some of the same materials, and we tend to share our excitement about the praxis *and* the cultural work of taiko. But each of us offers a different line in and a different way of configuring the relationships. Hopefully, the fellowship of taiko scholars has made this book better than it might have been.

Taiko effectively addresses Asian American needs for empowerment precisely because it is commoditized, mediated, and easily appropriated. Originally rooted in postwar Japanese American heritage politics, US taiko carries fewer and fewer specific meanings as more and more amateur players are neither Japanese American nor Asian American. Taiko teeters permanently on the edge of orientalist reabsorption (Taylor 2007, 140–60): no Southern California multicultural festival is complete without a taiko performance. Its slipperiness as a sign of authenticity is both its power and a vulnerability.

Each chapter in this book focuses on specific moments and practices. Chapters 1 and 2 reflect on a particular piece and some of the material objects that taiko players carry around and wear. Chapter 3 takes place within the huge circle dances through which Japanese Americans maintain cultural memory. Chapters 4 and 5 allow anger to surface. The latter addresses how some Asian American men draw on Japanese cinematic narratives and displays of physical prowess, exposing the Asian body to create old-but-new re-masculations. In chapter 6, I look at taiko players' valorization of pain (the pride taken in sore muscles and blisters) and the injury-without-end of the Japanese American incarceration. Chapter 7 addresses how taiko is reorientalized through commoditized celebrations of J-cool in a circuit of Pacific Rim goods and ideas—I take an irritated look at taiko as the new global groovy in my analysis of a car commercial. Throughout, I deploy postcolonial feminist approaches to consider how minoritarian anger refigures the body, whether through female taiko players' redefinition of "traditional" costumes or through new erotics of pleasure and participation. Intermittently, I reflect on the power and limitations of autoethnography. I attend closely to what taiko players say and do. I dwell anxiously on the hackneyed ethnic even as I look for signs that Asian American visibility matters.

Depending on how you count it, I am from the third generation of North American taiko players. I begin with the way the story is usually told. A Japanese martial artist named Seiichi Tanaka emigrated to the US in 1967, opened a dojo in San Francisco in 1968, and started teaching the contemporary tradition of Japanese drumming known as kumi-daiko or taiko. Many others have related the details (Varian 2013; Tusler 2003). Tanaka-sensei is one of the founding figures of North America kumi-daiko, and San Francisco Taiko Dojo remains a legendary organization. Tanaka-sensei instituted in the US a still-new "tradition" of drumming that emerged in Japan following World War II: in 1947, a young Japanese jazz drummer named Oguchi Daihachi returned home from the war and tried to play a piece on taiko at the local Shinto shrine based on embellished traditional matsuri patterns; in 1951 he founded Osuwa Daiko, widely regarded as the first kumi-daiko group. From the beginning, the music and the instruments reflected a combination of reconstituted traditionality and jazz sensibilities, the latter including solos and improvisation. In 1959, three Japanese musicians formed a Tokyo-festival-style (*Edo-bayashi*) kumi-daiko group and named it Yushima Tenjin Sukeroku Daiko, which eventually morphed into Oedo Sukeroku Daiko. Sukeroku performed in California in 1969, and Tanaka-sensei formed a close working relationship with its members that fundamentally informed his own style of playing and teaching. That same year, Tagayasu Den, a young Japanese "Marxist-Maoist agitator" (Bender 2012, 64), political organizer, and folklorist, founded the kumi-daiko ensemble Za Ondekoza on Japan's Sado Island with a group of idealistic young students who were disturbed by the postwar disappearance of Japanese traditional culture. Den developed a model for kumi-daiko as a way of life revolving around rigorous athleticism, communal living, self-sufficiency, and drum practice. His principle of *Sogakuron*—that "running and drumming are one, and a reflection of the drama and energy of life"[16]—is still the core of Ondekoza's philosophy and practice. In 1981, most of the founding members parted ways with Den (who maintained Ondekoza by recruiting new members) and founded Kodo, arguably still the most famous taiko group in the world, thanks to a relentless touring schedule.

Meanwhile, the Sansei activists Rev. Masao (Mas) Kodani and George Abe founded Kinnara Taiko at Senshin Buddhist Temple in Los Angeles in 1969. They were aware of Tanaka-sensei's activities four hundred miles away in San Francisco Taiko Dojo, but they were driven by Sansei rather than Japanese sensibilities and pursued an egalitarian Buddhist aesthetic that emphasized group improvisation. Rev. Tom Kurai and Kenny Endo were members of Kinnara for a short time. In 1973, PJ Hirabayashi and Roy Hirabayashi, a young Sansei couple, parted ways with San Francisco Taiko Dojo and founded San Jose Taiko to serve their local Japanese American community. Denver Taiko was founded by Japanese American activists in 1975, and its members sought training from San Jose Taiko, Tanaka-sensei, and Kinnara Taiko. The Japanese kumi-daiko master Etsuo Hongo founded L.A. Matsuri Taiko in 1977. Soh Daiko was founded in New York City by Alan and Merle Okada in 1979. At least three Japanese American Buddhist ministers played an important role in the formation of these early taiko groups: Rev. Hiroshi Abiko was a founding member of San Jose Taiko and later helped establish a group called Dharma Taiko at the Palo Alto Buddhist Temple; in New York City, the New York Buddhist Church chair Mamoru "Mo" Funai helped found Soh Daiko with the Okadas; and Kinnara Taiko remains fundamentally associated with Senshin Buddhist Temple and Rev. Mas.[17]

After Ondekoza performed in Seattle in 1980, local Japanese American and Chinese American activists started a taiko group there. More of Tanaka-sensei's students also formed their own groups, including Shasta Taiko in Northern California (founded by Jeanne Mercer and Russel Baba in 1985) and Sacramento Taiko Dan (founded by Tiffany Tamaribuchi in 1989). All these groups are still active and influential. In the 1990s the kumi-daiko scene grew considerably. Kyodo Taiko was established at the University of California, Los Angeles, in 1990, followed by Stanford Taiko and Jodaiko in 1992 (at Stanford University and the University of California, Irvine, respectively), thus kick-starting what is now known as the collegiate taiko scene. Although many of the early university-based groups had ties to Japanese American student clubs and Buddhist temples, they quickly became a magnet for other Asian American students. Portland Taiko was founded in 1994 by several former members of Stanford Taiko. The North American Taiko Conference (NATC) was first held in Los Angeles in 1997 and then every two years until 2011; after a pause, the Taiko Community Alliance has hosted it biannually since 2015. In 2005, there were perhaps 200 taiko groups in North America, with much smaller numbers in Western Europe and Australia; in 2016, the Taiko Census conducted by the Taiko Community Alliance documented 856 taiko groups, including 89 in Japan.

In short, taiko was picked up by many Japanese/Asian Americans in the 1970s and 1980s, especially on the West Coast, and subsequently became hugely popular in North America. North American taiko groups include college clubs, community groups sometimes based in Japanese Buddhist temples, all-woman groups, groups that emulate "Japanese" behaviors, groups that reject hierarchy, groups with entirely Japanese American members, groups with no Japanese Americans or Asian Americans at all, and more.

During the 2000s the North American taiko scene grew exponentially. More community-based groups were formed. More and more collegiate groups were founded. The first US-based professional taiko ensembles appeared in close order: TAIKOPROJECT was founded in 2000 and On Ensemble in 2002, both led by men then in their late twenties who had been very active in the collegiate taiko scene and wanted to keep going. These two ensembles were deliberately small and exclusive, unlike most community groups: one of their main purposes was to allow a select group of professional-level taiko players to perform mostly original work. Both quickly developed an intensive schedule of professional stage performance tours; their leaders almost instantly became coveted workshop teachers. Also in 2002, KODO Arts Sphere America (KASA) was created by Kodo's founding managing director. The organization describes itself as a nonprofit "grass-roots organization whose board members are also members of the North American taiko community" and whose "mission is to facilitate communication among community taiko groups, both in Japan and North America."[18] KASA's program director, Donna Ebata, has been a member of Kinnara Taiko since the early 1980s and is thus from the first generation of Japanese American taiko players.

Beginning around 2010, new groups appeared more and more rapidly. Links between the Japanese and North American taiko spheres intensified and the kumidaiko scene's deep primary location in Japanese/Asian American communities gave way to increasing numbers of groups focused on taiko as a practice rather than an extension of Japanese American communities. In 2011 the first annual East Coast Taiko Conference (ECTC), modeled on the NATC, was hosted by the collegiate group Yamatai at Cornell University, and it is now a well-established event, usually held on college campuses.[19] Asano Taiko U.S. opened in greater Los Angeles (Torrance) in August 2013. It houses the Los Angeles Taiko Institute (LATI), which offers classes taught primarily by two leading middle-generation American taiko players, Kris Bergstrom and Yuta Kato, and by a rich mix of visiting Japanese musicians, as well as practice sessions between classes, led by "coaches," or advanced performers.

Asano Taiko U.S. may be a game changer. The US outpost of one of the two major taiko companies in Japan, it instantly commanded attention with its showroom full of gorgeous taiko and two soundproof studios for classes. Behind the showroom is Kato Taiko, where the taiko maker Toshio Kato (Yuta Kato's father) repairs taiko and takes special orders. In 2014 Asano formed UnitOne, a professional taiko ensemble featuring top performers mostly in their thirties and early forties. When I attended the Twenty-Third Annual Taiko Gathering in August 2016—an event always held on the last day of Nisei Week in the JACCC Plaza in Los Angeles's Little Tokyo, with invited taiko groups performing thirty-minute sets—Asano Taiko came on near the end, featuring almost fifty performers from LATI's classes and workshops, and they performed a breathtaking set on their gorgeous drums. Asano Taiko U.S. may represent a certain formalization of instruction with its for-profit structure, as well as a consolidation of Japanese craftsmanship. Its massive, beautiful drums make other groups' small, lopsided, and often battered wine barrels look hopelessly amateurish, helping to nudge aside the DIY ethics and aesthetics that have guided North American taiko until now.

In the same year that Asano Taiko U.S. opened, the NATC faced a crisis. It had continued to grow and acquired a life of its own, with every other iteration hosted outside Los Angeles, including in Seattle and Sacramento. But just at the point when taiko players had come to rely on this biannual conference for authoritative instruction, its support structure was imperiled. The conference was one of many activities hosted and organized by the Japanese American Culture and Community Center in Los Angeles. For reasons too complicated to address here, the JACCC was no longer able to host the NATC after 2011. North American taiko players wanted and expected a conference in 2013, but the nonprofit structures established by the JACCC were essential to the conference's finances. In 2013 the NATC's Advisory Council created the Taiko Community Alliance and organized a three-day retreat to establish its mission and operations. The TCA hosted its first NATC in 2015, in Las Vegas.

Meanwhile, the World Taiko Gathering was held in Los Angeles in 2014, hosted by TAIKOPROJECT. Organized by Bryan Yamami, the founder and artistic director of TAIKOPROJECT, this conference was structurally identical to the preceding eight NATCs but carefully positioned to operationalize a "world" rather than a North American taiko scene. The event, which helped fill the void produced by the cancelation of the 2013 NATC, featured ensembles from Mexico, Europe, Asia, Latin America, and Australia, and the usual North American participants attended in droves.

As new groups proliferate, new repertoire has flooded into the scene and the understood categories of repertoire have become more explicit. Some pieces are anonymous, traditional and known to all: for instance, virtually every group has a version of "Matsuri." At the other end of the spectrum, the most accomplished professional musicians (like those in On Ensemble) continuously generate beautiful, intricate pieces that the taiko community admires but can't and wouldn't ever play. Some works can be learned and performed with permission, which often means learning directly from the originator, who is always acknowledged. Acknowledging ownership is increasingly emphasized without hardening the movement of ideas; rather, the praxis of respect now includes attention to where pieces come from. In the middle of this range of repertoire is a body of works that have been produced intentionally *for* the community of performers. Not coincidentally, many of these include bon-odori. Whether called open source, open access, or copyleft, a small but commanding number of pieces have been created since 2005 that deliberately fling the doors wide by declaring themselves authored but unowned.

TAIKO IN CRITICAL PERSPECTIVE

In this book, I follow taiko through Southern California and a few other places, including Japan. I focus on taiko in the US contexts I know best, which have been shaped by the neoliberal multiculturalism of California. Let me offer a brief over-view of the progression from liberal to corporate to neoliberal multiculturalism, which is now the defining framework for much US-based cultural heritage work. In the 1980s and 1990s, struggles in higher education over the core curriculum led to powerful new recognition of how systemic inequality generates multiple stories about history. While many areas of the humanities subsequently decentered the old canons, the newly diverse landscape was promptly rendered less threatening by retreating to the liberal humanist position that all subjects are created equal. Toni Morrison and Maxine Hong Kingston were assigned alongside Shakespeare and William Faulkner. In the 1990s and 2000s, the ideology of corporate mul-ticulturalism mapped this benign, nonconfrontational approach to difference onto the workplace and then onto global capitalist strategies. Neoliberal capital-ism posits that all relationships can or even should be defined in market terms. As Jodi Melamed (2006, 1) argues, neoliberal strategists deploy multiculturalism "as the key to a postracist world of freedom and opportunity." I refer repeatedly to the shaping force of multicultural ideologies on taiko because Asian Ameri-can culturemaking takes place within these terms, not despite them. When taiko groups perform in multicultural festivals, films, or TV ads, we not only fulfill those terms but provide pleasure. Neoliberal multiculturalism can make viewers feel good about themselves. These powerful and invasive ideologies irrevocably define North American taiko, but they don't provide the only possible narratives: performance can maintain other ways of knowing and generate essential strate-gies for cultural self-determination. As Will Kymlicka (2013, 99) writes, "If neo-liberalism has shaped social relations, it is equally true that those relations have shaped neoliberalism, blocking some neoliberal reforms entirely while pushing other reforms in unexpected directions, with unexpected results. In the process, we can see social resilience at work as people contest, contain, subvert, or appro-priate neoliberal ideas and policies to protect the social bonds and identities they value." As this book proceeds, I try to ward off the celebratory stories about taiko that neoliberal multiculturalism demands even as I discover the many ways that Asian American taiko practitioners reach deep and imagine otherwise.[20]

My primary research methodology was ethnographic, informed by participa-tion. I didn't set out to achieve bimusicality—the ethnomusicological practice of learning how to play an instrument as a formal ethnographic method, with sustained effort and long-term commitment—but that's where I ended up.[21] I ini-tially started taking taiko classes in 1997 not for research but because I was moved and compelled by taiko as an Asian American. I began to think of it as study *and* research after about a year of deepening engagement: I was consumed by it as a practicing musician and fascinated by it as an ethnomusicologist and Asian American studies scholar. Once I got past the initial learning curve (which took about a year), I wanted to get a lot better as a musician and I wanted a deeper understanding of everything I saw going on around the Taiko Center of Los Angeles (TCLA). I didn't realize it at the time, but those years were an important juncture in the North American kumi-daiko scene. It was the moment just before taiko suddenly and rapidly expanded. The first NATC was held in 1997, and I participated in it without fully understanding how historic it was. I was deeply involved with the TCLA, taking classes and eagerly committing to Satori Daiko, the center's performing ensemble, when Rev. Tom formed it in 1999. I routinely videotaped events and some of our rehearsals and performances, I began to formally interview Rev. Tom after a year or two, and I began to follow other taiko groups by attending as many performances as possible. I threw myself into taiko as both a practitioner and an ethnomusicologist. This simultaneous engagement was mostly easy and natural, though at times I knew I was more critical than some of my taiko peers. My ethnographic immersion in the taiko scene was necessarily autoethnographic. In this book I draw on my own experiences as a source of information, but I also locate myself in my ethnographic logos without making myself its focus. For me, autoethnography is a sustained commitment to metalearning (Dunbar-Hall 2009, 159). I am especially drawn to how autoethnographic work on music "frees the voice and body from the conventional and restrictive mind-body split that continues to pervade traditional academic writing," as Brydie-Leigh Bartleet and Carolyn Ellis (2009, 10) put it. Freeing oneself from that binary is neither simple nor entirely possible, but autoethnographic work on music can get inside the act of listening in ways that I hope ethnomusicologists will own as time goes on. Aurality offers extraordinary entrée into the body and can take us beyond the tired trope of embodiment.

Ethnography was only one part of my methodology, though the ethnographic impulse is evident in everything I do. I deploy close reading quite a bit, especially when unpacking a television commercial in chapter 7, because its critical techniques are already so virtuosically well developed. When reading video footage or still photographs, I offer ethnographic examinations that issue from my unitary subject position as an ethnomusicologist yet also a taiko player. I sometimes thought of my efforts as fieldwork, sometimes as rehearsal, and always as a lifelong commitment. I wrote a book (Wong 2004) about Asian American musicking during my early years of learning taiko. My ethnographic work with taiko players was an open-ended midcareer project. I never intended to go home afterward or to declare the research "done" in the ways made necessary when earning a degree or tenure. I was shaped by the postcrisis assumptions described by George E. Marcus (2009), who muses that most anthropological research since the 1980s has invited and expected incompleteness and derailment.

I have roamed around the kumi-daiko world but spent most of my time as a member of the TCLA and Satori Daiko. I have taken workshops with many of the extraordinary first- and second-generation North American taiko teachers, including Kenny Endo, Tiffany Tamaribuchi, PJ Hirabayashi, Roy Hirabayashi, and yes, Tanaka-sensei, for one *odaiko* workshop. Still, I have never studied at length with any of them, nor have I learned with any of the most famous taiko groups from the founding generation, such as San Francisco Taiko Dojo, San Jose Taiko, Kinnara Taiko, or Soh Daiko. Some taiko players may look askance at my knowledge base. As will become clear in this book, my teacher Rev. Tom Kurai (1947–2018) was in on the ground floor of North American kumi-daiko and the Asian American Movement, but he charted his own course. As a Zen Buddhist priest, he was not part of the extensive network of Jodo Shinshu Japanese American Buddhist temples on the West Coast which sustain the bon-odori tradition. He never created a nonprofit organization: the TCLA was a (modest) for-profit enterprise and part of how he earned a living.²² He was well known but not part of Tanaka-sensei's lineage. Heidi Varian's (2013) book is authoritative because it represents Tanaka-sensei's teachings; Shawn Bender's (2012) book is riveting because he learned from inside the *ur*-groups Kodo and Sukeroku. My book is not like either of those immensely important works. I have learned a lot and have walked through doors opened by my association with Rev. Tom, but at the same time my experiences—usefully, I think—don't reflect the authoritative, canonic core of North American taiko, if there is such a thing. Methodologically, this has been valuable, yet I sometimes felt acutely aware that I wasn't going to be able to tell the story of North American taiko in ways that some taiko players would want to hear it told.

While I hope that taiko practitioners will find at least some of their priorities reflected in these pages, this book is driven by broader critical concerns. I circle around six interrelated critical issues as I proceed.

First, I reflect on this extended historical moment in the early twenty-first century in which taiko has exploded into a global phenomenon. The viral expansion of taiko from a post–World War II invented tradition to the world music du jour raises questions of tradition, invention, ownership, and specific circuits of desire that have transported taiko from its most recent communities of origin (i.e., Japanese Americans) into Western Europe, Latin America, and now Southeast Asia and parts of East Asia. Taiko may be a globalized tradition, but I ask how, where, and why that happened.

Second, I address Asian American memory and community building in the troubled context of corporate multiculturalism in the backyard of the entertainment industry. It is no coincidence that taiko moves around the world as easily and nonarbitrarily as anime, video games, and manga. Taiko has expanded precisely because this is the historical moment when US neoliberalism has been normalized and the Pacific Rim is simply assumed to be an open field of exchange.

Third, I follow the trail of Asian American social justice work, from pilgrimages to the Japanese American incarceration camps to new articulations of Asian

American and Asian Canadian feminism. If some taiko practitioners seem a little too willing for taiko to be for "everyone" and thus not about memory and social justice, others choose to remember.[23]

Fourth, I explore taiko's restless movement between music and noise. Drawing from sound studies, I consider how taiko fills space with sound and operationalizes the formation of bodies politic. I argue that taiko's spillover from music to noise transforms taiko players' stunning corporeal discipline into an unruly invasive sonic presence that has political implications.

Fifth, I trace how taiko practitioners address cultural sustainability, through both intentional organization building and the broader play of "traditional culture," which is always mediated. Cultural sustainability is nominally about traditional practices but is really about community survival. Taiko is in no danger of disappearance, but as with all intangible cultural heritage, the question is how its communities of practice are defined and how they expand, contract, or vanish. I attend closely to the extraordinary ways that "the taiko community" engages in metareflection, hyperreflexivity, and incessant self-documentation, driven by a distinctively postwar Sansei preoccupation with history. I also address the work of music, including improvisation and generating new repertoire.

Sixth and by no means least, I listen to the cultural politics of emotion in taiko (Ahmed 2004). I have encountered few musics as profoundly about energy, joy, and passion. Having written that—and acutely aware that taiko is hardly unique in the ways it lifts, carries, and sustains people both collectively and individually—I ask how and why taiko practitioners and audiences feel so deeply. Emotion is political.

This book is shaped by these questions. Though I have separately enumerated them, they percolate throughout the book, surfacing and then resubmerging. No chapter is devoted to only one of these issues. Always I ask how taiko is a political project. It is hard not to notice that some taiko players, taiko groups, and taiko scholars deny or ignore how taiko is an Asian American political project.

People may first encounter taiko in a Hollywood commercial film, at a Japanese American Buddhist temple, in an arcade game, at a world music festival, on a college campus, in a car advertisement, at a multicultural civic festival, at a corporate reception, at the NATC or the World Taiko Gathering, or on YouTube. An all-inclusive approach to twenty-first-century taiko simply isn't possible, though I try to convey the richness of its scenes.

Taiko is a leisure activity for many of its North American practitioners, pursued in the hours outside a job or classes. Is it a First World practice, and does its dissemination signal a desire for a certain kind of class politics? Kumi-daiko materialized in postwar Japan at precisely the moment when that demilitarized nation was being reinvented by the US victor: its young Japanese originators were anxious about the disappearance of Japanese culture, but the very terms of that disappearance were bound up with a dramatic change in class formations. Taiko seems so quaintly and dynamically folkloric, yet its cultural specificity is inextricably interlaced with cosmopolitan ideologies about global circulation. Why has such a specifically Japanese form of performance traveled so far, and why is it pursued so passionately by such a broad range of practitioners, from those with Japanese heritage to those with no direct Japan connection at all? Taiko is far from alone in this: certain kinds of music and dance are practiced on a world stage, but such movement is never arbitrary.[24] If the *djembe* and didgeridoo are played in multiple First World communities far from West Africa or Aboriginal Australia, their enthusiasts pursue ideas about Elsewheres via heavily mediated conduits (Magowan 2005).

Taiko is spectacularly recognizable: its form is vivid, invasive, and "colorful" (that tired marker of the ethnic). That form is an accumulation of sonic and visual ethnic indicators. Beyond its splendid visuality, its sonic form is instantly parsed: the sound of many drums floods through any space, whether indoors or out. The literary theorist Michael Davidson (2008, 743) argues for a "cosmopoetics" of form that reveals the interactions of the cultural and the geopolitical under late capitalism. The cosmopoetics of taiko is based in a hardening of form that, at its most unthoughtful, allows for playful expansion but carries the terms of its own privileged First World, leisure-class empowerment. Indeed, it is precisely the hardening of form that makes taiko so instantly recognizable and nameable. Although kumi-daiko is irrefutably hybrid and has been since its postwar emergence in the hands of a Japanese jazz drummer, its practitioners often assert its authenticity, couched in a First World longing for a preindustrial moment outside history. García Canclini (2014, 17) urges us to "get out of this binary" between "epic accounts of the achievements of globalization" and "melodramatic narratives from the fissures, violence, and pain of interculturality." I hope my treatment of taiko as contemporary and intercultural is both theorized and matter-of-fact. I argue that one cannot address the epic expansion of kumi-daiko without referring over and over again to the original wound of the Japanese American incarceration.

I take a critical step in this book that I believe makes my work different from other scholars', and they may not agree with my position. I argue that taiko is well into a process of deterritorialization and destratification that reflects its location in late capitalist circuits of dissemination in precisely the manner posited by Deleuze and Guattari (1987). Both inside and outside Japan, taiko groups proliferate, but its practitioners generally sidestep fraught matters of class, commoditization, ownership, and mediatization. The Japanese American organizations that have supported the growth of the North American kumi-daiko scene are intensely focused on autodocumentation for just that reason. I deploy ethnography to address this process, focusing on specific people, places, and moments to understand how kumi-daiko is becoming less tied to place. Ethnomusicologists and musicologists

are only slowly beginning to address how and why certain specific musical practices go global. Some, like K-pop, were practically designed to do so. Taiko wasn't
and isn't, but it has gone global, unevenly and nonarbitrarily. The relationship
between late capitalist racial fantasy and commodified heritage is precisely what
makes taiko so uncontrollably popular, rendering replication easy and relying on
Asian American practitioners as willing accomplices.

I acknowledge that I have an incomplete understanding of *wadaiko* (traditional drumming in Japan), a California-centric understanding of the scene, and
no training in the Japanese language. My commitment to ground-level participatory ethnographic work is both a strength and a limitation. My strengths include
thirteen years (1997–2009) of passionate, immersive engagement in the Southern California taiko scene as a student and performer with the TCLA; five study
trips to Japan under the guidance of my taiko teacher Rev. Tom Kurai; and stints
as a guest member of Triangle Taiko in Raleigh, North Carolina (2005–6), as an
observer of Kokyo Taiko in Chicago for ten weeks (2004), as a bon-odori dancer in
innumerable SoCal Obon festivals, as a participant in the NATC (1997, 1999, 2001,
2005, 2009, 2011) and the ECTC (2012, 2014), as an observer at the World Taiko
Gathering (2014), as a participant in the intensive three-day planning workshop
for the Taiko Community Alliance (2013), as a passionately committed student in
the Summer Taiko Institute's Women and Taiko workshop (2017), and as a member of "the taiko community," that nebulous formation both real and imagined,
oft cited by taiko players. I know a lot about certain things and I don't know much
about others. The problem is that taiko means too much. Maybe it's in too many
places; maybe it's being forced to do too many kinds of cultural work.

MULTIMEDIA ETHNOMUSICOLOGY

This book is based in multimedia ethnomusicology: visual and audio analysis is
central to my purpose. Scholarship on performance must exceed the limits of any
given medium (Denzin 2003). The loud physicality of taiko begs for the thing itself,
but any research on performance should push at the limits of the page. The translative act of moving from performance to thinking about it is literally and inevitably mediated, and different media create different ways of thinking. Humanities
scholars have privileged one medium—the word. I was shaped fundamentally by
the 1980s humanistic turn in anthropology that involved embracing the word, so
I have no desire to leave it behind, but I believe a more restless attention to different media could reenergize ethnomusicology and related performance-based
disciplines. Ethnomusicologists take sound, movement, and materiality more seriously than scholars in many other disciplines, but we haven't yet realized the fullest
implications of our own interests, because we inevitably pull materiality straight
back into the word.

I am proud that this book will appear in an open-access digital format, which enables the multimedia ethnomusicology for which I am eager. Open-access and open-source work are the foundation of public scholarship. As mentioned above, a handful of taiko and bon-odori leaders have created open-source pieces with great intention, working toward a certain vision of community founded on collaboration and anticommodity processes. I am beholden to their model: they fashion works meant to live in the community and to travel far. I have learned from them and emulate them here. This book isn't mine; this book is part of a process. All faults and inaccuracies are mine, but I want this book to be available as widely as possible, and the open-source digital format offered by University of California Press is thus deeply appealing to me.

The Japanese American taiko community is intensely inclined toward self-documentation and self-narrative—even self-mythologizing. The institutionalization of the history of the Japanese American incarceration (1942–45) is the result of a successful political project to reclaim who gets to relate history (Creef 2004). Documentation and reading the past-as-documented are ubiquitous in the Japanese American community. When I use my own video camera or audio recorder to document events or to conduct interviews, I almost always feel redundant and as if I have somehow become part of a larger commemorative project whose terms I never agreed to. I document objects and interlocutors who have already been historicized and incorporated into a broad narrative.

This ethnographic study is thus already mediatized. The digital is no mere accompaniment to this book, nor simply a place to store rich media. The best multimedia books are significantly different from hard-copy or even e-books. The visual anthropologist Sarah Pink (2013, 6) calls for ethnographers to "reject . . . the idea that the written word is necessarily a superior medium of ethnographic representation. While images should not necessarily replace words as the dominant mode of research or representation, they should be regarded as an equally meaningful element of ethnographic work." Pink clears the way for closer attention to all the senses: she acknowledges that "visual anthropology" really demands the kind of sensuous anthropology imagined by Paul Stoller (1997). I aim to put my book's materials into dialogic relationships. Rather than "use" video, photos, and sounds to illustrate my text, I configure them to make visible the media-saturated environment in which all multicultural practices now circulate. An ethnography of racialized heritage work must put mediated representational practices front and center, not as "evidence" of ideology but as the very means for action and response. I assume that all parts of this environment are constituted through media practices—that there is no distinction between the thing itself and its mediated representation.

I wrote and designed this book in a mostly linear mode: my arguments build on one another as the book proceeds. Still, I don't think this book should necessarily be read in order. Reading changes all the time; some of you may read one chapter and nothing else; others may skip around to the parts you most care about. As Ken Wissoker (2013, 133) has written, "It is when we think of the book as media that we can begin to see how much this is a transitional, even disruptive and disrupted, moment in the history of the book." I wrote this book over many years and then rearticulated and reorganized it over several more. I think I have tried to make it into two different kinds of books: one is shaped by my generation- and history-bound knowledge of print monographs, and the other is an open-access digital book whose readership I don't want to control. I can't (yet) write with the "rhizomatic plurality" imagined by Wissoker (136), but the rising generations of taiko players might, and I look forward to that.

The sociologists Bella Dicks and Bruce Mason (1998, 2.2–2.9; Mason and Dicks 2001) cogently identify the ethnographic tensions between the death of the author and the shift toward more dialogic, open-ended forms of representation. As they put it, there are "two related areas of concern within 'post-paradigm ethnography': to rethink how ethnography's subject-matter is defined, and to radicalise how it is written" (Dicks and Mason 1998, 2.7). As a discipline, ethnomusicology has struggled with both those challenges. Ethnomusicologists have yet to address an additional problem: the (literal) absence of sound in our scholarship. One could say that this broad problem faces all scholarship of the live—the thing itself shudders and disappears. It is so ephemeral that we spend considerable critical energy creating an object that will permit sustained attention. We are fixed on two mechanisms: reading (a process thoroughly imbedded in a noetics of the printed word and the visual cultures that followed) and the act of translating across media. Refashioning the thing-that-is-studied is second nature to us; we do it almost automatically.

A serious critical multimedia scholarship is the single most unique and important thing performance scholars could offer to the humanities. By placing performance at the center of our critical gestures, we could fashion something profoundly different. I imagine a multimedia ethnomusicology along the following lines:

1. Sound and movement are incommensurate with word-based scholarly practices. The CD or DVD tucked into the back of a book cover reenacts this incommensurability; the website that "accompanies" the book text reinstantiates it. A multimedia ethnomusicology would reincorporate the word into the bachi strike on the head of the drum or the taiko player's shout.

2. A multimedia ethnomusicology cannot be described in a how-to manner: it can't be codified or outlined in a primer. The modalities will change continually. We can talk about different software platforms, but that isn't really the point. We must focus on what we aim to do, and assume that the means will continually change, often radically.

3. A multimedia ethnomusicology will necessarily create unstable objects that
    would be at once more aesthetic and more open ended. We could engage
    with our material and our interlocutors in a more playful, creative, respect-
    ful, and commanding manner via nontextual media.

The two most radical epistemological discontinuities offered by digital publication are the break with linearity and the intensified interaction between writer
and reader. Most scholarly electronic publications indulge in neither. Quite a few
electronic journals have enlivened the scope of scholarly music publications.[25] All
are noteworthy, but only a few make full use of multimedia possibilities. Most are
simply full of text, with an occasional graphic illustration or streaming audio file;
to put it another way, they feature lightly enhanced text. Ethnomusicologists have
used the internet for "virtual field sites," online textbooks, and digital pedagogy.
Suzel Ana Reily (2003, 190) notes, "Perhaps the area that has been least developed
within ethnomusicology pertains to sites that draw on the interactive potential
of the Internet as a means of exemplifying a given theoretical proposition," and
she points to Jeff Titon's 1993 website on the old-time fiddler Clyde Davenport
as a strong early example. Mark Slobin's simple but beautiful 2003 website on his
research in Afghanistan is a metamorphosis of his first book, *Music in the Culture
of Northern Afghanistan* (1976). The entire book is present as downloadable PDF
chapters, but the website doesn't simply replicate the book: it addresses a series of
critical issues through text, still images, video clips, and MP3 audio files. I am also
influenced by the anthropologist Shelly Errington and her course on multimedia
ethnography at the University of California, Santa Cruz. Errington suggests that
"thinking visually" and thinking through sound are key hallmarks of a multimedia
ethnography, and she argues that this requires the ability "to engage while inform-
ing."[26] These are some of the models that have inspired my book.

My multimedia ethnography attempts to resituate the place of representational
practices in our interpretive practice. The crisis of representation has paralyzed
ethnomusicologists, and we simply must step up to the terms of a Baudrillard-
ian mediasphere. As ethnographers, we must wade into it and make its terms our
own. Ethnography will become increasingly quaint and irrelevant if its noetics are
severely text centered; we cannot remain mired in the unidirectional quandary
of *How do I represent them?* Performance-centered research has the potential to
create new intersubjective relationships, but this will happen only if we urge it to
overrun our expectations.

I have tried to call forth that excess of hope here. You are welcome to buy a hard
copy of this book, but I hope you will read it online, in fits and starts. I hope you
will click on a link to a photo or a video and allow it to stream as you read so that
my words and the movements run into each other. If you are a scholar, I hope you
will hear how deeply inter- and intratextual my ideas are, built on the fine work
of other antiracist writers. If you are a taiko player, I can feel you reading over

my shoulder. I have felt you beside me for all the many years I have spent writing this book. You are my touchstone, my comrade, and my ethical base. I owe you. I wouldn't care so much about all of this if it weren't for you. I hope at least some of your finest experiences have been or will be like mine, and if you are driven by the sweat and rumble half as fast toward utopian hope as I was, well then, my work here is done.

Transition

Don

DON! Taiko players know what *don* means, whether trained in Japan, in North America, or elsewhere. *DON!* By itself, just the one syllable, it means a strong right-handed bachi strike on either a chudaiko or an odaiko. Not on a shime: that would be *ten,* not *don.* Of course, the left hand can also play *don,* but by itself the syllable implies an emphatic, assertive leading right-hand strike. You might well hear it as the last stroke at the end of *oroshi,* the dramatic drum roll that ends many pieces: the right and left hands alternate, starting very slowly, then gradually speeding up, then gradually slowing down again, and that final right-hand strike comes down only after a ki-filled pause and perhaps a sustained *kakegoe* (e.g., *i-yooooooo*), followed by *don!,* pushed powerfully and loudly into the drum with the entire body behind it.

The mnemonic *don* is part of an extensive system for vocalizing music, often for pedagogical purposes. Japanese music is full of mnemonic systems: not only can you "speak" nearly any kind of Japanese music, but there's probably a codified way to do it. *Kuchi shōga* (also sometimes rendered as *kuchi showa* or *kuchi shoka*) is the phonetic system for uttering drum strokes, whether taiko or *tsuzumi* (the small two-headed drum featured in the music for Noh and Kabuki). Kuchi shōga is meant to be heard, though it is also written down—in katakana, the Japanese syllabary, not the Chinese-derived kanji—for pedagogical purposes and as a performance prompt. It is and isn't fixed: a core set of widely accepted syllables is understood by most musicians, but new and idiomatic syllables are common, tied to specific performing ensembles or pieces. Although some of its meaning is contextual, each syllable may indicate several parameters at once: duration, volume, which kind of drum is being played, which part of the drum is being struck. *Don doro-doro-doro,* for instance, is a quarter note followed by six eighth notes, played in the center of the drumhead of either a chudaiko or an odaiko. *Don kara-kara-kara* is the same rhythmic pattern— a quarter note followed by six eighth notes—with *don* played in the center of the drumhead and the eighth notes played on the rim, with the bachi clattering brightly against the wooden frame. *Ten teke-teke-teke* is, again, the same rhythm but played on a shime daiko, with the bachi striking the center of the drumhead. A wide range of syllables indicate rests, including *su, ho, sa,* and *iya.* The rest, the space of silence or the absence of sound, is in fact often filled with sound as kuchi shōga overlap with the ki-filled shouts (*kiyai* or *kakegoe*) that are so characteristic of kumi-daiko and the Japanese martial arts. Silence is dynamic but often filled.

Musicians learn their parts by speaking or singing the shōga before touching an instrument. The body, the voice, and the mouth (*kuchi*) usually come first. *Kuchijamisen* is the system of onomatopoetic syllables used to teach koto (the thirteen-stringed zither), though the term suggests it derives from shamisen (*jamisen*) playing (Adriaansz 1973, 41–42). For instance, a distinctive melodic and kinesthetic pattern found in many shamisen pieces is signified by the mnemonic *terenton,* which Philip Flavin (2008, 186) describes as "the syllabic realization of *moro-bachi,* a melodic pattern created by a down-stroke plus up-stroke on the third string followed by a down-stroke, usually on the open second string." Blown instruments like the *hichiriki* and the *fue* have their own mnemonic systems. Kuchi shōga implies different parameters, from the production of sound on particular instruments to the pedagogical interface between student, teacher, and repertoire.

While kuchi shōga is centrally part of musical practice, its mnemonic syllables can also be used to describe a broader onomatopoetic world of sound beyond music. Not every kuchi shōga syllable is found in the extramusical world, but some are, and *don* is one of them. As I noted in the introduction, the compound word *pika-don* is a powerful example of a don sound that is now irrevocably part of the Japanese historical soundscape. Curious, I asked some friends and colleagues, mostly ethnomusicologists and all specialists in Japanese culture, What other things make a don sound?[1] They described an evocative range of contexts worth laying out in some detail, not least for the sheer delight of seeing/reading/hearing one soundworld but also because the array of meanings are connected, and that web tells us something about taiko. Or rather, taiko tells us something about the affective world of Japanese and Japanese American sound. I reflect here on the dialogic relationship between that affective soundworld and kumi-daiko. Sound and listening are interconstitutive, and languaging about sound constructs what we hear. As Ana María Ochoa Gautier (2014, 7–8) evocatively writes, "Listening is not a practice that is contained and readily available for the historian in one document but instead is enmeshed across multiple textualities, often mentioned in passing, and subsumed under other apparent purposes such as the literary, the grammatical, the poetic, the ritual, the disciplinary, or the ethnographic. If sound appears as particularly disseminated across different modes of inscription and textualities it is because, located between the worldly sound source from which it emanates and the ear that apprehends it, the sonorous manifests a particular form of spectrality in its acoustics." Languaging about the sound of taiko is part of the meaningful array of sounds musicians make. Significantly, it creates a dialogical space for how taiko players hear themselves.

Don implies something being struck. Thunder makes the sound *gorogoro* until it strikes the ground, at which point it sounds like *don*. *Don, don, don* is also specifically the sound of rain associated with thunder. *Don* is a deep resonant percussive sound, like knocking on a thick wall or door. A light knock on a door is *ton ton*, but if no one answers, your next knock might go *don don don*, with a deeper reverberation and more intent. *Don* implies something sudden with a powerful impact. When things collide—cars crashing together (*don to butsukaru*) or waves slamming against the shore—it sounds like *don*. A heavy kitchen knife repeatedly slicing or dicing something goes *dondondon*. *Don* also suggests something deliberate. Measured, slow steps, whether a giant's or a toddler's, go *don don don*. Godzilla's footsteps go *don* but are really more like *doshin doshin*, which communicates the impact of his foot followed by the shaking of the ground. *Don* signals resolve or confidence and can be used as a nononomatopoetic adverb, describing forward motion or progress while walking. In Japanese teenage film and television dramas, a male love interest may corner a girl and perform the *kabe-don*, a move where he slams one palm into the wall behind her—*don!*—while staring into her eyes and then asking her if she likes him.

Explosive things like fireworks, volcanoes, or bombs make the sound *don*, as do explosive beginnings: "Yoooi don" is uttered to mean *Ready, set, go!* before a race. A famous *enka* song (a form of Japanese popular music that draws heavily from traditional vocal techniques) titled "Dondon bushi" uses *don* to represent people exploding when they've been pushed too hard and too often (possibly referring to another enka song, "Dynamite bushi," which explicitly likens people to dynamite). Some songs include onomatopoetic lyrics: "Don-Pan Bushi," for example, is a *minyo* (folk song) from Akita Prefecture whose title and chorus imitate the sound of the taiko as *don-don, pan-pan, don-pan-pan*.

Don implies a deep dark timbre. In Kabuki, snow falling softly is depicted sonically by playing *don don don* on the odaiko. Japanese audiophiles may refer to *don-shari* sound, produced by loudspeakers with a heavy low tone and bright high tone. *Don* refers to the low tone and *shari* the high tone, and *don-shari* speakers are suitable for jazz but not classical music. Satomi Oshio[2] noted that *don* sometimes describes a low, faint sound in several traditional music mnemonic systems: when a tsuzumi makes a single weak sound, it mnemonically goes *don*. She also observed that *don* suggests a correlation between register and timbre: on shamisen, the sound of the open first string (the thickest and lowest in register) is *don*, whereas the second string goes *ton*, and the third, highest string goes *ten*. Noriko Manabe[3] mused that vowels convey information about relative register— *on* means a lower-pitched sound than *a or *en*—and consonants about volume: d^* implies a louder sound than t^*.

While the sound of a chudaiko or odaiko doesn't evoke all those meanings, its affiliation with them calls them forth. A taiko playing *don don DON* is part of a sonic world of large emphatic forces. Sara Ahmed (2004, 11) writes, "Emotions can move through the movement or circulation of objects. Such objects become sticky, or saturated with affect, as sites of personal or social tension." Don is saturated with associations. Does a taiko sound like don, or were taiko made to evoke don-ness? How does don make us feel? How does our understanding of the world make us hear don-ness in certain ways? Don is a sound of power, or a powerful sound, or a signal that power is present. Apparently, don is a feeling as much as a sound. The sound of don assigns the feeling of power to things and people. Don is Japanese but moves around the world with/in taiko.

1

Looking, Listening, and Moving

MUSIC AS A PROBLEM

Taiko is music, noise, visual spectacle, corporeal knowledge, and an archive of Asian American hope. It exceeds all these categories in some ways, but it is also subject to the many binary ideologies maintaining mind/body and music/dance as separate. The spectacle of taiko is shaped by powerful ideologies even as it sometimes challenges them.

The ephemerality of music poses a series of analytical challenges. Put simply, sound doesn't stand still: it moves through time. The sound of music is a moving presence that refuses to be pinned down for examination or revisitation. What *can* be examined are *representations* of sound—notated music or recordings, for instance—and there are many, many ways to analyze or to interpret those objects; indeed, entire fields are devoted to those projects (e.g., "music theory"). But the thing itself—"music"—is slippery, fleeting, and a significant ideological problem for ethnomusicologists (Wong 2014, 347–49).

"Music" is especially vexing for ethnomusicologists (as compared to historical musicologists, composers, or music theorists).[1] Ethnomusicologists study sound as culture: we approach music as part or even constitutive of culture.[2] (Musical) Sound is inextricably embedded in everything else that makes up culture and society. Some ethnomusicologists choose to focus on music as sound alone—that is, they spend their careers focused on the notes, the sounds, and trying to understand the relationships between rhythms, melodies, repertoires, and the like—but such ethnomusicologists are presently few in number. Most of us end up considering far more than the sound of music: we tend to believe that music makes sense only if you understand its relationship to political structures, religion, history, gender and sexuality, local and global economies, environment, social aesthetics. One might ask why ethnomusicologists seem concerned about so much *besides* the music. Ethnomusicologists are essentially anthropologists who study music, so we regard music as more than notes or sound: we understand it more broadly as performance, or as part of a range of expressive behaviors that are beautifully and exuberantly difficult to contain. As the ethnomusicologist Matthew Rahaim (2012, 1) asks, "What do we miss if we reduce music to sound?"

I have often *not* addressed formal musical structures, for instance in my scholarly work on the musics of Thailand and Asian America (Wong 2001, 2004). I am deeply distrustful of traditional music analysis, even though I know my sweeping generalization ignores the spectrum of possibilities presented by the field of contemporary music theory. I'm not alone in my uneasiness. The music theorist Fred Maus (2003) writes that music analysis sets up an opposition between "composition versus performance, music itself versus experience, structure versus embodiment." Taiko is a profoundly corporeal practice, yet taiko players are inexorably shaped by the aesthetic ideology that makes it possible to isolate the music from the rest of the sensorium, even when we generate a rhythm entirely shaped by how we want to swing our left arm in that phrase. The things I want to understand about taiko music are fundamentally at odds with the principles and ideologies of music analysis.[3] My work has been vulnerable to the criticism that I don't address the music itself. Naturally, I am profoundly affected by musical sound, but the music itself is never just the sounds or the notes. Taiko forces me to address musical sound because it is that and so much more. So the challenge is how we can address musical sound without activating all the old moves that objectify it.

Taiko is noise as well as music. While this is true of all music, percussion more easily spills over from one social category to the other. Percussion is notoriously difficult to record because it "goes into the red"—that is, the attack and fast decay create a sound signal marked by clipping, the distortion that occurs when an amplifier is overdriven. These technical and acoustic properties are also wonderfully metaphorical. Noise is part of percussion's radical potential. Caroline Polk O'Meara (2013, 15) writes that "noise has a dual status as a category at once inside and outside of musical systems of knowledge." The French and French Canadian tradition of *casseroles*—street protest percussion featuring pots and pans— is almost too synecdochic (Sterne 2012). I am certain audiences and performers are so thrilled by outdoor percussion traditions like samba, *samulnori,* and taiko because these powerfully activate the sound-body-environment relationship. The uncontrollable spread of the sound through bodies and neighborhoods suggests something a bit dangerous even as we delight in its careful arrangement into rhythms. As an ethnomusicologist I won't offer an essentialized theory of percussion, since all percussion and indeed noise, like all politics, is local. Avant-garde twentieth-century musics intentionally driven toward noise were often exploring futurist modes that rearranged the relationship between the body and agency, subjectivity, and experience. Noise has long played a key role in popular musics, and rock as a sprawling family of genres has long featured noise, from overloaded electrified timbres to noise rock as a genre. Indeed, O'Meara (2013, 14–15) argues that noise rock was a strategy to deconstruct and remake the rock tradition by deliberately rejecting any stable set of authoritative practices, but she also notes that noise as an intervention is constantly at risk of being reabsorbed as simply a different kind of order. Similarly, Kenneth Igarashi (1997) has explored how certain traditions of free improvisation are continually resituated as noise, and how noise as an intentional genre developed accepted practices in the late 1970s and early 1980s in New York City and the San Francisco Bay Area. Audiences, musicians, and sound engineers have complicated learned processes for identifying noise, filtering it out, or rejecting it. As Pamela Nash and Kevin Malone (2000, 105) note, "Noise is ever-present in the physical action of making and recording music. Players and listeners are taught to filter it out, composers pretend it doesn't exist, and recording engineers strive to reduce it in their medium."

Taiko is not explicitly conceived as noise by anyone I know, but its disciplined tumult is key to its affective hold over practitioners and audiences.[4] The experience of being inside its noise walks the line between pain and exultant delight in its din.[5] Loudness/volume alone isn't the only politicized parameter, though I note that one of my colleagues, an art music composer, has told me with regret that he can't attend the taiko class recitals because they kick his tinnitus into high gear. The inability to block out the sound of taiko—to silence it—can prompt extreme responses. Many years ago on my campus, in the middle of an end-of-quarter outdoor taiko class recital, a faculty member burst out of her nearby classroom, rushed over to Rev. Tom Kurai, who was leading the group, and literally shouted at him that we had to stop playing because she couldn't hear herself lecture. She lost it, you could say, and I was struck by how the noise shook her loose from any polite or reasoned response. Her perception of our playing as noise was both a matter of decibels and, I'm certain, an instinctively classed and racialized response. If Rev. Tom had been wearing a tuxedo, she probably would not have so easily claimed the right to shout at him while he was in the middle of leading a performance.

ANALYZING "ARANAMI"

Taiko activates relationships between order and disorder, and it forces a consideration of the organized structures of rhythm versus chaos. I will explore these issues by considering one "piece," though I intend to immediately complicate the very notion of the "piece" or "work" in several ways. Rev. Tom, my teacher and the leader of the taiko class recital mentioned above, created "Aranami" in 1997. Notice that I say "created" rather than "wrote": the idea of "writing" a piece of music is inextricably bound up with Western ideas of musical composition and music notation and immediately raises all the problems that I am writing against. It is generally assumed in the Western art music tradition that music is notated, that that notation is prescriptive (i.e., it tells performers what to do), that it was put down by an individual creator known as a composer, and that the notated object is more authoritative than any single performance. When Rev. Tom created the piece that he named "Aranami," he was the director of Kishin Daiko, a community-based taiko group in Southern California. One could say that he created "Aranami" "for" them, but as time went on he parted ways with Kishin and taught other groups, so "Aranami" was learned and played by a number of taiko ensembles, most recently Satori Daiko, to which I belonged.[6] The piece was thus disseminated by Rev. Tom, and according to the etiquette of the taiko world, each group plays only pieces that its members created together, that their teacher created, that they received directly from another teacher, or that are explicitly known as open source.[7] Anything else is a bit unseemly. In fact, it would be in extremely bad taste to "lift" a piece from another group by learning it from a recording without their permission. One could say that "Aranami" exists only in relation to Rev. Tom: no taiko player would play it without acknowledging that it came from Rev. Tom. (To listen to "Aranami," go to *http://wonglouderandfaster.com*.)

Was Rev. Tom the "composer" of "Aranami"? The simplest answer is yes, but the conceptual field defining a composer is historically, culturally, and ideologically complex. The Western art music tradition understands composers as individuals (as opposed to groups), who create pieces of music full blown, out of their imaginations, each of which is idiosyncratic and unique.[8] "Aranami" is and isn't utterly unique. Rev. Tom drew from a vocabulary of formulaic rhythmic motives to create it (see Lord 1960), and he employed one of four standard *ji,* or taiko "base lines," as they are called in English, to underlie it. That is, the small, high-pitched drum known as shime-daiko plays *teke-teke-teke-teke* (continuous eighth notes) throughout. The patterns that make up the piece are found in many other works for taiko, in many other groups: *don don don don, doko-doko-doko-doko, su-don su-don don,* and so on. Rev. Tom's compositional gesture lay in ordering these motives in a certain way, dividing them across different taiko in particular ways, and situating them in *his students*—"composing" with the expectation that these sounds would (at least initially) be played by the musicians closest to him. It is clear that he was proud of how widespread "Aranami" became, because this is metonymic of his impact as a teacher.

Rev. Tom regarded himself as the composer of "Aranami": he was quite aware of the Western art music complex defining pieces and composers, and he listed himself in concert programs as its composer, often including the year 1997 as its composition date. He gave the work a name—a title—to indicate that it had its own identity as distinct from other pieces for taiko. He always translated "Aranami" as "turbulent waves." By giving it a Japanese name, he located the work as Japanese American / Japanese. Sometimes he described "Aranami" as part of a "trilogy" with "Ame no Mori" (Forest of rain) and "Arashi" (Storm), because although they were not written to constitute a larger unit or group, they all have names that refer to water. Rev. Tom named many of his pieces after nature, in Japanese, and thus located himself within a traditional Japanese aesthetics of nature . . . which suggests that certain signs and symbols are coded across the Japanese American–Japanese divide and acquire power and significance in each culture via the logics of heritage and orientalism.

One could analyze "Aranami" using the tools of traditional Western art music theory, which would probably mean focusing entirely on rhythm and would also probably leave many traditional theorists at a loss, because the rhythms in themselves are not particularly "complex." A structural or formal analysis would have the same problems, as "Aranami" is quickly and easily described as having ten phrases or motives that are repeated four times, and then the piece is over. "Aranami" is a short work, as are most of Rev. Tom's compositions. Like many if not most North American kumi-daiko pieces, it is solidly in duple meter. Music theorists often treat percussion pieces as if they are entirely "about" rhythm, but one could also analyze their pitch and dynamics, which in taiko are related to the size of the drum. In "Aranami," Rev. Tom depicted crashing waves programmatically in at least two ways, through rhythm but especially through dynamics and pitch. Two phrases feature different-sized drums in a call-and-response pattern: the chudaiko play one line alone, and the lower-pitched odaiko answer with another. Also, the crescendos in some of the phrases near the end of the piece create huge, swelling waves.

Taiko players often learn pieces not only by playing them but also by "speaking" them—that is, by learning mnemonic syllables called kuchi shōga (*kuchi,* "mouth"; *shōga,* "song"), discussed in the introduction. (See figure 2, Rev. Tom Kurai's mnemonic notation for "Aranami," at *http://wonglouderandfaster.com.*) These syllables address only rhythm, and somewhat inexactly at that. Although these mnemonics are written down and then regarded as notation by taiko players, it would be difficult if not impossible to learn a piece from such notation: it is always necessary to hear the piece, whether played or spoken, to learn it. When taiko players "speak" through such mnemonic patterns as part of their learning or review process, they add a number of elements not present in the syllables themselves: they often move their hands as if they were holding drumsticks (*bachi*), to associate right-hand and left-hand strokes with particular syllables, and they "speak" dynamics not only through the volume of their voices but usually through relative pitch as well. A crescendo is mnemonically spoken by starting soft and low and ending loud and high. I would venture to say that this is how taiko players *hear* such lines when they play them on a drum.

These mnemonics are standard for taiko players. Many groups learn pieces orally, by rote. West Coast community groups use Western staff notation only rarely; when pieces are written down, mnemonics are most common, though a range of written techniques are used (e.g., some groups put the syllables in boxes, with each box representing one four-beat measure). *Don* means a quarter note at medium volume; *DON* is a loud quarter note; *doko* is two loud eighth notes, usually right hand followed by left hand; *tsuku* is two soft eighth notes, usually right hand followed by left hand; *teke* is two eighth notes on the small high-pitched drum (shime-daiko); and so on. The relationships between purely "musical" parameters of this sort are only part (and perhaps the least) of the ways that taiko players experience and understand the works that they play. There are other ways to understand the "work" of taiko, and I mean quite deliberately to play with the idea of the "work" as an isolatable musical object and the corporeal, sensual, spiritual, and political labor that goes into creating the complex of understandings called taiko. Another way of addressing taiko methodologically is through the body, which opens up a host of issues. Rather than think of music as a sound object, I want to move toward a conception of music as body: the movement of music through bodies over time, and between bodies (both within and across time), the placement of music within particular bodies and its generation by particular bodies, the linkages created between bodies through sound, and the metaphorical leap from the corporeal, material body to the body politic and the body of the community. Resituating the music object onto/into bodies has radical implications and would work for any "piece" or tradition of music; this methodology moves the discussion away from an isolated thing, which requires much focused effort to identify its shape and its boundaries, and instead toward the connective traces of processes and activities across time and space. It offers both a material and a metaphorical means for regarding the work of music—that is, the things that music does.

For taiko, the pleasure of such an analysis is doubled because this tradition is explicitly (emically) grounded in a social, philosophical, and political aesthetic of the body. Taiko is intensely physical, and it represents a corporeal aesthetic system that is both Buddhist in origin and decidedly contemporary in its realization. The kind of kumi-daiko I learned from Rev. Tom is explicitly based in Buddhist concepts linking the mind, the body, and the spirit via the principle of ki, energy. Ki is the vital energy that can be realized physically but is in fact mental and spiritual as well; it blurs and even collapses distinctions between the physical, the spiritual, and the mental.[9] The pragmatics of how ki is used and actualized in taiko comes from the Japanese martial arts, to which the taiko master Seiichi Tanaka (the founder and director of San Francisco Taiko Dojo) explicitly connected taiko by calling his school a dojo and drawing on such martial arts principles as ki and kata. His theories and approach are consistently activated by North American taiko practitioners to theorize the complex of mind/body/spirit that is viewed as central to taiko (Varian 2013, 81–95). The body is thus always more than the body: it is understood as a corporeal realization of vital principles that exist beyond the body, but without demoting the body to secondary importance. The primacy of *kata*, "stance," in taiko and the martial arts bespeaks this. Taiko practitioners give much attention to the body. At the very least, warm-up exercises precede all rehearsals, and the Japanese groups Ondekoza and Kodo are (in)famous for their extreme physical regimens, focused on long-distance running (Ondekoza members participated in the Boston Marathon before a full-length concert; Kodo apprentices are expected to run up to ten miles every morning before rehearsal). Preparing the body in these ways prepares the mind and spirit for the "work" of taiko. Bodily experience is something that taiko players like to talk about and to theorize. Blisters and aching muscles are honorable parts of the taiko experience, but they speak most deeply to the centrality of the corporeal/spiritual conjuncture in taiko (see chapter 6). Some groups bring beginning students into the tradition through physical exercises, introducing them to the drums and "the music" only after weeks or even months of bodily training. In her groundbreaking monograph on Japanese dance (*nihon buyo*), Tomie Hahn (2007, 67) emphasizes the organic links between ki, kata, and *hara,* the abdomen as the physical location for ki in the human body and the bodily site from which motion begins: "Japanese aesthetics and concepts of the body are integrally linked." The hara exemplifies this: it is located in a physical place on the body (just below the belly button), and all bodily stances (kata) emanate from it; although your kata may be technically correct, you cannot move with ki unless that movement begins in the hara. A drum stroke, a karate strike, and a dance step are all manifestations of ki that begins in the hara. The ki/hara/kata complex offers an approach to performance that is simultaneously physical, spiritual, and mental.

"Aranami" is a bodily experience, both individual and shared. Rev. Tom tended toward minimal choreography (unlike some groups, who put extensive effort into choreography for its own sake), with few unnecessary movements. In "Aranami," as in many of his other works, the individual players stay put throughout, standing solidly in front of each drum (whether shime-daiko, chudaiko, or odaiko). Playing "Aranami" makes you feel strong, and this is all in the upper body, since the lower body doesn't move at all. Starting out with strong, steady, repeated strikes (*don don don don*) rather than a more complex or involved set of rhythmic motives is strong; doubling the density of those repeated strikes (*doko doko doko doko*)—and thus doubling the effort—is strong. The repeated gesture of accented downbeats with the right hand is strong: the sensation of flicking out those accents—of raising the right arm a little more and then flinging the extra ki out along the arm, from shoulder to elbow, then through the forearm, snapped through the wrist and out the length of the bachi—is strong. Moreover, these repeated accents and the physical gesture creating them, just described, are a physical representation of a wave. Certainly, this happens too quickly to register visually for a viewer, nor do taiko players explicitly think or talk about the motion this way, but if you slowed down video footage of the right arm as it pushed out these strong accented downbeats, it would register as a retreating and advancing wave.

Another key gesture in "Aranami" is the four-count "rest" in the middle. Sonically, nothing happens in that rest except that the lone shime-daiko continues to play the base line (though one of our shime players is fond of jazzing up this measure). Again, a sound-focused analysis would miss the point of this "rest," which is anything but a rest. It is filled with the slow, considered movement of raising the right arm from the drumhead to full extension above the head. At its best and most ki-filled realization, raising the arm doesn't begin straight from the drumhead but is rather preceded by a quick pull back that allows the player to bring the bachi up from below in a scooping and arcing motion, literally pushing the bachi up, leading with its tip in a movement that actually *generates* a tremendous amount of ki as the arm goes up to full extension. You can feel your body fill up with additional ki if you do this. You find yourself instinctively inhaling through the entire motion, the entire measure, filling yourself up with air, expanding the chest. The next phrase—*SU-don, SU-don don*—is explosive for two reasons. First, its expenditure of ki matches and exceeds the generation of ki in the "silent" measure preceding it. Second, the half-beat "rest" at the beginning of the phrase—the first *su*—generates yet more ki, but in a slightly different way from the measure preceding it. Taiko players don't experience that half beat as empty: it is marked with the mnemonic *su,* and this may be literally shouted or may be sounded in the head, silently (though at this point there is no distinction between sound *heard* and sound silently *felt*). Furthermore, the movements most filled with ki always have a pronounced beginning. That is, the most ki-filled movements are propelled into motion via a slight drawing back or pulling up in a quick, small gesture that makes all the difference. In other words, the arm doesn't just start moving: an extra small movement gets the big movement into motion. It is like a kick start, and it too *generates* ki. Rev. Tom explained and demonstrated this in his classes; again, this is part of the theory of taiko and ki. The half-beat "rest" at the beginning of this measure should be filled with that kick start—that is, the arm should already be fully extended above the head as it arrives at the end of its arc from below, but in that split second of *su*, you raise your arm through the shoulder a few inches higher still. Indeed, that small additional lift starts all the way down in your feet— you may even lift up from your toes—and at this point it becomes evident that the lower body has not been immobile and uninvolved through all of this. Rather, that arc from below may be visually defined by the right arm, but it is galvanized by a slight pivoting rise through the legs and torso. The kick start involves the entire body, really: the reach upward is created from below, starting down at the toes and rising through the legs to torso to shoulder to arm to bachi. Rise up into the kick start and bring the right arm down on *don* at the same time as you explosively exhale . . . and as you simultaneously raise the left arm in a scissors motion to put it into position for the next movement. If you are doing this correctly, every- thing comes from the hara: certainly, your abdominal muscles should be tight and engaged, but your ki should burst out from your solar plexus and down your legs and out your arms and into your bachi and through your bachi into the drum.

This is a complex set of kinesthetic relationships, you might say, to create such a small moment. Yet it is metonymic of a bodily theory of taiko. It has taken me a long paragraph to unpack the physical movements in one measure of "Aranami," so this is a microanalysis at best, but it also addresses a number of assumptions. How should we think about the relationship between sound and movement? It is a problem of vocabulary and more: shall I say that the movement is "behind" the sounds, or that the movement "drives" the sounds? Neither metaphor really works. "Fronting" and "backing" aren't accurate descriptions of the sound-body relationship—the theory of ki makes that clear. Nor is sound simply a consequence of something more primary—movement isn't in the driver's seat of the sound machine. Rather, the circular, synergistic set of relationships between body, ki, and sound is made visible and audible when a microanalysis of this sort is offered.

The boundaries of "the work" in taiko are not always easily defined. My university campus has a club called Senryu Taiko that is run and organized by students; like many collegiate taiko groups in North America, they mostly create their own repertoire, but they learned "Aranami" from Rev. Tom around 1998, when they were still establishing themselves. When I saw them perform it in 2004, I didn't recognize it for a moment: the rhythmic patterns were "the same" as those I know as "Aranami," but the students had completely transformed the feeling of the work by creating their own choreography for it. Senryu Taiko used two kata (first diagonal, then facing the chudaiko) and utilized the space around their chudaiko in strikingly different ways than Satori Daiko, by shifting stances and deploying a broader range of strokes, such as large sweeping strokes that crossed in front of the body.[10] The overall effect was extremely graceful and physically lyrical, unlike the powerfully grounded and stationary effect of Rev. Tom's minimal choreography. The students always credit the "piece" as Rev. Tom's (e.g., on concert programs), but they perform it in ways that he never would have, that offer their own distinctive interpretation.

"The work" is thus something flexible and potentially open to rearrangement and rechoreographing, though in this case it retains its original attribution to Rev. Tom. This comparatively open-ended approach to authorship attaches "the work" to an originating individual, though it assumes a slightly different shape and character in its bodily realization by another group. Such difference isn't thought of as mere ornamental detail laid over "the work" itself. I literally didn't recognize "the work" as "Aranami" for a long moment when I watched Senryu Taiko's version of it, despite the fact that "Aranami" is part of me, heart and soul, since I have played it so many times over the years. I was disoriented for that long moment, suspended in a jarring sense of knowing but not knowing. It sounded familiar, but I didn't know what it was because its bodily realization was so different.

But this "analysis" needs to go further. Kumi-daiko is literally a group experience—few of us ever play alone, except to practice—and that needs to be part of any analysis. This is a tradition of massed drums, with no emic theory of how many are too few or too many. I played "Aranami" with approximately one hundred other taiko players in 1999 for the opening of the Pavilion of the Japanese American National Museum in Los Angeles.[11] The experience of the sound and the experience of playing are meant to be multiple: many sounds, many performers. Satori Daiko has eighteen members, and we are used to a certain density of sound. As in many amateur taiko groups, some but not all of us have "training" in music, which means that we don't all play with a metronomic sense of exactness or subdivision, and we don't play as a large group with an expectation of rhythmic precision—whatever that might mean. Some of our members have extensive

Western art music training, and the group's inexactness of attack and inability to control tempos with any certainty are sources of frustration for them. In this community of performers a diversity of ability is a given, though not all participants accept this with equanimity. Another way of putting it would be to say that the amateur taiko scene does not *discourage* participation based on a lack of musical training. It is assumed that playing makes you into a musician—not that you must be a musician in order to play. Musical chops are recognized and admired, but they are not the only criterion for being a "good" musician. Rev. Tom selected the members of Satori Daiko from his many classes, and he said more than once that solid playing ability in itself wasn't the only or even the main thing that he looked for: he chose students who had a good "attitude" as much as anything else, and that attitude is the thing often referred to as "the taiko spirit," a set of values that include a lack of ego or arrogance, the ability to work well with others, the choice to put the group before your own concerns, the will and desire to learn, and the motivation to work hard. When we rehearse, we go over the matters that contribute to good "ensemble" playing in other kinds of music (timing, choreography, dynamics, and so on), but we also attend to spirit. We are used to hearing quite a bit of flamming: we don't all come down on downbeats together in any absolute sense. We have limits to how much flamming we will tolerate for ourselves, but these limits are not the same as those for studio musicians. The relationship between playing with spirit and playing with metronomic exactitude has a wider envelope for us than for some other traditions.[12]

Playing with a group of other people has deep bodily implications. We are trained to look around us, at one another and at the audience; there is no notation in which to bury our heads or eyes. You become used to the sensation of hearing and feeling sound all around you. Taiko is invasive: a deaf musician could easily become an accomplished taiko player through the bodily reception of sound vibrations and visual cues. The shime or the *kane* (a small struck gong) cuts through the mass of other sounds, so "listening" in taiko is both selective and involuntary: you are subject to all the sounds around you but learn to focus on some over others.

But isn't a lot of music making like that? What do performers in any tradition hear, and how are they brought or socialized into certain kinds of listening? The multiplicity of sounds (notice that I am avoiding words like *inexactness* and *imprecision*) that is so much a part of amateur taiko groups is hard to talk about because taiko players are subject to the aesthetics of Western art music, which neither values nor encourages messy playing. But the theory versus the practice of taiko is an essential distinction, and the noise of messy, imprecise, unprofessionalized playing is quintessentially part of the political aesthetics of taiko. In flamming, I hear something besides an inability to subdivide: I hear the activation of the body politic.

Taiko has been central to Japanese American and Asian American identity work since the 1970s. Taiko posits strength, discipline, organization, group consciousness—the very things that define the Asian American Movement as a political presence. Not coincidentally, Japanese/Asian Americans turned to taiko during the decade when universities were creating ethnic studies programs and when the Japanese American reparations movement was defined, articulated, and operationalized (E. Yamamoto 2001). Taiko was part of an assertive new Asian American sensibility, and it came to represent not only Sansei confidence but also the political consciousness that being Japanese American is also being Asian American and that the incarceration affected all Asian Americans. The pan-ethnic gesture of "Asian American" is a coalitional grouping, not an erasure of history or difference. The cover of William Wei's important *The Asian American Movement* (1993), for example, features a photograph of a taiko player at a demonstration commemorating the death of Vincent Chin and protesting anti-Asian violence.[13] Taiko became a metaphorical *and* an actual manifestation of the Japanese/Asian American body politic, though the extent to which this is acknowledged or deliberately activated varies. Part of the power of the taiko body politic, I think, is the dynamic difference between Japanese American and Asian American as separate but interconstitutive and even overlapping identities. This is central to my own interest in taiko and was manifested in some of the sites where we performed. In April 2003, for instance, Satori Daiko played "Aranami" at the annual pilgrimage to the site of one of the ten Japanese American incarceration camps: Manzanar, in the high desert of central California. All these camps were in remote areas, and few have any remaining structures; most are now barren expanses of rock, grass, sand, and tumbleweed punctuated by the foundations of the barracks that housed more than 120,000 Japanese Americans from 1942 to 1945. Since the 1970s—that key period when Japanese Americans and Asian Americans got politically organized—former internees have arranged annual pilgrimages to these sites, keeping memory alive and linking past and present civil liberties issues. The pilgrimages always feature music, speeches, religious services at the camp cemeteries, testimony from the now-elderly surviving internees, and more. They are a compelling example of consciously created ritual. When Satori Daiko participated, we spent a long morning in the sun and desert wind surrounded by others determined to remember—former internees, young Asian American activists, local schoolchildren—listening to music and speeches and participating in an interdenominational religious service. We played "Aranami" with the snow-topped Sierra Nevada behind us, the hot wind in our faces, and the stirring, sobering presence of Manzanar's ruins around us. (See video 13, Satori Daiko playing "Aranami" at the Manzanar Pilgrimage, at *http://wonglouderandfaster.com*.)

What did "Aranami" mean in that context? One could riff on the programmatic meaning of turbulent waves and the metaphoric connection to advocacy and resistance, but these weren't Rev. Tom's original intent, nor were they brought up at the time—the work is simply part of our core repertoire, you could say, and its non-specific message of strength and power fit the bill. At another level, the sheer presence and sound of a taiko group—any taiko group—was the point, for all the metonymic reasons I have noted. At yet another level, we were there because Rev. Tom had worked with the founders of the Manzanar Committee in the 1970s, when he was drawn into the Asian American Movement and the Japanese American reparations movement, so our presence in 2003 was an extension of his personal history and his coming into political consciousness as a young Japanese American. Satori Daiko was one way that Rev. Tom participated in a body politic, and therefore we did too. "Aranami" became part of a web of associations: First World / Third World patterns of labor migration, the racialization of bodily economies, and the surveillance of these economies. This aggregative process is the mechanism behind political process: How do individuals draw together into formations? How does an idea become shared? How does a movement become political action? How is the body politic activated?

I now draw together the three parts of my argument into a methodology for how music might be addressed. Musical sound is a bodily product; attending to the body means taking experience seriously; experience is always individual but implicates the collective. The production of musical sound through the body politic is the thing most worth getting at, it seems to me, and a few key ethnomusicologists have focused on this challenge at both the micro and the macro levels.

I focused above on the dynamic sound phenomenon of musicians playing together in ways that draw on the sonic reality of multiple presences. Charles Keil (1994) argues that imprecision is centrally part of the excitement of live musicking: the micromoments of coming in and out of any exact or absolute conception of downbeat or pitch are what make the music dynamic, vital, powerful, moving, and simply interesting. He writes, "The power of music lies in its participatory discrepancies," and "Music, to be personally involving and socially valuable, must be 'out of time' and 'out of tune'" (96). By focusing on the moments when things don't line up exactly, he identifies the "discrepancies" that make performance alive and "participatory"; he prioritizes liveness, couching it in terms of a cultural "ecology" of life, identity, and performance that is both compelling and oddly romantic (97). Keil argues for peak experiences achieved through live performance with others, whether while dancing a polka or listening to the blues, as moments when we are "swept up," full of "euphoric feelings," and immersed in a "deeper and more satisfying knowledge of who we are" (98).

The ethnomusicologist Steven Feld's (1982) expansive work on a Kaluli community in Papua New Guinea also situates sonic multiplicity as a principle. In conversation with Keil (1994, 114), Feld posited the "lift-up-over-sounding" sonic aesthetic of the Kaluli as a world view or, as he put it, a "spatial-acoustic metaphor" that becomes more broadly and deeply a model for perceiving the world and relationships between everything in that world. The Kaluli most value musical sound and conversational speech that is dense and overlapping, drawn from their perception of the sonic and visual space of the Papua New Guinea rain forest.

In short, these two ethnomusicologists—who not coincidentally have worked together closely over the years—have both focused on how sound relationships map out the imbrication of aesthetics with everything else in a culture, from social ecology to environmental ecology and beyond. Both suggest that sound relationships matter, though always in locally specific ways. Both focus on how the sounds don't "line up," as it were, and they find important and epistemologically essential meanings in those overlappings and discrepancies. This is not to say that all musics everywhere contain their most profound meaning in mismatch and misalignment[14] but rather that the very terms of such values probably tell us—and the people making them—something important. This is more than a reiteration of homology models for music and culture.[15] Musical sounds have a synergistic relationship with the body politic and with the supercultural and subcultural interactions posited by Mark Slobin (1993). Sound and movement are realizations of the body's work as well as sites where the body is (re)formulated. The body in performance does a lot at once: it moves in obedience to supercultural imperatives, it recapitulates the terms of that obedience, it formulates the means for questioning and refusing those terms, and so on, and all this happens simultaneously. For instance, the ethnomusicologist Veit Erlmann (1996, 25) compares the work of the body in the late capitalist First World to its placement in the laboring Third World and argues that these locations outline different ways to understand "the work in the work of art." Which is emphasized, and which is most enabled: the agency of the body's work, or its control?

As the musicologist Christopher Small (1998, 213) puts it, any musical performance articulates a "whole set of ideal relationships" between sounds and between people. Small took a long look at the late twentieth-century phenomenon of Western art music as a cultural construction, and he didn't like what he saw. He reflected on the practices defining the performance and reception of symphony concerts and reluctantly concluded that they were "too hierarchical, too distant, and too one-dimensional for [his] taste." Arguing that the music we choose to make and listen to tells us what kind of world we want to live in, he came to the painful conclusion that the repertories which had been "a source of pleasure and satisfaction since [his] earliest days" no longer worked for him—that they went "counter to the way [he] believe[d] human relationships should be" (220). He insisted that the question for anyone must then be "Who am I that I should go on wanting to play and hear the works in this repertory?" As a young musician, I went through the same process of immersion in and identity formation through Western art music, and later, as an ethnomusicologist, I not only reached the same conclusion as Small but went in search of musics that constructed different versions of social reality and different models for ideal human relationships. As an Asian American ethnomusicologist, I think taiko provides a compelling template for a social, cultural, and musical reality that unambiguously emphasizes relational experience.

I realize that I *still* haven't focused on sound. One could say that I have written around it, circling around the thing itself, addressing the bodies producing the sounds more than the sounds themselves. Working through "Aranami" has shown me this: my own immersive experiences of the piece generated a pressing desire to understand how and why it is so thrilling to make its sounds and hear them alongside other people, both taiko players and audience members. Clearly, I am both unable and unwilling to talk about the sounds "themselves" as isolatable or meaningful. I have followed Small's lead in finding that for taiko practitioners, performance is more meaningful than composition, the experience of performance (and not the "music itself") is foregrounded, and the embodiment/enactment of sound creates affective, choreographic structures of meaning and effect that are just the opposite of the objectified structures at the heart of traditional music analysis.

In sum, these are the matters that can be pursued through "analysis": the primary values and the social vision driving the experience of music, whether hearing or performing. That experience may or may not be euphoric or one of flow—it may manifest in very different terms than those I described for taiko—but it will certainly hinge on the shift in sensibility from the individual to the collective and back again. I close with the sense that "Aranami" is and isn't something that holds still or something that allows analysis. It suggests that vestiges of the body and the work of performance may be found in a piece of music, but such a piece might better be regarded as a stopping-off point, a room with many doors. Attending to the sonic means redefining the act of listening.

LOOKING #1

Look at the group of photos taken by one of my taiko friends (video 1, montage of Gary St. Germain's photos, at *http://wonglouderandfaster.com*). Gary St. Germain and I—and about fifteen other amateur musicians, mostly Japanese American— were in Satori Daiko together through most of the 2000s. Now in late middle age, Gary is hapa haole (in his case half Japanese and half French Canadian). He is a public school music teacher, a rock and roll drummer, and a very serious amateur photographer. He has probably taken thousands of photos of Satori Daiko over the years. I told him I wanted to feature some of his photos in this book, and I asked him to send me around ten of his favorites. These are the ones he sent.

I looked at them and realized he hadn't sent any photos of our group, so I asked him if he could send some favorite photos of Satori Daiko in action, and he sent the ones in video 2, montage of Gary St. Germain's photos of Satori Daiko, at *http://wonglouderandfaster.com*.

These are all striking and even accomplished photos. I'm not sure they offer the story I want to tell about taiko, but I see a specific aesthetic at work in these images. I have been perplexed for some time about how to take critically effective photos of North American taiko, especially of my group. Documenting events in which you are actively involved is a practical and a political challenge. Do I step out of the action so I can capture it? Do I help serve food, carry equipment, talk with friends, or do I step away so I can document other people doing those things? Do I put my own sociality on standby or do I participate?

But I've been even more challenged by deeper matters. One can't *see* taiko without a lot of historical interference at work. I can't *see* taiko without reenacting and revitalizing other ways of seeing, including the colonial gaze and its contemporary cousin, the multicultural gaze. It is impossible to do visual documentation of any kind (still photography, video, etc.) without reenacting colonial and touristic traditions of looking. I can't *see* taiko. I am blind. I am frustrated because I am at the mercy of inculcated ways of *seeing* that have colonized my ability to look. Throughout this chapter, I mark this valence of *seeing* by italicizing it. This is the act of looking that I want but can't achieve. This is the ability to look at my friends in a way that refutes everything framing us: it is an intervention of the most basic kind, a willful act of performative perception that is at once unattainable and necessary. I want to *see* taiko, and my friends playing taiko, in a way that reactivates certain histories without being defined by them. I want to *see* the performance of difference through taiko in ways that quickly acknowledge the problems (orientalism, etc.) and then force an engagement with other narratives—other stories about performance and alterity.

I want an ethnomusicology that moves restlessly between media and assumes a translative shiftiness. This ethnomusicology takes performance more seriously than we have allowed. Ethnomusicologists always come back to the text as the ultimate medium of representation. We are excellent wordsmiths; we are adept at talking around the thing itself; we know how to speak "for" it; and we even know how to *stop* performance so that it can't move around, so we can control the moment and shape that we want to take in hand. We pay little attention to motion, whether through time or space.

I don't want to rehearse and retread and re-create the politics of display here. Hundreds of books and articles have been written on these matters, mostly since the 1980s, addressing the long reach of colonial surveillance and its contemporary presence in images published by National Geographic, Kodak, and Benetton. "Color" is a primary trope in these matters. Color is a literal value, in the sense that the more colors are in a picture, or the brighter they are, the better. Brighter and more colorful people enact a (social) aesthetic that positions variety as visually pleasing and geopolitically comforting. Brightness and cheerfulness are coterminous: clean, smiling, vivid people of color are fun to photograph, and their smiles mean that they are happy to be photographed and happy to be taken home in your camera. They are available, ownable, transportable, accessible. All this is old news.

PICTURES THAT MOVE

The image must be compelled to speak. How does the photograph—this still, silent object—become the thing itself? How can we choreograph it back into movement, let alone into sound? We need to dance with it and engage with it as if it were a partner in a duet.

Ethnomusicologists consistently use photographs in severely limited ways, often to say little more than "I was there" or "Here's an instrument. It has twenty-two strings." The work of Charles and Angeliki Keil (1992, 2002) stands out because they combine music and photography, often working with the photographer Dick Blau. I love Blau's photos of American polka dancers and Roma musicians, and the Keils' grounded words about them. Text and image interact; neither is primary; the frisson between the two is unexpected and stays with you beyond the page.

One of the few standard ethnomusicological monographs that pulls this off is Steven Feld's *Sound and Sentiment* (1982). Feld has experimented with audiovisual media in any number of ways, often pushing the boundaries of accepted practice and wisdom. He too is weighted down by heavy genealogies of "documentation," but he often turns this around and makes it work for him. Near the end of his book, he inserts two color plates that do important critical work. First, he offers a standard photo that gives the viewer the expected full, unobstructed view of a performer, allowing us to take in and own every detail of the man's costume. As Feld puts it,

> The first image has a form that is frequent and conventional in ethnographies. We assume that it represents someone doing what he normally does. With no further information about who is represented here or what he is doing, it is easy to take refuge in the structure of the image—conventional Western portraiture framed in a medium shot—and to assume that this framing is a significant way to depict a Papua New Guinean dressed in a ceremonial costume holding a drum. Further attention can then be directed to the costume itself, the body painting, the red and white feathers, and the palm leaf streamers.
>
> It is clear, however, that these things are not the meaning of the image, nor is the simple meta-message "the photographer was in Papua New Guinea and saw this costuming." The image could have been made at any number of places, and we have no other internal information to indicate the photographer participated in some event for which the costume was made and used. (233–34)

Then you turn the page and see something extraordinarily different. Feld writes:

> The second image is clearly not an attempt at iconic depiction, and only the deliberateness of its presentation here might lead one to decide that it is intentional and not a representation of incompetence. . . .
>
> [It] was very premeditated. Two days before the event at which it was made, I spent the day talking with Jubi and asked him to describe what was going to happen. I wanted to get a sense of the anticipatory feelings that accompany the planning and staging of ceremonies. At one point he remarked: "In the middle of the night, while the dancers continue, dancing and dancing . . . you get tired and lie down . . . and then, all of a sudden, something startles you, a sound, or something . . . you open your eyes and look at the dancer . . . it is a man in the form of a bird." I was taken by this description of that hypnotic, tired, dreamy sensation promoted by a long evening of song, as well as the implication that one is emotionally prepared to experience the ceremony in this way.

> Jubi's remark was the basis for the second photograph; I decided to use a meta-phoric convention from my own culture's expressive tradition in photography to make a synthetic and analytic statement about a Kaluli metaphor. (234, 235–36)

Turning the page from the first image brings the viewer into another world: the dancer is in motion, the photo is blurred, and the longhouse is dark. What might have been discarded as a bad photo is instead one of the most stirring moments in the book: the man becomes a bird before our eyes, dancing in the deep night. Feld explains that this was the only time he stepped away from his "imaging behaviors as an ethnographer" (1982, 236). He calls this attempt "co-aesthetic witnessing" (236) and describes the photo as an encore to the rest of the book, though it also forecasts his subsequent experiments with soundscape recordings and more. It is an effort to see differently and to participate in an aesthetic by doing more than just looking. The photo moves. The viewer (you or I) looks at the photo and sees not only Feld's shift in perspective but an invitation to see *with*.

Similarly, Louise Meintjes (2004, 176) uses a photograph to convey the power of the kick in Zulu *ngoma*. In this extraordinary photo by T. J. Lemon, the dancer Bafana Mdlalose is seen head on. His body fills the frame; a woman behind him is blurrily out of focus, so our eyes are drawn to nothing but him. His posture is impossible: at first you can't make out how the parts of his body can be where they are. His right foot is high above his head; the sole of his shoe dominates the top left corner of the photo. He is grimacing, and his stare is directed somewhere above the viewer's head: Lemon caught him in the exact moment of kicking his foot into the air, so his arms are down and his body is powerfully contracted. He is shouting; we can see his teeth and the lines in his forehead. We can't help but admire the musculature of his shoulder, his left arm, his left thigh, and the startling back of his right calf and hamstring. His posture is powerfully unnatural. The focused energy of the move clearly comes from the core of his body, but the photographer has deliberately left this dark, shadowed—the energy comes from a place we can't *see*. Mdlalose's entire body makes visible the physical effort of the kick—this key choreography of defiance. Meintjes describes this moment:

> Of the hardest hit they say in Zulu "*inesigqi!*" (It has power!). The hardest hit has power. The voiced palatal 'click' -*gqi* is an aural icon of the thud of the foot hitting the ground after a high frontal kick in the Zulu men's dance styles called *ngoma*. After a preparatory sequence, the dancer's right knee bends, his back arches, his head tilts back. He extends his right arm over his head as his left leg stretches back to prepare for the pick-up to the beat. The forward thrust of his left arm balances his taut and arching body. Then, as if a spring suddenly triggered, he kicks his left leg into the sky, curls his torso and shoots his right arm forward to balance his one-legged stance. His skyward foot thunders down onto the ground on the beat, *gqi!* Dust flies. He throws away the movement with his hands, in the recoil of his torso, with a flick of his head, and he saunters off. (174)

The relationship between the photo and Meintjes's vivid paragraph isn't clear. Is she describing this dancer, or is her description generic and the photograph an apt but nonspecific example of such a "high frontal kick"? Her purpose is to reintegrate sound, the body, and politics, and her justly famous article offers a compelling model. She unpacks how *ngoma* generates "that sense of total dense consolidation" of collective song, dance, and purpose (180). She articulates "the absolutely dialogic relation between the kinetic body and the sound as two expressive elements that collectively compose the form" of *ngoma* (184), and the similarities with taiko are strong.

Coaesthetic witnessing is a critical move that means the ethnographer has made an ontological commitment to try to *see*, which probably means feeling, knowing, listening, carrying things, and more. I aim to leave the documentary impulse behind and move instead to enact core values in every frozen moment. This is a shift in intent and position; this is a performative commitment.

HOW I DON'T WANT TO LOOK AT TAIKO

capture
take
shoot
snap
freeze

Photographs of performance are so predictable. It's as if photographers think they've been granted automatic access to people's souls and, worse, have already decided what (they think) they know about those souls before taking the picture. There are an impressive number of clichéd ways to look at taiko and to capture it. Most performance traditions have clichéd photographic expectations. The jazz sax player, always a cisgender man, is always captured blowing out a high note with his eyes squeezed shut. This is supposed to tell us that he is full of emotion, that he is putting "everything" into it, that body and soul are one and the same (a trope mapped onto any music with African American roots), that he is so deeply into the music that everything else has vanished, and so on. Classical pianists are photographed hunched intensely over the keys or in transport, with their head thrown back and eyes closed; they are never, ever, *ever* photographed smiling while they play.

Stereotyped ways to depict taiko players are clichés because they enact and maintain certain narratives about the tradition. The odaiko is generally the largest kind of drum in a taiko ensemble and is deeply connected to specific ideas about masculinity, strength, and authority. I write about these matters at great length in chapter 5, but here it suffices to say that men are far more likely to play virtuosic odaiko solos than women. Gendered ability is never "natural," though it certainly takes considerable upper-body strength to play above shoulder level. No rules decree that men should play the odaiko more than women; rather, a series of historically specific practices have hardened the gender associations between men and the odaiko, particularly the spectacular solos played on odaiko by members of the Japanese taiko groups Ondekoza and Kodo. As a result, playing lengthy virtuosic solos on this instrument is at once a sign of strength, stamina, gendered authority, and cultural authenticity. Following from that, many taiko players, especially men who want to be known for their abilities as soloists or as master teachers, tend to have their photographs taken at the odaiko, often from behind. They often display quite a bit of skin as well, partly in homage to Kodo but also to show off musculature. This kind of photograph thus tells a story about mastery, discipline, and roots: this stereotypical image depicts a body grounded in the most authentic practices . . . even when it's a woman doing it. When a woman is inserted into this generic taiko photograph (and she can be only an insertion, not an authentic presence), she is understood to aspire to the kind of fame and regard normally reserved for men in this tradition, especially in Japan. A few women—especially Tiffany Tamaribuchi—have effectively redirected and even disrupted this iconic image, but only by first evoking it (Ahlgren 2008). In short, this kind of photograph is endlessly restaged and reshot because it tells a story that certain people want and need. Some of those people are taiko players. Others are not, and they want to capture or consume an idea of taiko reflecting their need for particular kinds of authenticity or authority.

LOOKING #2: WHY IT'S HARD TO PHOTOGRAPH JAPANESE AMERICANS

As Joseph Jonghyun Jeon (2012, xiii) writes, the "dark trope in American history" is that "racializing objectification erases subjectivity." Asian Americans simply aren't *seen,* and when we are, the refracting lens of racialized logic ensures that something else comes into focus and our subjectivity vanishes. The exuberant visuality of taiko is necessarily, inevitably, and disquietingly in permanent negotiation with this dynamic. Many of my taiko friends are Japanese Americans who have lived in Southern California for much if not all of their lives. Their families are mostly from this area, and they are rooted in an extensive Japanese American community that stretches across some four generations and the sprawling suburbs of greater Los Angeles. Two degrees of separation is the most that anyone seems to have from anyone else. This extended community is framed by the historical fact of the Japanese American incarceration. Almost everyone has relatives who were interned; one member of Satori Daiko was born in an incarceration camp. The incarceration is a mostly unspoken but defining presence.

The incarceration camps were photographed in specific ways by specific photographers, and a small body of fine scholarship has emerged on this, particularly the work of Elena Tajima Creef. Ansel Adams's and Dorothea Lange's photographs offer contrasting approaches to *looking* at the incarceration, both critical but profoundly different from each other. Adams created aestheticized portraits of heroic American citizens, often in carefully composed arrangements of line and light. Lange went for messier images of drudgery and the weary work of incarceration. Both photographers assembled gripping bodies of documentation, each infused with certain political sensibilities—Adams's assertion of the "good" Japanese American citizen, Lange's thinly contained sense of outrage—but neither corpus can be described as coaesthetic witnessing. Both photographers were profoundly manipulative. Providing a political critique involved aestheticizing Japanese Americans in ways that are now part of *my* ability to *see* and to know. As Susan Sontag (2003, 76) wrote, "Transforming is what art does, but photography that bears witness to the calamitous and the reprehensible is much criticized if it seems 'aesthetic'; that is, too much like art." These beautiful black-and-white images of the emblematic wound to Japanese America are centrally part of what I *see* when I look at taiko.

Fast-forward fifty years to the present, through the civil rights era and the Japanese American fight for reparations. The problem of the incarceration has been solved and the predominant narrative in SoCal is multiculturalism and the celebration of difference. Multicultural festivals punctuate the landscape like bright smorgasbords, colorful and tasty and fun to see. Satori Daiko plays at festival after festival, in city parks, in blocked-off streets, in parking lots. My hard drive is full of the same photograph taken over and over again: we're on a stage, playing for an audience sitting in folding chairs or passing by with children in strollers and dogs on leashes, eating hot dogs or funnel cake. Everyone's having a good time. The sun is out. The same banner is behind us on stage, saying that we're in Gardena or Monterey Park or Ventura and that the festival's sponsor is Budweiser or Target or WalMart. The group waiting to come on is a Brazilian samba troupe or Chinese ribbon dancers or a local rock band. We're playing our hearts out, but it's the same photograph: We're part of a story that's being told about us. No, we're telling that story ourselves, whether or not we meant to.

I can't reconcile these images. I look at these pictures and I realize all over again that I can't *see*—I'm looking through someone else's eyes, like in those sci-fi stories where the protagonist has been transported into someone else's body. I don't want to be in this body. I want to be able to *see* in my own ways.

THREE WAYS OF LOOKING AT TAIKO

In his poem "Thirteen Ways of Looking at a Blackbird," Wallace Stevens offers this final way of looking:

XIII
It was evening all afternoon.
It was snowing
And it was going to snow.
The blackbird sat
In the cedar-limbs.

Time is suspended. Things are happening and are anticipated. A dark, vital presence punctuates this: the blackbird has a marked stillness and is a defining reference. The blackbird is to time and snow what a photograph could be to performance. It immobilizes the ephemeral things that are so beautiful and so important, but without judgment, violence, or desire. It is a cipher, but it allows time and action to continue to move, flow, and stir us.

Let me offer three ways of deploying still photography to learn something about taiko. I want to use photography to learn about taiko, ethnomusicology, ethnography, and difference all at the same time. I want to get beyond "I was there" and "This is what the musical instrument looks like." I want photography *not* to be self-evident. I want it to be more than an extratextual way of saying the same thing as the text. I want it to require conversation (both speaking and listening). I want looking, feeling, and understanding to be pushed into a circle of interconstitutive effort, *through* the text, through a cross-media circuit of translative exchange between the writer and the reader. It's meant to be a mutual effort in the way that a good conversation is shared work and shared play. Here are the three ways of looking at taiko:

1. This is what that moment feels like.
2. This is how that moment opens up.
3. This is how these moments come together.

I'll start with #1. If we really want photography to "capture" a moment, then we should put more thought into why some moments are worth capturing or are (in)appropriate to capture and why the temporal gesture of freezing/capturing/slowing/objectifying the ephemeral motions of performance is something worth doing. I have already addressed the problem of aestheticizing through the act of stopping and the kinds of beautiful violence wrought by the unitary eye.

The photo in figure 3 (Taiko Center of Los Angeles members playing "Amano," 1998, at *http://wonglouderandfaster.com*) was taken about a year after I started playing taiko; I don't remember who took it. It's been used countless times as a PR photo for the Taiko Center of Los Angeles. It catches us in a particular moment in a piece called "Amano," short for "Amanojaku," which is associated with a taiko group based in Tokyo. It isn't literally programmatic—we're not pretending to be *amanojaku*, the little demons who can convince people to act on their worst desires—but it uses some rhythms from Kabuki and has a dramatic choreography, seen here. The central phrase stops in the middle with a one-beat rest in which the taiko players freeze with their arms in the air. This is what that moment feels like: if you do it right, you use your entire body to push your arms into the air above your head, working up from the hara, drawing on the rootedness of your thighs and feet in basic kata position. You can do this only if you allow yourself to be relaxed and flexible, if you allow your entire body to move in a quick flow of related parts. You should think of your arms, hands, and bachi as arriving at a certain point—that is, you need to envision a point of arrival, with your bachi in a slight V so that they stop at dynamic point where they're about ten inches apart at the tips but feel as if there's electricity crackling between them. You STOP there, for a long second: everything should arrive and STOP. This is pure *ma,* an empty dynamic space that gives meaning to everything around it. Then you pull your arms down for six eighth notes—*DORO-tsuku-DORO*—and then repeat the gesture, thrusting your arms UP. When you arrive at that moment with your arms in the air, you can shout *Ho!* if you like, to punctuate it, to fill it, to help define the exact point of arrival.

The now-forgotten photographer caught me at that moment. I didn't achieve the right combination of flexibility and arrival every single time. "Aranami" is an aerobic piece to play, and sometimes I tired toward the end as the tempo sped up and it became harder to catch the moment just so. But this photo shows me arriving at ma perfectly. By *perfectly* I mean that my kata looks right, but I'm really saying that you can tell I got it from the look on my face as much as from my actual form, which is literally perfect (said in all humility—this was not always the case). On the left, Janet Anwyl didn't quite get it—look, the bachi in her right hand is still cocked, so she didn't think of pushing up using the ends of her bachi like arrows. On my other side, Irene Ogata got there but is trying too hard: look at how her shoulders are hunched up—you can see how stiff she is and how she's forced the movement rather than pushing up from the core. It's in her face too: she has a kind of blank, frozen stare that shows she's all inside her head, thinking too hard rather than directing her ki outward. I can tell you all this because I've been there and done that.

This is how that moment opens up. Any moment is set within many other moments, some of them side by side, others far away in space and time. Let me turn to another photo: figure 4, Audrey Nakasone airborne, at *http://wonglouderandfaster.com.* This isn't a great picture, but I love it because of the series of moments it offers. This is Audrey Nakasone, formerly a member of Satori Daiko. I miss her. It all ended in fraught ways, as it sometimes does in music ensembles when people care deeply about what they're doing and the terms on which they come together to do it. In short, she left the group, and it took us more than a year to get things back on track. She wasn't a trained musician, so her sense of rhythm wasn't perfect, but she had more ki than anyone else I've ever played with. She had already been playing for about ten years when I first started, so I looked to her as an authority, though she wasn't officially our teacher. Rev. Tom was our teacher and director, but Audrey was nonetheless completely in charge of our group. If she said "Get in line," we got in line. Sometimes this made me feel browbeaten and infantilized, but I still got in line, because she knew what she was doing.

This photo shows her jumping while playing, and it exemplifies her tremendous ki and her ability to channel it. It reminds me of how much fun it was to play beside her: she was always, *always* directed outward, and completely in the moment, and aware of whoever she was playing with. She was a tyrant, but she was also one of the most generous musicians with whom I've ever played. With some of my taiko pals, I feel as if they're waiting for me to do something wrong, but Audrey had the ability to pull the best playing out of each of us by connecting. Playing with some of my taiko friends feels like being bullied: they push the tempo on purpose and simply expect everyone to follow, for instance. Audrey sometimes bullied me with words, but only in rehearsals, and when we played together she created a positive connection that drew the best out of me and pulled me up to the next level.

When I teach fieldwork courses, I often ask my students to write an essay about one of their research photos, to get them out of show-and-tell mode. A picture isn't worth a thousand words: it will tell you only as much as you demand of it, and if you demand only that it retell old stories, then that's all it will do. John and Malcolm Collier (1992, 99–115) suggest several ways to treat photography as a kind of social action and *inter*action. For instance, they encourage anthropologists to use photographs in interviews—that is, the researcher and the researched should literally look at photographs together and thus disrupt the interviewer-interviewee binary—to prompt people to talk about themselves, their environment, and the things most meaningful to them. As the Colliers put it, this shifts the very terms of the relationship, by asking people to be "expert guides" rather than "the *subject* of the interrogation" (106). It also resituates meaning from the image back into the person looking at it. Photographs aren't self-contained: they aren't objects complete unto themselves, though a heavy history of aestheticized assumptions encourages this idea. They demand to be read, and my reading of this photograph includes attention to the relationship I had with Audrey, to sadness over a friendship lost, to a discussion of what ki is and how it works, to the dynamics of pedagogy and learning.

MOVING: THIS IS HOW THESE MOMENTS COME TOGETHER

We shouldn't expect photographs to stand alone. After all, the stand-alone photograph is basically a throwback to art history and the odd ways that the practice of aestheticized photography has been wed to the history of painting: early photographers often evoked the moves and expectations of painterly praxis, including the expectation that "an" image should have the legs to stand on its own, alone, as an isolated moment. Why should that be? The image is a moment extracted from many moments. So maybe we shouldn't force it to be a single moment. Instead, let me show you an afternoon—the long, beautiful afternoon of August 4, 2007, at Gardena Buddhist Church, a Japanese American temple in California. I share that afternoon with you to explain why taiko players need to know how to do bon-odori, the group dances that are part of the Obon ritual. I use photography to try to show you what it was like, on that afternoon, for *this* taiko player to dance and dance and dance. I will need to show you quite a few photographs, and most aren't Kodak moments—they aren't perfectly composed or balanced or even memorable. But why should we insist that any of them be so? Instead, I suggest that looking at this series of photographs will teach you what it was like, on that afternoon, to be a taiko player who went to participate in bon-odori to move through what some Japanese Americans say is the heart of Japanese American taiko, even though you are moving *to* taiko rather than playing it. I don't yet want to give you an encyclopedia definition of Obon or bon-odori. Both are touchstones throughout this book. Suffice it to say that these dances are both new and old, that they are always done in unison, and that it doesn't matter whether the people who dance them are good or not: the point is to participate. Obon is a kind of unintentional corrective to the SoCal multicultural festival. I don't offer it as more authentic; rather, it reflects the reality of existing Japanese American communities that are here, now, despite incarceration, despite out-marriage, despite the fact that the suburbs are the new Japantowns. Obon interfaces with the multicultural festival but is its vital cousin, reminding us that community is sometimes quite real and coherent and doesn't need to be stage-managed.

The dances are scheduled at the end the day, after you have presumably been at the temple for a while, probably watching and listening to taiko performances and buying and eating teriyaki, *dango*, spam *musubi, gyoza*, or shaved ice. It's five o'clock, and people are gravitating toward the side street that's been closed to traffic, where white lines have been chalked onto the asphalt, concentric ovals a block long. If you're a kid, you went bobbing for goldfish and are probably carrying one around in a clear plastic bag. You've checked out the farmers' market. If you're a member of the temple's Buddhist Women's Association, you've been in high gear for several days and are now working at a food stall. If you're a member of the temple, you've been running into acquaintances and chatting.

Participating in an event often means looking at the backs of people's heads. Dancing means you're in motion and can't make the moments into a single moment. Participating means taking "bad" pictures—photographs that are blurry, unbalanced, cluttered, unposed. Coaesthetic witnessing forces a willingness to discard the aestheticized terms of good photography once and for all. You—the reader—must flip through these photos in a suspended act of waiting to dance (see video 3, montage of Obon and *bon-odori* at Gardena Buddhist Church, August 4, 2007, at *http://wonglouderandfaster.com*). Most were taken between dances. Each dance lasted about five minutes and the entire event about two hours. In between dances, things stopped for three or four minutes while a new drummer climbed up into the *yagura* or the MC made sure the right CD was in the PA system. Everyone waited, still on the white lines. We chatted with one another. People came into or went out of the dance circle. That's when I took pictures. There are no photographs here of dancing (because I was dancing), save one near the beginning of the sequence. The woman in it stands with her hands folded in prayer, slightly to the left of the white chalk line in the street. She and her dance companions wear matching white *happi* coats with red borders—they're all from the same temple. Her face is solemn; her expression suggests something internal. She's praying, or rather, her face and her hands and her stance all say that this is "Bon-odori Uta," the dance done at the beginning and again at the very end of the evening. The dance *is* prayer, stately and a bit slow, with the hands in and out of *gassho:* they weave and sway, pantomiming a fish swimming. Gassho is several things at once: the gesture of putting the hands together in prayer, a greeting, an expression of ritual understanding that a Buddhist frame has been created, reverence. My photograph shows the woman in prayer—her hands, her face, her body, her place in a line of people doing the same thing. It's a "good" photo. But its presence here means *I* wasn't in gassho, which isn't good at all.

MOVING THROUGH THE IMAGE

Documenting Japanese American drumming demands a new kind of visual ethnomusicology. I have offered a series of moves that folds the history of the colonial gaze into a mindful practice of *seeing*. It is impossible to do visual documentation of any kind without reenacting colonial and touristic traditions of looking. These acts of looking are unavoidably part of the way the way that we see and thus part of the way that anyone—including taiko players themselves—is forced to "see" taiko. I offer an unbeautiful, uncelebratory visual ethnomusicology that acknowledges the guiding, spectacularized effects of colonial surveillance on our ability to see yet deploys visual technologies to try to get inside the performance of alterity from the viewpoint of a participant. I thus offer a willfully conflicted yet mindful attempt to document taiko as an intervention in those economies.

Reaching for a time-out-of-time is perhaps necessary here. The defining gaze can't be undone, it seems. As Rey Chow (1993, 51) puts it, "Because [the] 'originary' *witnessing* is, temporally speaking, lost forever, the native's defiled image must *act* both as 'image' (history of her degradation) and as that witnessing gaze." The moment before being seen retreats and retreats. My book doesn't stand silently on the page: it shudders and blinks and jumps. I hope it pushes at how ethnomusicology has depended on critical moves that limit how we are able to think about performance—that is, how we are able to *see* performance, and thus to *see* the serious cultural work that performance does. I dance with the camera. Sometimes it's in my pocket and sometimes it's in my hand. My I/eye has many fields of vision. I am trying to *see* more than I can ever, really, see—yet the effort itself is the performative task that begs to be attempted.

2

___

Inventories

The Material Culture of Taiko

The whole world goes into this drum.

—MARK MIYOSHI, JAPANESE AMERICAN TAIKO MAKER, *MAKING AMERICAN TAIKO*

I understand blackness as always already performed.

—MONICA L. MILLER, *SLAVES TO FASHION: BLACK DANDYISM AND THE STYLING OF BLACK DIASPORIC IDENTITY*

WHAT'S IN MY BAG

Let me show you what's in my taiko bag. The canvas tote I use to carry all my taiko paraphernalia just gave out after over a decade of use. It's red and has the distinctive TCLA logo silk-screened on one side (see figure 5, the author's Taiko Center of Los Angeles bag, at *http://wonglouderandfaster.com*). Luckily, my mother had bought one just like it from my teacher and was kind enough to let me have hers. She didn't play taiko but was a faithful audience member and supporter.

This chapter is not a taiko primer. I know what the early chapters of an ethnography are supposed to do: the genre dictates that the scene should be set, maps provided, and the histories defined.[1] This chapter will not give a tidy overview of, well, anything about taiko. This book will not begin with times past, summaries, or taxonomies. I begin instead with the things closest to me: the things I need to play and the attitudes toward them that I have learned from my friends and teachers. You *will* learn what's in my taiko bag: this is an inventory.[2] My bag is always full of what I'll need, plus a lot of detritus from rehearsals and past events. The main thing it contains is my bachi bag, a cloth bag full of drumsticks. Various teachers and local Japanese American craftspersons make bachi bags, but my mother made mine, from cotton cloth with the distinctive Japanese indigo wave pattern; it has a drawstring top and is very simple, but I love it.

THINGS

The material culture of taiko is rich and varied, and taiko players sensuously involve themselves in the material realities of drums, drumsticks, and clothing. They also spend a lot of time thinking and talking about the material things that are part of performance. Drums are, of course, central, but drumsticks are personal, since the drums are often owned by the teacher, whereas bachi are your own. Clothing is both communal and idiosyncratic: performance costumes are the result of agreement and often identical for the whole group,[3] whereas rehearsal clothing is individual but considered. In short, the artifacts surrounding taiko say a lot about the players' attitudes, beliefs, social aesthetics, poetics, and conflicts.

The world of physical objects outlines complex interactions between people, environment, and sociality. Physical objects construct and reflect values and aesthetics. Given the deeply physical performance praxis of taiko, its material culture is deep and well developed. The lives of material objects are fundamental to taiko practice, and human-object interactions are sites of generative meaning. The "things" that taiko players wear, brandish, strike, caress, wash, fold, and repair don't acquire meaning as much as dialogically instantiate meaning in both human bodies and the objects themselves. Object-subject relations aren't thing-human in taiko. As Bill Brown (2001, 4) argues, "The thing really names less an object than a particular subject-object relation." Some phenomenologists even suggest that objects have agency.[4] Barbara Bolt (2013, 4–5) notes that the new humanistic materialism in the arts is both a corrective to the modernist interest in the formalism of any medium and a challenge to the turn-of-the-millennium assumption that art is only discursive, constructed through language. At the end of the last century, ethnomusicologists rendered painstaking taxonomic schemes around the physicality of musical instruments, and this study, which they named organology, was in many ways a gesture of radical scientific relativism, leveling the field to make all musics worthy of serious attention.[5] The museum haunts twenty-first-century ethnomusicologists: its compendium of things is omnipresent. Although we spend most of our time with instruments animated by living bodies, we are uneasily aware of our instinctive trained impulse to describe and categorize the thing: *It's a directly struck barrel-shaped membranophone from category 211.222.1 in the Hornbostel-Sachs [1961] taxonomy, though it could also be categorized as 211.322, since it has two usable membranes.* Still, the twenty-first-century museum is a space in which objects are openly regarded as fraught interfaces between different histories,[6] and that drum is a dialogic animation of all its histories. The ethnomusicological object is overloaded with meaning. I reject its overdetermined transformation into an organological thing; no, I struggle with it. The humanistic turn toward the new materialism has opened a more porous understanding of things, along with a move away from the empirical objectification of objects and the assumption that the materiality of the world simply represents resources to be extracted for human use. The late capitalist assignment of value through networks of difference and need reveals how and why objects—including, especially, those regarded as laded with culture—move around in space and between different practitioners. For instance, given the exorbitant market value of traditional craft objects from Japan, locally made, wine-barrel *chudaiko* were first a necessity in North America but are now perhaps on the verge of being edged out through the strategic infiltration of Asano's gorgeous Japanese-made taiko.

The objects themselves, and the shadowy, shifting relationship between the rustic North American drum and the objet d'art Japanese drum, speak to a rich and troubling history of nations, bodies, global capitalism, and self-determination. Thuy Linh Nguyen Tu (2010, 5) writes, "Asian American culture always bears the traces of its material conditions. But for me, that materiality must be a central site of analysis, rather than simply a context for understanding the cultural text." Following her lead, we can see that the North American drum has an iterative relationship to the Japanese drum, but not vice versa. For North American taiko players, Japanese objects and the use of Japanese-language terminology are always indications of a deep need for cultural authenticity and affiliation. Taiko players' relationships to Japanese objects are often intimate and deeply meaningful. The anthropologist Takeyuki Tsuda (2016, 225–49) argues that taiko offers a "performative authenticity" (248) to Japanese Americans that addresses violent historical discontinuities. We fetishize Japanese objects as a way to address the gaps between past and present. INTERSTING IN RELATION TO FESTIVAL

My bag contains these things: a bachi bag with seven pairs of bachi; a *kane* in a small Japanese cloth bag; and a mesh bag stuffed full of first-aid tape, several barrettes, a small LCD flashlight for reading directions in the dark wings of a stage, my *tekko* (wristbands), business cards for the TCLA, foam earplugs for rehearsal, four *hachimaki* (headbands) made of, respectively, black, gold, blue, and red rope, and a bunch of business cards from people met during gigs. I didn't realize that I had so many bags within my bag. Have I absorbed the Japanese and Japanese American inclination toward wrapping things up?

The *kane* is a small bronze handheld gong. It looks like an ashtray or small saucer. It is more properly called an *atarigane* and is used to keep time because its sound cuts through the roar of even a large group of drummers. It is usually held in the left hand and is struck by a special bachi that has a small piece of deer horn at the end. Deer horn is hard enough to create a loud, clear, percussive sound but also soft enough so that it doesn't dent the kane. I don't often get to use my kane, since a lead musician usually does the honors (usually Rev. Tom, our teacher). After studying taiko for about five years, I started to offer workshops here and there for nonmusicians, and I realized that a kane is an essential means for cutting though the sonic chaos created by beginners. I bought mine at Miyamoto Taiko in Tokyo— it's the middle size, about four inches in diameter—and a little drawstring bag for it a few blocks away, in one of the arts and crafts shops for tourists that line Nakamise

Street, the lane that leads to the main gate of Sensoji, the famous Buddhist temple in Asakusa, in the old-town area of Shitamachi in Tokyo. The bag is a lovely little artifact of traditionality. It is in the "traditional" style carried by Japanese women before World War II but is made of a synthetic version of the knit cloth called *chirimen* and is an object meant to be bought by domestic or foreign tourists in search of traditional crafts. Each drawstring ends in a knot and a five-yen Japanese coin, meant to evoke the past. The bag is simultaneously traditional and orientalist, referencing certain ideas of Japaneseness. I had seen such bags several years before on a previous trip to Tokyo and knew one would be perfect for a kane.

My sakura-pattern hachimaki—a length of cotton printed in a classic red-and-white cherry-blossom pattern, already twisted into a headband—is always at the bottom of the bag, since I wear it a lot. A half-empty plastic water bottle is also down at the bottom. About twenty pieces of paper are stuffed in among everything else, including dog-eared charts from past performances, scribbled directions to past gigs, several old copies of *Rafu Shimpo* (the bilingual Japanese American Los Angeles newspaper) containing announcements about our performances, and advertisements from Marukai (a Japanese supermarket with several stores in greater Los Angeles). It's a mess. I know I should clean it out and archive things, but I rarely get around to it.

Lest you think my bag is unusual, let's see what Beverly Murata has in hers. Beverly is a longtime member of the TCLA and my good friend. On August 26, 2007, after a weekend of performances in California's Central Coast, Rev. Tom was driving his van back to Los Angeles, and I was squeezed into the back seat along with another TCLA member and a lot of drums. We were settled in for a long trip, so it was a good time to ask Beverly to show me the contents of her bag. Some of my best conversations with taiko colleagues took place in this van, on the way home from one gig or another.

Take a look at the ten-minute video 4, Beverly Murata showing the contents of her gear bag, at *http://wonglouderandfaster.com*. Rev. Tom is in the driver's seat, taking us south on the 101 toward home. It is still early in our four-hour drive. Sunlit hills roll by. I am in the back seat, and Beverly is in the front passenger seat. I ask her to show me everything in her bag, so she starts at the top and works her way down, showing me these items in this order: a Habitat for Humanity baseball cap; a black TCLA tank top, which she had worn earlier in the day for our performances; her long black "taiko pants"; an over-the-counter instant cold pack for sore muscles; a pair of dark blue *tabi* (shoes); a pair of dark blue tekko in a plastic Ziploc bag; two twisted rope hachimaki, one gold and one blue and gold; one hachimaki made from a sakura-pattern *tenugui* (thin cotton towel), already twisted and tied, ready to be slung around the neck; a folded red cotton tenugui with the TCLA logo on it; a copy of the notation for our signature piece "Okedo-mai," folded up into a square; several pieces of sandpaper in a Ziploc bag, for smoothing down bachi; a pair of earplugs in a plastic bag; a stretchy knee brace; a pair of tabi ankle socks with little red fish on them, bought in a Tokyo gift shop; a roll of first-aid tape, also bought in Japan, with adhesive on one side, much better than Band-Aids for blisters; a hairbrush; about eight TCLA business cards (Rev. Tom offers a thumbs-up at this point in the footage); a billfold with Satori Daiko business cards with her name on them, made the year before by fellow Satori member Harriet for each of us when we were preparing to go to Japan on a study tour; a small cosmetic bag with a purse mirror, Kleenex, elasticized hair ties, and a barrette; her black cotton bachi bag, with the TCLA logo and a carrying handle, as well as a big bright pink "B" taped on it (so she could easily find it in the dark of the wings during stage performances) and a pink plastic luggage name tag around the handle, attached after she once left her bachi bag behind after a performance; six pairs of bachi inside the bag, including a pair of *shime* bachi from Japan, several pairs of chudaiko bachi of different weights, and a pair of *okedo* bachi (wider at the base and thinner at the striking end), each with a little "B" written on the flat end with a Sharpie to easily identify them as hers; and finally, down at the bottom, a wad of empty supermarket shopping bags, just in case, and a folded-up piece of paper with directions to our performance the day before at the John Anson Ford Theatre. She also has a bottle of water in an outside pocket. I ask her what equipment she has left at home, and she says other costumes, more bachi, a hot-air comb, and "a metronome that I don't use!" She says she has taken several things out of the bag and left them at home for this trip: a small portable tape recorder for practices, useful when learning or creating new pieces; a whole folder of notated pieces; and the Satori dues book, where she keeps track of each member's quarterly dues.

Taiko players bring everything but the kitchen sink. We aim to be ready for anything and everything. We are ready for the pain (blisters, sore muscles) and ready for all the different drums in different pieces necessitating different drumsticks. We are ready for the heaps of drumsticks all jumbled together at the side of the stage, left there as we run from the end of one piece to the beginning of the next. We have an anxious determination to be ready for anything, which demands both flexibility and thorough, exhaustive preparation. There's always a "right" way to do things, and you need to prepare for that. You're going to need a lot of stuff in order to be ready. As Ruth Behar (2013, 4) writes, "Traveling heavy with my doubts and worries" is how we roll. We travel heavy both literally—look at Beverly's bag!—and affectively. Traveling heavy makes it possible to leap into the air at the right moment with the right bachi.

Bachi are a taiko player's most prized possessions. They come in many sizes and shapes, and serious players usually have many pairs. Bachi don't last forever: they get beat up (literally) and they break after some years of use. I always carry seven pairs with me and have another six pairs at home. I just looked back at an old journal entry about the bachi I was carrying with me then and realized how my arsenal has changed:

FROM MY JOURNAL, JUNE 8, 2003

I look over my bachi during a break in the dress rehearsal. I have so many now that they don't all fit in my bachi bag, so I keep the ones that I use only rarely in another bag—my odaiko bachi in particular, which are very large and still quite clean and undinged because I rarely play odaiko.

I have three pairs of chudaiko bachi, one pair of shime bachi, and two pairs of okedo bachi. I just got the second pair of okedo bachi because my original pair (about two years old now) are suddenly dinged to the point that the surface of the wood is splitting and chipping and could damage a drumhead. It occurs to me that I've never used them on okedo: rather, I use them for pieces when I'm moving between chudaiko and shime, e.g., in "Nightfight" and "Lion." My two heavier pairs of chudaiko bachi are impressive but give me blisters within minutes of continuous playing . . . which leaves me embarrassed and humbled, determined to use them more and thus to get used to their heft and their power. But in fact I never do. I keep returning to my earlier pair, which are from the Miyamoto studio. The gold lettering of the studio is part of what I like about them; I also love their slim denseness. But again, they've suddenly become grubby and are starting to split along their deeper dings. I compare them to my Miyamoto shime bachi. Same problem. I look closely and think about doing some serious sanding. That would take off the surface dirt and smooth out the dings, but would I be able to address the deeper dents that are leading to the splitting? I hate the idea of leaving this pair of chudaiko bachi behind. This was my third pair: The first—pine—I was proud to leave behind, as it marked a moment of advancement. The second pair—oak—pleased me—its whiteness, its weight. But moving on to the Miyamoto pair felt like a graduation, and I'm not ready to leave that moment. But that's laziness, because it's also an avoidance of the blisters that my other pairs will leave, reminding me that I'm not yet strong enough, not yet playing as much as I should.

I use my Miyamoto chudaiko bachi all the time. (See figure 6, the author's Miyamoto bachi, at *http://wonglouderandfaster.com*.) Miyamoto is one of the two major Japanese taiko manufacturers. I have been to Miyamoto's main showroom, in Tokyo's Asakusa neighborhood (they also have branch stores), four times now, and I always plan that visit for months because they carry at least fifty kinds of bachi. One of the walls is covered with little cubbyholes, each stacked high with bachi. There are bachi the size of baseball bats, and there are bachi that are thin and delicate. I would guess that they are made from about ten different kinds of wood. A little scale is placed beside the wall of bachi—the kind you might use to weigh letters for the post office—so you can make sure the ones you choose are exactly the same weight. You can spend a lot of time weighing bachi until you have exactly the right two: same weight, same color. Some but not all the bachi have the gold Miyamoto kanji on them. My shime bachi are so marked, and I love them.

AN INVENTORY OF THE TAIKO OWNED BY
REV. TOM KURAI

I don't own any taiko, though a few of my taiko mates do. Beverly, Harriet, and Harriet's daughter, Taylor, each bought their own okedo-daiko in 2003 when we were in Japan together: we have a signature piece that we play on okedo, so it was worth it to them. An okedo has a strap that goes over your right shoulder so you can move around while playing it, and our piece "Okedo-mai," written by a former Satori member, is very upbeat and has marvelous choreography in which we keep changing formation. It's a crowd pleaser. Harriet has a few other taiko at home for practice, I think, and so do several other Satori members: Ray has at least a chudaiko and a shime at home, and Judi has a shime. But none of us has more than several drums, and certainly not enough to do a performance of any scale. In most North American taiko groups, the taiko are owned either communally or by the teacher, so we are quite typical.

Rev. Tom owned all the Satori taiko, and he accumulated an astonishing array of equipment. He had two vehicles (a Ford van and a Honda minivan) to cart taiko around, and I often rolled around greater Los Angeles with him on the way to a gig, sometimes several in a single day. The taiko were all stored at Sozenji Buddhist Temple in Montebello, California, on the edge of East L.A. (See figure 7, taiko in the storeroom at Sozenji Buddhist Temple, at *http://wonglouderandfaster.com*.)

This temple was formerly a Christian church and was bought in 1976 by a group of Zen Buddhists who had parted ways with Zenshuji Soto Mission, a Buddhist temple in L.A.'s Little Tokyo. Zenshuji was founded in 1922 and was the first Soto Zen temple in the US. Rev. Tom's father, Shuyu Kurai, was the first priest in charge of Sozenji when the group left Zenshuji in 1971, and Rev. Tom succeeded him; he was ordained by his father in 1980, took over as Sozenji's resident priest in 1986 after his father died, and was formally named its abbot in 2001. The exterior of the temple looks like the church it was, and the interior features a main hall full of pews and a small raised stage at the front that holds the altar, a glorious sight, full of gold screens and lanterns. We held our rehearsals in a relatively small area at the back of the hall, behind the pews.

When you enter the temple from the parking lot, you are in a short hallway that leads to the main hall. Four small rooms with closed doors line this hallway. Rev. Tom's office and a general storeroom were two of these, and the other two were taiko storerooms, heaped high with equipment. A small hallway on the other side of one taiko storeroom became a spillover storage area. In 2002, Rev. Tom owned the following:

2 thirty-four-inch-diameter odaiko
3 twenty-eight-inch-diameter odaiko
7 fifteen-gallon chudaiko
10 thirty-gallon chudaiko

4 hira-daiko
5 shime-daiko
9 okedo-daiko
3 Thai odaiko
4 Thai chudaiko
10 uchiwa-daiko
1 hanging flat gong
1 bag of assorted noisemakers, including *naruko* (wooden festival clappers), *binsasara* (traditional Japanese clappers made of approximately seventy-five small pieces of wood strung together on a cotton cord and sounded by snapping them in a wavelike motion), and rattles

As noted, some of the chudaiko were from Thailand: they were manufactured as drums for use in Theravada Buddhist temples but were very similar to the drums used in Japanese Buddhist temples . . . which are very similar to the chudaiko and odaiko used in kumi-daiko. Some of the small (fifteen-gallon) chudaiko were made by Stanley Morgan, a White American taiko teacher.[7] A few of the shime were bought in Japan, though one was American made and had heavy iron bolts rather than the traditional ropes holding the heads to the body. The uchiwa, single-headed frame drums called fan drums, were arranged in sets of three on two stands for a few pieces, mostly for special effects; they were Japanese made, but the stands were made in the US, and their decorative ribbons were designed and attached by a former Satori member.

This list doesn't include Rev. Tom's stands, of which he had more than one for each drum. Many were made by Stan Moyer, Harriet's husband and Taylor's father. Stan didn't play taiko but lent his craftsmanship to our group. He installed wheels on older stands (to facilitate easy onstage movement) and designed strikingly simple and elegant stands for various taiko as Rev. Tom added them to his collection. Some of the stands were used for only the most important stage performances, such as two massive ones for odaiko that were heavy and time consuming to set up and break down but were beautiful, could support our very largest odaiko, and were rock solid.

Chudaiko can be played on two kinds of stands. There are actually far more than that, but the two most standard in North America are the flat stand (*beta*) and the slant stand (Sukeroku style). Each requires a different stance (kata) and bodily technique. We mostly used slant stands until a taiko controversy in 1999—to which I will turn in a moment—led Rev. Tom to put them aside and instead use beta stands. I had studied taiko for just two years at that point and had played only on slant stands: my entire kinesthetic sense of taiko was based on those stands and that kata. Left foot forward, left knee bent, left thigh parallel to the floor, right leg back and straight, right foot at a 90 degree angle to the left foot, arms scissoring across the body along a diagonal plane, right hand leading with an overhand strike, left hand following with a backhand strike, torso upright, head turned to the left toward the drumhead, rear end tucked in, abdomen (hara) tight and engaged, the entire body flexible. I had spent two years working on the complexities of this kata. Fundamentally asymmetrical, it felt strange, unnatural, off balance, and awkward for a very long time. It made me aware of every part of my body. No sooner did I feel I had gotten one part of my body under control than I would realize that some other part had slipped out of place. The slant stand placed the body into a certain kata. The stand created the kata; the stand dictated the kata; the stand forced the body into a stress position; the stand tortured me; the stand created new strengths in different parts of my body; the stand deserted me. In 1999, many North American taiko players learned that it wasn't just "a" kind of stand but was created by and emblematic of one taiko ensemble, Oedo Sukeroku Daiko, the first professional kumi-daiko group in Japan. At the North American Taiko Conference that year, the artistic director of Sukeroku had a letter read aloud (by Tanaka-sensei) to the assembled participants in which he asserted copyright ownership and asked that North American groups pay royalties or stop using the stand. The stand wasn't a kind of generalized traditional culture: it was created and unique. It was art and it was owned.[8]

Within a month, Rev. Tom put the slant stands away and had us play on beta stands instead. The upright beta stands require a kata so much more symmetrical that it seemed ludicrously easy: the right and left arms both strike in the same way, overhand on a vertical axis. Rev. Tom commissioned more beta stands. We played on the same chudaiko as before but were brought into a new bodily relationship with them through the beta stands. The slant stands were quietly stacked up in a hallway storage bin. As the years went on, our group and many others gradually reintroduced slant stands into our practice. I don't know whether anyone paid royalties to Oedo Sukeroku Daiko as requested. The slant stand controversy made it clear that taiko culture was actively made rather than infinitely up for grabs and open to all. The material realities of slant stands changed our bodies and our relationship to Japanese performers. Japan was not only authoritative but was watching and correcting us. It forced a difficult conversation about respect, authority, ownership, and community that led to the creation of explicitly open-source repertoire by younger-generation performers, as I discuss in chapter 3.

Harriet and Shirley, another Satori member, designed and sewed bags for most of the taiko. Since the drums were constantly hauled around—in and out of vehicles, on and off stage—they needed protection. Shirley's bags were black polyester canvas with the TCLA logo silk-screened on them; they had straps on the sides and elastic around the top rims and round, flat tops with Velcro fasteners. Harriet designed clever bags for several okedo featuring zippers and slots where the okedo strap comes out to become a carrying strap. She also designed and sewed an amazing set of octopus-like bags for Stan's odaiko stand parts, which had crossbars that could easily get misplaced. In short, a lot of homespun effort went into all the equipment that surrounded and supported the taiko. Some types of these items could have been bought from various Japanese or American taiko makers, but they would have been expensive and might not even have fit our particular taiko, since there are no prescribed volumes or diameters for American taiko.

Setting up for rehearsal or packing the van for a performance was a group activity. Take a look at video 5, Satori Daiko members packing the van for a performance at the John Anson Ford Theatre in Los Angeles, August 22, 2007, at *http:// wonglouderandfaster.com*. Notice how almost everyone participates: what appears to be chaotic is quite organized. We had all performed many, many times and were familiar with the routine. Someone—Harriet or Rev. Tom—had created a list of the equipment we would need for this performance. We knew it was best to haul the equipment into a big pile, double-check that it was all there, and only then start carrying it out to the van. Getting it all to fit was another matter, and Rev. Tom was often inside the van organizing things as we handed equipment to him. The result was an impressive three-dimensional jigsaw puzzle of equipment, sometimes stacked to the ceiling. I am inside the van lifting and pulling on odaiko stands as Rev. Tom pushes them from outside. Somehow it all fits, though the van is literally full to the ceiling.

After he closes the van's doors, he jokingly refers to the "ritual" of packing the van, and in fact that evening, like every practice and performance, ends with a ritual (see video 6, closing circle, at *http://wonglouderandfaster.com*). Even though the night is getting late, notice that almost no one leaves until the van is packed and Rev. Tom has called out "Circle!" and we all stand in a circle. He says, "Otsukaresama deshita," and we respond "Otsukaresama deshita" in unison—thank you for working together, good job, take care, good-bye—and bow.

We knew this equipment in so many ways. We had a profoundly tactile relationship with it. Certainly, we knew its characteristics through playing the taiko— we knew which drums had become dull and nonresponsive because they had been played for so long, and we knew which okedo were uncomfortably heavy and which were wonderfully light, and we knew which stands were so short that you had to maintain a superlow kata if you wanted to look right, and we knew which shime had holes in them from heavy use. We also knew what it was like to carry a heavy chudaiko a long way, for instance for a reception gig at the Walt Disney Concert Hall in Los Angeles that involved trudging down endless halls or for the infamous gigs at the L.A. County Fair, where the distances grew in the telling, through what seemed like miles of crowds. We knew how to balance odaiko stands on our shoulders and then walk so they didn't bang us in the legs. We knew how to sling an okedo or chudaiko in its bag over the shoulder and then pick up as many stands as we could manage. We knew how to stack as many as three odaiko or chudaiko on a little dolly and wheel the tower of taiko down a hallway, one person pushing and another alongside to steer and keep the drums on the cart whenever we bumped over thresholds or electrical cords. We were familiar with the little aches and bruises on our bodies the next day, which were the evidence that we knew these drums in more ways than one.

MADE IN THE US?

The material culture of taiko is in constant movement between North America and Japan. Objects from Japan such as bachi, clothing, and above all taiko are prized in deep ways. But it is precisely the taiko themselves that are often insanely expensive by North American standards and thus beyond the reach of many North American taiko groups. A few performing groups are sponsored by the leading Japanese taiko makers—Asano Taiko donates taiko to TAIKOPROJECT and On Ensemble, for instance—but most North American groups make their own drums or buy them from North American taiko makers. The North American craft of taiko manufacture has become a distinct tradition and often creates group bonding through the hours spent sanding, soaking, stretching, and gluing the wine barrels and cowhides that become taiko.

Japanese and North American drum-making techniques are interrelated rather than utterly distinct, but North American taiko making became a craft tradition unto itself in the early 1970s. The key difference is that Japanese taiko are made from a single piece of wood: a section of tree truck laboriously hollowed out. Large taiko like odaiko are thus made from very large and old trees. Miyamoto and Asano are famous for buying spectacularly large, old trees and seasoning the wood until it can be transformed into stunningly large odaiko. Such taiko are expensive, due to the accumulation of cost that begins with the purchase of carefully chosen logs and their transport from anywhere in Japan or beyond to the taiko factory. Very few North American taiko makers have attempted this kind of work. Beginning in the 1970s, most used old wine barrels, and a long and now standardized process of disassembling, reassembling, and refinishing the barrels is well documented. Soaking cowhide and then stretching it over the reinforced rims of the barrel follows another set of established techniques.

The documentary *Making American Taiko* (Kim, Boch, and Miyagawa 2005) offers a particularly rich picture of early taiko making in the US. In it, the Kinnara Taiko members Rev. Mas, Johnny Mori, and George Abe describe their practical need to make their own taiko, given Japanese drum prices; they were thus the first North American group to make their own taiko. Tanaka-sensei says that he didn't know you *could* make your own taiko and that he learned the techniques from Kinnara. That is, as a Japanese immigrant, he regarded taiko making as a craft known only by a specialized few. He doesn't say so in the documentary, but taiko making was originally the purview of the Buraku, the caste still considered unclean by some Japanese because of their professions as butchers and leatherworkers; they face considerable discrimination in Japan even today. As Alan Gamlen (2003) points out, Japanese taiko players have long been admired, but the Buraku taiko makers have remained shadowy background figures. In the 1980s, politicized Buraku reframed social discrimination against them as a human rights issue, and in 1987 a group of young Buraku formed a taiko group—unthinkable in traditional Japan—that they named Ikari (anger).[9] Taiko are thus embedded in horrendous histories of discrimination; they are products of the structurally abject; they have been transformed into art objects and luxury goods. North American taiko makers have recast taiko as treasured material repositories of cultural knowledge, but it bears asking, What knowledge? Whose knowledge? Why do so few North American taiko players talk about the Buraku as central to what we do?

As Abe succinctly puts it in *Making American Taiko,* a group of taiko players deciding to make their own taiko "wouldn't happen in Japan," for all these reasons and more. Throughout the 1970s, North American taiko groups went through a long process of experimenting with and exchanging taiko-making techniques. PJ Hirabayashi, the codirector of San Jose Taiko, said "We knew we couldn't be 'authentic,'" but this freed them in certain ways. Looking back to the 1970s, the Japanese American taiko maker Mark Miyoshi said that "everyone in the country at that time was making drums," but as Mori, who also played taiko in the interethnic fusion band Hiroshima, put it, "Mark took it to another level," by going to Japan and studying drum making. His beautiful handiwork is considered some of the very best in North America.[10] Rather than use wine barrels, Miyoshi now carves his own staves with meticulous care and exactness. Victor Fukuhara, another taiko maker and a member of Kokoro Taiko in Long Beach, California, is more categorical in describing his own work, saying, "We don't make it at all traditional—we make it [the] American way." In fact, some Japanese taiko players now come to the US to learn from American taiko makers because the craft is so closely guarded in Japan.

The members of Stanford Taiko, the first collegiate taiko group (formed in 1991), undertook an intensive effort in 2003 to make their own taiko, traveling to learn the process from the Hawaiian ensemble Zenshin Daiko. They then posted an impressively detailed manual to Stanford Taiko's website.[11] One of the first things Senryu Taiko at the University of California, Riverside, did when it formed in 1998 was to make two odaiko, which are still in use more than twenty years later. In other words, some collegiate groups have chosen to participate in the tradition of drum making even though the 1970s are long past and there are now easier ways to obtain drums. Stanford Taiko's remarkable manual says nothing about *why* the club members were driven to learn how to make their own taiko; in fact, its website dates the genesis of the club to the first taiko made by its founding members, in 1992.[12] Implicitly, the manual's authors seem to carry forward beliefs from early North American taiko groups (some twenty years before them) that making taiko enacts respect, creates group bonding, offers tactile access to the tradition, and earns a group the right to play taiko.

Despite the emphasis on taiko making in North America, the prestige of Japanese objects there is undeniable. I have absorbed these values. I could buy wooden dowels at Home Depot and easily make my own bachi, but I am fiercely attached to my Miyamoto bachi. My pleasure in handling them is both sensuous and romanticized. These bachi have a wonderful, dense heft and are perfectly balanced, but my pleasure in them goes beyond their performance as drumsticks and into the realm of heritage production. I am not Japanese American but in certain ways am moved by roots values as much as any North American taiko player. In significant ways, however, I reject the roots trope that drives so much North American taiko. The Japanese origin of taiko and the contemporary circuit of exchange between Japanese and North American taiko players are both undeniable. I am more than a little keen to see taiko reframed as a transnational genre rather than a simple heritage industry, and even keener to see it acknowledged as a distinctively Asian American form at precisely this moment when more and more non–Asian Americans participate with each passing year.

The material culture of taiko plays out all possible binary relationships that art objects maintain and trouble. As Barbara Kirshenblatt-Gimblett (2001) argues, the dynamic dichotomies of gift/commodity, alienable/inalienable, art/artifact, and art/commodity are constantly at work when material culture is assigned value. These dynamics shape taiko players' attitudes toward their objects. Until recently, for instance, very few North American taiko groups owned a (spectacularly expensive) Japanese-made taiko: these gorgeous drums are doubly constructed as commodities, first through postwar Japanese economies of craftsmanship and the elevation of traditional objects to art/craft/prestige items, and then again through a Japanese American valorization of such items as heritage objects. When Japanese taiko manufacturers bestow their products on North American performers who have carefully cultivated their ties to these companies, the gift of such prized and expensive craftwork elevates the standing of the group and the performers lucky enough to own these prestige objects.

CLOTHING MAKES THE TAIKO PLAYER

The clothing worn by taiko players in rehearsal and in performance is central to the material culture of North American taiko. In chapter 5 I return to the sartorial imagination and consider how clothing charts powerful new ways to perform gender through ethnicity. Ethnomusicologists and dance scholars have paid surprisingly little theoretical attention to clothing. Clothing is one of the single most public forms of performative identity construction and a central physical means through which taiko bodies speak. It is also a chosen platform for how the body is spatially constructed and then able to do its work.

Taiko groups make considered decisions about their performance clothing. Most choose to have their performers dress identically, though some distinguish between men's and women's clothing. Some call these garments *costumes* and others *uniforms*. The vast majority draw from Japanese festival clothing styles, though some only emulate those styles rather than reproduce them. These garments thus create a dynamic tension between Japanese and Asian American identity, both for those wearing them and for audiences. The clothes seem to make statements about the ethnic and racial identity of the people wearing them, even if they sometimes set up visual contradictions (when the person in the clothes doesn't phenotypically code as Asian). Dorinne Kondo's (1997, 56) thoughts on Japanese high fashion could just as well describe North American taiko costumes. She reflects that the Japanese fashion industry in the 1990s was transnational in reach and "simultaneously rife with essentializing gestures that refabricate[d] national boundaries." Similarly, Thuy Linh Nguyen Tu (2010, 131) argues that Asian American fashion designers "fit awkwardly into the economy of Asian chic" because the very discursivity of "Asianness" makes them complicit in that economy's long life if they deploy its symbols. (The "Mandarin" or "Chinese" collar and the "Nehru" jacket are examples of how Asian clothing styles have become "mere" style, or Asian chic.) Likewise, transpacific taiko costuming is often self-consciously traditional while embedded in the circulation of Asian chic: its signifiers of Japaneseness activate proliferating cultural associations and are often tweaked into chicness by North American groups—by wearing mass-produced athletic tops over traditional wrapped cotton leggings (*kyahan*) and tabi, for instance. Taiko costumes are wildly diverse in style yet in fact often based on a combination of actual matsuri clothing and matsuri-inspired styles, sometimes made by skilled members of North American taiko groups. Matsuri styles—or ideas about matsuri styles—have become transnational through taiko, among other means. Japanese heritage clothing has a tense relationship with Asian chic.

In 2003, Rev. Tom owned the following costume items for TCLA performers:

30 sets of traditional *matsuri-gi* (festival costumes), consisting of *koi-kuchi* (colorful "koi mouth" half-sleeve shirts—so called because of their koi-mouth-like sleeve openings), aprons (*hara-gake*, literally "stomach coverings"), *jika-tabi* (footwear with heavy-duty rubber soles), tekko, and hachimaki
30 TCLA logo *happi* coats, in three colors
11 TCLA logo *happi* coats, red with black trim
18 custom-made vests and hachimaki for Japan tour
20 custom-made T-shirts for Japan tour
40 sports T-shirts, in two styles
10 designer (individual) T-shirts with jeans for the Hidano Concert at the Aratani Theatre

Almost all North American taiko groups use head and foot gear that are distinctively Japanese. Hachimaki are made from a long rectangular piece of cloth (usually cotton) that is folded and/or twisted and then tied around the head. Some groups use specific kinds of knots and dictate whether the knot appears at the front, back, or side of the head. The tabi worn by most taiko players are two-toed cotton shoes with rubber soles. They fit very closely and look like mittens, with the big toe separated from the rest. Tabi have no heel or arch support and thus place the wearer solidly in contact with the ground. They are surprisingly comfortable. I feel strong in my tabi: I feel connected to the earth and ready to jump around and play. I am on my second pair. Both were dark indigo (the color chosen for my group by Rev. Tom). I bought my first pair directly from Rev. Tom when he outfitted Satori Daiko in 1999, and they lasted about eight years before the seams on the big toe and heel started to give out. In Riverside, a local Korean shoe repairman stitched them closed but warned me that they would last only a while longer, so when Satori visited Japan in 2006, I bought another pair, identical, at the festival clothing shop near Sensoji temple. On that same trip, Beverly and I went to a Japanese hardware store and bought gardeners' jika-tabi in the same indigo color but with rubber soles that extend up over the tops of the toes so they're very strong. But I've scarcely worn them. I actually feel a bit heavy-footed in them, in a way that seems contradictory to taiko. If I ever need to play on a rainy day, though, they'll be perfect.

In performance, Satori members also wear a Japanese-made apron (hara-gake) traditionally worn by craftsmen, likewise in indigo. It covers the chest and abdomen, stopping midthigh, and its straps crisscross the back. It has a wonderful deep pocket that extends from the waist all the way down, and I rely on it for all sorts of things: I stick my bachi in it between pieces when I need to move a taiko, and I keep my cheat sheet listing the program order there when we perform long concerts. If I have to emcee, I put my watch in there, so I can keep an eye on the time.

Wearing these articles of Japanese clothing creates an ellipsis between Japanese and Issei identities. Of course, non–Asian American audiences don't see this and simply perceive the clothing as quaintly or colorfully Japanese. But the articles of Japanese clothing most commonly worn by taiko groups are workers' or laborers' clothes which speak in two ways at once. They are still worn by the Japanese in the nostalgic and self-consciously authentic contexts of contemporary festivals where tradition is showcased and maintained, but they were also worn by the many Issei who were farmworkers. Barbara Kawakami's (1993) wonderful study of Issei plantation workers' clothing in pre–World War II Hawai`i documents the kinds of garments that immigrants brought from Japan and adapted for the hard work in the sugarcane fields. Seen in this context, the indigo tabi, hara-gake, and tekko worn by taiko players reclaim their functional origins: these garments once protected Issei men and women from the sharp stalks of sugarcane, just as they now serve practical functions for North American taiko players. Kyahan, heavy cotton leggings, were once a simple, sturdy, functional form of trousers designed for individual fit by wrapping and tying, and are now worn by some taiko groups (though not many, because synthetic leggings are ubiquitous in North America thanks to athletics). In significant ways, North American taiko players dress for the *work* of taiko and thereby reembody histories of immigrant labor. We do not wear silk kimonos. We do not look like geisha, nor like we are about to conduct a tea ceremony. Only a few taiko groups wear clothing associated with samurai, such as *momohiki,* the broad pantaloons that create a powerful expanded silhouette. Most taiko players are dressed for industrious working-class movement and sweat. The clothing we wear evokes not generic Japaneseness but rather specific histories of class and manual labor. We return to the rural working class, the class embodied by the Issei—but most taiko players view the clothing style as Japanese rather than the working-class first-generation immigrant.

Most North American taiko groups wear stretchy black pants, easily available from everywhere and anywhere, from Nike to Kmart to Lululemon. What we wear on our legs is often categorically neither Japanese made nor Japanese derived. Many taiko groups allow their members to choose (and purchase) their own stretchy black pants within certain parameters (length, tightness or looseness, etc.). The ubiquity of black stretch pants and leggings, whether meant for running or for yoga, speaks to a historical juncture when the First World has refabricated leisure athleticism, and elasticized mass-market exercise clothing made in the Third World and marked up to First World prices is thus abundantly available. What we wear on our legs connects us to this sphere and all its problems. The athletic body is marked for class, race, and, to a great extent, gender: expensive brands like Lululemon and Athleta are primarily directed toward upper-class White women, with concomitant pricing.[13] We render ourselves ready to move at a certain cost, literally and figuratively.

The *happi* coat—a loose cotton jacket with wide sleeves, worn open over the rest of your clothing—is another matter. It is an item of Japanese festival clothing, of course, but in North America it is literally a blank canvas for color and branding, and for Japanese American communality. Most temples design their own happi coats, sometimes with a crest or logo, and in *bon-odori* circles the coats of temple members dancing together can create visual blocks of sameness in the big circle of variety. Many taiko groups also create their own happi coat design. The happi coat is about public presence: virtually no one I know wears one during rehearsal, let alone in daily life. It's a sartorial symbol of connection and performativity, and an axis between Japanese and Japanese American identity. I miss wearing the TCLA happi coat: since I stopped performing in 2009, I dance at Obon happi-less, showing all too clearly my lack of connection, my lack of affiliation and a home. I'm far from the only dancer in a happi coat–less state—actually, the majority of dancers aren't part of temple contingents—so I must remind myself that it's my own longing for community, and occasional self-consciousness over having left a longtime home, that is really what these reflections on happi coats reveal.

Last but by no means least, T-shirts are centrally important to North American taiko culture. Although they are obviously inexpensive, easily personalized, and comfortable, their place in the performance of the taiko body is deeper than that. Certainly, the T-shirt has a long history as work clothing, but since at least the

1960s it has been a canvas for identity work.[14] The taiko community has taken this to extraordinary lengths. Every group not only has "a" T-shirt but often makes special tees to mark occasions. Groups create logos not least to feature them on T-shirts, and during the 2000s such logos were often in a graphic design style that I regard as Sansei, drawn from Japanese icons and crest styles or deploying kanji in deliberately contemporary fonts or calligraphic styles. Taiko T-shirts are an iterative part of the DIY ethos that defines North American taiko generally (e.g., groups make their own taiko, design and sew their own costumes, and write many of their own pieces). They are unique to each group or event, and their value is directly tied to that uniqueness (see figure 8, wall of taiko groups' T-shirts, *Big Drum* exhibit installation, Japanese American National Museum, Los Angeles, 2005, at *http://wonglouderandfaster.com*). Contemplating someone else's taiko T-shirt with envy shows that you feel you missed out on something. Few taiko players would wear a T-shirt bearing the name of another group unless some kind of explicit connection were at play. No rules dictate this: it's simply a matter of identification, with a whiff of etiquette—even though many groups sell their T-shirts as an informal kind of publicity and a way to fund-raise. As the anthropologist Brent Adam Luvaas (2012, 22) writes, the DIY ethos is inevitably "both of and against capitalism": it pushes idealistically and even rebelliously against the mass market of things and experiences even as it is shaped by them. These T-shirts are so easily and inexpensively designed and ordered thanks to sweatshops and factories elsewhere, whether in the Third World or in Los Angeles.

My final inventory for this chapter is my personal collection of taiko T-shirts—a fitting way to reflect on the sedimented global aesthetics of North American taiko. The T-shirt—any T-shirt—is already deeply embedded in global clothing manufacturing economies (Rivoli 2005). I have fourteen T-shirts, though I thought I had more; for some time I resisted acquiring more, though now, in the spirit of full-on folkloric collection, I regret that. I have found that other taiko players take similar pleasure in their taiko T-shirt collections. Emma Hyeon Jin Valentine posted a photo to Facebook on August 29, 2018, with the note "I don't think I've ever nerded out this much about folding clothes . . . but . . . my drawer of taiko shirts is beautiful!!!" (see figure 9, Emma Valentine's taiko T-shirts, at *http://wonglouderandfaster.com.*) She lives in Saint Paul, Minnesota, is a member of Ensō Daiko (formerly Mu Daiko), and works at TaikoArts Midwest, so her T-shirts reflect her circles.

My T-shirts are also from the groups with which I spent the most time, especially the TCLA and Satori Daiko (see video 7, stop-action of the author's T-shirt collection, at *http:// wonglouderandfaster.com*). I have three black TCLA T-shirts. One is faded from fifteen years of washing but is my favorite because it feels good (soft and broken in) and *I* feel good in it—I feel like the taiko player I was at the height of my abilities. Wearing it transforms by sense of my own body. The second one is identical but unfaded. I gave it to my father, and he wore it for a year or two

before he died in 2000, at which point my mother gave it back to me. Somehow I
don't wear it as much as the other one, so it's still nearly pristine. The third was my
mother's, and she shortened it, so it fits the best of the three. My black TCLA tank
top was for performances, and it's never occurred to me to wear it informally, even
though I haven't performed since 2009. My single generic Satori Daiko T-shirt was
created for one of our trips to Japan, though it doesn't say so; my other Satori tee
says "Japan Tour 2006" below the group's name and the TCLA logo. Last but by
no means least, I have a black TCLA T-shirt labeled "Hollywood Bowl June 2011,"
from the night we opened for Yoko Ono and the Yellow Magic Orchestra.

I have three T-shirts from my year with Triangle Taiko in Raleigh, North Carolina. Two of them I've worn to death; the third I'll probably never wear, because
each member of the group signed it with a permanent market at my going-away
party before I returned home to Southern California. I would hate for their names
to fade. My sojourn with them more than a decade ago was brief, but I wear those
T-shirts proudly and fondly: I wear my connection to them. I wear my gratitude
that they took me in when I was far from home. The rest of my T-shirts are a
hodgepodge, but each reflects a personal connection to an event or group. I have
an On Ensemble "Foundation Team" T-shirt because I contributed to one of their
fundraisers. I attended the East Coast Taiko Conference at Wesleyan University
in 2012 and came home with a striking T-shirt (incorrectly labeled "Eastern Taiko
Conference"). Brenda Joy Lem gave me a beautiful T-shirt from her group, Inner
Truth Taiko Dojo in Toronto. My *Big Drum* T-shirt commemorates that historic
exhibit at the Japanese American National Museum in 2005–6. I have two T-shirts
from intercollegiate taiko groups. One is Stanford Taiko's T-shirt commemorating their annual concert in 2006. I think I bought it when I was at Stanford for
the 2011 North American Taiko Conference and the shirt was marked down to
almost nothing, but I've actually never worn it—it feels disloyal to UCR's Senryu
Taiko. I treasure my Senryu T-shirt. It's faded and has two bleach spots right in
front, but I wear it often. It marks a coming-of-age moment for Senryu, when they
first hosted the Intercollegiate Taiko Invitational (the twelfth annual iteration)—a
very significant arrival, because until then only the older, established collegiate
groups (Jodaiko, Stanford, and Kyodo Taiko at UCLA) had hosted it. Just looking at it makes me feel proud and oddly competitive in the ways that come with
the collegiate territory. Finally, I like my T-shirt commemorating the 2011 NATC
at Stanford but have worn it perhaps once. That weird bear on the back probably
means more to Stanford University folks than it does to me.

My T-shirts were made in Honduras, Mexico, and El Salvador; I acquired them
in California, North Carolina, and Connecticut, and I have worn them in many
places. They are part of a widely dispersed set of shared practices that are well
established in the North American taiko scene. Like all inexpensive, mass-produced T-shirts, they reflect unmarked ideas about sameness (they are ungendered
and come in three or four basic sizes; I don't reach for the ones that hug my rear

in irritating ways because they're too long). Each has been carefully made special through color and printed design. Each reflects certain values about taiko as a local activity. T-shirts offer vivid evidence that the North American taiko community is dynamic, creative, and flourishing. As Lynn Neal (2014, 203) writes, "I suggest we entertain the notion that the T-shirt functions as *the clothing of democracy*." T-shirts allow any taiko group to assert its difference from other groups while its members display their shared identity. The T-shirt is an essential blank page on which to write belonging and difference.

WHAT, WHERE, AND WHY THINGS MATTER

The material culture of North American taiko is profoundly directed toward the making of new selves in environments already about difference, often—but not always—in direct interplay with Japan as the authentic elsewhere. Monica L. Miller (2009, 5) has written about African American "stylin'," the exuberant aesthetics of black men costuming themselves to create new selves that were not slaves and not abject; she argues that the "black dandy" strategically played/plays with adornment in ways that unseated "normative categories of identity," sometimes radically, while those stylish men were also vulnerable to the "politics of consumption and consumerism."[15] In North American taiko communities, the prevalence of DIY values conceals the extent to which our material culture is embedded in First and Third World production and consumption. In the twenty-first century, taiko players generate and recirculate fetishized heritage objects in endlessly dynamic and creative ways. The strong aesthetics of instruments and costuming and an insistence on a certain visual intelligibility make taiko profoundly physical. Its thingness plays out across an Asian Pacific unembarrassed about its late capitalist flows of goods and styles. Miller suggests that the "self-fashioning" of the Black dandy simultaneously creates new, experimental bodies and new fashion (221). In contrast, taiko players work very hard to conceal their experiments. Our materialities are spectacularized as traditional and authentic. Our pleasure in the "specific unspecificity" (Brown 2001, 3) of Japanese stylin' is doggedly unthoughtful in some ways, but those materialities are also an exuberant showcase for how thingness and globalized movement are interconstitutive. Who made your drums? A Japanese craftsperson, a US undergraduate, a Japanese American woodworker, or a Buraku artisan whose name is lost to time? The cosmopolitan reach of artisanal commodity creation is impressive; the resulting taiko are sometimes gorgeous, sometimes rustic, and always considered. What are you wearing? Who made it? What does it feel like when you grip the ground with your tabi and feel your happi coat swing loose as you shout a *kakegoe* and leap?

Transition

She Dances on a Taiko

It began with a woman dancing, exposing herself, laughing and making others laugh. She's clever—a problem solver. She's not young and beautiful. The other woman is young, beautiful, and important, and she's hiding in a cave; she's pouting or despondent or terrified, depending on who's telling the story. The world is in peril without her: Amaterasu, the goddess of the sun, who despaired and cast the world into darkness by hiding in a cave.

All the other deities gathered outside the cave and begged Amaterasu to come out, but she wouldn't.[1] The old woman Uzume had an idea: she began to tell jokes and stories. The other deities sat down to listen, their attention now focused on her rather than on the despondent sun goddess. At the center of the circle, Uzume climbed on top of a washtub and began to sing and dance. As she danced, she beat out rhythms on the tub with her feet, and as her song became increasingly ribald, she opened her gown, flapped her wrinkled breasts at the crowd, and pulled her kimono hem high, flashing her privates, laughing and singing. The deities roared with laughter. She was good. She was bawdy and scatological, and she was both very funny and the object of her own joke—an old woman exposing her wizened body even while using that body to save the day.

And it worked. Amaterasu realized that no one was paying any attention to her, heard the gales of laughter, and started to wonder what all the commotion was about. What was she missing? She peeked out of the cave, and a beam of sunlight shot into the crowd. *Come join us!* Uzume called, swinging her breasts and dancing faster. Amaterasu slipped out of the cave and light burst into the world, filling the sky and shining over the gathered deities. Wily Uzume: the crafty old woman had saved the day, and the world.

North American taiko players know this as our origin myth. The birth of taiko! Some groups create little skits retelling the story; Rev. Tom often recounted it when emceeing, filling time between pieces. Taiko players almost always call this

"The Legend of Amaterasu," but to me it's clearly about Uzume. She's the one who danced on the taiko and saved everyone. But she's old and inappropriate, while Amaterasu is beautiful and needed.

All the deities in this story are kami, the Shinto spirits who fill the natural world. Amaterasu is one of the primary kami, whereas Uzume is a much lesser kami, of laughter and mirth. In certain accounts, Uzume's dance was the very first kagura, one of the powerful ritual dances still performed at Shinto temples.[2] In some accounts, Amaterasu's brother the storm god destroyed her loom and killed one of her handmaidens, so she was frightened and traumatized when she fled to the cave. The various versions of the story suggest a web of values around female power, which generated both taiko and kagura.

Taiko was the brainstorm of an old woman. It wasn't played loudly or power-fully then. She sounded the washtub with her feet and exposed her body as an object of bawdy ridicule. Like clowns everywhere, she knew how to flip expecta-tions, utter the unspeakable, and activate that second of shocked comprehension when you think *Did she just—?* and then collapse into laughter. Clowns speak truth to power and get away with it because they're so damn funny. Uzume knew exactly what she was doing.

The first taiko performance was a solo comedic dance meant to trick the power-ful. An old woman saved the world.

3
_____

Dancing the Body Politic

Obon and Bon-odori

THE BODY POLITIC

Participating in the huge unison circle dances at Obon gatherings has been my most profound experience as a taiko player, repeated many times every summer at many temples. It's all about dancing, not about playing taiko, though it has taught me as much about taiko as actually playing has. Bon-odori are the dances at the heart of the Obon festival. I haven't played taiko much since 2009, but every summer I go to the Southern California temples to dance. Sometimes I go with friends, especially taiko friends. Sometimes I go alone, because I know I'll see taiko friends there. Really, I just go to dance. No one is alone when dancing bon-odori.

In July 1997, only a few months after I started learning taiko with Rev. Tom, he told the members of my beginning class that we would play a piece for the annual Obon festival at his temple, Sozenji. The day came and we were all nervous. It was my first Obon. In between helping with the bingo game and moving folding chairs, we all kept going over our little piece in our heads and doing air taiko together. Before the outdoor taiko recital, we were told there would be group dances. I figured I would just watch, but no. Audrey Nakasone was busily herding taiko students to and fro, but she had a sixth sense for certain things. She grabbed my arm though my happi coat and said, "Just dance. You have to dance." I said, "But—," and she said, pushing me into the circle, "No. This is important. Everyone should dance, especially taiko players."

Perhaps I have romanticized bon-odori. Certainly, I bring heavy hopes and expectations to it, but the dances carry an explicitly utopian purpose, realized through praxis. You are supposed to dance and thereby to lose your ego. In the act of getting over yourself, you vanish into the messy, unwieldy, colorful, beautiful, awkward totality of the crowds that dance together. You become the body politic because you are part of it. Community and self are collapsed. Hundreds of people dance at the Southern California Obon festivals, mostly Japanese Americans. A few of the temples have small gatherings, but most have huge gatherings, especially the fifteen Jodo Shinshu temples linked in the Buddhist Churches of America (BCA). Sometimes a thousand people dance together; minimally, three to five hundred. Community is not abstract in this environment. The sight of hundreds upon hundreds of people making the same movements is powerful—even more so, feeling one's own movements amplified through hundreds of other bodies.

Bon means Obon. It comes from the Ullambana—"Urabon" in Japanese—Sutra, which tells the story of a monk who danced for joy when he released his deceased mother's soul from hell by making merit (a force accumulated through good deeds) for her. Most Japanese American Buddhists say that Obon is the annual ritual when the living should remember the dead. The dance scholar Judy Van Zile (1982, 1) writes, "O-Bon is usually translated into English as the Festival of Souls, the Feast of the Dead, or the Festival of Lanterns. Traditional belief maintains that the souls of the departed return to earth to be with the living during O-Bon. Thus, although the occasion honors the dead—what might be considered a sad occasion in Western cultures—it is a joyous event celebrating the temporary return of souls and happiness at their achieving a higher state of being." Rev. Masao Kodani (1999, 9) observes that Obon is also called "Kangi-e, or the Gathering of Joy . . . meaning the Joy in the Dharma or the Joy in the Truth of Life and Death. It is thus a gathering of joy which embraces all things, living and dead—a memorial service of joy." Rev. Patti Usuki of West Los Angeles Buddhist Temple has written that Obon "is not, as some mistakenly believe, to welcome back the spirits of the dead. Instead, it is a time of gratitude, giving, and joy in the Truth of Life. Hence, it is also known as Kangi-e, or the Gathering of Joy." She also notes that bon-odori may have "evolved from the Nembutsu Odori of dancers who played instruments while chanting 'Namo Amida Butsu'—I take refuge in Infinite Light and Life, Immeasurable Wisdom and Compassion—symbolized by Amida Buddha."[1] In Japan, Obon takes place at the same time all over the country, from the thirteenth to the seventeenth day of the seventh month (July or August). Many people return to their families then, so the train lines spill over with travelers. In Japanese American practice in California, Obon extends over a two-month period, since temples take turns celebrating it, to maximize cross-temple attendance. The effect is an extended, sustained period of celebration, as well as hard work for the host temples.

Odori means "dance," and bon-odori are thus the dances for Obon.[2] Sojin Kim (2014) writes that dancing bon-odori is about "remembering the ancestors, appreciating past and present relationships, enjoying the moment, and acknowledging the impermanence of life." In the early afternoon, the host temple holds Hatsubon, the "first Obon," a Buddhist service that marks the first anniversary after a death and is attended by those who experienced loss during the preceding year. Most Jodo Shinshu temples in California celebrate Obon as a one- or two-day event that combines a carnival fundraiser with Hatsubon and bon-odori. The rituals of Hatsubon and bon-odori are thus surrounded by food and booths, cultural exhibits

and demonstrations (of, e.g., ikebana and martial arts), a yard sale of donated sec-
ondhand household items, stage performances (of taiko, *enka*, etc.), bingo, and a
farmers' market of seasonal fruits, vegetables, and potted plants. This often con-
stitutes the most significant fundraising of the year, and temple members put a
huge amount of work into planning Obon. Food preparation alone takes weeks
of organization and then long days of work just before the festival. I once spent
eight hours in the afternoon and evening before Obon in the kitchen of my teacher
Rev. Tom Kurai's mother, filling and folding wontons so they would be ready for
deep-frying the next day.

In Southern California the dances take place in the early summer evening, often
from 6:30 to 8:30 PM. They are always held outside, since it virtually never rains
during the summer in Southern California. Most temples stage the dances in their
parking lot or in an adjacent street blocked off to traffic. Ahead of time, as part of
the temple's extensive preparations for the Obon festival, congregation members
sweep the area and spray-paint white lines on the asphalt—huge concentric circles,
at least two and up to four if the area is large enough. A tall wood tower called a
yagura is erected in the center, at least six feet off the ground and sometimes much
higher. Yagura were originally watchtowers or turrets in castle or fortress walls,
and they have historical connotations of keeping watch, though this isn't their feeling in bon-odori. In Obon, a yagura is a ritual band stage: a small platform at the
top, about ten by ten feet and sometimes smaller, is accessed by climbing a ladder.
The platform is empty except for a chudaiko. Volunteers spend hours stringing
lines of electric lights from the yagura to the perimeter of the dance circles—like
spokes in a wheel—and hanging paper lanterns from them. Temple members can
make donations to have a deceased family member's name attached to a lantern,
often in the shape of a dangling rectangle of paper that flutters in the breeze. Bon-
odori begins with a brief Buddhist service led by the resident ministers, who often
climb up into the yagura and say a few words through the PA system while the
dancers stand waiting, lined up on the white stripes.

I love how bon-odori shapes certain corners of Los Angeles. At Nishi Hongwanji Buddhist Temple in Little Tokyo, the white lines for the circles are painted on
the parking lot asphalt (see figure 10, the parking lot at Nishi Hongwanji Buddhist
Temple, looking toward the temple, and figure 11, the same parking lot, looking out
toward Vignes Street, at *http://wonglouderandfaster.com*). You could say that the
space—which otherwise looks like just another parking lot—is in a perpetual state
of readiness for the dances. The circles wait to be populated with the choreography
of the community.

Every year, the lead dance teachers in the region choose eight dances for the
season. About six other dances are perennial favorites and are always featured,
such as "Tanko Bushi" (discussed below), "Tokyo Ondo," "One Plus One," "Shiawase Samba," and the dance that begins and ends the event, "Bon-Odori Uta,"
to which I will return. The dancing starts when the sun is low and the shadows

are long. The dances are performed in succession, one after the other, all the way through, with a break in the middle when everyone runs off to buy *dango* (Okinawan doughnut holes) or shave ice, or to redeem the drink ticket given to each dancer in thanks for their participation (see figure 12, the author's drink ticket from Obon at Hompa Hongwanji Betsuin, Los Angeles, July 2015, at *http://wonglouderandfaster.com*). By the last few dances, the sun has set, the lanterns glow in the dusk, and the area looks magical.

The Obon schedule in Southern California is extremely organized, thanks to the structure of Jodo Shinshu Buddhism in the US. The BCA's Southern District has fifteen temples, across California's Central Coast, the Central Valley, greater Los Angeles, and Arizona. The Southern District Dharma School Teachers' League (SDDSTL) coordinates the annual dance set for all the Obon festivals in the Southern District, making it possible for dancers to participate fully in Obon at one another's temples. Indeed, the entire idea is to create a fixed schedule of Obon so temples aren't competing against one another.[3] Between the third week of June and the first week of August, no more than two or three temples hold their annual Obon on any given weekend. The larger temples host the festival over two days, Saturday and Sunday, with bon-odori on both evenings; smaller temples offer only a single day of festivities and dancing. Some people attend only the Obon festival at their own temple; many go to at least several others. Taiko players seek out as many as possible because kumi-daiko performances are almost always given in the hour or two before bon-odori, featuring the resident taiko group if there is one and often one or two other invited groups.

GETTING READY TO DANCE

In 2015, Obon was the main focus of my summer, for both research and pleasure, so I faithfully attended the dance practices at Nishi Hongwanji. My aim was to finally learn the dances so I wouldn't (as I always told myself) spend yet another summer stumbling through them. To my surprise, the practices at Nishi began only a week before the late-June start of the SoCal Obon festivals. Somehow I had pictured classes that went on for months, carefully leading the attendees into the dances move by move. Instead, the sessions were truly practice, not class, open to any and all but implicitly directed toward participants with some degree of bon-odori experience.

We met in the parking lot, in the actual space where the bon-odori would take place. The teacher, Elaine Fukumoto, was outfitted with a wireless mic; she stood in the center of our circles, near the platform that would be transformed into a yagura during the two days of the festival. She quickly reviewed the moves before each dance by walking through them, and then we went right into it: the music started and we were off. I (along with some others) had not memorized the moves from Elaine's brief demo, so I kept my eyes fixed on the inner circle of about six advanced dancers. The session took place in such a large space that I consistently wasted time trying to figure out who I could follow most effectively without having to look over my shoulder, which inevitably flummoxed me with left-right orientation problems. Finally, I began to trust in whoever was in my line of sight. The practice was truly that: running the dances one by one in a full ninety-minute session with a short break in the middle—pretty much exactly what a "real" bon-odori session is like, and with the exact same recordings played. It worked—or at least it worked well enough for me. After three practice sessions (Tuesday, Thursday, and again the following Tuesday), the dances that at first seemed utterly mysterious and difficult were becoming familiar, even if I was still just getting it at about the time when the recording ended and the dance was over. (See figure 13, T-shirt sold by Venice Hongwanji Buddhist Temple to fund the Venice Fujinkai Buddhist Women's Association, at *http://wonglouderandfaster.com,* for evidence that I was not alone in my struggles to learn the dances.)

The dances I already knew were a complete pleasure: "Bon-Odori Uta," "Bambutsu no Tsunagari," "One Plus One," "Shiawase Samba," and of course "Tanko Bushi." I finally got comfortable with "Ei Ja Nai Ka," PJ Hirabayashi's composition and choreography. When dancing "Bambutsu" in the third practice session, I felt the joy and emplacement that come with moving without thinking, as if I were part of a much bigger whole.

Curiously, the practice sessions weren't particularly social. I had imagined people hanging out and talking about the dances, but most participants were intent, focused, and matter of fact. Many were middle-aged women; most came with at least one other person—a friend or family member—with whom they kept to themselves. About forty people were present, all Japanese American or Asian American except for one White man. During the break I chatted with people, often starting with an acquaintance or a nearby stranger, but I found that I was virtually always the initiator when talking with strangers. People were friendly but distant. I thought that everyone would already know one another as members of the temple, but some participants were outsiders to Nishi, who came strictly to practice the dances. I didn't feel at all awkward or out of place, since many people didn't seem acquainted, but it wasn't the bustling space of enthusiastic love for bon-odori that I had expected. Instead, the participants' quiet focus and choreographic purpose bore out their commitment. They were there to get the dances down so they could move with grace and confidence at the events to come.

I have been dancing bon-odori since 1997 but am an interloper and an amateur. For years I showed up at Obon festivals in sneakers and informal summer clothing and relied on borrowed fans (uchiwa), since the temples always have a box of them available for those dances (you take one for one dance and then immediately return it to the box before the next dance). Sometimes I remembered to wear a tenugui, a thin cotton towel knotted around the neck like a bandanna, ready to use it in the appropriate dances. I own three tenugui. One was a present from a

Japanese friend, and another is a plain length of white cotton covered with spon-sors' names from an Obon at Zenshuji Buddhist Temple that I bought for five dol-lars. I bought the third in Nishi's bookstore in July 2015: it was the last one, so the clerk kindly discounted it from ten to four dollars.

On June 27, 2015, at Senshin Buddhist Temple's Obon, the first L.A.-area festi-val of the season, I ran into Rip Rense and Annie Chuck, two friends of mine to whom I'll return below. They are avid bon-odori dancers: they go to Obon virtu-ally every weekend during the summer months. I complimented them on their clothing. They both looked terrific—informal but put together, with colorful happi coats and polka-dot tenugui (see figure 14, Annie Chuck and Rip Rense at Senshin Buddhist Temple's Obon, June 27, 2015, at *http://wonglouderandfaster.com*). Annie had her tenugui around her neck, and Rip had twisted his into a hachimaki. I was suddenly envious. Without really thinking about it, I had assumed that you got dressed up only if you were a temple member and therefore wore a happi coat emblazoned with your temple's name and logo—basically for home-team pride. Many women and a few men, mostly Japanese Americans, wore *yukata*—colorful cotton summer robes like kimonos but decidedly informal. I've worn yukata when staying at Japanese hotels and guesthouses (*ryokan*), but I can't imagine wearing one in public, let alone dancing in one. I fingered Annie's lovely happi coat, which was obviously her own personal clothing—it had no temple name or crest on it. As far as I was concerned, wearing Japanese clothing was a measure of Annie and Rip's seriousness about bon-odori and Jodo Shinshu, and their clothes were not the kind of japonaiserie I address elsewhere in this book. Seeing my envy, Annie suddenly said, "You should dress up!" I found myself eyeing dancers' clothing in a different way after that. Though most participants at the Nishi practices dressed informally (T-shirts, jeans, shorts, sneakers), some middle-aged Japanese Ameri-can women there wore simple Japanese indigo wrap-front jackets. By the third ses-sion, I was emboldened enough to ask one woman where she had gotten hers—I immediately liked its understated *sashiko* (white cotton embroidery) patterns. She said she had gotten it at the Uyeda Department Store, on East First Street, just four blocks away.

Step by step, I was entering a deeper level of intent. I started bringing my own fan, which was by no means an elegant uchiwa but had a lot of personal meaning because it was a souvenir from a trip to Japan with Rev. Tom and Satori Daiko in 2006 (see figure 15, the author's dance fan (*uchiwa*) from a trip to Japan with Satori Daiko, at *http://wonglouderandfaster.com*). At Senshin's 2015 Obon, I asked a woman where she had gotten her *kachi kachi* (bamboo castanets), and to my surprise she pointed to the rear of the temple and said, "Right there—in the temple bookstore!" I went straight over and spent fifteen minutes with a Japanese American volunteer clerk, who showed me some eight sets in three sizes (small, medium, and large). "A temple member made them," she said, and I put two and two together. "Was it George Abe?" I asked, naming the well-known taiko and shakuhachi (Japanese bamboo flute) player who was a founding member of Kinnara Taiko and Senshin Buddhist Temple. "Yes!" she said. I bought a large pair for thirty dollars and now bring them to every bon-odori practice session and Obon gathering (see figure 16, the author's *kachi kachi,* made by George Abe and bought at Senshin Buddhist Temple, at *http://wonglouderandfaster.com*). Whenever I attend an Obon, ready to dance, I wear a small backpack to keep my fan and kachi kachi with me; my tenugui is around my neck. I wear a bright red happi coat I bought at the Uyeda Department Store.[4] I'm starting to think of myself as a bon-odori dancer.

MAKING A BUDDHIST TRADITION

As Sojin Kim (2014) puts it, "Each weekend, upon the asphalt of temple parking lots across Southern California, lined up in concentric circles and trying to stay within the lanes spray painted on the ground, the dancers move more or less in time with the music. . . . Swaying their arms and stepping to the beat of the taiko, keeping the circles in motion, they reinforce the connections between the past and present, among the people participating, and to a sense of place—all this by just dancing." Like taiko, bon-odori is often talked about and affectively experienced as if it were very old, but the Southern California tradition is in fact not old at all.[5] As Linda Cummings Akiyama (1989, 96–97) has painstakingly researched, the dances were introduced and established in the 1930s by an immigrant Jodo Shinshu minister, Rev. Yoshio Iwanaga, and his Nisei musician wife, Chizu Helen Iwanaga (a pioneer in Japanese American Buddhist music). At that point, Obon was not a regular or prominent observance in California's Jodo Shinshu temples; after deaths, memorial services were held at the proper time and were mostly attended by Issei. Rev. Iwanaga came to the US specifically to teach Buddhist music (*doyo buyo*) and bon-odori to Buddhist Nisei youth. Invited to California by a Buddhist minister who was already focused on work with youth, he was automatically connected to the network of Jodo Shinshu temples. The first bon-odori on the mainland was held "in the auditorium of the San Francisco Buddhist Temple in 1931" (Kodani 1999, 9), and by 1936 that city's bon-odori had become so large that it was held outside, on Buchanan Street in Japantown. He taught doyo buyo first at the Stockton Buddhist Temple in the Central Valley and then at the temples in San Francisco and San Jose. From 1931 to 1933, Rev. Iwanaga worked out of Nishi Hongwanji in Los Angeles and was invited to teach bon-odori at many temples up and down the length of California. He was later assigned to the Stockton temple for a time and then to the one in Watsonville.

In the 1930s and 1940s, most of the Issei had been in the US for only two, three, or at most four decades, and many were originally from the central and southern parts of Japan. Rev. Iwanaga carefully arranged and introduced dances from those regions and then spent years simplifying and rechoreographing them. He also created entirely new dances, built from a vocabulary of folk-dance movements and set to Japanese recordings. Interviewed many years later (in 1988), his widow, Helen Iwanaga, described his process as creative. Akiyama (1989, 69) writes, "He would often take a basic Japanese dance movement and then do an improvisation from it . . . , adding a curved path of an arm gesture, a body tilt, or a step pattern. If he wasn't completely satisfied with a section of his choreography, he would have his wife repeat the phrase on the piano, over and over until he felt the choreography was the way that he wanted it." Akiyama argues that Rev. Iwanaga used "school-taught *minyo*," or the minyo (folk music) arranged and taught in the Japanese public school system in the 1920s and 1930s (118). That is, he transmitted a tradition of revised and mediated rural materials rather than unadulterated Japanese folklore. The parallels with late twentieth- and early twentieth-first-century kumi-daiko are obvious and suggest dynamic, long-term processes of shaping and reshaping Japanese expressive practices.

Rev. Iwanaga's dances are still in the Southern California bon-odori repertoire, but they are not part of a self-consciously stable tradition. Rev. Masao Kodani, the longtime minister at Senshin Buddhist Temple, has written extensively about Obon, bon-odori, and taiko as *horaku,* or Buddhist practice. As one of the founders of Kinnara Taiko (established in 1969), Rev. Mas (as he is known) is widely regarded within the North American taiko community as a knowledgeable and principled community-based practitioner-scholar. Over some fifty years he has generated an impressive amount of writing and a corpus of primary materials including documentaries and instructional films.

Bon-odori is a very old ritual practice but has been continuously reconstituted. For centuries in Japan it was associated with the rural labor class and was participatory, with no professional dancers. Rev. Kodani (2009) writes that it was banned in Japan from approximately the 1860s to around 1912—that is, from the early Meiji era to the early Taisho era (1912–25); he notes that the Meiji government felt bon-odori "encouraged licentious behaviors," whereas the Taisho government lifted the ban as part of a national return to "an emphasis on what it meant to be Japanese." He also observes that the years immediately following the lifting of the ban featured a surge in creative activity focused on bon-odori, "especially in the cities, where new, more western-influenced Bon-odori was created." Akiyama (1989, 110) describes the Taisho era as "a period of intellectual and artistic freedom," when Obon festivals became popular again and were held in towns and cities rather than just the rural countryside.

I draw extensively on Rev. Kodani's thinking and writing about bon-odori not only because he has thought so deeply about it over some five decades but also because his approach to it has influenced many Japanese American Buddhists in Southern California and beyond. His Sansei sensibilities are often evident in his unapologetic focus on Japanese American community maintenance. He became a minister at Senshin Buddhist Temple in 1968 and served as its head minister from

1978 to 2013; he was a founder and longtime member of Kinnara Taiko. He and Nobuko Miyamoto—the legendary activist and musician mentioned in the introduction—have collaborated on seven contemporary bon-odori songs/dances,[6] so he has intentionally contributed to the tradition of Japanese American (rather than Japanese) bon-odori with focus and thought. He was also a key writer and generating force for the booklet and CD *Gathering of Joy,* a compendium of Japanese American bon-odori songs (Kodani 1999).

Over the years, Rev. Mas has written repeatedly about Obon and bon-odori in the monthly newsletter sent to members of Senshin Buddhist Temple. (See figure 17, page from Senshin Buddhist Temple's monthly newsletter, at *http://wonglouderandfaster.com.*) His list of values and directives was published in the newsletter in June 2012 (Kodani 2012) and is worth reading in its entirety. Rev. Mas's thinking is deeply informed by the Japanese American experience and by Jodo Shinshu Buddhism. The radical egalitarianism that marks Kinnara Taiko as a group is largely the result of Rev. Mas's commitment to the principles of Jodo Shinshu, which shift spiritual emphasis away from monks and toward everyday practitioners. He has written that the Jodo Shinshu sangha is therefore not its community of monks but rather the "fellow-travelers in the Dharma," or all practicing Buddhists, especially the laity (Kodani 2010b); he consistently refers to Senshin members (who might be called, in Christian terminology, the temple's congregation) as "the Senshin Sangha." His principle of *tada odore,* "just dance," is well known in the Southern California Japanese American Buddhist community.

Rev. Mas (Kodani 2010a) notes that Senshin is unusual because, from its founding in the 1950s, it separated the fundraising carnival from bon-odori and in the 1970s stopped holding the carnival entirely. Since then, the bon-odori at Senshin has focused on dancing alone, with generally only a single booth, selling drinks for thirsty dancers. As Rev. Mas has written, "If you came to Senshinji's *Bon-odori,* you came to dance, and if you came and watched, you were urged, sometimes taunted, to dance by the dancers."

His list of fourteen things that "Bon Odori in America is not" (Kodani 2012) is thus both typical and unique. Without question, Rev. Mas has put his personal philosophy of Obon and bon-odori into words in a way that few other Japanese American Buddhists have. This is not to say that the huge community's Buddhist and non-Buddhist practitioners don't have equally deep and thoughtful understandings of what the dances mean, but most express this through practice rather than words. In my experience, those who choose to dance would generally agree with most of Rev. Mas's assertions, though they might also learn new things from his list.

The state of mind—or the mind-heart-body-soul oneness posited by Buddhism—generated by participation in bon-odori is profound. It is worth quoting Rev. Mas (Kodani 2010a) at length on this point because he articulates communal understandings in a way that draws them into sharper relief:

The essential thing was to dance, not showing off, not being embarrassed, but to forget the self long enough to "just dance", and in that moment of just dancing to suddenly remember and sense a deep connection to our deceased loved ones and, on a deeper level, to all things living and dead. It is a "*tariki*-like moment" where everything is perfect and in its harmonious place. And when you come out of that moment, everything old becomes suddenly new, it has a new vibrancy that is seen individually and communally. Bon Odori is after all and at long last—not just a summer festival to eat, drink, be merry, and make a few bucks—it is a religious event celebrated by a religious community by members living and dead.

Rev. Mas focuses here on the individual experience of dancing bon-odori with others. It is remarkably like Mihaly Csikszentmihalyi's (1990) concept of flow— that ideal state of complete absorption in an activity, when time and your ego fall away—and of course this is no coincidence, since many ritual/performance acts are meant to create just such a collapse of distinctions between self and other, then and now, here and there. *Tariki* is a Japanese Pure Land Buddhist concept usually translated as "other-power," meaning the power of the Amitabha Buddha; it is the opposite of the "self-power" (*jiriki*) which is the useless arrogance of the human condition.

I hasten to add that bon-odori is not at all mystified. Practice sessions are offered annually at many temples for a few weeks, held at least once if not twice a week in the temple auditorium, leading up to the beginning of the Obon season in late June. Anyone who wants to attend these free sessions is welcome. Many of the most focused and serious attendees are older women, mostly Japanese American, who are the kind of dancers you want to be near if you aren't sure of the steps, because they know the dances inside and out. They are as prepared as one can be: they have their own uchiwa and kachi kachi, they wear matching temple happi coats, and they dance together at any Obon. In 2016, many wore matching LED-lit plastic rings on their fingers, so their hands created a wave of bright, blinking light as they danced. They look good in every possible way. They exemplify the Japanese value placed on doing things correctly.

Bon-odori is instantly metaphorical. The dancers are and aren't in unison—a perfect metonym for the Japanese American Buddhist community. The key principle is simple: everyone is dancing the same steps and moving in the same direction (usually counterclockwise). That unison is beautiful to see as hundreds of arms rise together in waves or as hundreds of bodies take a step toward the yagura together, making the great circle suddenly contract, and then step back outward, making it expand again. Still, the unison movements are full of differences, despite some of the dance teachers' hope for sameness. Differences—some subtle and others glaring—mark (some might say mar) the dancers' movements. Rip and Annie, respectively a White American Buddhist and a Chinese American Buddhist, are a couple who dance in virtually all the Obon festivals in Southern California, as mentioned above; they are true bon-odori devotees. As members of West Los

Angeles Buddhist Temple, they wrote a short essay, "Why We Dance at Obon" (Rense and Chuck 2006), in which they describe "the variety of dance styles on display: the robust, flamboyant and sometimes free form stylings of some of the men; the economic grace of the ladies; the classical flourishes of some of the more serious students; the exuberance of the young people; the confused steps of the little kids. They are all beautiful." I couldn't describe it better. These participatory discrepancies are the life of the tradition.

TAIKO AND BON-ODORI

Bon drumming is notoriously different from the kumi-daiko that reigns supreme at this historical moment. *Bon daiko* is accompaniment, whether to bon dancers or to a minyo group of singers and perhaps a few other instruments (shamisen, etc.). In North America, the clear majority of bon drummers are men; a few women are now featured, as I will explain, but for now I will refer to the drummer as *he*.[7] He stands far up above the dancers and indeed everyone else, alone on the yagura. He wears a happi coat and hachimaki; he usually plays a chudaiko. He plays very sparingly, just accenting the main rhythms of the dance, with a relaxed minimalism. He stands not in formal kata but often in a flat-footed, casual stance. His moves are unfussy and understated. He is literally the heartbeat of the dance.

I just realized that I'm describing George Abe—not a generic bon drummer— since I have mostly seen *him* play bon daiko over the years (see figure 18, George Abe playing *bon daiko* at Higashi Hongwanji on the *yagura*, at *http://wonglou-derandfaster.com*). Abe is the preeminent bon drummer in Southern California. He is invited to play at any number of Obon dances—not all of them, but many of the main ones, including, of course, Senshin's, plus those of Higashi Honganji and many others. Rev. Mas remembered the bon drummer at Senshin during his youth: "It was a man named Mr. Inouye who . . . my prejudice is he's the only decent *Bon-odori* taiko player that I've ever come across. But he used to play as a kid and so he played really well. . . . He was here and George is his successor. George played with him year after year and got the hang of it and so he's probably our best *Bon-odori* taiko player." For Rev. Mas (Kodani 2004, 29–30),

> *Bon-odori* taiko is really hard because it's not supposed to be heard. It backs up the music and the dancers, so it's not "listen to this" kind of performance, whereas taiko is. It's stage taiko. But *Bon-odori* taiko is this kind of heartbeat that's supposed to support the dancers and to do that, you have to know the dance and the music and not be . . . "check this out," you know. So in that sense, it's very hard. And the worst players of *Bon-odori* taiko are taiko players because they're the exact opposite—"check this out!" you know. So it's the exact opposite.

The Southern California bon drummers whom I have seen since 1997 play along with the recordings that are the main soundtrack for bon-odori—that is, not with live musicians.[8] Rev. Iwanaga sometimes played taiko to accompany his bon-odori dancers, and Akiyama (1989, 32) notes that he too played along with recorded music. The Japanese American bon-odori as known today is largely the creative legacy of Rev. Iwanaga, and since 1930 it has evidently meant dancing to the sound of commercially recorded songs and a live bon drummer who follows the recording. The recordings are distinctive: their sound is quintessentially part of the bon-odori soundscape. Many Sansei dancers have told me that they remember scratchy old LPs played at their postwar childhood bon-odori, followed in the 1970s by dubbed cassette recordings that grew distorted and wobbly as the years passed. The decidedly imperfect and lo-fi sound of the songs was part of their charm and acquired a nostalgic sheen over time. By and large, the same commercial recordings were used over and over, because dancers were used to them. Virtually all were from Japan and featured Japanese musicians singing in Japanese.[9]

The system for distributing the fifteen or sixteen songs and dances selected for the season is impressive, effective, and part of an informal Japanese American dissemination structure. Given the DIY ease of assembling digital materials, the songs are compiled on uncopyrighted compact discs and sold for a minimal amount by the BCA Bookstore.[10] For instance, one CD in my collection was clearly home-made, with a label saying "2014 SDDSTL OBON SONGS." The fifteen song titles were listed on the CD's face, and the CD's plastic case was completely unadorned except for a simple adhesive label on the back also listing the titles. Likewise, an annual instructional DVD is often made so everyone in Southern California can learn the same dances. Over the years it has become increasingly professional, featuring narrated, step-by-step footage of each dance performed by a couple, to show male and female movement styles, as well as front and back views. One can also watch the two dancers perform each dance all the way through without stopping, to the recorded music. Like the CDs, these DVDs are available through the BCA and are widely disseminated by the temple dance teachers, who make it available during the weeks of dance practices in the late spring to anyone interested.

Kumi-daiko is not at all the same as bon drumming, nor is bon drumming generally taught in Southern California kumi-daiko classes. At the Nishi Hongwanji Obon festivals in July 2014, 2015, and 2016, each bon dance featured one of six to eight young drummers, all in their teens; the emcee announced their names. Most emulated the spare rhythms that Abe has made familiar. None had his relaxed weightiness—not yet. The taiko teacher and SDDSTL lead dance teacher Elaine Fukumoto, long associated with Nishi Hongwanji as its kindergarten teacher and much more, told me that she had witnessed a long procession of bon daiko training at the temple over the years. Since the Nishi Hongwanji Obon is the biggest in Southern California—up to a thousand people routinely participate in its bon-odori over two nights—it makes sense that this temple would address the need for good bon daiko. Elaine said she vaguely remembered an older man playing bon daiko on the yagura decades ago, but when he stopped, others tried to learn without success. In the 1990s, the temple member Rick Taketomo (who played with Kinnara in its early years) taught the dharma school students bon daiko on a volunteer basis. He would start in February and work with some fifteen youths. He did this for many years, with the youths taking turns drumming for bon-odori, but many people quietly felt that their playing didn't have quite the right feeling and was even a bit robotic. Elaine then stepped in herself; as she wrote to me, "I then took the bon daiko on myself with a couple of other people. I had Rev. Mas's philosophy in mind and did a lot of 'research' online. I played for a couple of years, bringing in some guest players like George Abe. [But] it interfered with my opportunities to dance." She said nothing about gender, but this was significant: I know of only a few women who play bon daiko. Rev. Hiroshi Abiko, a taiko player himself, sometimes played bon daiko, taking turns with some of the older youths. When he retired, Yuki Inoue, a coleader of L.A. Matsuri Taiko, a friend of Elaine's, and a Nishi Hongwanji member, volunteered to teach bon daiko to the dharma school youths. At Elaine's request, Inoue asked Abe for guidance and then began teaching. The youths I saw on the yagura in 2014, 2015, and 2016 were the result of this long process. Yuki told me that most of her pupils weren't musicians or even kumi-daiko players but rather dharma students recruited to ensure youth participation. She laughingly admitted that they were neither terribly good nor committed to the project until they actually accompanied live bon-odori: she said rehearsals were sometimes musically chaotic as they played along with the recordings but that things tended to come together at the event. One of Yuki's students, a teenage girl, told me at a bon-odori practice session in 2015 that it was her second summer playing bon daiko and that she hadn't really "gotten it" last year but was now excited about participating in such a central way.[11]

In sum, bon daiko is profoundly different from kumi-daiko, and kumi-daiko players may exhibit exactly the wrong approach to it . . . but some Japanese American community leaders now teach a handful of young kumi-daiko players how to do it. Most kumi-daiko players know nothing about bon daiko; those who do know that it is a deep corner of taiko which few get to enter, though it isn't clear why bon daiko is so difficult. No one refers to it as ritual drumming, but quite clearly that is what it is. It has been played to scratchy and distorted recordings of Japanese popular songs since the 1930s. It disappears into the exuberance of the crowds and the tumult of the recorded music. When you dance, you feel the drumming as much as you hear it. Few spend much time looking at the bon daiko player despite his—or her—prominent place at the center of the circle, high above the dancers.

RUPTURES

Without question, Japanese American bon-odori is the result of a series of ruptures. It did not emerge out of the mists of time, though in some ways it is a very old practice. While Obon is observed without bon-odori in some parts of Japan, many Japanese villages and small towns have a folk dance associated with it. When Rev. Tom Kurai took members of Satori Daiko on a study tour of Japan in 2003, for instance, we attended Obon in Tsubetsu, a small town in Hokkaido, where we participated in a long, mesmerizing evening when townspeople danced the same bon dance over and over, for hours (see video 8, *bon-odori* in Tsubetsu, Hokkaido, 2003, at *http://wonglouderandfaster.com*).

In Japan, bon-odori traditions first appear in the historical record in the fifteenth century and were widespread and popular by the seventeenth-century Tokugawa period (Kodani 1999, 7). By and large, though, the Issei did not transport a rich tradition of bon-odori to North America: the practice was interrupted during the Meiji era. Rev. Kodani writes,

> In the Meiji Period (1868–1912) the Bon Odori was banned as it was thought to encourage immoral behavior, especially among the unmarried young who were permitted to fraternize unchaperoned during the period of the Bon Odori. The ban came at a time when the Meiji government was desirous of showing the western world that it was as civilized and advanced as any country in Europe, albeit basing that definition of civilized on western standards. It was a period of intensive copying of western clothes, habits, and mores.
>
> An inordinate number of babies were in fact born nine months after the Bon Odori during the Tokugawa period and the Japanese designation of October as the wedding month may possibly derive from the necessity for an expedient marriage before pregnancy became too obvious. Because of the ban however, much of Bon Odori music and dance was lost. (8)

Akiyama (1989, 126) notes that in the 1930s, Rev. Iwanaga worked with temple ministers and lay leaders to ensure that bon-odori was explicitly defined and experienced as Buddhist practice, choreographing a procession of bon-odori dancers being led into the dance circle by the temple ministers, who wore their formal Buddhist robes. As she explains, "One minister would then lead everyone—dancers and audience—in *gassho*, a gesture of gratitude, and the reciting of the *Nembutsu*, repeating the name of Amida Buddha. After the *Nembutsu*, the dancing would begin."

Jo Anne Combs (1979, 1985) and Minako Waseda (2000, 116) have documented the so-called "*ondo* craze" or "*ondo* boom" of the 1930s in Japan and "the great popularity of newly composed, commercial *ondo* songs," used to accompany "the street *ondo* dance." Waseda notes that record companies routinely released *ondo* (Japanese folk music) songs in competition with one another and that choreographic instructions, often featuring little stick figures, were included with the records. Many ondo songs were immediately exported to the US, so the transpacific circulation of materials between Japanese and Nikkei audiences was extensive. Waseda also found that a few Japanese American recording companies commissioned new ondo, including "Rafu Ondo" in 1935, named for *Rafu Shimpo*, the leading Japanese American newspaper, based in Los Angeles, and "America Ondo" (118–20).[12]

Rev. Iwanaga was visiting Japan in 1934 (and took lessons in *nihon buyo*, classical Japanese dance, during that stay) when "Tokyo Ondo" became a hit, and he immediately choreographed it for bon-odori when he returned to California. "Tokyo Ondo" is still a standard today at most Southern California bon-odori: it is often included in the set even if it was not rehearsed as part of that season's dances. It was a secular dance sensation in Japan *and* California in 1934 and became a Japanese American bon-odori song and dance that same year through Rev. Iwanaga's efforts. The craze swept both sides of the Pacific. Combs (1985, 143) notes that "Tokyo Ondo" was performed in 1934 at a Japanese American Citizens League (JACL) fundraiser in San Diego and at various wedding receptions, disseminated to Southern California Japanese American communities almost immediately as popular culture and as ritualized secular dance.

During World War II, bon-odori was such a fraught spectacle of Japaneseness that it had to be managed in any number of ways. Japanese Americans self-policed their public presence. Lon Kurashige (2002, 68) mentions that in 1941, only several months before the Pearl Harbor attack, the official costumes worn by ondo dancers in the Los Angeles Nisei Week parade were made from cotton, to honor the boycott of Japanese silk, while *Rafu Shimpo* recommended that no Japanese clothing whatsoever be worn in public, to prevent confusion over American loyalty. Emily Roxworthy (2008, 132) muses that assumptions about "racial performativity" deeply shaped that last preinternment Nisei Week ondo, forcing its participants to "dance for their citizenship and freedom" in barely concealed ways. Pearl Harbor realized their worst fears.

From 1942 to 1945, Obon and bon-odori were held in most of the internment camps.[13] Rev. Iwanaga, his family, and his Watsonville congregation were confined first in the Salinas Assembly Center and then in Poston War Relocation Camp II in Arizona. I have found no photographs of the Poston Obon, but the camp newspaper attests to its celebration, and I wonder whether Rev. Iwanaga organized the bon-odori there. Striking photographs document bon-odori at several of the other camps. Bill Manbo's 1943–44 photographs of bon-odori at the Heart Mountain Relocation Center in Wyoming are gorgeous (see Manbo and Muller 2012). Startlingly, they are in color—they were shot with Kodachrome—and their soft pastel hues are hauntingly vibrant compared to the black and white of the famous camp photos taken by professional photographers like Ansel Adams, Dorothea Lange, and Toyo Miyatake. The careful composition (and even staging) of images by War Relocation Authority (WRA) photographers is now well established (Creef 2004). Manbo was interned along with his wife, their young son, and his wife's parents, and he took photographs as a hobby. His photos of the bon-odori are lovely: most offer close views of young women dancing. In one, most of the women wear a kimono with obi and zori with white tabi; a few wear sneakers or oxfords with their kimono. Spectators surround the bon-odori circle, especially young men in Western clothes (T-shirts, jeans, cardigans, etc.; see Alinder 2012, 90). One shot shows a small, informal circle of teenage girls, all in kimonos, smiling and chatting with one another (Manbo and Muller 2012, 54). Another was taken from just outside the outermost of two concentric bon-odori circles (Manbo and Muller 2012, 60). Two young men in yukata, with tenugui around their necks, blurrily unfocused, were caught as they clapped. The camera was focused on the inner circle of dancers and a simple yagura about six feet high. Its small stage is empty— no performers, no instruments, no taiko. A wide ladder gaily decorated with red bunting is propped against it. Lengths of rope sporting triangular pennants of different colors emanate from the yagura. A white line in the sand marks the inner dance circle. Teenagers and small girls dance on the line, mostly in bright kimonos (red, pink, blue), though three young girls standing together wear American dresses and bobby socks. The yagura is surrounded by a bench, and the eye is drawn to the men who sit on it: they appear middle-aged and are all formally attired in white shirts, several wearing ties, several others wearing suit jackets, several wearing Panama hats. Are they Issei men, sitting in a place of authority while the girls dance?

The traditional arts (nihon buyo, koto, shamisen, *nagauta,* martial arts, etc.) were a cultural dividing line in the camps between Buddhist and Christian Japanese and Japanese Americans and between Issei and Nisei. The more Americanized Nisei focused on marching bands, Boy Scouts, baseball, dance halls, and big bands (Yoshida 1997). Bon-odori in the camps looked and probably felt traditional in the face of the traumatic distinction drawn between Japanese ethnicity and US citizenship, but in fact at that point it was still a recent development in Japanese American Buddhist practice. Its widespread adoption in the camps points to how quickly it took hold on the West Coast and how much the internees needed diversion, entertainment, and the powerful connective force of participatory performance (Turino 2008). It was also a performative statement about the internal politics of Japanese Americans. Kurashige (2001, 392) has described the "two factions" in most of the camps, one exemplified by JACL members, who argued for a pro-US assimilation into American culture, and the other offering a more nuanced and often more resistant position. The second faction was reframed as "pro-Japan," and these "internees not only espoused antiwhite sentiments but also disparaged community projects and resented Manzanar's white staff and administration. These people flaunted their preference for Japanese culture by listening to Japanese music, singing nationalistic songs, and dancing folk dances." Roxworthy (2008, 124) argues that "Japanese traditional performing arts flourished in particular among the Issei as a corrective for WRA educational policy that often attempted to instill ethnic self-hatred in the second generation of Japanese American children interned at Manzanar and other camps." Kurashige (2002, 50–51) reflects that ondo was a way to bridge Issei-Nisei conflicts in the 1930s. Bon-odori thus served as a sign of difference between Japanese Americans *and* helped some of them to perform unity and cohesion.

After the end of the war and the gradual closure of the incarceration camps, some Japanese Americans reestablished themselves on the West Coast, while others relocated to the Midwest. Bon-odori was part of their cautious cultural regrouping. Akiyama (1989, 39) notes that Rev. Iwanaga's dances "were dispersed to areas throughout the country" in the postinternment years. A major Jodo Shinshu event in San Francisco in 1948 featured one thousand bon-odori dancers on the plaza of the Civic Center (40). Nisei Week was reinstated in Los Angeles's Little Tokyo in 1949, and Kurashige (2002, 119–20) quotes a *Pacific Citizen* article that announced, "The race-baiters have been routed and the songs and dances of Nisei Week serve to wipe out the memory of bitterness and frustration of the mass evacuation experience."

Rev. Iwanaga died in 1950 at the age of fifty, not long after choreographing "Fresno Ondo" to music composed by a Japanese American Buddhist woman, Chieko Taira—possibly the first bon-odori set to music by a Japanese American. Akiyama (1989, 43) describes how California temples continued to teach and perform Rev. Iwanaga's dances until around 1955. At that point, each of the eight BCA districts began to make idiosyncratic adjustments to the dances. As part of the extended postwar Japanese American effort to move from the working class into the middle class, some temples arranged for nihon buyo instructors to teach bon-odori. These classical dance teachers elevated the choreography of the folk dances and shifted the emphasis from simple participatory dances to more elaborate, professional presentations. Kurashige (2002, 144) notes that the professionalization of the dance teachers began to push out amateur participation by 1954. Other temples stayed closer to the rural, minyo feeling and simplicity of the bon-odori imagined and created by Rev. Iwanaga. They used minyo recordings from Japan and sometimes engaged minyo teachers.

In sum, bon-odori addressed different needs in the Japanese American community in the mid-twentieth century. In Rev. Iwanaga's hands, it was an invented tradition from the moment he introduced it to California to keep Niseis engaged with Buddhism. He used already mediated materials to create his dances: he drew from minyo dance moves that had already been reorganized and rechoreographed for Japanese schoolchildren, and he and his wife worked creatively to assemble the minyo dance vocabulary into pleasing arrangements. His dances and the recordings that traveled seemingly straight from Japan to California percolated through Los Angeles's Little Tokyo at a time in the 1930s when the Japanese American community was struggling to address US anxieties about its public performance tradition (Nisei Week). The fraught war years changed and didn't change the dances: in the incarceration camps, bon-odori was a means to reconstitute community and cultural identity, to perform a colorful but unthreatening difference from the non-Japanese communities surrounding the camps, and to try to bridge Issei-Nisei generational differences. In the years immediately following the war, bon-odori helped constitute new communities in the Midwest and on the East Coast. On the West Coast, meanwhile, new class aspirations changed bon-odori from participatory to presentational staged performance. My sense is that bon-odori has never settled. On the contrary, as the Japanese American community has faced dramatic cultural challenges and undergone rapid change, bon-odori has offered a choreographic language and the promise of cultural cohesion in response to the needs of the moment. In Japanese America, it has had a uniquely (though shifting) North American cultural formation, but always built with Japanese materials. The Japanese American body danced and dances to Japanese recordings. From the 1930s to the 1950s in particular, Japanese American bon-odori was transnational in awkward ways that challenged ideologies which conflated ethnicity with national identity. Bon-odori seemed Japanese even as it outlined difficult Japanese American realities. Given the rapid cultural and political changes it has moved along with, its meanings were and are sedimented and accumulative.

"BON-ODORI UTA"

Are you ready to dance? "Bon-Odori Uta" is always the first and last dance, framing the Gathering of Joy at each temple. At a macro level, it also frames the annual Obon season in Southern California, since it is the last dance at the Nisei Week closing ceremonies in L.A.'s Little Tokyo. *Gassho* is built into the dance—it is the emblematic Buddhist gesture of placing the palms together in prayer, request, gratitude, and reverence. It is all those things at once.[14] Clasping your hands in gassho "expresses" those modalities and, more deeply, readies the mind/body/spirit to offer them. When you recite the Nembutsu—*Namu Amida Butsu* (I take refuge in the Buddha of of Immeasurable Life and Light)—you do it three times, holding your hands in gassho at chest level.

"Bon-Odori Uta" was choreographed by Rev. Iwanaga and was probably first danced in 1934. Rev. Kodani (1999, 12) describes its genesis:

> When Rev. Iwanaga chose music for the Bon-odori, he selected pieces which he thought were in tune with the spiritual meaning of Bon-odori. In addition, if he did not particularly like the choreography that accompanied the record, he did not hesitate to re-choreograph it. This he did with the song "Bon-odori," written in 1934 by the Buddhist Music Association of the Honzan, or mother-temple in Kyoto, which today is the first and last dance of almost all temple Bon-odori. Rev. Iwanaga created a dance of simple and elegant movements which everyone could pick up and dance. It is still considered the most beautiful of our Bon-odori dances. Over the years this Bon-odori has changed, especially in Southern District where several of Rev. Iwanaga's basic dance movements have been added to the original. Nevertheless its simple beauty is still preserved.

Haa – Bon wa na, *yoi sa,* Bon wa ureshiya Wakareta hito mo, *arase- yo hohohoi* Harate kono yo e, *ha,* Ai ni kuru	Ahh – Bon, how pleasant Bon is. Those who have parted from us Come to meet with us again, on this clear day.
Haa – kumo no na, *yoi sa,* kumo no aida kara Urayamashi geni, *arase- yo hohohoi* Odori mini kita, *ha,* Otsukisama	Ahh – the clouds from between the clods An envious moon, comes to see the dancing
Haa – Odori na, *yoi sa,* odori odoru nara Tebyoshi tatake, *arase- yo hohohoi* Choshi tsuke nakya, *ha,* Uta mo denu	Ahh – the dance, if you dance the dance Clap your hands If you don't take up the spirit of the dance The song will not come forth.
Haa – Koyoi na, *yoi sa,* koyoi deta tsuki wa Shinnyo no tsuki yo, *arase- yo hohohoi* Oya no goshoraku, *ha,* Mite kurasu	Ahh – this evening, this evening's moon A moon of True Thusness We spend this evening contemplating The religious devotion of our parents.
Haa – Odori na, *yoi sa,* odori nembutsu Ki mo karugaru to, *arase- yo hohohoi* Asu no kagyo, *ha,* Ku ni naranu	Ahh – the dance, the dance of Nembutsu The lightness and ease of spirit There will be no pain in tomorrow's labor.
Haa – Mura yon na, *yoi sa,* mura no obon yo Oemma sama no, *arase- yo hohohoi* Akai okao ga, *ha,* Wasuraryo ka	Ahh – the village, the village Obon The red face of Emma (King of Death) is forgotten.

Rev. Iwanaga took a brand-new Japanese Buddhist song and created a dance for it drawn from his understanding of minyo dance vocabulary. Neither the song nor the dance was old or traditional in any literal sense; rather, both were (re)composed from familiar materials. But both were absorbed into Japanese American practice as self-consciously traditional. Akiyama (1989, 32) writes, "In Northern California today, Reverend Iwanaga's choreography of 'Bon Odori' still frames the dance portion of *Obon* Festival and was referred to at one temple as 'the most traditional dance that we do.'" She reflects that very few people now know who choreographed it, and she notes that "'Bon Odori' has become a traditional, unauthored dance to the thousands of people who dance or see it" (126). The Buddhist Musical Association of Japan commissioned the music,[15] and the lyrics, by the composer Seisui Fujii, are about Obon, bon-odori, and Buddhist belief. The Japanese lyrics and English translation are above, with the kakegoe in italics (Kodani 1999, 27).

"Bon-Odori Uta" is performed counterclockwise. *Uta* means "song." Akiyama (1989) refers to the song and dance simply as "Bon Odori," and her description of the dance movements suggests she thinks it has a metaperformative function and is an enactment of Japanese American Buddhist community. She writes from a position of deep experience. Her account of the choreography and its meaning for many Japanese American bon-odori dancers is exactly right, and I can do no better:

The dance is very simple. Following the line of direction, the dancer holds a flat fan in the right hand. Each dancer moves slowly, stepping on the right foot with slightly bent leg, facing away from the center of the circle. The dancer then touches the left foot in place while straightening the right leg; at the same time each hand traces a half circle, arms moving from low to side to place high on both sides of the body ending with palms facing up. This is a traditional *minyo* movement motif and is performed three times, first on the right foot, then left and right. When the dancer steps right she faces away from the center of the circle and when she steps left, she faces the center. Next, all dancers step left and face the center of the circle. The dancer touches right foot in place as the hands are brought close to the body at waist level, palms up. The dancer pauses momentarily then steps forward on the right foot, sweeping the fan toward the center of the circle, then stepping back of [*sic*] the left, followed by the right foot stepping in place as the free hand claps the fan in front of the body and then to the left. The dance then begins again.

The slow, short dance phrase is repeated over and over. Midway through, as everyone is moving together, there is a sense of community, of being carried along by the motion of all the other dancers. Even those who have never seen the dance before or who don't consider themselves good dancers are able to join in during "Bon Odori". The number of dancers swell when "Bon Odori" is performed for the last time. In Northern California, this is the time when people from the audience, both Japanese and non-Japanese, are most apt to join in the dancing.

"Bon Odori" reminds the members of the temple that the dances are also part of a larger religious observance. The music and choreography have a reverent quality. While the audience talks and jokes during the other dances, there is a sense of attentiveness during "Bon Odori" even though very few people today understand the lyrics. It leads everyone into the festival, and then, at the end it provides a sense of closure. Following "Bon Odori", a minister of the temple leads the participants in the *Nembutsu*. The event is thus framed in religious ritual. (127–28)

This dance and its music move communities (literally and affectively) in ways much like taiko does: both have accrued significant meanings. The dance has been rechoreographed, collectively reconstituted, and its history is remembered in certain ways and forgotten in others. The sound of the remastered yet still slightly distorted recording to which it is performed immediately draws the dancers into a state of ethnicized Buddhist collectivity and readiness. We dance, in the words of the poet Garrett Hongo (2004, 459), "as if it were a memory," an experience "of [our] own dreaming," powerful because it is the result of individual and collective effort that has been lost, rediscovered, transformed, and reauthored.

BON-ODORI AS PILGRIMAGE

Bon-odori is danced for many reasons. Since the very first pilgrimage to Manzanar, in 1969, circle dances—both ondo and bon-odori—have been performed at the remote sites of some internment camps as a contemporary commemorative ritual articulating memory and resistance in a distinctively Sansei way.

Angered by the Vietnam War, inspired by the Civil Rights Movement, and mystified by Nisei silence about the internment, a core group of young Sansei—many of them still activists today—organized a bus trip to Manzanar in 1969. Victor Shibata was the young activist who suggested calling the trip a pilgrimage, or "a journey back, to pay our respects," as Warren Furutani says in Tad Nakamura's (2006) documentary *Pilgrimage*. This first pilgrimage was emblematic of the early Asian American Movement: urgently informed by the need to reclaim Asian American history, its participants were also trying to create and sustain new political collectivities.

Photographs and film footage of dances at the first pilgrimages are compelling. I'm not entirely comfortable calling them ondo, though most archival accounts describe them as such (see figure 19, Manzanar Pilgrimage *ondo*, 1970s, at *http:// wonglouderandfaster.com*). *Ondo* is a generic Japanese term for secular, minyo-derived street dance and is used, for example, in "First Street Ondo," featured in the annual Nisei Week in L.A.'s Little Tokyo in August. While I know that dance teachers could discuss the similarities and differences between ondo and bon-odori for hours, my sense is that the key distinction is context and purpose. I argue that the pilgrimage dance circle was (and is) bon-odori, not only because it is the same as the dances performed at Obon but, more important, because its purpose is so clearly connected to commemorating, honoring, and remembering the dead.

The religious studies scholar Joanne Doi (2003) explicitly connected the 1996 Tule Lake Pilgrimage to Obon. She describes the long bus ride to the site as integrally part of the experience, full of passengers' discussions, the folding of origami cranes in preparation for the memorial service, and Japanese box lunches. For her, this all sparked a feelingful set of associations: "The atmosphere of food and community brought back memories of the familiar church bazaars that resembled the Obon festivals that remember and honor the dead during the summer months" (278). Tule Lake is an especially fraught site in the already troubled arena of the internment camps because No-No Boys (those who answered no to questions 27 and 28 of the infamous "loyalty questionnaire" administered to all Japanese Americans in the camps), "disloyals," and political activists were incarcerated there. In historical perspective, it is now viewed as important precisely because its internees were known for their self-determination and resistance. Contemporary participants in the Tule Lake Pilgrimage are thus aware of its extraordinary place in the trauma of the incarceration, and they pay homage to its history of struggle. Doi writes, "Remembering the forgotten dead of Tule Lake reconstitutes the living and dead as community, reminiscent of the Obon midsummer festival that marks the temporary return of the spirits of the dead" (284). She cites Obon as a way to reconstitute Tule Lake's internees as a community willing to speak against injustice.

Doi takes it even further, describing this annual gathering as a "post-colonial pilgrimage" (275), in which the relationship between Japanese Americans (and

Muslim Americans) and the US nation-state is haunted by histories of paranoia and discrimination. The act of visiting the site—or playing taiko or dancing in it—addresses the incomplete or even reluctant effort to enter the nation-state on its authoritative terms. If the moment of rupture, trauma, and separation is in the past, the present is not yet in a state of completion.

Nakamura's lovely *Pilgrimage* builds up to bon-odori in an extremely moving way. At 16:29, this documentary shows the ondo circle at the 2005 pilgrimage, but only after interviews with participants have demonstrated how the pilgrimages since 9/11 have explicitly connected Muslim American and Japanese American civil rights issues. After clips of interviews with young Muslims at the pilgrimage, the dancers are seen with the stark white Manzanar monument and the snow-capped Sierra Nevada behind them. A young woman in a plaid shirt and jeans spins joyously in place, and I recognize the move and her exuberance—she's dancing "Shiawase Samba"! The next brief clip shows the circle dancing "Tanko Bushi," with an experienced dancer in the foreground and, behind her, many first-timers finding their way into it. Nakamura then quickly alternates color footage of the dancing from 2005 with black-and-white ondo footage from the 1970s, to startling effect. His editing reveals the additive meanings of dance, pilgrimage, and memory. (See figure 20, *bon-odori* in a Manzanar Pilgrimage, 1970s, at *http://wonglouderandfaster.com.*)

I participated in the Manzanar Pilgrimage twice (in 2003 and 2007), during a particularly uneasy period when two problems dominated: post-9/11 threats to civil liberties and the transfer of Manzanar to the National Park Service (NPS). In a spectacular example of coalition politics immediately following 9/11, the JACL argued that Muslim Americans should not bear the brunt of xenophobic fear, and from then on the Manzanar Pilgrimage routinely included Muslims American participants (many from the Council on American-Islamic Relations) and paid explicit attention to the parallels between post–Pearl Harbor nativism and 9/11 xenophobia. Almost a decade before, the establishment of Manzanar as a National Historic Site in 1992 had put official and unofficial memories into a direct relationship borne out through every aspect of the park and the pilgrimage: the pilgrimage had been created to assert the importance of unofficial memory, history, and experience, so the hyperofficial process of setting up the national park and all its exhibits juxtaposed different kinds of commemorative processes. From the beginning, the NPS evidently embraced the pilgrimage as part of the site's meaning and significance (and lists it on the park's website as an annual event), but what the anthropologist Christina Schwenkel (2009, 12) calls "recombinant history," "the interweaving of diverse and frequently discrepant transnational memories, knowledge formations, and logics of representation," is more deeply part of bon-odori than ever in the pilgrimage ondo circle. Unlike the post–Vietnam War context addressed by Schwenkel, the pilgrimage is not explicitly focused on reconciliation. Redress and reparations demand profoundly different performatives. Bon-odori nevertheless stretches to include coalition groups as well as NPS rangers who dance in full uniform.

"TANKO BUSHI"

The ondo circle is the last part of the pilgrimage's two- to three-hour program, which also features speeches, music (songs and always a taiko group), the roll call of the camps, and an interdenominational service held in the cemetery in front of the Manzanar monument. The dance offers a transition out of collective sorrow and anger into participatory joy and determination, enacting a different kind of commemoration in a long morning full of remembrance.

"Tanko Bushi" is almost always one of these dances. Sometimes it is also danced as part of the Manzanar at Dusk program. Indeed, it is danced in most Japanese *and* Japanese American Obon gatherings. Its ubiquity is striking because it carries no inherent or ever-ready symbolic meaning. It is originally from Fukuoka Prefecture (in the south of Japan), but its specific regional identity seems only superficially part of its popularity. Terence Lancashire (2011, 63) notes that it was a folk song sung by female workers in the coal mines in Tagawa, Fukuoka Prefecture, and that a schoolteacher named Ono Hoko rearranged it in 1910. His version was recorded in 1932 and by a famous geisha in 1948, then by the singer Otomaru in 1957, and so on. It was featured in the 1957 film *Sayonara* starring Marlon Brando. The song has gone through repeated rearrangements and remediations. The dance has been thoroughly rechoreographed but during my years of participation was always performed to the same commercial recording, featuring the *enka* singer Suzuki Masao.[16] This recording's dissemination is nothing short of astonishing, and it has jumped across a range of technologies from its original form as a 78 rpm record.

The dance offers a straightforward programmatic representation of coal miners' work. As Akiyama (1989, 120) writes, "'Tanko Bushi' is one of several bon odori depicting the work of coal miners. It has become extremely popular with people in Japan and with Japanese Americans and is performed on social occasions such as Japanese American picnics as well as during Obon Festivals. The song and dance was also popular among American soldiers in Japan after World War II." "Tanko Bushi" is a dance that can be featured in nearly any context. The series of moves are always explained as literal depictions of first digging for coal (to the right, then to the left), tossing a shovelful over the shoulder (right, then left), shading the eyes to look at the sun (or moon, depending on the teacher) while stepping backward, pushing a cart loaded with coal while stepping forward, and then throwing the coal onto a heap (by casting both hands down and away from the body while stepping in toward the center of the circle). Some teachers say the final gesture opens a gate. As in most bon-odori, the dancers move counterclockwise. "Tanko Bushi" is extremely simple: it is almost a primer for basic odori gestural vocabulary.

Despite—or perhaps because of—its simplicity, several sources describe the choreography in detail. A website devoted to bon-odori and featuring the Japanese dance teacher Yoshiko Ikemura Sensei offers this step-by-step explanation of the dance, in English that conveys the feeling of the Japanese from which it is clearly translated:

Tankobushi (炭坑節) is the most popular Bon Odori Song. All Bon Odori Matsuri always play this song. So, it is this basic and simple dance which everyone can dance easily.
Tankobushi "The song of Coal Miners"
(walk counterclockwise)
Song: Masao Suzuki.
Level: 01 Very Easy
Type: Basic
Move:
Face your stomach to the walking direction.
Count Four when music starts.
Clap, clap and clap.
grab your hands just like you are grabbing a scoop for coal mining.
Dig, dig (right),
Then, dig, dig (left).
Carry coals. Carry coals.
You are getting out from underground.
Then you see beautiful moon. watch it two times.
Push your lorry. Push your lorry.
Then, open gate. Then, back to clap clap and clap.
Repeat.[17]

This version relies on video and text to convey the details of the choreography. In her lovely little book documenting the bon-odori repertoire in Hawai`i, Van Zile offers detailed schematic drawings of the dances, including a set for "Tanko Bushi" (see figure 21, schematic drawings for "Tanko Bushi," at *http://wonglou-derandfaster.com*). Similarly, the children's book *Bon Odori Dancer* (McCoy and Yao 1999) provides illustrated instructions for the dance after telling the tale of Keiko, "the clumsiest girl in her Japanese dance class," who is consumed with anxiety over her two left feet but eventually performs with grace and confidence at her local Obon festival. "Tanko Bushi" is thus both frequently danced and much documented, across a variety of media (as are other bon-odori choreographies). First a regional dance about women's labor, it became a kind of catchall for traditionality and an invitation to participate thanks to its simplicity and intelligibility. That minimalism allowed it to travel far, through the bodies of immigrants, through a transpacific flow of sound recordings, and then through the internet. Japanese American political practice transplanted it into both secular invented ritual and a fiercely new kind of sacred heritage: as danced in the desert dust and under the hot desert sun, "Tanko Bushi" in situ in the Manzanar Pilgrimage is an invitation to participate in oppositional memory. It is an integral part of sustained remediated heritage work that asserts uncomfortable histories without explicitly connecting the dots. Women once worked in the coal mines in Fukuoka and marveled at the beauty of the sun or the moon when they emerged from underground. Now Japanese Americans, Muslim Americans, and NPS rangers dance together in the space of injury.

CREATING NEW BON-ODORI

At the time of this writing, Los Angeles's Little Tokyo serves a bustling combination of contradictory needs, from tourism to Buddhist space to a grassroots anti-development movement focused on cultural self-determination. Post-1970s Little Tokyo is an ongoing experiment in Japanese American community making.[18] The neighborhood was designated a National Historic District in 1986 but has nonetheless been threatened by outside financial interests and gentrification. Several nonprofit community organizations—including the Little Tokyo People's Rights Organization, the Little Tokyo Anti-eviction Task Force, the Friends of Little Tokyo Arts, and the Little Tokyo Service Center—have pushed back, arguing over and over that the neighborhood should serve the needs of Japanese Americans, from housing for the elderly to community-based athletics.

The proxemics and body politic of bon-odori are all over Little Tokyo. During the nine months of the year outside the Obon season, visual hints keep the dances close by and mark the spaces where they could materialize. Tile images of dance hats from northern Japan are embedded in the asphalt of the First Street and Central Avenue intersection, reminding one that the street is as much a site of the annual "First Street Ondo" as a thoroughfare. The beautiful courtyard between Second and Third Streets outside the JACCC was designed by Isamu Noguchi as a public gathering place.[19] Its circular shape is designed for bon dancing, which (among many other things) has repeatedly taken place in the plaza since it was finished in 1983. I view it as a bon-odori circle waiting to happen: the bricks are arranged in concentric circles, and I have seen bon-odori performed there many times, enacting the principles of community in a charged space of Japanese American self-determination. Like most of Little Tokyo, the plaza reclaimed Japanese American presence after World War II. (See figure 22, *bon-odori* fans etched into a crosswalk in Little Tokyo, Los Angeles, at *http://wonglouderandfaster.com*.)

Taiko and bon-odori are key symbols of postwar Japanese American presence. The mural at Central and First Streets titled *Home Is Little Tokyo* (2005) sums up the hundred-year history of the neighborhood and the twenty-first-century emphasis on certain forms of cultural heritage (see figure 23, *Home Is Little Tokyo* mural, Little Tokyo, Los Angeles, at *http://wonglouderandfaster.com*). In keeping with the tradition of community murals, this was the result of a painstaking process of consultation and execution, "the culmination of three years of work by almost 500 individuals, groups and organizations": the muralists, Tony Osumi, Sergio Diaz, and Jorge Diaz, solicited ideas for the content from community organizations, and the public painting involved hundreds of people.[20] Three taiko players drum joyously on the left. On the right, among others, a girl dribbles a basketball, another girl wears a karate gi, an activist raises a sign supporting the Little Tokyo Recreation Center, a young man carries an elderly Issei man, a Latino shopkeeper displays vegetables for sale—all these figures speak to the neighborhood's complex history and needs. A bon-odori dancer stands in their midst: a woman in a pink yukata holding an uchiwa, arms raised in the moon position.

Inspired by the principles of the Asian American Movement, at least three Japanese American women have created new bon-odori dances with accompanying music, and each has done so in deeply informed ways, activating bon-odori to build a self-consciously Japanese American participatory culture from traditional materials. Nobuko Miyamoto, PJ Hirabayashi, and Michelle Fujii (whom I introduce in more detail below) have offered new approaches to bon-odori that build on almost a century of music and dance, reassembling traditional materials in vivid and original ways that the West Coast Japanese American Jodo Shinshu community has embraced. Since the 1970s, Sansei reclamation and ownership of bon-odori has driven a number of vibrant experiments, all framed as dynamically part of the tradition rather than as contemporary departures. As already mentioned, Miyamoto and Rev. Mas Kodani have created a number of original songs and bon-odori choreographies outlining specifically Japanese American issues and concerns (Asai 2016).[21] Similarly, Hirabayashi's music and dance for "Ei Ja Nai Ka" address the history of Asian American laborers.[22]

Each of these artists has carefully defined the context for their new works. All have been at pains to indicate that their songs and dances are meant to live in the community and that their purpose is inherently participatory. The audience for "Omiyage" is the most explicitly outlined of any taiko piece I have encountered. *Omiyage* means "gift" in Japanese and often refers to the small gifts you offer when you are visiting someone or give to friends and family when you return from a trip. This work was designed as a gift to the taiko community and is carefully listed on various websites as conceived by Bryan Yamami, composed by Shoji Kameda, and originally performed (quite spectacularly) by TAIKOPROJECT. Kameda has stated that "Omiyage" is

> a piece that I originally wrote for TAIKOPROJECT and have since released under a free art license as a gift to the North American Taiko community. Bryan Yamami first conceived of a piece called "Omiyage" for TAIKOPROJECT (re)generation that TAI-KOPROJECT would workshop to the various communities it would visit. I have Kris [Bergstrom] to thank for expanding the "Omiyage" concept in terms of releasing

it under a free art license. My work and On Ensemble's music and recordings are released under a more restrictive creative commons, attribution non-commercial, share-alike license, but I often have interesting conversations with Kris regarding free art and admire his commitment to the concept. I wanted to do something under the free art license and "Omiyage" was a logical choice.[23]

Bergstrom (2008, 2011) has written at length about free art licensing and copyleft. Significantly, the core group of musicians who generated "Omiyage" and "Korekara" (discussed in the next paragraph) had all grown up with kumi-daiko, were leaders in collegiate groups, and went on to shine in the professional TAIKOPROJECT or On Ensemble. Their impressive knowledge of taiko history and culture led to their emphasis on open-source work. I view it as a generational response as well, since the pieces are unabashedly contemporary yet familiar, exuberant yet based on recognizable kumi-daiko rhythms.

In 2005, the NATC created a Song Committee, made up of Fujii, Bergstrom, Walter Clarke, and Yuta Kato, and charged it with creating a piece for the biannual conference. The result was "Korekara," which is now played all over the world. It is always described as "composed" by Fujii and Clarke, and Bergstrom, Kameda, Kato, and Hitomi Oba are listed as "artistic advisors." As a collaborative effort, the music and dance were taught in workshops led by all those musicians during the spring of 2005, hosted by different taiko groups across Southern California, and were performed at that year's NATC by over eighty local taiko players. The notation was included in the participants' packets, and in the explanatory notes accompanying it, the Song Committee wrote,

It's YOUR song!

We hope *Korekara* is considered a successful and interesting piece that piques the interest of members of our community. ~We hope to see new versions of the song, tailored to the different taiko styles among us. . . . ~We hope you will take *Korekara* and make it your own. ~In doing so you will be contributing to a creative pool of taiko music for our community, free to be learned, practiced, performed, and enjoyed by all!

In one workshop I attended—hosted by Hikari Taiko—Fujii, Clarke, and Bergstrom carefully and efficiently broke the piece down into component parts, teaching the sections first through kuchi shōga and air taiko before moving on to the dance (see video 9, Michelle Fujii, Walter Clarke, and Kris Bergstrom teaching "Korekara" at the Southeast Japanese School and Community Center in Norwalk, California, 2005, at *http://wonglouderandfaster.com*). Fujii is known for her training and her ability to make traditional moves contemporary, and she had choreographed "Korekara" for taiko players in a unison counterclockwise circle, like bon-odori. Since then, I have seen it performed many times by many groups.

Fujii is Japanese American and was in her mid-twenties in 2005, and Clarke is African American and was then in his early thirties. Both have had leadership positions in several key Southern California taiko groups. Fujii came up through the vibrant collegiate taiko scene and went to Japan for several years after college to study traditional dance and taiko; she was at that time a member of two recent, cutting-edge, young taiko groups in greater Los Angeles, On Ensemble and TAIKOPROJECT. Clarke had studied taiko for several decades and was a long-time member of two Los Angeles taiko groups, Kishin Daiko and Kodama Taiko. "Korekara" was a response to controversies over narrowed access to taiko repertoire. Fujii and Clarke wanted to teach "Korekara" to as many Southern California taiko players as they could during the two months before the big conference in 2005 and then to debut it at the conference's opening ceremony. Their idea from the beginning was that the piece would be in the public domain, not owned or controlled by any individual or ensemble. They thus created a wholly new category of taiko repertoire, driven by the political economy of its historical moment.

The impetus behind this public domain piece lay in sharply delineated tensions between a Japanese taiko group and its concern over how North American taiko groups were using its material, which led in 1999 to a new level of discussion about such issues as Japanese and North American taiko relations, cultural ownership, and authority (Wong 2004, 223–25). "Korekara" was a response to that debate, put forward by taiko players for other taiko players, with little explicit acknowledgement of its generating circumstances but lots of then-recent history just under the surface. It is emblematic of a North American taiko subjectivity that overlaps with but is distinct from Japanese practices. It has a deep and self-conscious base in heritage: on the West Coast, it is difficult if not impossible to play taiko without engaging directly with Japanese American culture and history, which means knowing something about the incarceration, Obon festivals, the reparations movement of the 1980s, and the Asian American Movement generally.

"Korekara" sounds and looks simultaneously Japanese and Japanese American. Its base pattern is a classic festival rhythm, which broadcasts a joyously upbeat mood immediately understood by any taiko player, and indeed by many Japanese Americans. The dance section is instantly recognizable as a bon-odori dance, albeit an utterly new and decidedly contemporary one. It evokes and could potentially be absorbed into Obon practice as a bon dance. It is performed in a large circle, in unison, and features certain movements (wiping sweat from the brow, *yama*/mountain) found in many bon dances. (See video 10, Michelle Fujii teaching the "Korekara" dance to taiko players at the Southeast Japanese School and Community Center in Norwalk, California, 2005, at *http://wonglouderandfaster.com.*)

In short, the dance vocabulary for this piece, its spatial arrangement, and its upbeat mood instantly activate the joyousness of Obon and of Japanese American community. "Korekara" debuted at the taiko conference in Los Angeles on July 15, 2005 (see video 11, "Korekara" debut at the North American Taiko Conference in Los Angeles, July 15, 2005, at *http://wonglouderandfaster.com*). I videotaped it (though I wanted to perform!), and I know the piece quite well because I participated in three of the workshops leading up to this event.

"Korekara" was designed to make a performative statement about repertoire and community ownership. It was not meant to be a radical recontextualization: its two composers are well versed in North American taiko history and clearly see themselves as participants in that tradition; it's equally evident that they see taiko as having a past as well as a future (which they are trying to help shape). "Korekara" emulates bon dances, but it is *part of* that tradition, not on the outside looking in. As with all performance anywhere, the thing being performed and taught is a palimpsest, a multilayered historical artifact of movements across many times and places. Taiko carries connections to postwar Japanese nationalism, Japanese American politicization, and more. "Korekara" addresses a community embroiled in discussions about its own sources of authority, and it was put forward by two taiko players eager to push those discussions in a productive direction. By creating a contemporary bon dance and its music, they added to one of the key bodies politic of the Japanese American community.

DANCING WITHOUT END

I now experience the sadness of the end of the Obon season. The season follows a predictable arc. The last Obon festivals at Southern California temples are always held on the first weekend in August, followed by a two-week hiatus and then the large street ondo featuring bon-odori during the Nisei Week closing ceremony. Dancing down East First Street in Little Tokyo is beautiful and meaningful, but it feels very different from the temple gatherings. As this is the last chance to dance bon-odori for a year, large numbers of aficionados turn out. We dance with the spirit of Obon, but it's hard not to feel a little melancholy—it's like the day after Christmas, when the ephemerality of the season's beauty is evident and fully appreciated as part of its significance.

Some bon-odori are well known; others are revived and retaught; others are made anew. The new/old inauthentic/authentic bon-odori tradition is spectacularly alive and well. It is sustained by a Buddhist organizational structure of pedagogy and dissemination that reaches more than ten thousand dancers every summer in Southern California alone. The dances are imbued with traditionality yet constantly made contemporary, and young dancers are always boisterously present in the circles alongside the statelier, middle-aged and elderly dancers. I love all of it and particularly enjoy a rambunctious recent tradition I've encountered since 2014 at Nishi Hongwanji, Higashi Hongwanji, and the Gardena Buddhist Church. After the first hour of dancing, there is a fifteen-minute break, when dancers flock to the food and drink booths. The intermission ends when, without any fanfare, a recent pop hit is suddenly put on the PA system, and one by one, dancers line up and spontaneously perform any of the more well-known bon-odori to the song. Everyone falls into the same dance once several people have found their groove. In August 2014 at the Gardena Obon, we danced "One Plus One" to Pharrell's "Happy" (rather than the Japanese song usually used, sung by Suizenji Kiyoko). "Happy" is just a shade faster, so the dance felt slightly frantic but also dizzily fun, like playing musical chairs. In July 2016 we danced "Tanko Bushi" to "Uptown Funk."[24] At some point further back, I remember dancing "Tanko Bushi" to Michael Jackson's "Thriller"—or was it "Billy Jean"? These transitional moments in the evening are never announced, but after a minute or so all the dancers have returned, the concentric circles have re-formed, and suddenly hundreds of people, from small children to octogenarians, are dancing to the sounds of the top ten. This giddy choreographic moment reconstitutes the circles. It's the history of Japanese American bon-odori from the inside out—the groove and not-quite-in-unison body politic that bring us together every summer.

Transition

Unison and Circles

Dancing in circles. Playing in unison. Both are performance practices that create sociality. A circle may have a leader, but the bon-odori circles don't. Bon-odori circles are directed inward, toward the taiko in the tower. Sameness and difference. Some music and dance traditions assume that everyone does things differently; others insist on sameness; yet others celebrate the tension between the two. The space of performance creates separation or connection: the proscenium stage versus the powwow circle. None of this is simple, and the binaries I seem to suggest are never just that. Participatory discrepancies abound within sameness. Kumi-daiko often oscillates between ensemble unison playing and breakout improvised solos. Bon-odori never features solos but rather assumes unison movement while allowing for individual flourishes. The circles for bon-odori are embedded in the landscape of L.A.'s Little Tokyo: brick circles built into the courtyard connecting the Aratani Theatre and the JACCC, white paint circles on the asphalt parking lot outside the Nishi Hongwanji Buddhist temple. The circles are always there, ready to be activated.

4

Good Gigs, Bad Gigs

Drumming between Hope and Anger

The members of the TCLA performed constantly. Rev. Tom received a steady stream of requests for performances and was always making sure he had enough of us ready to cover the demands. He juggled who was available, the maximum or minimum number of people needed, the required skill level, and so on. He emailed a list of new requests to TCLA members every few days, and most Satori Daiko practice sessions ended with him going through the list of upcoming performances and asking who could go. Most of us were eager to play in public, but we had to consider not just the date and time but how long a drive would be involved, since most of us worked or were in school. See video 12, Rev. Tom Kurai and members of Satori Daiko discussing and volunteering for upcoming performances, August 2007, at *http://wonglouderandfaster.com,* for example: following an intense practice session on an August night and just before packing the van for an important concert the next day and a weekend of performances out of town, we milled around, simultaneously chatting, waiting, and responding ("I can go!").

This is not a celebratory chapter about how taiko provides a key means of empowerment for Japanese Americans and other Asian Americans. My writing in the 2000s (Wong 2000, 2004, 2008) focused on that performative efficacy, and I stand by those publications. As time went on, though, I faced the reality that I sometimes performed in extraordinarily racist and orientalist venues with Satori Daiko. What are the ethnographic implications of participating in racist and racialized practices? How do performers deal with, address, accept, and critique the presentational frames within which they do their work? As cultural workers, taiko players are inherently engaged with knotty representational politics in ways nicely close to the ground. Indeed, they do their work in a particularly loud, sweaty, and athletic way, which is central to taiko's attraction for me. I now roll up my sleeves on matters I have avoided in my more congratulatory work on taiko: how and why we perform in so many contexts and venues that are deeply

[handwritten marginal note: WE FORGET THAT PEOPLE HAVE A LIFE OUTSIDE]

problematic, rife with orientalist framing, expectation, and determination, and whether the emphatically politicized Asian American body posited by taiko can be reconciled with the performance venues available to us. We don't always play at Asian Pacific Islander heritage-month events or at political demonstrations or at API culture nights. How, then, do taiko players address the space between intention and racist reframing? And how does this implicate the politics of grounded ethnographic practices?

Rev. Tom depended (in part) on taiko for his living, which raises the question of whether playing in preferred circumstances—that is, in contexts where a post–civil rights, post–Asian American Movement political sensibility can be assumed—might often be the exception, a privilege, and a tough way to make ends meet. More habitually, we played in fairs and festivals that were put on by corporate or civic institutions and self-consciously directed toward the promotion of a certain idea of multiculturalism—usually the flabby liberal version dedicated to having us all just get along and feel good while we think we're doing it, with ethnic food, music, and dance as an essential apparatus.[1] As an ideology and a set of institutionalized strategies, multiculturalism is deeply imbedded in late capitalist frameworks of value, so it is hardly surprising that the labor of taiko is is co-opted by institutions that are not genealogically connected to social justice practices.

Japanese American taiko walks a certain line between new ways of being Asian American and more troubled histories of folkloric practice. Nostalgia for authentic Japanese practice is ever-present in taiko—in our costumes and in our efforts to connect to Japanese taiko masters. Yet Japanese Americans and other Asian Americans are not alone in our longing for authentic culture. The anthropologist Marilyn Ivy (1995, 55) addresses the power of nostalgia in postindustrial Japan, arguing that traditional Japanese material culture has a particular affective weight for the "new Japanese" (*shin Nihonjin*), the third postwar generation, who grew up "in an Americanized, affluent state in which certain things Japanese appear more exotic than products of western civilization." These Japanese goods are literally called "nostalgia products" (*nosutarujii shōhin*) and are regarded as a kind of postmodern hip with elements of camp, kitsch, and the retro (56). I would say that taiko is not quite a nostalgia product but draws its power from the same ideological source. Ivy traces these newly commodified sites of the vintage as "mere" style (58), in the postmodern sense, back to the New Japanology, the resurgence of folklore studies in the 1960s and 1970s—which is, not coincidentally, when the kumi-daiko phenomenon took off. Ivy argues that folklore is possible only with the disappearance of the object of study—that its reconstitution as a textualized, "studied" object emerges only at the moment of its vanishing (66–67).

In this chapter I compare two events at which Satori Daiko performed, to lay out the wide spectrum of critical possibilities in which taiko players must be adept and to show how I attended to what my fellow taiko players said about their own multifocal awareness. On April 26, 2003, we performed at the annual Manzanar

Pilgrimage, a quintessentially Japanese American event that is as politically positioned as it gets. A year earlier, in May 2002, we were hired to play in a daylong dragon boat race in Laughlin, Nevada. I set up an unapologetically overdetermined spectrum here: the Laughlin event was outrageously racist, and the Manzanar Pilgrimage continuously reconstructs a fraught memory and operationalizes civil rights discourse as a racialized political strategy. I focus on how my taiko friends talked about both events because some of the most important political work that any of us do is often at ground zero, in the one-on-one interactions where we talk, don't talk, generate new means of response without having planned to do so, or make self-consciously strategic efforts to assert new spaces, new voices, and new choreographies.

PILGRIMS AT MANZANAR

The Manzanar Committee has sponsored the Manzanar Pilgrimage for over thirty years; it is all volunteer and incorporated under the laws of the State of California as a nonprofit educational organization. Many of its founding members were integrally involved in the redress and reparations movement that resulted in President Ronald Reagan signing an apology in 1988 to Japanese American internees for the violation of their civil liberties and an acknowledgment of the unconstitutionality of the Japanese American incarceration camps during World War II. Every year since 1969, several hundred people (mostly but not entirely Japanese American) from all over California and beyond annually come together at Manzanar—this dusty, remote place—to assert memory, anger, and a commitment to social change.

Playing at Manzanar was profoundly moving. The ten of us from Satori Daiko who made the two-hundred-mile drive into the Mojave Desert to do so knew it was a deeply important event, and it was doubly meaningful for us because Rev. Tom was one of the first taiko players, along with Kenny Endo, to perform at a Manzanar Pilgrimage, in 1975. Our participation in 2003 was thus part of a KINGSBURY lineage, directly connected to Rev. Tom's founding presence. The incarceration camps and the reparations movement are centrally part of the Japanese American experience, and it is an honor for any taiko player to be part of this pilgrimage. Participation is a gesture of homage, memory, political placement, and commitment to continued social change. It makes you part of a much bigger conversation. Standing in the sun and the wind for several hours in the Manzanar cemetery, with the snow-covered Sierra Nevada mountains behind us and a crowd of at least five hundred people in front of us, was curiously intimate: we were so far away from everything, and the sense of being in a remote, isolated place was terribly strong. You knew that anyone willing to go to the effort of being there that day had to be pretty committed, so everyone was very informal and familiar with one another. You assumed that you shared certain things: sadness, outrage, injury, determination. The ritual of the event was prearranged, with quite a few former internees, by then quite old, offering testimony of what it was like in the camps and reflections on how to think about issues of civil liberties in a broader, contemporary context. Musicians performed between the speakers (a folk-rock group, a Dylanesque balladeer, and the taiko players). The roll call of the camps included one banner for each camp carried into the cemetery, followed by a commemorative service featuring Shinto, Christian, and Buddhist priests. Many participants approached in procession to light incense and place a flower on the Manzanar monument. Finally, hundreds of dancers formed a huge bon-odori circle (see figure 24, Rev. Tom Kurai playing *odaiko* for the *ondo* at the 1975 Manzanar Pilgrimage, with the pilgrimage organizer Sue Embrey dancing in the right foreground, at *http://wonglouderandfaster.com*). The experience didn't end there: it went on as we returned to our cars sunburned, windburned, and covered with the dust of Manzanar, and then followed the long dirt road back out to Highway 395. We saw small groups of people scattered over the empty acres of the site, many standing and staring at what little is left—cement foundations, rock gardens. Later, in the small, nearby town of Lone Pine, I was struck by the fact that all the motels and restaurants were full of Japanese Americans, and thought how odd, ironic, and triumphant that is.

We played. (See video 13, Satori Daiko playing "Aranami" at the Manzanar Pilgrimage, at *http://wonglouderandfaster.com*.) To play with that much history hanging on us! It was humbling, exhilarating, invigorating, inspiring. To play with Mount Whitney and the Manzanar monument looking over our shoulders; to play with those small, stony graves a few steps away. To play for a crowd that understood we were playing for a Japanese American political, historical, and cultural agenda—a crowd that wouldn't mistake us for "Japanese" or "oriental."

Playing taiko at the Manzanar Pilgrimage was ideal: we had an informed, politically astute audience, with the understanding that we weren't on objectified display—there was no museum-like sensibility framing cultural meaning as authentic and contained—but rather were part of the fabric of the event and, more deeply still, were there to help generate a certain spirit of strength, assertion, and affirmation. In the Japanese American community, it's understood that taiko has performative effects.

The annual return to Manzanar is defined as a pilgrimage for several reasons. Pilgrimage is usually an act of worship, a means of enacting devotion by moving through space and place in ways that redefine both sites and the routes to them as sacred. Philip V. Bohlman (1996) and Paul Greene (2003) have theorized pilgrimage as a practice that maps sound onto movement and vice versa. The Manzanar Pilgrimage certainly does that: the program involves lots of music, and taiko is central to how a postincarceration Japanese America—both in and beyond the pilgrimage—is constituted and reconstituted. But questions remain: Why frame the movement as pilgrimage? Why juxtapose activist organizing with pilgrimage? Why even suggest that this remote site of transgenerational trauma somehow be a place of ritual memory?

None of the informational literature I have found addresses the genesis of the use of *pilgrimage* in relation to the camps—and in fact, *all* the incarceration camps are now annually revisited, remembered, and resituated in this way, under the rubric of pilgrimage. Pilgrimage is more than a metaphor. Why visit Dachau or Auschwitz, Wounded Knee, Hiroshima, the museum of the killing fields in Phnom Penh, or the place in my town, Riverside, California, where a gay man was killed in a hate-driven knifing? To remember, of course, and to commemorate, but reinhabiting a site as a performative act makes memory into a political strategy.

Unfortunately, Satori Daiko spent most of its time embroiled in the nostalgia industry as defined by multicultural show biz. We swung pendulum-like between very different performance contexts. At one end of the spectrum was the Manzanar Pilgrimage. At the other were absurdly orientalist events defined by japonaiserie of the worst sort. In between were a range of engagements that, at best, contained elements of both extremes.

There are no pure spaces for Japanese American or Asian American self-determination. Still, the Manzanar Pilgrimage came close to being one: it defined the preferred outer end of our activities, an ideal location, audience, and Asian American performative possibility. Yet it teetered on the edge of a new kind of nostalgic redefinition. In April 2004, Manzanar was officially opened as a national park. This was the end of a long process of recalibrating meaning and acknowledgement, as acres of empty, federally owned fields were named California Historical Landmark #850 in 1972, then redesignated in 1985 as a National Historic Landmark, still known by hardly anyone except Japanese Americans, and then as a National Historic Site in 1992, and finally, under President Bill Clinton, made into a national park, with a visitor center, exhibits, interpretive trails, and the whole nine yards. Manzanar has become part of an official metanarrative about a benign nation-state that makes mistakes but is big enough to acknowledge them. This is a different kind of nostalgia than the heritage play of taiko. It reframes Manzanar as a place that we can visit to feel safely angry about social injustice because we already know the end of the story: that injustice was recouped. What was wrong was made right. The very fact of the national park bespeaks this and performatively makes it so. Manzanar becomes a nostalgic souvenir of this inevitability.[2] There are postcards (the souvenir par excellence), but what else? As Barbara Kirshenblatt-Gimblett (1998) argues for the museum and visitor center at Ellis Island, the nostalgic gesture is one of ownership and control, of folding troubled histories into a single story owned by all. Nostalgia renders it harmless, solved—a story with closure.

So it was poignant to play at the Manzanar Pilgrimage in April 2003, because evidence of the national park was already manifest, including the presence of more than a few rangers in khaki and olive drab. Two were at the entrance to the camp off US Route 395, stopping each car and ascertaining participation in the pilgrimage. And they were armed, as are many post-9/11 national park rangers. It shook me up to be stopped by anyone in uniform at the entrance to this site of all sites, but then I was instantly embarrassed to be so affected—two knee-jerk responses in quick succession—because of course I recognize how essential the National Park Service is to the protection of tangible heritage. The next day, though, I met Mo Nishida, one of the original organizers of the pilgrimage and a central figure in the redress movement, now a wiry, suntanned man in his seventies, and he said it made him flat-out furious to find armed federal officials as gatekeepers of Manzanar. With nostalgia comes forgetting. Is that forgetting purposeful or merely thoughtless? Isn't thoughtlessness itself a performative act?

We played; we listened to the speeches; we joined the bon-odori circle that grew larger and larger as hundreds of participants joined in. Two of the head rangers were pulled into the dance, and they followed along gamely, awkwardly. To me, their participation—though well intentioned—was heavy-handed, unsubtle, and clumsily symbolic. It was a choreographic move from the ideological script of the multicultural festival, in which the culture bearers put on a show and then invite the audience onstage to learn a dance.

I have long insisted that I want to focus my research on Asian American self-representation, but in fact it's difficult to hold the line. Detailed works like James S. Moy's *Marginal Sights: Staging the Chinese in America* (1993) and Robert G. Lee's *Orientals: Asian Americans in Popular Culture* (1999) were central to the construction of Asian American studies because structural racism and orientalist praxis are (at least partly) the impetus for Asian American experiments with self-determination. William Wei (1993, 47–58) summarizes the problem of "selling out" when Asian Americans perform in popular culture. From the San Francisco nightclub Forbidden City (Dong 2002, 2008, 2014) to Philip Kan Gotanda's play *Yankee Dawg You Die* (1991), Asian Americans have continuously explored whether representation can be controlled in any way or at any level. Sometimes it seems like any Asian American cultural worker is always already co-opted until otherwise asserted. Between 1999 and 2009, Satori Daiko played in

- many, *many* multicultural civic events, such as festivals in parks or on main streets
- a corporate reception at the Staples Center in Los Angeles that sported an "Asian" theme, with young Asian American women dressed up as geisha, a sumptuous spread of Asian foods, huge papier-mâché Buddha images scattered throughout the area, and Whites as the majority of attendees
- numerous API history-month events on local college campuses
- a city-sponsored "night out" with no specifically Asian or multicultural theme
- a birthday party with a "Japan" theme at a private home, for a group of White American young professionals, who wore yukata, ate sushi, and toasted one another with sake
- the grand opening of a Japanese Mitsuwa supermarket in Gardena

- quite a few Lunar New Year festivals, from Chinese to Vietnamese
- the annual dinner sponsored by an association of API pharmacists who work for Kaiser Permanente (a large HMO)
- the grand opening of the Japanese American National Museum's new Pavilion in 1999

Some of these are of course completely heinous, which raises the question of why any self-respecting Asian American would agree to participate in them. As the historian and museum curator Jack Tchen has commented, "Sadly, part of what it means to 'become' American is to enact these racist traditions" (K. Chow 2014). Why did the members of Satori Daiko allow ourselves to be presented as fetishized commodities? Could we have refused to participate in the most appallingly exoticized settings? After all, the boycott has been one of the most critically informed gestures of refusal available to minority communities. Any boycott is powerful because it theorizes the connections between political presence and capitalism.[3] "Not buying" becomes "not selling out," and withdrawing capitalist compliance thus becomes metaphorically and *actually* an act of self-determination, even a sign that collapses the apparent space between theory and praxis or politics and commerce. It reveals the corporate capitalist base that defines spheres otherwise imagined to be purely in the realm of "culture."

My activities with Satori Daiko provided a gateway to both the best and the worst of the Asian American experience in Los Angeles. I had the chance to see the Japanese American community at work from behind the scenes, I had entrée to vibrant Asian immigrant neighborhoods through their public events, and I met any number of leading figures in the Asian American arts, but I have also seen the dark side of corporate multiculturalism *and* astonishingly old-fashioned yellowface play and orientalist fantasy at work. At one level these spheres are separate, but at another they were joined together by my taiko group. We showed up and played the same repertoire regardless of the context.

The critical theorist Meyda Yegenoglu (2003, 2) suggests that an "ethics of hospitality" undergirds the logic that "allows" the work of immigrant labor forces and "non-normative citizens" of all kinds. She argues that liberal multiculturalism is a "regulative principle" that might seem to invite the creation of new kinds of democratic spaces but may actually prevent new political formations from emerging, by policing the very terms for presence. Drawing on the work of Appadurai, Hall, Dirlik, Spivak, Jameson, Žižek, and especially Derrida, Yegenoglu posits a "reorganization of diversity" that "revalorizes both the local and the global" while creating new conditions for containment (5, 6). She combines Žižek's and Spivak's ideas to show that liberal multiculturalism is central to the workings of global capitalism: difference has been resituated as somehow inherently resistant, making it necessary to reassert the relationship between difference and transnational commodity capitalism by "rethink[ing] globalization and the . . . valorization of particular identities as a double gesture of capital" (7). As Yegenoglu puts it, "[This version of] multiculturalism is based on a disavowed and inverted self-referential form of racism as it empties its own position of all positive content," allowing a "Eurocentric distance" that ensures the "foreclosure" of any other politics (11, 12). The trope of hospitality is central to corporate globalization because it establishes a tolerant welcome to the other while maintaining the terms and authority of the host—for instance, immigrant labor forces are welcome if it is understood that their presence, movements, and rewards will be limited. Discussing multiculturalism as "merely" an ideology that has swept through education and the arts ignores the crucial ways that it has enabled new global flows of goods and people that are channeled along prescribed paths. Whereas the corporate language of globalization emphasizes a free and open-ended circulation of capital, specific ideas of the "local," "difference," and "identity" are activated to circumscribe some movements, as well as to facilitate others. Some of the more atrocious circumstances in which my taiko group performed were not simply new forms of the old story of yellowface but rather imperialist choreographies newly reconstituted as a politics of entry and empathy.

The praxis of pilgrimage and the practice of taiko are conjoined activities that formulate and perform a politicized, assertive Sansei social aesthetic. Whereas taiko is a nostalgia product in Japan, Japanese American taiko is doubly constructed as both a practice imbued with a longing for roots, heritage, and authentic culture and, simultaneously, as part of the Asian American project of reparations and redress. These apparently contradictory purposes were both operative in the pensive work of playing taiko at Manzanar. Our participation in the 2003 pilgrimage drew on the nostalgic, originary power of taiko even as we offered commemorative gestures of refusing forgetfulness.

The absorption of liberal multiculturalist logic into the very means of performance has dreadful implications for the ethnography of performance as a utopian project. For me, there's a lot crowding in on this, including Kamala Visweswaran's important reconfiguration of fieldwork as homework; the phenomenological collapse of self and other that some have argued as a possibility for the ethnography of performance; and the feminist effort to resituate the inevitably asymmetrical relationships created by the ethnographic encounter.[4] I focus here on the ethnography of response, the ethnography of critical reflection, and an informed rejoinder to racist practice, racist containment, and racist master narratives. Becoming pilgrims helps taiko players remember; we assert memory through the noise of competing nostalgias.

FOLLOWING THE DRAGON BOATS

Taiko is consistently featured as a festishized commodity in the cynical play of corporate multiculturalism. Let me give you an example illuminating the challenges that are necessarily part of any attempt to opt out of commodity capitalism through boycotts or refusal.

The first annual Dragon Boat Festival in Laughlin, Nevada, was held on Friday and Saturday, May 10–11, 2002, and Satori Daiko was hired to provide orientalist trappings. I turn to this event with hesitation, because it's too easy an object of analysis; after all, anyone in Asian American studies is skilled at unpacking obviously racist practices—this is one of the first things we learn how to do in any ethnic studies course. Yet there's a certain pleasure in doing this kind of critical work, because the logic of racist representation is predictable, so the elegance and devastation of the critique are really the point. Five of us from Satori Daiko piled into Rev. Tom's van: Audrey, Lani, Elaine, Rev. Tom, and I. It's a long, hot drive from Los Angeles to Laughlin, which is a small town on the banks of the Colorado River, ninety miles south of Las Vegas. Like most Nevada towns, it's there for its casinos, which line the riverbank, one after the other.

The dragon boat races are a business. In this case they were overseen by FMG Dragon Boat, one of several such companies in North America that roll into town complete with the boats, paddles, life vests, and coordinating staff (including several emcees). The teams are made up of local folks who are essentially plugged into the event. (See figure 25, Dragon Boat Festival program, at *http://wonglouderandfaster.com.*)

FMG Dragon Boat uses the trope of team spirit to argue that dragon boat racing encourages group work and cooperation and that this, of course, has payoffs in the workplace. In Laughlin, the teams were mostly from the casinos: the Golden Nugget team, the Harrah's team, and so forth. A notable exception was the team of Las Vegas Metro Police officers (who were conspicuously fit and focused). The casino employees were doing their civic duty by contributing to this charity event, which was really a means to promote the casinos while encouraging the employees to have organized fun together (which would in turn up productivity). In short, the event combined a liberal multicultural narrative of celebratory difference; the paradoxical conflation of charity and the phantasmatic promise of the casino as a site of capitalist overabundance; a kind of participatory, Disneyesque, World Fair re-creation of other times and other places; and an exultant display of working-class spirit.

Each team consisted of twenty-two rowers and a drummer who sat at the prow and provided a beat for them to pull to. All the teams had come up with T-shirts decorated with dragon motifs, "oriental" fonts, and so forth. One team's drummer wore a coolie hat. Another team wore matching aloha shirts with hats of woven grass, and they marched to their dragon boat chanting "Ka-bunga! Ka-bunga! Ka-bunga! Ka-bunga!" which was clearly meant to sound strong/primitive/ritualistic/whatever. Yet another team wore matching Viking helmets with plastic horns. The prevailing logic connected the Chinese to the oriental to the primitive to vague, undifferentiated Otherness. Framing all this were the sports-bar behaviors of the teams and their followers. Howling and shaking fists in the air were a constant. The teams kept coming back to two kinds of chants: Queen's anthem "We Will Rock

You" and the time-honored GI call-and-response marching chant with dragon-appropriate lyrics. It was all about kicking butt.

We played taiko on Friday night for the opening festivities and then all day Saturday during the races, with a final performance on Saturday night for the closing ceremony and the announcement of the winners. It was hard work: we played for a total of five hours on Saturday, with lots of waiting in between, plus hauling the taiko back and forth between locations. During the races we had to maintain a big distance between ourselves and the dragon boats. In the first race we were too close, sonically speaking, because our "noise" interfered with the contestants' ability to hear their own drummer(s), and an Arizona Wildlife officer told us in no uncertain terms to keep away from the races—he pulled up beside us in his boat and shouted this at us. Did I mention that we were on a boat? It was not a dragon boat: we performed on a small pontoon with just enough space for the five of us to drum while the driver steered and kept us moving. For the rest of the day we stayed a good half mile behind each race and then followed along, playing for people on the banks, all by ourselves on our pontoon. By the time we reached the end of the Laughlin Mile (and the last casino), towboats were pulling the now empty dragon boats back upriver for the next race, and our pontoon driver would turn around and likewise plow back up the river against the current to the starting line, where we would wait for the next heat to begin. Basically, we spent the day going up and down the same mile of the river, playing between races for the tourists watching from the banks and from casino balconies overhanging the river. By the end of the day I was tired, sunburned, and in a state of grumpy desperation from too many hours of invisibility and inaudibility in a panoply of orientalist excess.

The next morning before hitting the road, we went for a buffet breakfast at the Colorado Belle casino. After eating, we started talking about the experience and ended up having a very reflective conversation about how taiko is all too often inserted into seriously problematic events. The before night I had muttered something about the whole thing being orientalist in the extreme, and it turned out that the word was new to my taiko friends, but they immediately got the concept. They brought it up again after breakfast, and we spent quite a while just enumerating the many ways that the event was over the top: the facts that virtually everyone in the race was White, that we were kept out of their way, that the specific ethnic and national backgrounds of the dragon boat races and taiko were collapsed into the "oriental," and so on. For my companions, our race was the metonymic point of departure: our "Asianness," their "Whiteness." I know that my taiko friends don't believe their cultural authenticity lies in some sort of racial coding; rather, race was their shorthand for identifying what was so obviously and overwhelmingly wrong with the event.

We all agreed that we hoped we would be invited back, if we could change how we were framed. Rev. Tom's livelihood was partly dependent on gigs, and this was an extremely good gig, at least in terms of the pay. But we didn't like the way we had been kept at a distance or on the sidelines; we had been positioned as colorful background activity. While we were treated with professionalism, we were always very aware that we were hired help.

I spoke with Elaine and Audrey several months later and asked them to reflect on both the Manzanar Pilgrimage (from which we had just returned) and the Laughlin dragon boat races. Both women were then in their midforties and were the unofficial leaders of our group, respected and looked up to for their vision and their skills, both as taiko players and in working with people. At that time, Audrey had been a taiko player for about fifteen years and was assertive and quite verbal (she still is). Elaine had then been a taiko player for six years but had studied traditional Japanese dance since childhood; she is quiet and thoughtful and often has extremely perceptive things to say. She immediately said that the Manzanar and Laughlin events were "like apples and oranges." Audrey completed her thought, observing that "Manzanar was for pilgrimage—spiritual, memorial." Both women described the experience of playing there as "uplifting" and further noted that they thought our presence there as taiko performers was meant to create that feeling and response in the audience. As Elaine put it, "We added to the spirit of the whole event. I think [the organizers] wanted us to create emotions: to remember the past, to look towards the future—I think they wanted that emotion there, and to keep the feeling 'up.'" They agreed that we were at Manzanar for "a cause, a purpose," whereas we were just "token Asians," even "froufrou," in Laughlin. Audrey said, "Laughlin was not fulfilling—it was probably one of the least fulfilling events I've done. The people watching us were just drinking beer, you know. It's like we were token. It's like that's how they think Asians are. People were there to have a good old time and drink. But when we play at Tet festivals and other local Asian festivals, the people are there for *culture*. At Laughlin, they were just there for a good old time. The reason they came was completely different." DECENTERING (AMBIGUITY)

The arc of connections between ethnographic effort, participation, and response is exactly what I think can serve as a located critical model, including and surpassing the ethnography of Asian American performance.[5] The critical gesture must exceed a simple refusal to be implicated (the boycott): it must acknowledge the troubled and inevitable power of othering narratives while effecting a ludic self-consciousness—a playful awareness that those narratives need not call us into being. That is why performance is a responsive site for such considerations: it offers nested, enfolded articulations of the status quo *and* interventionist vocabulary, often at the same time. I thus offer a grounded ethnography of performance and I attend closely to the particularities of time, place, persons, voice, and body, placing myself within the sphere of action and practice. The ethnography thus takes on the salient characteristics of performance: it moves, it has a bifocal consciousness and is twice behaved, it joins theory and praxis, it enacts the paradox of captured liveness. It allows mutual incursions. That means not checking out when the going gets racist, and it requires writing acquiescence as well as resistance. If it is an ethnographic leap of faith to get onto that pontoon and to drum in the wake of the dragon boats, then that's where some of the most important and trying work may be done.

5

Taiko, Erotics, and Anger

PLAYING

Taiko is a perfect social and musical space for me, and pleasure is at the heart of its perfection. Taiko was central to my social life and to my sense of myself as an Asian American woman. Let me offer you two moments in 1999 that, considered together, smashed open and revealed the relationships between taiko, pleasure, and anger.

Moment #1. The group I play in, Satori Daiko, is in rehearsal at Sozenji Buddhist Temple in Montebello, California, where we practice every Wednesday night. We have been working on the details of how to rise together from kneeling up to playing position in the middle of a piece, and it has involved painstakingly coordinating the speed of rising, the placement of the arms into ready position, and the small movements of the arms that get us back into playing position. We try it again and again, discovering more details that require coordination and agreement. Each time, another movement transforms into a single choreographed motion, while others are still a wave of ragged, separate actions. We talk, we argue different possibilities, and we try it again. I'm on odaiko, opposite Rocky; Elaine is nearby on chudaiko, directly in my line of sight. The seventh or eighth time we try it, I'm watching both Rocky and Elaine at once, and I notice that Rocky has risen infinitesimally faster than I have but that Elaine and I were synched; once up, all three of us move our arms together: one-two-three-*out!*-five-six-*back!*-*up!* We're locked in: we move as one. It is a small moment of perfection, and it breaks over me—a brief, intense burst of satisfaction.

Moment #2. Rev. Tom Kurai, Jacques,[1] and I have an outdoor noontime gig at a nearby junior college. Jacques is White, a native French speaker, and from Switzerland; he's an excellent rock drummer and has studied taiko for about a year. It's hot. We set up four taiko in the shade, on the grass under a tree. We have a forty-five-minute set—a long stretch when it's hot and there are only three of us to carry the show. We go through one piece after another; Rev. Tom talks into the mic between numbers, and Jacques and I shift around among different taiko

118

as he addresses the crowd. After a few pieces, I suddenly realize that Jacques isn't adding any kakegoe—I'm shouting by myself, since Rev. Tom is on the shime. We swing into "Shiawase Bushi," an upbeat festival number that involves lots of kakegoe and movement in between rounds when we are supposed to click our bachi over our heads while either dancing in place or in a circle or switching drums. Since there are only two of us, I automatically dance in place, and as I pivot in a circle, I catch sight of Jacques on odaiko behind me. He's just standing there—no dancing, no kakegoe, just waiting to start playing again. Afterward I ask him why. He says, "Well, Tom doesn't do it, so I didn't either." He knows perfectly well that a different standard applies to the shime player, who must keep the baseline going. I say, "But that left me all alone out there." He sets his jaw and looks at me challengingly. "Oh," he says, "so you're giving me a hard time?" Later, as I drive home alone, I vow to myself not to take any more gigs that mean being in close quarters with Jacques.

One moment of intense pleasure, another of anger and irritation. In rehearsal at the temple, we spent most of our time collaboratively working out the series of movements, and the cooperative effort was part of the social pleasure of playing together. This doesn't mean that the group is completely egalitarian: it isn't, nor does anyone expect it to be. Elaine and Audrey have an unofficial authority: whenever Rev. Tom isn't present, we look to them for—what? Not the final word, because that's not what they want to provide. They sense when we've reached consensus, and they call it. We wait for them to call it.

Irritation. Jacques felt that he wasn't required to shout kakegoe or dance: he regarded those things as additions to the "music," which for him meant (I think) hitting the drums. Nor did he like being questioned about what he chose to leave in or take out. He concluded that I was challenging him, so he challenged me back. This made me decide to avoid playing with him as much as possible.

Pleasure, satisfaction, anger, and resentment are all located within configurations of difference that are the bedrock of taiko in North America. In the early 2000s, approximately 75 percent of North American taiko players were women, and although this taiko scene was and is multiethnic, most of the practitioners were of Asian descent. For me, getting swept up in taiko had everything to do with gender and ethnicity: I have encountered few things as stirring as the sound and sight of Asian American women moving with coordinated strength, assurance, and discipline, and making a lot of noise as they do so.

I am watching a videotape of San Jose Taiko (1998) in performance, and there is something about this line of women moving in tandem, opening and raising their arms, lunging forward in choreographed joy, that calls forth an affective response from me. I watch, and I feel their movements in my own body. I experience no simple reflection of their power and joy—rather, they instantiate something that I would return to them if we were in a room together. I would shout kakegoe at them as encouragement. My heart rate quickens. Watching them makes me want to play.

Jacques is a White European man. Most of the members of Satori Daiko are Asian American women. Jacques was in his late twenties, Swiss, and a "drummer"—he played drums in a rock band. He was the one member of Satori Daiko who consistently didn't get it. I could go on and on about how he didn't get it. The point is, he didn't, and it drove me crazy—and this has everything to do with how gender and ethnicity are lined up between us. White man, Asian American woman.

PLEASURE

Only certain areas of music scholarship discuss pleasure. Traditional scholarship locates pleasure in musical Others: in women, in people of color, in the queer, in the working class. The kinds of music that call pleasure forth are problematic: they are of the body, they delimit sites of possible threat and unruliness, and they are always, always devalued. Popular music studies is one of the few areas that consistently acknowledges and celebrates musical pleasure, regarding it as intrinsically part of many musics' significance. Taking musical pleasures seriously is a radical move that signals anti-canonic intentions.

That said, scholars are more apt to focus on the pleasures of spectatorship than on the pleasures of performing. I suspect that this is unwittingly based in certain understandings of how power and performance play out in the elite imagination—for instance, the performer is seen as controlling the situation and the audience is the receptacle for the performance. This logic leads to a focus on the pleasure of the audience, the spectator, or the fan, because this is the site where the performers', composer's, or choreographer's intentions are realized. Critical work on spectatorship thus often focuses on revealing how fans' pleasures are in fact resistant, which shows that fans aren't passive but rather are embroiled in constitutive acts of interpretation. While all this has opened reception studies in fundamentally useful ways, empowering the spectator reinscribes the asymmetrical power relations of the spectator and the performer—whose relationship can be critically reclaimed only by investing the spectator with powers similar to those of the performer.

Reading the interviews in *My Music* (Crafts et al. 1993), I am struck by the abundance of sentences beginning with "I like" or "I love"; the forty interviews show that people *want* to talk about how and why certain musics give them pleasure, whether the pleasures of intense sadness or the voyeuristic pleasures of immersing oneself in a music video by Tina Turner (94, 157–58). Similarly, critical work on sports spectatorship offers some of the most focused considerations of fans' pleasures, for what could be more unrestrained, unruly, and unapologetic than a sports fan? The emblematic sports fan is not only male and working class but completely over the top in his enjoyment.[2] John Fiske (1993, 82) presents a Foucauldian analysis of "sporting spectacles" in which the inversion of surveillance and discipline creates the terms of pleasure. Describing a stadium as an "inverted panopticon," he suggests that fans' peak experience is the rush of giving themselves over to the moment, together, when the power of watching is reversed and knowledge is generated "horizontally," within a group, rather than "vertically," within the usual structures of hierarchical authority. The fans' pleasure is both collective and experiential: "Crucial to sports fandom is an intensity of feeling, a passion, and a loss of control which are produced by an embodied way of knowing that is rooted in the body's presence in the experience that it knows" (88). The intensity of collective pleasure is resistant precisely because of its base in body and experience, but Fiske also notes that "this localized power exists only in the spaces created by inverting an imperializing power-knowledge over others" (91). Fiske's discussion of the power dynamics of pleasure provides a useful contrast to the place of pleasure in taiko: he ultimately seems to feel that sports fans' experience of pleasure is an ephemeral response that does little to change the status quo, whereas I believe that Asian American women's pleasure in taiko offers the terms for social change.

Wayne Koestenbaum's work offers other parallels to the pleasures of taiko. In *The Queen's Throat* (1993), he provides one of the most sensuous and slyly unfettered accounts of fandom to date, connecting the opera queen's body to excess of every sort. He describes the act of listening as an intensely physical pleasure that joins gay fan to performing diva, and suggests a mimetic connection between them—a kind of listening that coalesces into participation, identification, and sensual pleasure all at once (31–32, 42). This link is unidirectional: the diva receives nothing in return from the gay listener; rather, she is in an exalted sphere of her own. Nonetheless, Koestenbaum describes a kind of pleasure that is posited on a real connection between performer and spectator and based in complete identification and shared experience, in which performing and listening become part of an interconstitutive whole that is deeply (homo)erotic.

GENDERED PLEASURE IN TAIKO

I turn now to the mysterious peak experience and the frustration of thwarted pleasure. Asian American women are drawn to taiko for real reasons: the construction of a body redefined as strong, disciplined, and loud works against overdetermined gendered orientalist tropes that position Asian and Asian American women as quiet, docile, and sexually available (Wong 2000). Taiko offers a compelling space to Asian American women because it posits an empowered collective social body in gendered and racialized terms. I refer to this deeply physical and profoundly political process as the erotics of taiko. Asian American woman taiko players tend to care passionately about taiko; they don't just *like* taiko—they usually *love* it.

There are pleasures and pleasures in taiko. In rehearsal with my group, that small moment of complete satisfaction with beautifully synchronized movement is one kind: the pleasure of details well executed, in tandem with others. Then there are the pleasures of collaboration and discussion. The other kind of pleasure is the rush you get only in performance, and we are all familiar with it. We know when it happens. It is both private and public, lone and shared. It is mysterious and addictive. We talk about it because it feels so good when it happens and because we know *how* it happens, but explanations are adequate only up to a certain point.

The peak experience is a moment of pronounced, intense feeling that marks a good performance. Taiko is high-energy—this is one of the first things that anyone would notice about it—but the specific form that that energy can take fascinates the taiko players I know. We talk about it. It is called ki, and it is central to taiko and to the Japanese martial arts. I asked two of my classmates—both women—to talk about it with my tape recorder present, and I would like to share our conversations; these words were informed by shared experiences over several years.[3] Both Harriet and Beverly are Japanese American women who were raised as Buddhists, which informs their ways of thinking about taiko; I will come back to this point.

Harriet Mizuno-Moyer is a Sansei woman who was then in her midforties; her then-eleven-year-old daughter, Taylor, was also in the group. I caught Harriet during a break in rehearsal and asked her to talk about how and why taiko feels good to her, and she said it was a matter of energy:

Deborah Wong: What does it feel like, that energy?

Harriet Mizuno-Moyer: It's not like an exercise energy, where you tire yourself out, running around the track, or aerobics or something. It's not that kind of energy. When you're hitting the drum, and your hits are all at the same time, it's almost as if that energy is coming back at you. So that's different, because you're getting something in return, somehow, whereas when you're exercising, you're not getting anything back in return—you're just expending energy! When you hit the drum, it seems to me like feedback, where you get more energy. It's more of a mental than a physical energy, for me.... If it were just physical, it would tire you out so you couldn't play. As that song's going along, and it's really cooking, you almost feel like you have more energy as that song goes on—but then when it ends, you go, Oh gee, I'm really tired! [*laughs*] So I don't know if it's the same kind of energy as exercise energy. I don't know what it is—if you would call that mental or . . . I don't know. Maybe a little bit of both.... A long, long time ago, I used to play tennis, and I used to play every single day. After about a year of this, I finally got to the point where my serve felt just really good. You could feel it . . . I never attained that level in very many other things, but I remember what that serve felt like going in, every single time. It's the same type of thing—it's a real high feeling. But it takes so long to get there! I feel really lucky, because I'm not very athletic, to have that feeling. You hit that ball, and you know it's going to go in. It's the same with taiko: you get that sort of high.

Harriet outlined the energy-pleasure principle as regenerative and both physical and mental: it arises from the emotional and kinesthetic satisfaction of practiced activity. Her description of it as a kind of "high" is similar to Victor Turner's (1986, 54) and Mihaly Csikszentmihalyi's (1990) formulation of "flow," an ideal state of "total involvement" that is utterly and intensely satisfying.

I asked Beverly Murata to describe the connection between energy and the group. She is a Sansei woman who was then in her early fifties and had played taiko for about fifteen years.

> **Beverly Murata:** When you're really in the groove—when the whole group gels—you have more than the sum of your energy. You feel each of your individual energies, but when it's all joined together, it's more than just the sum. It all comes back to you, and it gives you 125 percent of the energy. And then you feel a real connection between body, mind, and spirit. But that's when it's really together—that's the ideal state. You know when it hits—the group knows it. It's a group consciousness by that time.
>
> **Deborah Wong:** How do you know it?
> **BM:** It just—everything clicks. It falls into place, the timing's on, everybody's at the same level of energy—it becomes a group level of consciousness at that point. It's more than just an individual thing.
>
> **DW:** What does it feel like, physically? Can you describe the sensation in your body?
> **BM:** It's almost like there's no separation between the mind, body, and spirit, for me. Everything just becomes one unit, so you're not thinking about what you're doing, you're not telling your body what to do. It's all one total unit. It's kind of like: spirit comes into your body, flows through, and it's out. So it's all at once, it's everything. It's almost like you don't think any more. [*pause*] Yet you do. It's like total consciousness without mentally thinking, if that makes any sense.
>
> **DW:** That's not a contradiction in this case.
> **BM:** No. It's like the Zen thing: when you get to that mental state where it's just peace, oneness, and energy flowing. So there's no separation between the different aspects of who you are.

Beverly drew certain distinctions between the circulation of energy within the individual performer, between members of the group, and between performers and audience. However, she noted that the exchange and expansion of energy was similar in all three cases. I asked her if the physicality of effort and exertion had anything to do with it:

> **DW:** Are you aware of your heart going *thumpity-thumpity-thump*?
> **BM:** Yeah. Oh yeah! And you're sweating—you can't breathe! [*laughs*] I'm talking about the *peak* experience. If it goes on, then you're really tired and your muscles start aching and all that, but I'm talking about when you hit

that peak, that's what it's like for me. It's a oneness. But those other things happen too! Oh yeah. [*We both laugh.*]

DW: How long does, or can, that peak state last?
BM: It's hard to say . . .

DW: Can it be fifteen minutes, or is it just a flash?
BM: It varies. It depends on my energy level. When you're actually on during a performance, it's a little easier to sustain, because there's an energy exchange with the audience. It's like a cycle. You give out, and the audience gives to you, and it flows around—it's a cycle. So it's easier to sustain that energy level, whereas [during rehearsal] you don't have that exchange from the audience, so it's a different flow. And then you have audiences that are duds. It's audiences that are really excited that create that energy. You can feel that difference too.

Many of the Asian American women I know who play taiko describe that kind of peak experience in similar terms: they say that their most pronounced moments of pleasure emerge from the interaction between performers or between performers and audience. It goes further: many Asian American spectators describe a similar response. At UC Riverside, one of my colleagues, a Sansei scholar, told me that watching or listening to taiko has always been a singularly powerful experience for her, and her comments suggest that the exuberant pleasure of performers' peak moments is communicable. My colleague has known taiko for most of her life—growing up in the Bay Area, she routinely heard San Jose Taiko at the annual Obon celebration in San Jose's Japantown—and she said that as far back as she can remember, it has called forth a nearly unbearable excitement in her, as well as responsive tears. The upwelling of strong emotion that goes along with watching or listening to taiko has always been part of her experience; it doesn't last through the whole performance but surges up in response to the arc of pieces that sustain and carry forward long-repeated rhythmic and choreographic sequences. Her strong emotional response suggests that we need to reconsider the "vicarious": the cresting waves of power and pleasure are confined to neither performer(s) nor spectator(s) but rather move dynamically and synergistically between them.

Key moments of pleasure are thus moments of power, but for most of the women I know, power in taiko is not situated along vertical lines of authority (as discussed by Fiske; see above) but is generated by collective action. In the Euro-American experience, pleasure is usually associated with the sensual—with the body—but Harriet and Beverly each described a kind of exuberant, transcendent pleasure that did not rely on the mind-body divide for its power but rather issued forth from the connective synapses that blurred mind-body, performer-audience distinctions: the dynamic loop between those binaries apparently creates the potential for the kind of peak experience that taiko players live for, and that experience is transcendent in the Buddhist sense, not the Western Romantic sense.

Several elements are necessary if that peak experience—that joy, that most sublime pleasure—is to make its appearance: a receptive audience, and an ensemble of taiko players working together as a group.

In Satori Daiko, there was a fly in the ointment, a bull in the china shop. Perhaps Jacques was there to clarify the terms of my perfect social space, because he disrupted it: he often ruined my perfect space when he was in it. Jacques was a good musician and a bad taiko player. He was a rock musician—a "drummer"—so he had a strong sense of meter and rhythm. But he tended to disregard the things that make taiko more than drumming: kata, kakegoe, the group social aesthetic, and the devaluing of personal ego. One of the most experienced members of the group said to me privately that she thought he was a drummer, not a taiko player, and this is one of the more dismissive things one taiko player can say about another. Jacques had a bad kata or none at all, depending on how you look at it; he virtually never added kakegoe; he didn't bother to learn many of our pieces, preferring to be given flashy solo moments when he could improvise; he didn't spend much time socializing with the group—he left when the rehearsal was over, if not before; he challenged anyone beside Rev. Tom who had authority in the group. I left some rehearsals and performances in a complete silent fury over him. Getting to me was part of his disruptive power. He messed with my pleasure and thus made me angry: he prompted a rage in me that could have consumed us both because it emanated from dangerous intersections that are gendered and racialized.

You can understand my rage only if you understand my pleasure. These specific moments of anger and irritation circled around one member of our group—a White European man—who periodically challenged the value system that maintained the terms of pleasure for the Asian American women in the group. I know I was not alone in my outrage, but I run up against the ethical limits of both friendship and ethnography at this point: the group social aesthetic was so strong in our ensemble that it took us a long time to begin talking among ourselves about Jacques's disruptive presence. I won't tell you what my classmates said, nor can I tell you what went on in Jacques's head, though an ethnography of failed understanding, and of the dangerous differences that made my taiko group an imperfect utopia, is now visible.

Anger indicates where strong values are being challenged; anger tells you where to listen if you want to know what's really going on. Black feminist critics like bell hooks (1996) and June Jordan (1992) address the profound feelings of rage that are interpolated with their passion for social justice. Writing about rage is risky: it too easily spills over into shared territory with fighting words, and Patricia Hill Collins (1998, 79–94) argues that the performative (and legislative) effort to prevent effects by silencing insults is, in the end, conceptually limited—"censuring selected elements" (87), as she puts it, simply reinscribes and duplicates powerful binaries. Moreover, the targets of hate speech are most apt to respond not with violence but with "anger, flight, and silence" (85).[4] Jacques' words and behaviors may seem insignificant—he didn't really do anything except insist on having his own way. I reacted as if to fighting words, with anger, flight, and furious silence. The depth of my outrage was triggered by the fact that he was a White man; it takes a White man to *not* get it in the ways that he didn't; did he not get it *because* he is a White man?

When Jacques asserted virtuosic solo drumming over unison group drumming and refused to be absorbed into the cooperative aesthetic that deemphasizes ego, the Asian American women in Satori Daiko responded with frustration, irritation, and (in my case) fury that he meddled with our pleasure. Pleasure raises the stakes, and this troublesome White man's resistance may well have stemmed from his own awareness that the gendered and racialized terms of my/our pleasure defined his exclusion from it—and part of his pleasure lay, possibly, in his rejection of our terms. For me, writing this was an act of critical reclamation and grudging recognition that his encroachment on my pleasure created alternative sites of gratification which were politicized in troubling ways. Nevertheless, part of my pleasure in taiko lies in exploring its politics through the performative act of writing—and by writing my irritation with this man.

Two years after I vowed to stay out of close quarters with Jacques, Rev. Tom created a small group-within-the-group. One night in October 2001, he simply told Rocky, Gary, Jacques, and me to start coming an additional evening each week to rehearse so he could create some new works. The four of us were the ones in Satori who had "musical" training—so we could play complicated rhythms at fast tempos. Working closely with these three men presented me with all sorts of new challenges: they were so pleased to be playing complicated rhythms at fast tempos that, to my mind, they became, well, guys playing drums. The faster and more accurately the four of us played, the less I sometimes felt like a taiko player. They stopped maintaining kata and they didn't shout kakegoe; they just played fast and loud.

But then Jacques started growing on me. He had questions. He wanted to know more about the nature of ki, and he asked Rev. Tom about the "taiko spirit," a thing referred to frequently by practitioners that sums up the value placed on group effort, putting the group before yourself, placing your trust in the group. He was asking about the right things. Soon it wasn't as easy for me to complain about him. Taiko's values were rubbing off on him. He was changing, or taiko was changing him: it began to resituate his White/Swiss/rock-drummer subjectivities. Angela Ahlgren (2018, 83–110) writes about White presence in the North American taiko scene with depth and perception, addressing how some White players learn about Asian American history through taiko, how others wield the disruptive power of White fragility, and how "whiteness interrupts audience expectations" (90) in productive, anti-orientalist ways. Jacques was not immune to taiko's social aesthetics.

North American practitioners must continually address challenging issues around material identity. The big questions of identity politics are played out through the body, and this creates real vulnerabilities. For me, Satori Daiko was a utopian space perpetually teetering on the edge of complete compromise. We wrote new pieces and argued over how far we could go before we would no longer "really" be a taiko group. That's not taiko, Audrey says, that's just drumming. OK, we say as we gather together, what if we do it like *this*?

Pleasure is thus political. The social aesthetics of pleasure may be exalted or gritty, a matter of gatekeeping or immersive inclusion, but they simultaneously maintain and construct the terms for relational power and are thus no simple thing. Music isn't always about pleasure, nor is pleasure always rooted in the sensual body, which is why ethnographies of pleasure are important and necessary. Taiko in Asian America redefines women's bodies and positions gratification as a collective endeavor. The erotics of taiko rewrite difference and authority and rechoreograph the relationships between the sensual, the mind, the autonomous spirit, and the disciplined body. If I vanish into the sweat and ache of loud collective effort and Jacques stands aside, whose pleasure is the more acute?

GLAMOROUS WOMEN AND TRANSNATIONAL FEMININITY

I was a fan before I ever saw them play, let alone met them in Japan. A friend gave me their poster, knowing that I was interested in gender and the taiko tradition, and I kept it on my office wall for quite a few years.[5] These women were saying something about femininity and taiko, and they were stunningly glamorous. Those costumes, that attitude! *Honō* means "fire" or "passion" in Japanese; *daiko* means *taiko*, or "drum." The group's name could also be transliterated as "Hono-o-Daiko," with the prefix *o* before *Daiko* meaning "big" or "great." Honō Daiko is an extraordinary Japanese taiko group, and I reflect here on an encounter between it and my Southern California taiko group in 2001 that suggests the construction of an Asian and Asian American feminism through taiko. How taiko empowers women is at once more compromised and more interesting than most practitioners will allow. Forms that draw on essentialized signs challenge the narrow, perilous space between reinscription and social transformation.[6]

Glamour is charisma with style, magnetism with panache, and allure with élan. Women with feminist glamour have style, confidence, and answers. They're way past messing around with conventional ideas of beauty. They say what they think, and what they think is that the power structures defined by gender relations still need work, at both the micro and the macro levels.

When we met Honō Daiko in 2001, Satori Daiko had seventeen members, twelve of whom were women, as was quite typical for North American taiko groups. At that time, about 75 percent of all US and Canadian taiko players were women, and most of them were of Asian descent. Most North American taiko groups were made up of both men and women, though a few were all female by design.[7] None of us in Satori Daiko had feminist glamour, though I know that some women in our audiences have felt differently. Few if any of Satori's members self-identified as feminists, and many did not want to acknowledge the shaping force of gender and race in our group, or in taiko generally. Part of taiko's North American mystique is its connection to multiculturalism and the fact that it can be learned by "anyone." It is understood that one absorbs interesting and useful things about Japanese culture in the process of learning taiko, including the values of self-discipline, respect, and cooperation. This ethos makes it hard to face up to difference.

In August 2001, Satori Daiko went on a two-week taiko tour of Japan, led by Rev. Tom. It was the first of several such trips we took with him. We went to taiko festivals, had workshops with notable taiko performers, and visited taiko factories. It was an extraordinary experience, but it was not unprecedented: we all understood its purpose, because other North American taiko groups have done it too.

The globalization of taiko has taken place along an inner circuit of understandings. First, taiko is always already more "authentic" in Japan than in Asian America, which Japanese, Japanese American, and Asian American taiko players tacitly understand. North American taiko players make the journey "back" to Japan to partake of that authenticity and cultural capital. It's an aura that rubs off on you, even if the taiko tourist has previously only attended festivals as a spectator. Even in simply witnessing at the site of the source, one is understood to have been transformed and to "know" something more about taiko than North American practitioners do (or can). This journey staggers under the weight of its colonial baggage. It is troubled by a curious neo-orientalism, defined by exoticism, and imbued with primitivist longing. Its genealogy is directly tied to the history of the Asian martial arts in the West: we will go sit at the feet of the taiko masters, just like every single one of the Karate Kids and every Euro-American martial arts action hero. We will accept their teachings without question. They will be stern and strict, and they may ridicule us, but we've seen the movies, so we know the drill.

The movement of taiko study-pilgrimage is unidirectional. North American taiko groups go to Japan in search of authentic knowledge, but Japanese taiko groups come to North America only to teach or tour, not to study.[8] Much is at stake in maintaining a clear center of "the tradition." As the ethnomusicologist Linda Fujie (2001, 94) has written, however, the Japanese ideological origins of kumi-daiko are complex. She notes that taiko is a post–World War II phenomenon that quickly become a national symbol. She describes how, in the early 1970s, a group of university students gathered around the musician Den Tagayasu, the founder of Ondekoza, and, as she succinctly puts it, "the *taiko* drum became the center of an experiment for young urban Japanese, many of whom were disillusioned with the competitive, materialistic world of postwar Japan and were searching for some deeper meaning for their lives." She describes their efforts to create "a kind of social and cultural utopia around the drum and drum playing" which was based on certain ideas of the "traditional" and traces their reworking of Japanese instruments and musical material for the stage in ways that troubled some of the very "traditional" musicians from whom they claimed to have learned (96). Not only did they skirt the traditional system of instruction (close, sustained contact between teacher and student), but they quickly became regarded as culture bearers of "traditional music" as they joined the international circuit of festivals and concert halls. Fujie describes their ties to traditional Japanese folk musics as "exaggerated to some degree. Taiko groups create the aura of centuries-old historical tradition and present themselves as bearers of this tradition" (97–98).

The slippage between taiko as a sign of the national ("Japan" and "Japanese culture") and as a sign of diasporic ethnic heritage (Japanese American culture and history) sets up pesky possibilities for misunderstanding and devaluation. Some Japanese players view diasporic Japanese American culture as inauthentic and watered down. Naturally, Japanese American and other Asian American taiko players see things otherwise: through the lens of the Asian American Movement and with an understanding of diasporic identity construction as dynamic and ongoing, they view North American taiko as related to Japanese taiko but ultimately different because its history, placement, and cultural functions are necessarily distinct. Fujie focuses productively on the relationships between the local, the national, and the international (in the sense of international concert and festival production) in Japanese taiko; if you consider that the same interlocking network of loci are at work in North American taiko, and then that Japanese and North American taiko are in close interaction, it's clear that the dynamics of located and imagined meanings are entangled indeed. North American groups draw on a body of representational practices that are similar but not equivalent to those of Japanese groups, and their investment in the "traditional" overlaps with that of Japanese groups but ultimately has a very different weight, in the context of anti-Asian North American colonial histories of discrimination, containment, assimilationist cultural policies, and so forth.

This ponderous representational work is passed back and forth between Japanese and North American taiko players. In that exchange, orientalist and exoticist signs are recirculated. Samurai values provide an orientalist imaginary for both the Japanese and Westerners, in which the Tokugawa era (1600–1868) is configured as quintessentially premodern and precapitalist. In taiko, a twentieth- and twenty-first-century educated urban middle class on both sides of the Pacific conflates shared orientalist understandings of "Eastern" praxis with Buddhist values and Bushido (the way of the warrior).[9] Taiko isn't only a nostalgic museum for imagined Tokugawa-era practices, however. Its postwar identity puts it in traffic with the commodification that is part and parcel of the international performance circuit: when Kodo and other Japanese taiko groups go on concert tours, they export traditional Japanese culture. They perform tradition, though the nostalgia on which audience enjoyment relies is not the same in Japan as in the First World West. As Marilyn Ivy (1995, 245) notes, the Japanese nostalgia industry busily fetishizes and reifies key concepts even as this very process "reveals the presence of a wish: the wish to reanimate, not simply fix, the past at the moment of its apparent vanishing." Taiko is an exemplar of this process: its practitioners are more than historical reenactors.

HONŌ DAIKO AND THE SAMURAI BODY

During our trip through the taiko tradition in Japan, Rev. Tom arranged for us to take a workshop at the Miyamoto studio in Tokyo, home of the chief taiko-making rival to Asano Taiko Company. The teacher, a famous middle-aged master musician named Kiyonari Tosha, was one of the founders of Sukeroku Taiko and was trained in *hayashi* drumming. He spent a lot of time addressing our clumsy, undisciplined American bodies. He promoted a sternly still, controlled stance (kata), and he thought we all moved our hips too much: he made his point by swishing across the room in a parody of queer effeminacy, all loose hips and wrists. As the group lesson went on, he said to several of us, "Forget you're a woman!," though it wasn't clear (to me, at least) what that might mean. Play more stiffly and less fluidly, more strongly and less softly, more assertively and less gently? Something like that.

Our encounter with Honō Daiko was at the other end of the gendered taiko imagination. Honō Daiko is a professional group of three women taiko players. It was founded in 1985 by Akemi Jige, who has remained in the group while other members have come and gone. Honō Daiko was eventually hired (full time) by Asano, which makes some of the best taiko in Japan. The three women play pieces they compose themselves, which are characterized by complex, driving, asymmetrical rhythms (like 3 + 3 + 3 + 3 + 2 + 2); close, turn-on-a-dime coordination of parts; exquisite timbres and dynamic utilization of their drums; and breathtaking physicality.

Their athleticism jumped out at us. Those bodies! Their performance instructed us in a new way to watch women's bodies with pleasure. This wasn't a scopophilic pleasure of eating up their bodies with our eyes: we were enjoying their arms and shoulders, not T&A. For a taiko player—particularly a woman taiko player—watching the movement of muscles in their arms, shoulders, and backs was mesmerizing, and it generated a deep desire to look like that, to play like that, to move like that. Nor was it like watching women body builders who heft iron like men: the women of Honō Daiko played with grace, flexibility, and expressivity, realizing the metric and synergetic complexity of their pieces with their bodies. Jige said, "We don't use a lot of *furi* [movement, or flourishes]. We play naturally, according to the body. You should learn pieces so that your body knows them. We use a lot of concentration and focus and energy."[10]

Ahlgren (2011, 199–200) attended a Honō Daiko performance in Michigan in 2011, about which she writes,

> As the house lights fade and the stage lights come up, the four women who make up Honō Daiko sweep onto the stage in their bright red gauzy costumes and mesmerize

us with their virtuosic performance. Rather than the happi coats, aprons, and tabi that many taiko groups wear, these performers wear tightfitting sleeveless tanks with thick straps that criss-cross in the back and red skirts that flare dramatically like long tattered ballet tutus when they take their wide, barefoot stances. The small but imposing women—two with short, spiky hair and two with hair piled atop and spilling from their heads—stare out at the audience aggressively while their hands fly across the drumheads.

Although I do not know anything about these performers' identities, their performances certainly invite feminist and queer spectatorship. The drummers—two very feminine and two with androgynous looks—ooze sensuality, their torsos literally undulating as they took turns playing the large odaiko center stage. As I watch one performer arch her back impossibly far during a solo, I can see two girls who performed with the kids' class in the front row, flinging their bachi into the air and swaying unabashedly along with Honō Daiko's thrilling performance. Beside me, Clare sits amazed, and whispers, "I've never seen anyone *move* like this before!"

Jige did not go the folkloric route of seeking out "traditional" teachers (as Kodo and Ondekoza did). Her first teacher was an old man in Fukui-ken, where she grew up; she learned the basics from him, but after that she was on her own. Nor has she (as far as I can tell) tried to establish herself as a sensei, a teacher, a transmitter of "traditional" knowledge. She is a full-time professional performer—one of very few taiko players who have such a postfolkloric occupation in the New Japanese world of nostalgia products.

The three members of Honō Daiko are Asano employees, on the Asano payroll to show off their drums. They are not the babes seen in US car commercials: they aren't mere accessories, because they actually *drive* those drums—they haul right into fifth gear in a matter of seconds. They showcase Asano's beautiful merchandise, and they are basically part of Asano's apparatus of domestic and international commercial success. They rehearse in the Asano studio on weekdays from 10 AM to 5 PM. We spent three hours with them at the Asano main factory. They performed for us in Asano's drum museum before teaching us drills focusing on particular techniques and then a new piece (see video 14, Satori Daiko workshop with members of Honō Daiko, at *http://wonglouderandfaster.com*), after which we got to ask them questions for half an hour.

Honō Daiko's remarkable costumes stand out dramatically in the wistfully nostalgic world of "traditional" taiko clothing. Costuming is not a mere appendage to performance, and stage clothing of any sort carries deep symbolic and historical meaning.[11] Honō Daiko's costumes provide a striking angle on the relationships between gender, tradition, and a woman's body redefined by taiko. As I described in chapter 2, most taiko groups, whether in North America or Japan, wear costumes based on traditional Japanese festival clothing.[12] Honō Daiko has put a lot of thought into its costumes, using them to draw the eye to the players' bodies in certain ways while allowing for fierce movement. As Jige said, they have had several of their own costume designers, including a woman and now a man who designs some of the accessories on their clothes.[13] Jige has been centrally involved in generating ideas for their costumes. She explained, "Rather than being beautiful or pretty, we wear costumes that show the arms on purpose, because that's very visual—to see them moving. It's easier to move our arms too!" All their costumes expose their arms, shoulders, and backs. They often wear tank tops. But whereas their tops are all formfitting, their lower bodies are often enveloped in trousers or pantaloons that enlarge their body space and create a sense of being bottom heavy and massive. Their black satin trousers evoke the bulky pants known as *hakama,* which originated as an outer garment to protect samurai warriors' legs from brush when riding a horse.[14] Samurai in the Tokugawa era wore clothes that created an enlarged body, or a silhouette that extended the boundaries of the body, without adding a lot of additional movement through swaying cloth (in the way that certain ball gowns are meant to extend and amplify dance movements, for example). When the women of Honō Daiko wear hakama with tank tops, the effect is dramatic because it suggests samurai drag—women wearing warrior men's pants—but this is mediated by the decidedly un-samurai-like exposure of their unadorned upper bodies. Shawn Bender (2012, 157–60) writes at length about how their manager at Asano Taiko hired a designer to provide the women with freedom of movement—unlike the women in Kodo and Ondekoza, who often perform in confining yukata—and to draw attention to their muscular upper bodies.

The odaiko is the only drum played with one's back to the audience and, even then, only for solo pieces. Such works—like Kodo's "Odaiko," whose display of the male body is discussed below—self-consciously put the performer's strength and stamina on display. Honō Daiko usually includes an odaiko solo as part of its program, and in this case the women simply follow the masculine conventions for spectatorship: cover the lower body but wear tops that expose a large part of the back. An odaiko solo piece is the most deeply gender marked of all repertoire, which has made it the focus of extra effort from a few women taiko players.[15] If some of Honō Daiko's costumes redefine the female body in masculinist terms, one set of their stage costumes takes risks (less successfully, I think) in the other direction. I have seen photos of Honō Daiko members performing in formfitting white tank tops and huge, gauzy white trouser-skirts, almost bridal in effect. I have seen these costumes only in photos—never in performance—but they clearly combine the evening gown with the same principles of exposed upper body and covered, massive lower body as Honō Daiko's other costumes. In this case, however, the effect is self-consciously feminine, even referred to as "dress design" in the group's press materials. In one photo, Ayano Yamamoto carries off a striking combination of muscled strength with a bodice that seems designed to outline one breast. The image's effect relies on its resemblance to black-and-white glamour shots of the 1930s–1950s, but its surprise lies in the no-shit directness of Yamamoto's gaze and the drumsticks in her left hand. What at first appear to be evening gloves are in fact tekko, bands that provide support to the player's wrists. She's ready to hit the stage running.

The bodies that Honō Daiko's costumes define and display are not mere frames for clothing but rather additional fields for reconfiguration and experimentation. These women are ripped: they are impressively muscled—read: strong—without crossing the line into drag (if a reconfigured musculature can be considered a kind of drag akin to that of clothing). Honō Daiko's members do not seem to equate muscled strength with the masculine. Or do they? If their sartorial play with gender crossing is in conversation with Japanese haute couture, then their staging of the woman's body is genealogically linked to other cross-gendered forms of Japanese drama (Morinaga 2002; Robertson 1998).[16]

Although women are the overwhelming majority in taiko on both sides of the Pacific, the advent of a small, virtuosic, professional all-woman ensemble was a new development. Honō Daiko's emphasis on bodily discipline is striking, and two of the four members of the group since its inception have had the short hair, direct gaze, and glamour of Takarazuka's *otokoyaku* (women who perform male roles in all-female revues). I have no idea what their sexual orientations may be, or whether their fan base attaches a same-sex erotic charge to their public image. Still, the confluence of their muscled strength, mastery of the male domain of the odaiko solo, and musical chops puts them in a league all their own.

During our Q&A session, I asked Jige what she thought women bring to the taiko tradition. (See video 15, Q&A between Akemi Jige and Satori Daiko, at *http://wonglouderandfaster.com*.) She replied:

> When I first started, there weren't that many women in taiko, but as a woman, I wanted to play. I wanted to play the big odaiko. So when I first started Honō Daiko [in 1986], there were two women playing, and when people saw that, they were really surprised by it. That's the way it started. It wasn't a conscious thing—I just wanted to do it, and then another woman joined me. They used to make fun of women, so that's why we tried harder—we trained hard. We started out playing at hotel parties—private parties—but little by little, people started to appreciate us.
>
> Generally, a man's body is not as flexible as a woman's—men look stiff when they play.[17] *Chokusen* is a rigid way of playing. [*She leaped to her feet and bent backward as if playing a tall odaiko.*] *Kyokusen* is fluid, flexible.[18] Some men are able to do this [play in a kyokusen way], and they look really good when they do. And when you play that way, visually it looks better, and you can play with more speed. If you're too rigid, you can't play very fast. And it looks better. From the audience's point of view, it looks like that person is really struggling [if they play in a chokusen manner]. But if you're using kyokusen, it's more fluid—it's more dynamic, visually, it's more beautiful.

Jige didn't explain whether she thinks this is a matter of nature or nurture, but she clearly believes that there are real and very evident differences in men's and women's playing and that women's kyokusen is preferable: it looks better and it allows you to play better. Notice that she mentioned the way it looks no fewer than five times in six sentences: she clearly prioritizes the visuality of performance and the pleasure of the gaze. She is trying neither to emulate nor to put on the body of a man, even if she uses essentialized categories of choreographic essence to make this point.[19]

Bender (2012, 161–69) suggests that the gender balance in Japanese taiko might be shifting toward more women participating, with more and more amateur and community groups that are 50-50 men and women, even though male standards about the taiko body and authority remain the norm. He notes that the "tightly bound femininity" of the women members of Kodo and Ondekoza may be on its way out, but audiences still bring strongly gendered expectations to bear on performers, wanting women to be cute rather than strong and sometimes responding to Honō Daiko's strength, power, and volume with distaste (162).

SATORI DAIKO'S WOMEN BACK AT HOME

We left the workshop a bit star-struck and full of ideas for new pieces. Honō Daiko's fluidity, controlled power, and *style* had us all rather enthralled, even the men. The assumption that women's groups sacrifice power and precision for a kind of feel-good, inclusive, amateur enthusiasm remained unspoken, but an alternative model was suddenly in front of us, and it left us both humbled and thoughtful. There are only a few Asian American or other North American women in taiko even remotely like Honō Daiko's members, and it bears asking why, though I acknowledge Tiffany Tamaribuchi, Kristy Oshiro, and Raging Asian Women as North American examples of women who play taiko at a professional level with unabashed strength. The transnational movement of taiko and the valorized practice of the taiko study tour put me in a place to consider alternative kinds of women's performance. Compromised though it may be, taiko is the primary site for my own experiments with an embodied feminism of performative sound and movement, and the intersubjective possibilities of performance in an era of globalization are precisely what afford this space its potential. The intersections of the local and the global—the Japanese local, the Asian American local, and the brief confluence of these two spheres through the study tour—met at the site of Honō Daiko's performing bodies.

My friends in Satori Daiko did not normally spend a lot of time thinking or talking about gender. One of the four men in the group routinely disseminated outrageously sexist jokes to the rest of the members by email. My open interest in such matters was the target of bemused joking and occasionally outright dismissal. At the workshop, when I asked Jige about the presence of women in taiko, one of the Satori Daiko members (a woman) teasingly said, "That's a very Debbie question!"—in other words, there she goes again.

This changed suddenly and dramatically in the summer of 2002. A reporter for the *Los Angeles Times* contacted Rev. Tom: she had discovered that the majority of taiko players in North America are women, and she decided this would make a good feature. Rev. Tom referred her to me, and she openly located her interest in the topic in her own Chinese American identity and courses she had taken in Asian American studies. She attended one of our rehearsals, where she spent quite a bit of time interviewing two mother-daughter pairs in the group, at my suggestion. The resulting article was both informed and astute, and it had the effect of allowing and even encouraging the women in Satori Daiko to think about gender as a central force in the group and indeed their lives. The pleasure of appearing in a major newspaper and the resulting attention from admiring colleagues and friends opened up a space for thinking about taiko and gender, and I got the strong sense that the reporter's ability to draw these women's experiences into a certain configuration was surprising, affirming, and thought provoking for them. For instance, the reporter asked probing questions about whether any of the women were contradicting gendered behaviors instilled by their parents, and one member had a perfect example:

> When LizAnn Shimamoto was 12, her mother forced her to take an etiquette class, where Shimamoto learned all the things a "good girl" should be, how to be "ladylike" and "mild-mannered" and above all, quiet.
>
> Now, at 39, Shimamoto yells.
>
> She yells while playing the odaiko, a drum roughly the size of a refrigerator. She yells as if she's sending a message across the Grand Canyon. She yells because it gives her a sense of power, because it's fun and because it encourages her fellow drummers—including daughters Amy, 14, and Grace, 11—to keep the beat. Of the 18 performers in Shimamoto's group, Satori Daiko, 13 are women. It's a breakdown reflected in Japanese drumming, or taiko, groups across North America: About two-thirds of the roughly 150 taiko groups are composed of women, especially Asian American women. Many of these women have snatched up bachi, or wooden drumming sticks, to rediscover their roots—and to redefine their roles as women.
>
> "What we're doing is contradictory to what a Japanese female has traditionally been taught to do," said Shimamoto of Monterey Park. "It's a mirror of what's happening culturally."
>
> Once "extremely meek and shy," Shimamoto plays taiko with a grin on her face as wide as Julia Roberts'. She moves her feet wide apart. She raises the bachi as if they were nunchuks and pounds the cowhide-covered barrel. She pants. She sweats. And of course, she belts out an occasional kake-goe, or yell, to support her daughters. (Chan 2002)

After that, my friends frequently made comments about "woman power." In our pre-performance huddle at an outdoor festival a few months after the newspaper article appeared, one woman member shouted, "Women of Satori!" and several others responded, "Yeah!" This cautious step toward an explicit feminist understanding of taiko was a sea change.

Having spent so much time looking at the body and its trappings, it is worth returning to the fact that the members of Honō Daiko are musicians and make music. Without divorcing the bodily politics of taiko from its sounds, Honō Daiko's repertoire focuses tightly on a kind of virtuosity distinct from that of the loud, massed "power taiko" that defines most community-based ensembles. Honō Daiko's technique—both the command of complex rhythms and the kinesthetic control of timbre and dynamics—is strikingly and deliberately different from the spirited but inexact playing of most amateur groups (i.e., the clear majority of taiko groups on both sides of the Pacific), setting this ensemble apart as extraordinary. Honō Daiko has a foot in a different world—the world of the "professional" musician, the "trained" musician, and all the status markers that follow—resituating its musical product and practitioners as part of the classical arts, in contradistinction to the folkloric.

Taiko practitioners' uncritical valorization of tradition and our circulation of neocolonial feudalistic imaginaries are integrally part of our celebratory story about ourselves. Yet I would not dismiss these attitudes as invented, quaintly sexist, or "merely" enacting nationalist projects of folkloricization in the global arena. Our gender politics are conflicted. Taiko practitioners, overwhelmingly women, are routinely inserted into male costuming and absorbed into master narratives of a feudal (read: patriarchal) past. Taiko also offers liberatory possibilities for choreographing new kinds of gendered, racial, and ethnic identity. These contradictions are frustrating, seductive, and exhilarating. It may be necessary to unfetter ourselves somatically first, then intellectually—to enact what's envisioned before it can be articulated.[20] Jige said, "Learn pieces so that your body knows them," even as she was redefining that knowing body hard at work in the transpacific arc of memory and movement.

ASIAN AMERICAN MASCULINITY AND MARTIAL ARTS

The Japanese martial arts shape taiko indirectly but powerfully and persuasively. Taiko and martial arts each move back and forth across the Pacific continuously, through film industries, the imaginations of spectators, and the bodies of practitioners. Some men address Asian American masculinity through taiko and martial arts. Some Asian Americans study martial arts, but many, many more follow them in film, especially Hong Kong genres. Rev. Tom loved Japanese films about samurai, and he believed this shaped his moral universe and his relationship to taiko. I explore how martial arts–inflected values percolate through taiko, though this connection isn't always obvious or direct. In one notable case, though, it was quite direct. Taiko practitioners believe martial arts values are part of a certain teacher's legacy, and I address their sometimes conflicted opinions about the power and influence of that legacy. Finally, I consider the links between some Japanese approaches to taiko and their relationship to ultranationalism.

I have already argued that taiko offers new ways for Asian American women to come into voice and to assert a new bodily awareness; I turn now to how Asian

American men performatively redefine themselves with taiko, through the thicket of interrelationships between taiko and martial arts.

HE'S HUNG

In 2004, my then-thirty-eight-year-old cousin Eric sent me an email: "Oh yeah; speaking of AA stereotypes, that whole William Hung thing with *American Idol* just had me cringing!!! (I don't watch that drivel but I heard about it on the news.) I thought, this guy just set the perceptions of Asian males back an entire generation. Engineering student? Buckteeth? Nerdy fashion? Speaks with a slight accent? Yep, this is the frame of reference for all of middle America now. And of COURSE the Fox network purposely picked this guy cuz he DID fit the stereotype . . ." In early February 2004, the UC Berkeley student William Hung appeared on *American Idol,* performed the Ricky Martin song "She Bangs," and went down in flames. He was a caricature; he was a nightmare of Asian male stereotypes. The judges laughed at him. He was the self-image that all Asian American men carry in the back of their heads: nerdy, awkward, ridiculous, unattractive to women, and so on and so on. Yet his failure on *American Idol* gave him an unexpected fame. Almost immediately, websites devoted to Hung sprang up, celebrating, commemorating, and mocking him (sometimes all at once), replete with video clips, photographs, further news and information. Hung became a celebrity: in the wake of his internet fame, TV talk shows and record producers began to pursue him. The narrative inevitably comes around to the stereotype that all Asian men have small dicks. Hung was being idolized, but why and how weren't completely clear. Was the joke on him and expanded to supersize? This was the revenge of a public that knows they too will never win on *American Idol*—an uprising of losers everywhere, an identification with Hung's emblematic everyday unglamorousness (Meizel 2009).

The Western gaze configures Asian and Asian American men through a constellation of race, gender, and sexuality: they are effeminate, castrated, demasculinized. David Henry Hwang's *M. Butterfly* and a flood of critical work on it critique the historical processes that established Asian men as not-masculine and the contemporary practices that maintain this trope, including an endless parade of popular culture representations that repeat, reenact, and reify it.[21] A great deal of scholarly effort has gone into unpacking the historical patterns of labor migration and American legislation that created the Asian or Asian American man. As David Eng (2001, 17) writes, "Asian American male identity is historically and increasingly characterized by critical intersections in which racial, gendered, and economic contradictions are inseparable." It is a short distance from the feminized occupations of laundry worker, houseboy, and cook to the bottom that the Asian or Asian American gay man must always be. Maintaining Asian and Asian American men as always less than masculine contains a perceived threat to the US workforce: the Chinese coolie and the Japanese CEO are both forever overrunning the American economy. The emasculated Asian or Asian American man is thus a key strategy in the management of US ethnic minorities, just as the hypersexualized African American man was a key strategy for justifying the twentieth-century lynchings that used terror to contain an emergent workforce.

L. H. M. Ling's (1999, 283) virtuosic exploration of global "hypermasculinity" offers critical tools that can be used to consider the confluence of gendered values within taiko in Asia and North America. She borrows the term from Ashis Nandy (1988), who notes how colonizer and colonized together generated "a reactionary, exaggerated form of masculism" in India as British authorities feminized the disenfranchised ("women, the poor, homosexuals"). On the other hand, the West perceives economic development in the Asian Third World as aggressive, controlling, authoritative, and masculine, and Ling argues that postcolonial rejections of the West's emasculating force have deepened rather than rethought such tropes of hypermasculinity. When many Asian countries emerged from World War II, successful modernization, industrialization, and globalization was conceived in hypermasculine terms, even when built on the foundation of readily available female labor forces. The neocolonial dynamic behind a postcolonial response is full of internal contradictions yet still powerful. Ling views the Asian acceptance and reenactment of hypermasculinity as fallout from colonialism. As Asian countries assert new structures for economic self-determination, they sometimes rely on gendered models of development. Still, the old binary of the West versus the rest is no longer clear. As Ling writes, "The Other under global hypermasculinity is not outside, alien, or policeable but inside, familiar, and all too unmanageable. Put differently, global hypermasculinity brings 'in here' what's 'out there'" (299).

So there are several stories about Asian and Asian American masculinity and several ways of responding to the stories that are out there and all too many ways to understand how colonial and orientalist ideas about Asian nations, cultures, and people are gendered, sexualized, and racialized. The means of response cannot be disentangled from the master's tools, but redefining the terms requires memory, pleasure, awareness, fandom, movement, and organized rejoinders. Taiko offers all that and more.

TAIKO IS OUR BRUCE LEE

On February 12, 2004, Rev. Tom and I were eating lunch and talking about taiko, samurai flicks, and rehearsals when he suddenly declared, "Taiko is our Bruce Lee!" I provide a detailed biography of Rev. Tom in my book on Asian American performance (Wong 2004) but revisit his personal history here to explore why he loved samurai films. (All of Rev. Tom's remarks in what follows are from my interview with him over that lunch.) His father was a Japanese-born Zen Buddhist minister, and his mother was a Kibei Nisei, an American-born Japanese educated in Japan. Rev. Tom was born in Japan in 1947 and emigrated to the US at the age of five (in 1952) when his father was given a position at a Zen Buddhist temple in Los Angeles. He was thus technically an Issei but had the sensibilities and political views of a Sansei, though he was bilingual and in certain ways bicultural. He played and taught kumi-daiko continually beginning in the late 1970s and spent 1980 to 1983 in Japan studying traditional folkloric music and dance. Rev. Tom was in his thirties when he decided to follow his father's example and become a Buddhist minister; he was probably the eighth or ninth generation in his family to take on this calling, and he supported himself through a combination of taiko teaching, taiko performance, and Buddhist ministry.

Between the ages of six and about twelve, Rev. Tom watched Japanese films with his father almost every weekend in local movie theaters. They went to the Linda Lea theater most often, on Main Street in downtown Los Angeles (see figure 26, Linda Lea movie theater in downtown Los Angeles, 2004, at *http://wonglou-derandfaster.com*). They both loved *jidai-geki* (period films) but followed *chambara*, swordfight samurai movies, most avidly. Young Shuichi—as Rev. Tom was then known—liked everything about chambara: the stock/repertory actors used in film after film made by the Toei Company, the great costumes, the soundtracks of modernized, orchestrated minyo (folk music) and enka. The formulaic nature of the plots was also a source of pleasure: the hero gets into trouble, must take revenge on someone, and at the end makes a long speech about what the bad guy did and why he, the hero, has no choice but to respond. That long speech was a high point: Rev. Tom remembers that it was often delivered "in Kabuki style! Very stirring!" and preceded the final struggle between the hero and the villain. Chambara movies were about chivalry and honor, no matter what the class of samurai. The setting was usually Edo, old Tokyo. Shuichi liked the clarity of the chambara moral universe. Reflecting on it, Rev. Tom said, "I never really examined Bushido . . . but I knew what it was, from the subtitles." He remembered that as he got older (when he was in junior high), some chambara had darker themes: films that were critical of Bushido, about generations upon generations of lordly abuse of retainers and the ethical dilemmas created by these abuses. Rev. Tom said, "When I was a kid, I used to play with swords, pretend I was a samurai. I also liked westerns and had a cowboy outfit, toy cap pistols . . . Unconsciously, I liked the idea of justice, you know? Justice prevailing. In a lot of the stories, the underdog wins, finally at the end, and I guess I related to that aspect of it. Coming to this country and not knowing English, I felt kind of inferior and self-conscious." Chambara and the American westerns of the 1950s had deep genealogical connections through the international film industry, of course, but in this case an immigrant boy was drawn to both and performatively played at both. He had comic books with samurai characters and trading cards with cowboy characters.

He got involved with the Asian American Movement when he was in his twenties and saw that the implicit class code of Bushido conflicted with the movement's radically democratic ideals. Rev. Tom joined Kinnara Taiko in Los Angeles in 1976 at the age of twenty-five, less than a year after he first played taiko in the Manzanar Pilgrimage. He said that Rev. Mas Kodani, the head minister at Senshin Buddhist Temple in South Central Los Angeles and a founder of Kinnara Taiko, once told him that one of his inspirations for becoming a taiko player was watching the film *Muhomatsu no issho* (*Rickshaw Man;* 1958, directed by Hiroshi Inagaki), in which Toshiro Mifune is the poor title character, who also plays taiko in the Gion matsuri.[22] In other words, Rev. Mas—a notable and influential American taiko teacher—had been deeply influenced by the depiction of a Japanese taiko player in a Japanese film. Mifune is of course an iconic figure, inextricably linked to the image of the cinematic samurai. One cannot watch Mifune playing a humble rick-shaw man in 1958 without simultaneously seeing filmic shadows of him as a ronin, a rogue samurai: a certain overlayering of affective understanding takes place as Mifune carries forward his earlier roles into his modest rickshaw man so that the honor, strength, and determination of every samurai he ever played are channeled into our reception of him as a drummer in Gion. Relating the film to his own experience, Rev. Tom told me,

> Before going to Japan, I had an image of what I thought a taiko player was: I thought they represented honor, and they were like the new hero of Japan. . . . My ideal im-age—though not my inspiration—of a taiko player was [the Mifune] character in that movie. It was kind of a replacement for my hero, the samurai. There was no way I was going to become a samurai, right? Besides, I got politicized and found it wasn't that cool to be a samurai, so being a taiko player . . . Of course I wasn't thinking about it like this, but now I'm reflecting that I do feel kind of like a hero, a role model, as a taiko person.

When he became more seriously involved in the Japanese American reparations movement and the Asian American Movement, the caste system that defined samurai culture began to look different to him—feudal, and in fact not cool at all—so he sought out social justice values in other practices. I asked Rev. Tom whether there was any remaining connection between taiko and chambara, samurai, and Bushido for him. He answered, "But I do feel something when I'm playing—something that covers my entire *being.* And it's something . . . from that culture, from Japanese culture, that I feel." I asked, What *is* that? He said, "I feel inside—it's the energy, the ki. I'm pretty sure, though I never had any discus-sions with martial artists, that it's the same thing martial artists feel when they do their thing. Because I feel a sense of balance. It's a good feeling. You can see it in other people, whether they have it or not, even beginners, if they have it or not, or the potential."

Samurai, taiko, films, and ideas of honor and justice are interwoven and repre-sent a circulation of values and images back and forth between Japan and Asian America for more than a century. The border is there only to be crossed again and again; nothing stays still.

BROTHER BRUCE WAS ON MY WALL

I have thirteen Chinese American first cousins—eight men and five women—born between the early 1950s and the early 1970s. I asked them by email to tell me about Bruce Lee: was he a hero to them, was he a role model?[23] Suzanne, a bit older than I, responded to my initial query in a matter of hours:

> [My brother] Kevin still regularly takes Seattle tourists to where Bruce Lee is buried.
>   I don't remember posters around our house, but we were the few folks that watched *The Green Hornet* so we could see Cato in action . . . & especially the episode of Batman where they were guest "heros" . . . & he beat up Robin!

Some Asian Americans watch and listen to American popular culture—films, television shows, music, and so forth—searching for the presence of Asians and Asian Americans, keeping our eyes and ears open for the occasional or fleeting presence of Asian American faces and voices. We attend to them when they appear, and since we know that these appearances are likely to be brief and contingent, we learn how to spectate *against* certain mainstream, racist American understandings of how and why they're present at all. If Cato was unfortunately just another Chinese houseboy in certain ways, well, *we* knew that he was "really" Bruce Lee under that chauffeur's hat and that he was going to kick the crap out of the bad guys.

My cousin Eric also responded immediately to my query. Lee meant and means a lot to him:

> Very interesting topic. VERY fascinating man. The answer is YES, brother Bruce was on my wall. As his books and bios, etc., are on my shelf. . . . In fact, there is a poster of him in my office CUBICLE. He remains some sort of archetype for me, lurking somewhere in my unconscious levels. I thought about this before, why the appeal, why the fascination with ol' Bruce. Sure, the destruction of the weak Asian male stereotype has a lot to do with it.
>   But there is the sheer magnetism of his presence. No doubt, if you see any of his films on the BIG screen, not a videotape or DVD on a TV set, you can definitely see there was something charismatic about him. Plus, I found the philosophical aspects of his art, his Eastern influences and spirituality, to be something that helped me feel some sort of connection to really being Chinese. Sure, that sounds strange, but as a pre-teen in the 1970's, knowing that you were different and one of the few minorities in the neighborhood, it helped build a sense of pride. . . .
>   I never consciously wished that I were white so I could fit in better or to make me feel that I was fully accepted. . . .

> Even into my 20's, Bruce still had me fascinated. I read more of his books that were published by his family. I'm STILL fascinated with the guy to this day. If a new book comes out, I may or may not pick it up, but I'm always interested. No doubt, he is/was a role model for the PHYSICAL awareness of self. He was an incredible specimen of fitness, complete with this raw, powerful energy in his graceful movements. Let's face it, he was a badass. Half the movie theater would be full of black kids, who

really loved him too. It wasn't an overstated machismo, but it was the epitome of masculinity in some respects.

Eric was openly trying to find a way into "really being Chinese," because at that time—the 1970s—any authentic sense of the Asian American was still emergent. While he explicitly identifies the issue of physicality and physical presence, he also notes that he didn't want to be White, nor did he look to White models of machismo. At the same time, Blackness is part of his memories: the African American teenagers who were there in the theaters with him. Yet he apparently didn't look to Shaft or Superfly (African American action heroes of the time) for models either. The crossover occurred in the other direction, with young African American men looking to the Chinese martial arts for new ideas about strength, power, invincibility, and justice. Amy Abugo Ongiri (2002, 36) has written at length about how African American men idolized Chinese martial arts figures in the 1970s. She argues that African American audiences "wanted to see the underdog win through a differently articulated body politics that stressed discipline, restraint, and self-determination rather than a cartoonish display of brute force" like those featured in many blaxploitation films of the period. Lee and the huge number of Hong Kong martial arts movies offered heavily mediatized ideas about a feudal past and an uncomplicated world of honor with clear principles, generated by a film industry framed by late colonialism, high global finance, and late Cold War anxieties. Vijay Prashad (2001) acknowledges the orientalist fantasy driving African American empowerment through mediated martial arts but still views this type of spectatorship as the beginning of an Afro-Asian political formation that represented a new kind of coalition building at a moment when it made all the difference: he emphasizes the ethnic-political bridge that he believes martial arts formed between Asian Americans and African Americans in the 1970s. The play of representation thus ran deep in that movie theater where Eric and those African American teenagers looked to Lee for ideas about how to be strong, how to triumph as the underdog, and how to stand up to injustice.

My cousin Matt, then in his early forties, wrote back with similar memories. He too referenced the experiential importance (in a prevideo era) of going to movie theaters and watching Lee in an interethnic context:

> i was a huge bruce lee fan.
>
> at about 9 or 10 yrs old i used to go with my dad and [my brothers] nu and kim to the summer film festival at the u[niversity] of mich[igan]. students were gone for the most part, summer kids, locals, but it usually was full. i think it cost $1.50. that was maybe in '71 or '72.
>
> 'enter the dragon' is the one I remember the most. he kicked chuck norris' ass bad. and chuck was bigger physically.
>
> that was very empowering to a 9 yr old chinese kid. i was an ABC [American-born Chinese] skinny pip-squeak who took ymca martial arts. i remember getting a

t-shirt with bruce lee printed on it in his famous 'enter the dragon' pose in front of some snake shaped graphic twisting like dna. it was the bomb to me. . . .

i continued to go to the movie fests each summer and usually they showed a number of bruce lee movies, and i went to as many as my dad could stand. when he died rumors flew—kick to the head, natural causes—i was crushed again. today i live in san francisco close to haight st. where lots of young culture brews and blooms, i can still see bruce lee t-shirts on the kids now. to me he was my symbol of attitude, courage, confidence. and one of my very few heroes.

to this day i have back at home in mich. in my childhood home posters of bruce, nunchocks (real ones!) on the wall, silver stars (for fighting!), and even some nun-chocks i made in wood shop at my jr. high school—they didn't know.

Twenty-five years later, my cousins Matt and Eric both look back to their preteen fascination with Bruce Lee and talk about it in terms of their formative iden-tity as young Asian American men. Like Suzanne, Matt remembers an emblem-atic moment of Lee beating up a White man—and in each case, not a White villain but rather an authoritative White hero (Robin, Chuck Norris). In these moments, the status quo slipped a little, temporarily but noticeably. Lee resitu-ated racial hierarchies of which my young cousins were already aware, and what's more, Matt and Eric understood that he was doing it *for them*, as Chinese Ameri-can youth thinking about masculinity. Further, both have moved on in certain ways. Just as Rev. Tom realized that samurai culture doesn't transfer perfectly into Asian America, my cousins recognized the limits of their fandom . . . but the latest biography may still be purchased, and the posters and nunchucks haven't been thrown away.

Of course, Lee is, and perhaps has always been, so thoroughly and powerfully mediated that some can see Asian American men only as simulacra of him, revers-ing the distinctive ways that Asian American men become stronger through spec-tating by recasting them as inevitably Asian rather than Asian American and as irremediably foreign and exotic. Rev. Tom wasn't into the martial arts or Bruce Lee. He did study kendo briefly as an adult, but that was mostly to accompany his young son to lessons.

Deborah Wong: Did you have a Bruce Lee poster on your wall?
Rev. Tom Kurai: [*laughs*] No! But I thought he presented a very positive image for Asian American men. I mean, I wasn't distraught over his death, but I thought it was a sad thing—I thought, Gee, that's too bad. [*pause, remembering*] In fact, I was picked up by a Black woman because she was a Bruce Lee fan. This place called Baby Lions where [the Japanese American jazz band] Hiroshima used to play, a nightclub. And we went to see a mar-tial arts movie, just one date.

DW: How long did it take for you to realize why she was interested?
TK: Well, I knew from that first date.

DW: [*I'm in stitches. I can't stop laughing.*]

TK: She kept talking about Bruce Lee: Do you do karate, do you do kung fu, and I just said [*in a small voice*], No, I don't.

JAPANESE HYPERMASCULINITY

Tanaka Seiichi, or Tanaka-sensei, as virtually all North American kumi-daiko players call him, was born in Tokyo in 1943 and emigrated to San Francisco in 1967.[24] He studied the martial arts extensively in Japan and then took up taiko in his twenties, first with Oguchi Daihachi of Osuwa Daiko and later with the renowned group Oedo Sukeroku Taiko. In 1968 he founded his own dojo, where he taught martial arts and then taiko, and in a remarkably short time his taiko classes had filled up. Tanaka-sensei is regarded as the father of kumi-daiko in North America; some of his best students, now middle aged, were originally members of San Francisco Taiko Dojo and have since established their own kumi-daiko groups based to differing degrees on his philosophies and methods. Tanaka-sensei represents the most explicit pedagogical pairing of kumi-daiko and martial arts (social) aesthetics in North America. He is an exemplary transborder subject but in very different ways from Rev. Tom.

Stories and anecdotes circulate about Tanaka-sensei's teaching methods.[25] He is known as tough and demanding in ways perceived as authentically "Japanese": Tanaka-sensei has exceptionally high standards, and these standards are drawn from the Japanese martial arts. He places a strong emphasis on correct kata and on drills. His teaching philosophy is explicit and codified:

THE ESSENCE OF SAN FRANCISCO TAIKO DOJO

GRANDMASTER SEIICHI TANAKA FOUNDED SAN FRANCISCO TAIKO DOJO IN 1968 BASED ON THE PHILOSOPHY OF UNITY OF MIND, BODY AND SPIRIT. INFLUENCED BY CONFUCIANISM AND HIS TRAINING IN THE CHINESE MARTIAL ARTS, HE EMPHASIZES THE IMPORTANCE OF RIGOROUS PHYSICAL, MENTAL AND SPIRITUAL TRAINING.

心 - KOKORO

In martial arts, seika tanden is considered to be the central force of KI energy and is located about three fingers below the navel. KI is the life energy that must flow from the performer to the drum. Another important concept is I or mindfulness/consciousness. Both I and KI must come together for taiko to have life and expression. . . .

技 - WAZA

Tanaka Sensei believes in preserving the oral tradition of passing songs on through words. Taiko songs are not learned through a notated score. Playing taiko is an act of communication. When taught through words like "don" and "tsu-ku" the passing on of songs is also an act of communication. By speaking the song, the spirit of the song can be conveyed. Ultimately, the sound of the drum must communicate this spirit. . . .

体 - KARADA

Physical strength and endurance is important. Running, push-ups, sit-ups, finger crunches and other exercises are necessary to develop power and stamina. Dojo members repeat basic drills over and over. However, strength training is never separated from training of the spirit. "When you have played with all your strength and you feel tired, that is when you can truly begin to play, tapping into the energy deep within you," teaches Tanaka Sensei.

礼 - REI

Basic communication always begins with a greeting. At San Francisco Taiko Dojo, students learn the importance of greeting their instructors and each other when meeting or taking leave, with an energetic "Ohayogozaimasu" or "Oyasuminasai". Taiko students always bow to their teachers and when entering or leaving the dojo, a place of study and discipline. The bow and the audible greeting convey appreciation and respect. The attitude is vital when approaching the drum.[26]

Other stories note Tanaka-sensei's "traditional" emphasis on men over women: it is common knowledge that women must work harder to earn his approval. His student Tiffany Tamaribuchi, the director of Sacramento Taiko Dan, is a case in point: stories circulate about how hard it was for her, how she stuck it out, and how she earned her place as one of his primary students.

Rev. Tom never studied with Tanaka-sensei but did see him teach. I asked Rev. Tom what he thought Tanaka did that was especially effective for many of his male students, and he answered,

> He intimidated them, needled them, and you know, like an army drill sergeant: *What's the matter with you? You're so weak!* Just belittling. He did that more to the people who had the most potential. If he didn't think you were that good, he didn't spend that much time on you. Japanese American men didn't last very long in that situation, you know. Caucasian men did, because they thought that's the way it's supposed to be. Because many Japanese American men have already been exposed to that kind of thing and they've had enough of that. His emphasis was always on basics, would have people work on the same thing over and over and over again.
>
> I think a lot of Tanaka-sensei's students who have gone on to start their own groups use a lot of the same methods. Not the same methods, but the same structure, organizational structure—the dojo system. There's a *kohai* and *sempai* [relationships in a hierarchy in which the senior person has both authority and responsibilities]— . . . a lot of emphasis on seniority.

Tanaka-sensei's gendered authority didn't transfer easily from a Japanese to a Japanese American teaching environment. Some Japanese Americans had already experienced such authoritarian models in their own families and were in search of something less hierarchical. On the other hand, the imaginative force of orientalism enabled Tanaka-sensei's teaching method to work *across* race and culture: Rev. Tom thought White American men were more likely to accept the terms of an absolute authority that they perhaps viewed as authentically "Japanese" and therefore beyond discussion, making it even more powerful and attractive for them.

San Francisco Taiko Dojo has both men and women, but starting in the 1990s the odaiko has been played almost entirely by men, especially in the group's signature piece, "Tsunami." Concert footage of this is thrilling: the final section features a series of men, each more muscled than the last, taking turns playing odaiko solos.[27] The atmosphere is fierce and aggressive, and the speed, energy, and intensity of the piece escalate as it proceeds. Bender (2012, 172) offers a trenchant analysis of how a few Japanese schools of kumi-daiko (out of many) have promoted a connection between taiko and Japanese nationalism, which some Japanese find uncomfortable. He describes one Japanese taiko player who "expressed concern at how, in her view, taiko performance evoked the militarism of wartime Japan." Let me turn to Bender's account in some detail. In looking closely at how and why Oguchi Daihachi created the Nippon Taiko Foundation (Nippon Taiko Renmei) in 1979, he discovered direct links between Oguchi's taiko activities and right-wing nationalism, not least through the patronage of Sasakawa Ryōichi:

> Such large-scale organization requires substantial financial support, which the Nippon Taiko Foundation secured through the Japan Shipbuilding Industry Association (Nippon Senpaku Shinkō-kai), now known as the Nippon Foundation (Nippon Zaidan), an organization that was endowed by the wealthy entrepreneur and philanthropist Sasakawa Ryōichi. Sasakawa, who died in 1995 at the age of ninety-six, was one of the most notorious figures in modern Japanese history. He was an avowed nationalist and a member of Japan's *kuromaku,* a term derived from the theater to refer to the influential figures manipulating Japanese business and politics from behind the scenes. Many Japanese I encountered viewed Sasakawa suspiciously, and his connection to the Nippon Taiko Foundation gave a number of drum groups pause. Concerns about its sources of funding even made some reluctant to join the organization. (180)

Bender reinterviewed Oguchi, who reflected on Sasakawa's politics and his own agreement with them. Oguchi told Bender,

> Sasakawa was the kind of person who represented the spirit of old Japan. He believed strongly in respect for one's ancestors and in piety toward the gods of Shinto and Buddhism—the kind of person who represented the spirit of the old-time soldier, one who accepted the Imperial Rescript on Education without question.[28] He was the embodiment of *kokusui* [ultranationalism]. Some people call this "ultra right-wing"; if so then I, too, would consider myself to share this sentiment. Sasakawa knew that in every temple and every shrine in Japan, there is a taiko drum, that in this taiko

> lives the heart and soul of Japan and the spirits of departed ancestors. By encouraging people to learn about taiko, Sasakawa believed that more individuals would come into contact with and learn about the Japanese spirit. (182)

At the time of Bender's writing, the Nippon Taiko Foundation had over eight hundred taiko groups—many but not all Japanese kumi-daiko groups—but he also reported that certain taiko players openly resisted the kinds of standardization and control that they felt emanated from the foundation. In 2002, Oguchi published a taiko textbook that Bender views as a transparent and troubling attempt to create a national "Japan taiko" that could well flatten out the rich variety of regional taiko styles that have marked kumi-daiko until now.

Through his connection to Oguchi, Tanaka-sensei and his approach to taiko represent a meeting of postwar Japanese identity struggles with economic recovery. When Tanaka-sensei became a key player in Asian American kumi-daiko, the martial arts values of his version of taiko—imbued with gendered nationalist sentiment and shadowed by patriotic fervor—in some cases ran head-to-head against a completely different set of values generated by the politics of the Asian American movement. Asian American taiko players looking for a performative means to oppose histories of racism and containment will likely refute social models reliant on an uncritical acceptance of gendered hierarchy. Tanaka-sensei thus labors under a heavy load. As part of the postwar Japanese push to create what became an economic miracle, he participated fully and deeply in the ideological struggle to think about Japan in new ways and to enact that nation performatively in diaspora. If his participation in an arm of global hypermasculinity smacks uncomfortably of a kind of ultranationalism, it is for real reasons.

My Chinese American cousins were fascinated by Bruce Lee but never pursued the martial arts—let alone taiko—to any extent. Rev. Tom studied the martial arts only briefly but did make a life out of taiko and says that taiko is his Bruce Lee. Tanaka-sensei drew on a version of taiko imbued with patriotism and certain martial arts principles. These three Asian and Asian American male situations are not directly connected, and perhaps my effort to connect them is too speculative and too reliant on intuition. Asian American men growing up in the 1950s through 1970s were looking for new models at a historical moment when there was a shift in the tide: Pacific Rim popular culture channeled certain iconic images and understandings of powerful Asian men into the imaginations of Asian and Asian American men generally.

The construction of a powerful Asian American man of principle and honor has taken place along the sometimes parallel, sometimes intersecting tracks of mediated martial arts and taiko. My point here is to suggest a troubled but often empowering confluence of ideas about Asian masculinity whose transnational circulation has had markedly different effects in different places, times, and men. Certain forms of Japanese nationalism were elided with masculinity during a period of economic recovery. When those forms were carried into Asian America at a different historical moment, their meaning and power changed. I haven't even told you about my oldest cousin Christopher's fascination with the writer Yukio Mishima in the 1970s—another physically powerful and charismatic Asian masculine icon whose force is troubling for precisely these gendered, racialized, and imperialist reasons. Nostalgia has shaped ideas about Bushido for at least a century, but the oblique movement of Bushido values into North American taiko suggests both a powerful need for performative models and their vulnerability to orientalist reappropriation. Surely it is possible for Asian and Asian American men to participate in the public sphere in ways that are mindful of the play between queerness and militarized threat, and to step forward with unequivocally big . . . drumsticks.

BARING IT ALL FOR TAIKO

As the American studies scholar Masumi Izumi (2001, 44) has written, "In Japan taiko is commonly associated with masculinity. A taiko player's typical image is a muscular man with *hachimaki* (bandanna) and *fundoshi* (loincloth)." When male taiko players perform almost nude, wearing only a minimalist item of "traditional" clothing, they redefine Asian masculinity. Humor, nudity, and spectatorship assert a heterosexist masculinity that is haunted in North America by expectations of Asian effeminacy.

The fundoshi is a (very) small article of Japanese clothing. Worn today at Japanese festivals, it is a self-conscious reference to the past. Indeed, traditional Japanese clothing in a postwar context is deeply mediated and immediately invokes nationalism and Japaneseness without rejecting modernity. The fundoshi is a loincloth worn only by men. It is a long piece of (usually) white cotton about one foot wide and approximately six feet long that is pulled between the buttocks so it cups the genitals like a jockstrap and is then twisted and tied around the waist. The buttocks are bare but the genitals are concealed. Mutsuro Takahashi (1968, 149) writes that the fundoshi is "a cloth possessed of great spiritual powers" and describes how to put it on:

> Put a short end of the cloth over one shoulder with a few inches hanging down in back, and let the long end hang down in front. Pass the long end between the thighs, tight against the crotch; hold it firmly in place against the very end of the backbone; and fold it at a right angle. Still holding this fold with one hand, bring the cloth forward around the body so it crosses on top of the short piece, and continue on around to the back. Draw the end under the right-angle fold and pull it in the opposite direction. Now take the short end from the shoulder and let it hang down in front. Pass it between the thighs, thus forming a double-layered pouch, and bring it up in back; pulling the entire arrangement snug, tie the two ends together, after which any surplus can be tucked into the waistband. . . . And the fundoshi is complete.

Some men in Japan wear fundoshi and short, brightly patterned jackets (happi coats) in festivals, especially in massed processions carrying Shinto altars called *mikoshi* through the streets in ritual performances of strength, devotion, and drunkenness. Samurai wore fundoshi under their armor. Until World War II, Japanese men of all classes wore fundoshi as underwear, but the middle and upper classes switched to elasticized Western underwear when American goods and values flooded the country during occupation. In postwar Japan, the fundoshi carries powerful meanings that conflate masculinity, cultural authenticity, and national identity. It is also an object of fascination for non-Japanese: emblematic of an unashamed Japanese physicality untainted by Western Puritanism, and a little ridiculous. Online English-language discussions of fundoshi lead inevitably to jokes about wedgies and more. The fundoshi encapsulates what is most different about Japanese men.

In the Western imagination, the Japanese are famous for their matter-of-fact attitude toward nudity. However, Japanese attitudes toward mixed-gender nudity changed profoundly in the mid-nineteenth century, influenced by Western values. Public baths are still popular but have been gender segregated since 1872. Exposing the body has had strong class connotations: some laborers worked in fundoshi, but samurai didn't appear nude or semiclothed in public. In his introduction to the book *Naked Festival,* Yukio Mishima (1968, 14) proudly addresses the "uniquely Japanese" festival traditions that featured massed men in fundoshi carrying a large shrine through neighborhood streets to the sound of taiko. He wrote rhapsodically about male "sacred nakedness," reflecting on changing Japanese attitudes toward the nude male body in response to Western contact.[29] With the full-on romanticism, nationalism, and primitivism for which he was famous, Mishima claimed that the men who donned fundoshi and ran through the streets during the festival returned unapologetically to Japanese values. He declared that they

> have cast off the yokes of modern industrial society. Blue-collar workers from huge factories, bank tellers, construction workers—they have bravely cast aside all clothing in favor of the ancient loincloth, they have reclaimed their right to be living males, they have regained joy, fierceness, laughter, and all the primitive attributes of man. If only for a day, thanks to their healthy young bodies, thanks to our primitive past they are once again the essential man.
>
> Nor is it merely strength and life that fills these bodies: even if unconsciously, by means of the festival they have regained the sanctity of their flesh.

Ondekoza (and Kodo) created the odaiko solo that became the model for all other odaiko solos, and it looms large in the taiko imagination. Paul Yoon (2009, 102) writes, "The odaiko solo, as heard and seen in performances by Ondekoza and Kodo, is perhaps the most iconic image of taiko." Bender (2012, 91–93) argues that the odaiko solo and a muscled masculinity are now inseparable. When members of Ondekoza first wore fundoshi in performance, they were making a point about tradition and class identification, even though many of them were university educated. Bender offers a fascinating explanation of Ondekoza's decision to wear fundoshi while playing "Odaiko," the exemplary solo, and he discusses it in the context of a long progression of performance decisions that ultimately transformed "Odaiko" into the group's most iconic piece. Based on his own ethnographic interviews and other journalistic coverage, Bender relates that Ondekoza members hadn't worn fundoshi in performance until Pierre Cardin saw a photo of them participating in 1975's Naked Festival and requested they wear fundoshi when performing at his theater in Paris. Den Tagayasu wasn't initially open to the idea but eventually gave in, and French audiences (especially gay men) responded with standing ovations. As Bender puts it, the fundoshi "became a kind of stage 'costume' that emphasized the impressive bodies of the male drummers, not just the movements and sounds these bodies produced" (93).

Kodo is also famous for its fundoshi-clad performances, linked to specific repertoire. The group's versions of "Odaiko" and "Yatai Bayashi" are in many ways identical to Ondekoza's (and indeed, many other groups' versions are based on theirs at this point). Yoshikazu Fujimoto's performances of "Odaiko" are legendary. Born in 1950, he is Kodo's most senior performing member, and as the Kodo website states, "In 1972 [he] joined Sado no Kuni Ondekoza, and when the group became Kodo in 1981, he was one of the founding members. For many years, he stood center-stage as the group's featured O-daiko player and center-man for the Yatai-bayashi climax."[30] His performance of "Odaiko" filmed in 1992 is stunning in every way.[31] Fourteen minutes long, it makes the physicality of the performance breathtakingly real and is utterly typical of how Kodo has performed "Odaiko" for at least thirty years, if not longer; its particular drama is in the confluence of the staging (darkened stage with spotlights on the individual performers), the choreography (five performers below, still, looking up at Fujimoto), and the eye of the camera as it roams up and down Fujimoto's body, taking in the curve of every muscle. This version also acts out an explicit hierarchy of male performers: the other men, all younger and more junior within the group's structure, are staged so they focus respectfully on Fujimoto, their eyes on him, their bodies turned toward him, and their stillness designed not to distract. Yoon (2009, 102) writes,

> For many, the odaiko solo is the embodiment of power. The size of the drum, the volume, the endurance of the player all manifest this power. Power is etched on to the performer's body as taut musculature and scarcely a trace of fat. In performance, a single stage light shines on a solitary, fundoshi-clad drummer kneeling before an enormous drum, which is several feet in diameter. Rising solemnly to his feet, he unhurriedly, but purposefully, raises his bachi (stick) and locks one arm straight back. As if pulsing with electricity, his raised right arm twitches slightly before he quickly strikes one single note and lets the vibrations wash over the audience. His measured and deliberate movements punctuate the gravitas of the art form. Gradually he speeds up as he moves into the main section of the piece. Performances, which can

last anywhere from 5 to 25 minutes, typically follow a *jo-ha-kyu* structure, and so speed up significantly toward a finale. For the soloist, the odaiko solo is a marathon, requiring stamina and strength in addition to musicality. Interestingly, in wearing nothing but a *fundoshi*, it is not simply the musical element on display, but also the performer's body. The musicality of the performer, though captivating, is clearly not the *sole* point of interest.

Kodo members also wear fundoshi for "Yatai Bayashi," a spectacularly taxing piece originally from the Chichibu festival tradition, played on large chudaiko set on the floor: each player sits on the floor facing one drum head, straddling the drum's body and leaning back at a forty-five-degree angle, striking the taiko with special thick bachi. As in "Odaiko," the performer's body is exposed to dramatic effect, with every muscle and sinew on display: the musician's core (hara) must be in top condition to make it through this grueling piece. I invite the reader to look for online video of Kodo playing "Yatai Bayashi" in fundoshi. I have watched the 1995 DVD *Kodo: Live at Acropolis* many times. Its rather brief version of "Odaiko" goes straight into "Yatai Bayashi"—Eiichi Sato finishes his solo, bows briefly to the audience, and then leaps down from the odaiko platform and seats himself at the center chudaiko. He and two other men wield the special "Yatai" bachi, which look like short baseball bats. As the piece goes on, they grimace and bare their teeth—theatrically?—as they lean back and pound, making the physical effort as visible as possible. They are covered with sweat. Your eyes are irresistibly drawn to their bodies: they have muscles everywhere, in places you didn't even realize the body *had* muscles. You even find yourself looking at how their muscular big toes grip the bodies of the chudaiko. They lean back even farther. Can't you feel your own abdominal muscles tighten sympathetically?

Yoon (2009, 100) summarizes the problems facing Asian American men: they are inevitably seen, thanks to popular American caricatures, as effeminate, weak, servile, and deeply unsexy unless proved otherwise. Whether the houseboy or the nerdy model minority, the Asian American man never gets the girl. Yoon argues that searching for "positive performed or mediated Asian male body-types often requires looking (usually literally) to Asia. In stating this I don't mean that negative stereotypes from Asia are absent, only that positive stereotypes typically flow from Asia into the Asian American imagination and not the other way around." Taiko does and doesn't solve this problem. In some ways it offers Asian American men a way to be Asian or Asian American *and* strong and commanding. Yet women dominate North American amateur taiko: at the time of this writing, perhaps 60 percent of all North American taiko players were women, though a majority of taiko teachers are men; until around 2010, 75 percent of North American taiko players were women (Walker 2016). In no way are male taiko players marginalized within the taiko community, but these demographics create yet another way that Asian American men must work harder for visibility. The film scholar Peter Feng

(1996, 27) has argued that American popular culture consistently renders Asian American men invisible, often in inverse proportion to how much it puts forward Asian American women as emblematic of Asian American culture.[32] He writes, "American popular culture is notoriously male-centered. For Asian Americans, however, the situation appears to be reversed, which may be yet another reflection of the power of the dominant culture."

The young Asian American men I know who play taiko in fundoshi rehabilitate Asian American masculinity in ways at once historically informed, deeply playful, and adept at seizing on the changes wrought by the transnational movement of cultural tropes. The playfulness is a defining strategy, an emotional valence, and thoroughly mediated: their mischievousness emerges from the intersection of popular culture and folkloricized practice. The humor on which they rely is related to the powerful Japanese trope of cuteness but is assertively masculine and distinctively ironic in a manner that marks it as irrevocably Asian American rather than Japanese. It offers up a beautiful (heterosexual?) male body for display. This body demands to be spectated in two ways. First, the audience screams and performatively asserts that this body is an object of desire. Second, this body is acknowledged by both the audience and the performers as a joke, or as a playfully ironic and knowing agent that transforms the known trope of the strong, relentless, unbending Japanese man into a platform for a new kind of Asian American masculinity. That is, the trope on which it is based isn't dismantled, rejected, or discarded: instead, its power is acknowledged, revealed as inappropriate, and then reasserted as the foundation for a masculinity that is all that *and more*. This playfulness offers commentary that simultaneously confronts and backs away from the problem of racialized effeminacy. This is not generic ludic play: in this case, it is an acknowledgement of how the Asian American man is already inarguably gendered, raced, and (de)sexualized. Yet the question remains of whether this is an extension of the Asian or Asian American giggle—the self-deprecating step back from confrontation.[33] Why is playfulness the chosen strategy? Why not anger, ugliness, or a thousand other possibilities? To try to explain all this, I need to draw together the matter of onstage nudity and the Japanese social aesthetic of cuteness.

At the same moment when those Asian and Asian American male bodies are established as objects of desire, their playfulness—signified by those little twitches of the hips, the twinkle rather than the smolder in the eyes—intersects with and signifies on the powerful presence of Japanese popular culture cuteness among Asian American youth. Japanese cute fashion emerged in the 1980s and has both evolved and been exported. As Sharon Kinsella (1995, 243) writes,

> Cute fashion was . . . a kind of rebellion or refusal to cooperate with established social values and realities. It was a demure, indolent little rebellion rather than a conscious, aggressive and sexually provocative rebellion of the sort that has been typical of western youth cultures. Rather than acting sexually provocative to emphasise

their maturity and independence, Japanese youth acted pre-sexual and vulnerable in order emphasise their immaturity and inability to carry out social responsibilities. Either way the result was the same; teachers in the west were as infuriated by cocky pupils acting tough as Japanese teachers were infuriated with uncooperative pupils writing cute and acting infantile.

Childlike cuteness pervades Asian American youth culture, though neither uniformly nor in simple emulation of Japanese youth. It surfaces in particular circumstances, usually as a kind of passive resistance to adult and/or quotidian expectations (e.g., an undergraduate girl will simply giggle rather than answer a professor's question). Ethnic minority groups generally deploy two kinds of humor, "conflict humor," focused on intergroup relations, and "control humor," which ridicules "deviance from the group's norms" (Rinder 1965, 118). The playful, fundoshi-wearing Asian American man activates both at once, performing cuteness and sexiness to the delight and understanding of his peers in the audience: he pokes fun at his own desirability at the very moment when he is literally an object of desire in the spotlight.

Fundoshi cuteness is at once outlandish and self-consciously historicized. Any subject wearing striking clothing from the past makes a statement about their own present. The art historian Anne Hollander (1978) argues that portraiture featuring subjects in historical clothing (e.g., Italian Renaissance painters' depiction of classical Greek dress) is inevitably about the subjects' contemporaneity. Further, in the visual arts, the clothed figure is in dynamic conversation with the nude. Hollander shows how the nude body emerges through artists' understandings of contemporary fashion: clothes literally shape, constrict, weight, pad, and expand ideas about the body. In earlier chapters, I addressed the variety of Japanese and North American taiko costumes, from the prevalent eighteenth- and nineteenth-century Japanese festival costumes to recent experiments that extend women's bodies in dramatic ways. Exposing the body in taiko performance has a particular history. Women rarely do it, and women revealing bare arms and shoulders is a very recent development, mostly adopted by young players and always as a spectacular display of strength and fitness. When young Asian American men wear fundoshi—that most inarguably Japanese item of clothing—they are stating that they are *not* Japanese.

Asian American masculinity is always in conversation with effeminacy. These young men gender Asian America by engaging implicitly rather than explicitly with long histories of violence and emasculation. They offer a whimsical response that flies in the face of expectation and inverts its "authentic" source. They perform a bodily humor that is decidedly not Japanese yet not wholly Asian American either. It is wrought by the globalized movement of people, musics, and ideas about gender and nation. Displaying themselves in this way for these audiences could happen only in an environment produced through transnational warfare, empire, and capital. A cheering audience's response creates a new emplacedness, wherein the fundoshi-clad Asian American man is reracialized twice over: his ludic display rejects the militaristic masculinity of the Japanese taiko player while riding on its strength, and it rejects the emasculating gaze of a mainstream non–Asian American audience while insisting that his desirable presence be constituted through spectatorship. It walks a dangerous line, always on the edge of reifying scopophilic practices and infantilizing the very body that is willing to spoof itself. Emotion, gender, race, and place are thus actively constituted through the sounds of these bodies at play and at work.

Transition

From My Journal—Learning and Playing "Miyake,"
May 8, 2006

I've been working on "Miyake" for four months now, and I love it. It's a "traditional" Japanese piece from Miyake Island, but I'm keenly aware that it's been arranged, rearranged, and folkloricized from top to bottom. Nonetheless, it's thrilling to work on a piece that's so iconic for North American taiko players. For this Asian American woman, "Miyake" is so *Japanese.*

It's the stance, first and foremost—the kata. It pushes the body in extreme ways. Look at video 16, Triangle Taiko performing "Miyake," at *http://wonglouderand-faster.com*. The taiko is placed on a low stand so that you're striking it at approximately hip level, and you must lower your body accordingly. I love this stance for several reasons. First, look at the beautiful (and perfect) diagonal line outlined by the performer's left leg and raised right arm. It's utterly dynamic. Second, look at how the bachi are situated: the left bachi is wound around the neck so that the arm has an impressive torque when unwound and flung at the drumhead. Look at how the performers hold their right bachi at a strong 90 degree angle to the body. This is so different from how we usually hold our bachi: normally, the drumstick extends out from the hand and follows the line of the arm, lengthening it in a graceful and dynamic way that channels ki in an almost electric manner. In "Miyake," holding the bachi in a 90 degree angle doesn't stop the movement of ki; instead, I think it has the effect of bunching ki up in the hand. Holding the bachi like this is incredibly strong *looking* and strong *feeling.*

Lowering the hips puts all your weight on your thighs. This is emblematic of a more general taiko principal that isn't usually realized in such a strenuous manner: the body's center of gravity is kept very low in taiko, as in many of the Japanese bodily arts (classical dance, or nihon buyo; martial arts; etc.). All your ki comes up from below—from the earth, from your hara. The hara is the center of your ki. It literally means "belly" or "stomach," and your energy and vital force are located here, just below the navel; it is explicitly theorized in dance, the martial arts, and taiko as the locus of, well, everything—your physical comportment and your spiritual and mental energy. Paying attention to your kata inevitably means lowering your hara, and that usually means bending the knees and putting your thighs to work.

The "Miyake" kata is particularly low, challengingly so. As if that weren't difficult enough, you continually shift your weight back and forth between your left and right legs while playing. Ideally, "Miyake" is performed by two players on one drum, one on either side. They play the same thing but in mirror image, taking turns. I learned "Miyake" from the right side, so I'm accustomed to leading off its central rhythmic motive beginning with my left bachi. The player across from me, though (usually Masaki when I played this with Triangle Taiko) does just the opposite, leading with the right hand, and the "sticking"—that is, which strokes are done by either the right or the left hand—are precisely opposite for each of us.

The central rhythmic motive for "Miyake" goes like this (from my perspective as a player on the right side of the taiko): I start out by springing up from a crouching position (more on that below) and getting into ready position, which means left leg straight and right knee bent so that all my weight is on my right thigh. My feet are flat on the floor, as they should be throughout. They're both pointed outward at about a 135 angle from the straight line I imagine beneath me. I'm looking at the drumhead. In "Miyake," your attention really needs to be on the drum, nothing else—no looking out at the audience, no smiling. This is a seriously inward piece. It's just me and this drumhead. My arms and bachi are as described above: my left arm is wrapped around my neck from in front so that the bottom of my left bachi is next to my right ear, and it's wrapped so tightly around my neck that I can see the other end of the bachi in the peripheral vision of my left eye. My right arm is fully extended, horizontal to the floor, and its bachi is also horizontal to the floor, held at a right angle to my arm.

The first stroke is from my left hand. Without shifting my weight—without moving anything except that arm—I unwind my left arm and extend it full length so that it connects with the center of the drumhead. If I've gotten my spacing right, I am in exactly the right place, exactly one arm's length away from the drumhead. Of course, it's necessary to get this exactly right from the get-go—from the moment I spring up from my crouch—because there's no time or allowance for shifting around and getting repositioned. That would be completely amateurish and out of keeping with the strong, exacting focus of "Miyake." "Miyake" is about strength, perfection, and focus. I unwind my left arm, let the bachi snap forward carrying the weight of my arm, and DON, it connects with the drumhead and bounces back three inches, ending in a 90 angle to my arm, which I hold straight. I stay in this pose for a second. It's a frozen moment—so much ki went into that one stroke. Letting that ki resettle in a split second of inaction is essential: it's a small second of *ma,* that stillness and silence which defines action. Then I lift my left arm about six inches, from the shoulder, so that it is exactly horizontal to the ground. Locking into this kata is incredibly satisfying: both arms are now fully extended and parallel to the ground, and that gesture of raising the one arm and freezing is powerful. It's like brandishing both bachi—*grrrr!*—but without the loss of control that would result from merely enacting power rather than *being* power.

But this lasts for only a second. In one coordinated movement, I sweep my right arm across my body and strike the drumhead at the same time that I shift my weight to my left knee, pivoting my weight onto my left thigh. And then, in one more series of simultaneous movements, I move back into my original position: my arms swing back to the right and end up as before, right arm fully extended and left arm around my neck. My weight pivots back onto my right leg and my right knee bends deeply as my left leg extends straight. I'm ready to start over.

All that has taken approximately four seconds, and I'm only halfway through the first motive. Now I hit the drum twice—left! right!—in quick succession, and I shift my weight from right to left leg at the same time so that it fully arrives on my left leg when I strike with my right hand. This is very satisfying because that second strike—*DON!* (right)—has the full weight of my body behind it. If I do this move correctly, it feels fantastic: the literal weight of my body is flung through my right arm and out my hand, and it barrels along the full length of my bachi and out its end, *DON!* It's what things should feel like all the time if your kata were always perfect.

But this movement isn't finished until I pivot out of it and back into ready position, back where I started . . . and that must happen very quickly. I will need to execute this complete set of moves all over again in one second. It took a lot of ki to do just this much, and now I need to do it again. I fling myself away from the drum. I arrive back in ready position, and this time I've pushed my hara even lower and my right knee bends even more deeply and my god it hurts, but I'm determined to get *into* and then *hold* this kata for a priceless, perfect second. I'm still staring intently, only, at the drumhead, but if I've done it right, I can feel the audience respond even without looking at them. Ki rolls off them and over me—I feel it. Their ki is saying, *This is strong, this is dramatic.* I'm already breathing hard, but their ki floods into me and I'm reenergized, I'm ready to do it again, and again.

6

Pain and the Body Politic

Taiko Players Talk about Blisters and More

The taiko players I know are driven by a sense of mission. They tend to feel that taiko is one of the most compelling things anyone, anywhere, could do. They spend little time engaged in reflexive consideration of the deepest terms of their own engagement—they are too busy playing. For an invented tradition so thoroughly embedded in political histories, taiko has given rise to narratives astonishingly devoid of anger or pain, which most taiko players seem to prefer. Indeed, the Southern California taiko scene is overwhelmingly a leisure environment filled with upper-middle-class Asian American amateurs who are willing to cite pride in heritage but are consistently unlikely to acknowledge the radical conditions that taiko prophesies.

Taiko players are less and less likely, as time goes on, to address the specific circumstances that drew young Japanese Americans and other Asian Americans to this loud, exuberant form of performance in the 1970s and 1980s. Taiko was seized upon in California by Sansei, third-generation Japanese Americans, and then by other young Americans of Asian descent, when the Asian American Movement emerged, alongside other identity movements of that period. Anger over the Japanese American incarceration of 1942–45 was one of the drivers for the movement: that trauma helped create the political category of the Asian American. Lapsing back into silence about those hurts is the price of success.

I turn to the injury as a site of pain. Martha Stoddard Holmes and Tod Chambers (2005, 136) write that "a cultural history of pain . . . is the history of pain's cultural products." I begin with an inspection rooted in praxis and transmission, woven through with the ache of wrong and the dull stupidities of repetition. This is a self-examination: I evoke the proactive practice of checking your own breasts for lumps. This willing reflexivity means recognizing one's own body as a place of injury and memory. Taiko has left its marks and its sounds on/in my body.

SELF-EXAMINATION

For twelve years I played taiko several times a week. I now hear a persistent rustle in my left ear—a low vibrating hum that sounds every two or three seconds. It starts softly and then gets louder and stops. Then it does this again, and again, endlessly. I'm aware of it only when I'm in quiet places, especially lying in bed at night, when I sometimes listen to it with mixed horror and pride. After rehearsals it thrummed loudly in my head and would take a while to subside to its usual quiet purr. It sounds nothing like taiko, but it is an aftereffect, an echo of the loud sounds I immersed myself in for so many years.

My hands are a map of taiko past and present. Blisters and calluses come and go. I came to love the progression of playing a lot, several times a week, so that blisters formed and hardened into dry scabs and eventually became calluses. Every few months I achieved the perfect calluses, depending on our performance schedule: four on my right hand (the hand that works the hardest) and one on my left. Three on my right hand were at the top of the palm, at the base of my middle, ring, and little fingers, and the fourth was about three-quarters of an inch below my index finger, further into my palm. At their best, all four of these calluses were hard yellow bumps, sometimes with dark subterranean spots left over from blood blisters. My left hand usually got only one callus, at the base of my little finger. If I didn't play much—say, only once a week for rehearsal—the calluses worked loose, gradually peeling off and leaving soft new skin behind that was a blister waiting to happen. That's how I thought of my soft hands: as a blister waiting to happen. The absence of callused labor both was a mark of shame and anticipated pain that would again lead to pride.

Two of my fingers have stiff joints, probably from old fractures. Sometimes you whack your hand by accident when you play. I can't say how many times I've done this—more than I can count—but I'm familiar with the sharp impact and a buzzing feeling of numb shock, and then the throbbing pain that follows. If I hit myself, it was usually during a performance, but I never stopped or acknowledged it—I kept playing, and the heart of that stoicism was the effort never to break out from the group. At least two of those whacks resulted in what I'd guess were small fractures: the joints (in my right index finger and, another time, my left thumb) turned dark red and hurt quite a lot for quite a while. My left thumb now clicks when I flex it— I've picked up the habit of flexing it because it's pleasurable to feel the stiffness pop out and the thumb's full range of motion open. My right index finger is another matter, though: it's permanently stiff. When I make a fist, I can almost but not quite get that finger to wrap itself closed—it won't go the final fraction of an inch.

My pride is macho and masochistic. It comes from a world where pain is a sign of effort. Why didn't we wear earplugs? you might ask. Of course, we should have, and I should have asked Rev. Tom to make it a policy for his classes. It's not the aural damage I'm proud of—it's the fact that taiko has left its mark on me.

LOCATING THE BODY POLITIC

I have written elsewhere about taiko players' constant conversations about joy (Wong 2004, 195; 2008, 76–77). Joy is a central fact of the taiko experience—especially for Asian American women—and I don't mean to downplay it here, though I have been too ready to theorize it as a performative mechanism for empowerment. The play of pain and masochism is equally important in taiko praxis. The experience of, and pleasure in, pain defines the very body that then exults in its own presence. To bring this into view, I draw connections between the Japanese American incarceration, Asian American identifications, the cross-generational effects of pain, Japanese postwar ideas about the Japanese body, and Japanese American ideas about Japan.

Taiko makes possible the formation of a loud Japanese/Asian/American body politic in the postincarceration public sphere. Moving from the particular to the collective body is the key challenge in ethnography: the researcher must explain how the people she knows represent something bigger than themselves that is shaped by hierarchies of authority and control. As scholars of performance, we easily intuit how an individual body helps create a body politic through performance, yet this is also the matter most difficult to explain. And whose body politic? A body politic is always present, even in moments when the state is benign and distracted. Writing during the Iraq War, Judith Butler (2004, 25) asked why the body is regarded as autonomous and our own. She questioned whether an assumed bodily integrity is organically related to self-determination and whether a politics of the body can "open up" or foreclose connections to other bodies:

> Constituted as a social phenomenon in the public sphere, my body is and is not mine. Given over from the start to the world of others, it bears their imprint, is formed within the crucible of social life; only later, and with some uncertainty, do I lay claim to my body as my own, if, in fact, I ever do. Indeed, if I deny that prior to the formation of my "will," my body related me to others whom I did not choose to have in proximity to myself, if I build a notion of "autonomy" on the basis of the denial of this sphere of a primary and unwilled physical proximity with others, then am I denying the social conditions of my embodiment in the name of autonomy? (26)

Is there a taiko body politic at this historical moment, two generations out from the Japanese American incarceration, during an interlude when (many) Japanese Americans are part of a privileged upper middle class for whom taiko is a leisure activity, when Asian Americans are thoroughly ensconced in the US imagination as model minorities, regarded as flush with educational privilege and transnational capital . . . and when taiko players of European descent are flocking to the drums, eager to believe that anyone can play taiko? At this precise moment, how does taiko provide an ideal stage for exploring the distribution of pain across generations and bodies, shared through anger and memory?[1] Surely a body politic can be varied, mixed, assorted, ungainly, poorly assembled, awkward, and straining at the seams. Sometimes I think that too many kinds of people claim the right to be part of the taiko body politic.

FAILING AT FORM

Japanese Americans regard Japanese taiko players with respect, envy, resentment, and defiance, all at once. Japanese American, other Asian American, and indeed non-Japanese taiko players generally deeply romanticize Japanese taiko. It is always more authoritative than American taiko, and the line of interest and exploration is almost entirely unidirectional: it is understood that North American taiko players need to know as much as they can about Japanese taiko, but the reverse is not true. As a result, the relationship of North American practice to Japanese form is both apprehensive and submissive.[2] A North American taiko player should emulate Japanese kata (stance), but this sets up an anticipation of failure because North American taiko is never authoritative. Yet innovation and other changes are ubiquitous: few North American taiko groups choose to play only Japanese repertoire, and many are composing new pieces and deliberately creating specifically North American repertoire. The dance scholar Thomas DeFrantz (2005, 660) offers a useful example of how insurgents like these can participate in a high-status practice. He shows that the Alvin Ailey American Dance Theater succeeded because its Black company achieved both "mastery of form" and "deformation of mastery," terms borrowed from Houston Baker—that is, through Ailey's choreography, the company embodied and enacted both an expert mastery of dancerly technique informed by ballet genealogy and a distinctively African American sensibility that signified on those forms.[3] Similarly, North American taiko players invoke Japanese form but comment on it through change, extension, rejection, and even parody. The unspoken but always present relationship between the authoritative original and its feisty, inauthentic, immigrant offspring is constantly at work.

Yet the Japanese body isn't stable either. The anthropologist Laura Spielvogel (2003, 39–40) argues that the body has long served as "an extension of the nation" in Japan and suggests that Japanese attitudes toward sports offer a window onto Japan-US relations. The militaristic Japanese government enforced standardized callisthenic routines in the first half the twentieth century, promoting "a nationalist spirit . . . encoded in the body through a repetition of form," based on the Zen principle of the deep interrelationship of the body and spirit. This body was effectively defeated and rendered "diseased and starving" by the American military, which then nursed it back to health using Western principles of hygiene and medicine that transformed the corporeal national spirit into a modernized body, ready to engage with democracy and global capitalism. American aerobics and fitness clubs were imported to Japan in the 1980s and became popular among leisure-class women by the 1990s, and Spielvogel argues that these clubs produced a thin but muscular body that represented a powerful conflation of values: health and beauty could be attained in spaces for middle-class women who were otherwise subject to pervasive patriarchal expectations of selflessness and domestic service (84–85). Yet the shift was not a straight line from the militaristic, disciplined Japanese body to a commodified, modern, disciplined Western body. The role of pain in both suggests through lines that trouble any tidy narrative of postwar total transformation. As Spielvogel writes, "Like martial arts training, fitness clubs demand working through pain and discomfort to achieve a sense of accomplishment" (87).

The regard that North American taiko players have for the Japanese taiko body often involves a tacit admiration for extreme practices. The Japanese taiko player's body is unnaturally strong: it emerges out of rigorous denial and endures pain without acknowledgment or admission. That body is always rebuking the North American taiko body. The North American body is often flabby, old, and out of shape. Maceo Hernández, a Southern California taiko teacher, reportedly tells his students to "play through the pain." He's Mexican American, not Japanese American, but he was trained in Japan by the influential group Za Ondekoza, undergoing an extraordinarily intense and sustained socialization as a taiko player while still a teenager. A documentary about Hernández details his rigorous physical regimen, as well as the loss of his left leg after metal pipes rolled off a truck and landed on him while he was out running (Esaki 1993).[4] Ondekoza's extreme approach to the body is deeply admired by most taiko players but rarely imitated. Ondekoza was one of the earliest Japanese kumi-daiko groups, and its members set the bar with a physicality that fascinates both audiences and amateur players: they practice an excessive fitness that is framed as necessary for the best playing. They ran incessantly, beginning the day by running six or more miles. Ondekoza's philosophy is based on "Sogakuron," the idea that running, music, and meditation reflect life energy and are therefore closely related.[5] For their international debut, in 1975, they ran the Boston Marathon and then played a concert at the finish line. Since then, they have completed many "running tours" and "marathon tours," in which combine extraordinary long-distance runs with concert performances.[6] During their Marathon Live Tour in 2002, the group ran the almost four hundred miles from Sado Island to Mount Fuji and gave three concerts en route. And so on.

The anthropologist Shawn Bender (2012, 179–82) has argued that taiko was associated with ultranationalist, militarist fascism in prewar Japan (see previous chapter), and Tatsu Aoki, a Japanese American *Shin Issei* improviser, told me he thinks taiko is "totalitarian" in the way that it models discipline and obedience, even though it also offers tools for social presence and identity work.[7] The imagined Japanese propensity for aesthetic and physical extremity haunts North American taiko players. But for Japanese Americans, that extremity is also a strategy for reconstitution: it is a means of reaching back to a body uninjured by incarceration or US history.

TALKING ABOUT PAIN

In 2007, many of us in Satori Daiko were feeling our age. Those of us in our forties and fifties were beset with physical problems, some caused by taiko and some not, all of which affected our playing. LizAnn had had hip replacement surgery a year after arthritis left her with bone rubbing on bone. Judi had rotator cuff surgery for one shoulder and was planning to have it for the other; she didn't play at all for four months. Harriet had shoulder problems too. Rev. Tom's knee had been bothering him for at least five years. A student in one of his other classes left somewhat bitterly because of shoulder pain.

I asked several of my taiko friends about pain and taiko. I don't know any taiko group that has specific policies or preventive measures for repetitive stress injuries, nor is it my purpose to call anyone out for the problem, nor do I think the deeper affective understanding of pain should (or could) change. Taiko players warm up and stretch and have extensive techniques that prepare the body physically, mentally, and spiritually for the work of playing. The following conversation shows how my friends and teacher regarded pain as the price of taiko.[8] For them pain was a sign of real effort, was located in minute corners of the body that could be addressed with precision, and was evidence that you were playing wrong. Some of these attitudes are contradictory precisely because they are rooted in a very strong belief system that outlines affective relationships to the body.

We had just played a gig in San Pedro—a private birthday party—and were in Rev. Tom's van, waiting for everyone to finish packing up so we could all go find a restaurant and have a late dinner. While sitting in the dark van, I asked Shirley and Beverly whether they ever experienced pain as taiko players. Both were in their fifties and had played for many years. Listen to audio example 2, interview with Shirley Gutierrez and Beverly Murata about taiko and pain, February 22, 2007, at *http://wonglouderandfaster.com*, transcribed here:

Shirley	I don't get pain playing taiko.
Deborah	What about blisters, don't you get blisters?
Shirley	Yeah, but that's hardly pain...
Deborah	That doesn't count as pain?
Beverly	My arm – I don't know what I did to it, but it still – I keep injuring it.
Deborah	You keep injuring your shoulder?
Beverly	It starts here, and it keeps going –
Deborah	Your right shoulder?
Beverly	– down my arm.
Deborah	Really? When does it hurt?
Beverly	Like tonight when I was playing. When I do a lifting-up motion.
Deborah	When you raise your arm above your shoulder?

Beverly	That's right. No, even just like this –
Deborah	Like that, wow. As high as your shoulder. What do you do when it hurts?
Beverly	Hm?
Deborah	What do you do when it hurts? You're playing, and it hurts – what do you do?
Beverly	Just keep playing! [*laughs*]
Deborah	Just keep playing! [*We both laugh out loud.*]
Shirley	You can't stop once you start.
Deborah	Why not? [*We all three laugh more quietly.*] [*pause*] I mean, are taiko players all a bunch of masochists? That's what I'm wondering – that's what I'm after here.
Beverly	Yes.
Shirley	Yes.
Beverly	[*laughs*] The show must go on!
Deborah	[*laughs*] [*pause*] But – have you always had that pain in your shoulder?
Beverly	No, it's been like the last couple months.
Deborah	Oh, it's recent.
Beverly	It gets better, and then it gets worse, and then you know, it gets better…
Shirley	[*quietly*] Maybe it gets better when you rest it.
Beverly	And then I lift up something heavy and I think I just re-… do whatever injury…
Deborah	Is it only when you play taiko?
Beverly	No. It's when I lift – lifting… [*she gestures*]
Deborah	Like – lifting a… briefcase. [*Beverly nods*]
Deborah	OK. Do you think it's taiko-caused, or… something else? [*She nods.*] OK. OK. [*to Shirley*] You never get blisters??? Get outta here!
Beverly	I get little blisters.
Shirley	Weeell – a little bit, but not…
Beverly	Especially if I haven't played for a little while.
Deborah	Yeah, exactly.
Shirley	But if you get a blister forming, if you just, like, put a pin in it and let the water out, and then it doesn't pop and then it doesn't hurt.
Deborah	OK. What about if you play, like, the next day?
Shirley	If I play the next day, you have to catch it before it… [*very precisely*] popssss….
Deborah	So you have this whole… technique!
Shirley	And then it doesn't hurt.
Deborah	Really?!
Shirley	The only reason it hurts is because it pops and then you've got all that other stuff exposed.
Beverly	Right.
Shirley	But if the skin doesn't break and pop, [*whispers*] it doesn't hurt.

Deborah	So you do have a method basically, you don't apparently pick at them or anything like that. You just carefully pop them with a little pin...
Shirley	Yeah. You just, like, in the little corner, just put in a little hole and sssssquish out the water... [*pause*] That's it.
Deborah	That's it.
Shirley	And then it doesn't pop and it doesn't hurt!
Deborah	Wow. I need to take lessons from you or something, cuz...
Shirley	But you know, if you let it pop, then it's gonna hurt – all that skin underneath, exposed...
Deborah	It's raw.
Shirley	That's when it hurts.
Deborah	Do you ever get blood blisters?
Shirley	Nnn-no.
Deborah	Never! Dang. All right, where do you get blisters when you get 'em?
Shirley	Just like maybe... Around here.
Deborah	Oh really? That's pretty different from where I get them... What about – have you been playing a lot recently? Have you gotten blisters recently? [*She shakes her head.*] OK. Do you get pain anywhere else, ever, anytime, when you play?
Shirley	I used to, lifting up taiko... I don't anymore.
Deborah	Do you know why you don't anymore?
Shirley	Uhhh... I think – well, my physical therapist said –
Deborah	Oh!
Shirley	– it was probably pain from playing taiko, so he said take it easy for a couple of months.
Deborah	So hold it, you went to a physical therapist!
Shirley	No! I was going to a physical therapist before –
Deborah	Oh!
Shirley	– but since I was there, I thought, you know what? When I reach back, sometimes it hurts up here, so [*unintelligible*]. But if you, like, take it easy on taiko for a couple of months, you'll find that it's gonna be a lot better.
Deborah	Wow. What do you think he meant by taking it easy?
Shirley	Not... playing all out.
Deborah	All out. OK. [*Several other members of Satori Daiko get in the van and the doors are closed.*]
Shirley	It came at the time when we had a holiday, so we had a break.
Deborah	A natural break?
Shirley	Yeah.
Deborah	So it actually got better...
Shirley	Mm.

Deborah	Not to be nosy, but was that when you were going about your knee…?
Shirley	Mm. So I said, you know what? Can you work on my shoulder too?
Deborah	Hmmm. What did he do when he worked on it?
Shirley	Ummm… Stretching it, and massaging it… And I was doing some exercises on the machines.
Deborah	Oh wow, so you had several things you were up to. Did he tell you to keep doing any of those things, just as a preventative thing?
Shirley	Ummm… no.
Deborah	Just stop playing taiko for a while! [*laughs*] Oh my gosh. So the knee thing wasn't related to taiko, right?
Shirley	No.
Deborah	OK. Do you ever hurt the next day, after playing?
Shirley	Uhhh – not the next day. Only from carrying the drums.
Deborah	[*laughs incredulously*] How do you know it's that! [*Rev. Tom starts up the van. We're on the move.*]
Shirley	Well, it's usually my back!
Deborah	Ohhh, OK. You never ache the next day? OK, this woman is unreal…
Rev. Tom	[*From the driver's seat.*] Huh?
Deborah	I'm asking Shirley about pain.
Rev. Tom	Pain!
Deborah	She doesn't hurt the next day, ever.
Rev. Tom	Oh. From taiko?
Deborah	Just from – what did you say? Just from –
Shirley	– just from carrying the taikos.
Rev. Tom	From carrying the taiko…
Deborah	Something's wrong with this picture! Beverly, do you ever hurt the next day?
Beverly	Yeah.
Deborah	Me too. Where – where do you hurt?
Beverly	It depends on where I played wrong. [*cackles*]
Deborah	Where you played wrong? What did you say?
Beverly	Well, you know… If I play odaiko – [*unintelligible*]. Then I hurt here…
Deborah	Oh. Yeah. [*pause*]
Rev. Tom	You know, even though we played forty minutes tonight, I'm not going to feel it tomorrow. But when we played that four minutes – four minutes! –
Beverly	Yeah, but you played really hard.
Rev. Tom	– four minutes at the – where was it – at the Biltmore Hotel? And the next day I was sore.
Deborah	Really?

Rev. Tom	Yeah.
Deborah	What's the difference?
Rev. Tom	Because! I played, like, 200%.
Beverly	He was playing really hard!
Deborah	Oh, 200%!
Rev. Tom	On odaiko.
Deborah	Whhhhy did you put yourself out that day? Why –
Rev. Tom	'Cause there were only –
Beverly	– Four of us.
Rev. Tom	Four of us.
Deborah	Oh, OK.
Shirley	He only had four minutes of fame.
Rev. Tom	There was a really big crowd.
Deborah	Big crowd, big room.
Rev. Tom	I wanted to make, you know, a big impact in the shortest amount of time.
Deborah	So you hurt the next day.
Rev. Tom	Yeah. You know, it's not the length of time – it's what you put into it.
Deborah	Ohhhhhh, OK.
Rev. Tom	It's what you put into it. [*We all laugh quietly and knowingly.*] So what does that say, Shirley??? [*Loud laughter all around.*]
Shirley	It might say I'm in better shape than you are!

Notice the constellation of values around pain. Injuring and reinjuring yourself is business as usual. The expectation that you *just keep playing* even if you're hurting is both understood and a matter of amused self-awareness. Notice Shirley's precise attention to blisters and her pleasure in emptying them to prevent pain. Her rhythmic enunciation of prevented pain (*and then it doesn't pop and then it doesn't hurt*) and her onomatopoetic enjoyment of removing the possibility of pain (*just put in a little hole and ssssquish out the water*) are striking. She's talking literally about the matter of blisters, but it's hard not to hear at least a little metaphorical sensibility at work (*But you know, if you let it pop, then it's gonna hurt—all that skin underneath, exposed . . .*). Beverly and Rev. Tom agree that post-performance soreness is the result of either playing incorrectly (tensely) or playing "hard," all out, which is a good thing. *What you put into it* is presumably what you get out of it, and in this case, more is more, and the mark of success is pain.

Far more research has been done on music as therapy than on music and pain. Indeed, taiko is often referenced as a kind of ersatz therapy—how many times have I been told "You must get rid of a lot of stress by hitting those drums!"—and sometimes literally wielded as therapy and intervention for at-risk youths and the mentally ill. Broader Western ideas about music as a panacea frame such assumptions.[9] But if taiko wears out the body in certain ways, and if it tears and ruptures our hidden anatomical structures that are most drumlike, then this is the cost: you have to give it your all; its noisy pleasures are earned only at a certain expense.

JAPANESE → JAPANESE AMERICAN PAIN

As I discussed in chapter 5, the Manzanar Pilgrimage was a rare example of taiko players returning to a site of damage and playing through it. Conversely, Japanese culture is famously full of pain, self-denial, and extreme ascetic practices. Writing at length about the bodily enculturation that took place during his Japanese taiko training (specifically through the practices of two groups, Sukeroku and Kodo), Bender (2012, 131–32) argues that disciplining the body is always about specific social orders. Kodo makes apprentice musicians sit *seiza* at meals, in the traditional Japanese position with legs folded under the body, feet tucked under the buttocks, hands resting in the lap. "Even though the pain was intense," Bender writes, the explanation for this rule was that the practice rid young apprentices' bodies of the Western habit of sitting in chairs and thus returned them to traditional habits, and indeed they were told that they would "get used to it." Kodo's training process attends to all aspects of apprentices' movement, from opening and closing doors to eating with chopsticks, in order to discipline their bodies into mindful, efficient, and "Japanese" habits; all movements are conceived of as part of the experience of playing taiko. Kodo's performances enact a body totally dedicated to taiko.

Taiko is an extreme sport, but this will not impress dance scholars, who are deeply familiar with the masochistic imprint left on their entire discipline by ballet. The Balanchine regime may be a specific oddity in a long history of differentiated practices, but it is an extension of ideologies more than a hundred years old. Balanchine's anorexic, White, North American ballerina has a large presence, given her frailty. The psychologist Jock Abra (1987, 33) writes that ballet is utterly defined by pain, injury, and weariness. But its pain-filled praxis is supposed to be invisible. One could cite many other kinds of performance that memorialize and channel real pain and injury, from Khmer court dance in diaspora to rituals of commemoration at the Vietnam War Memorial in Washington DC. As Judith Hamera (2002, 65) writes, "Dance technique offers more than protocols for reading the body; it is also a technology of subjectivity, a template organizing sociality, and an archive that links subjectivities and socialities to history. As archive, technique contains and organizes the traces and residues dance leaves behind, and out of which it forms again: injuries, vocabulary, relationships." The bodily techniques of any social practice thus contain and reveal the "sociality" of the community in movement, and the codification of motion in technique is at once history making and history telling.

Injury is especially likely to be woven into choreographic principles. Elaine Scarry (1985, 279) argues that inflicting pain is about unmaking, so she notes that "achieving an understanding of social justice may require that we first come to an understanding of making and unmaking." Understanding taiko as an Asian American form of making thus requires equal attention to what has been unmade, and a critical engagement with the techniques that disarticulate(d) the body politic.

Karen Shimakawa's (2002, 4) formulation of Asian American abjection as a spectacle of the US nation is useful here because she opens up the abject as a dynamic, shifting formation central to national identity.[10] Drawing from Kristeva, she argues that the Asian American as repulsive Other is necessary to any sense of the norm, writing, "I utilize *abjection* as a descriptive paradigm in order to posit a way of understanding the relationship linking the psychic, symbolic, legal, and aesthetic dimensions of national identity as they are performed . . . by Asian Americans." Like Shimakawa, I aim to address "the complex relationship between affective experience and cultural expression in the formation of Asian Americanness," by interrogating a form whose participants continually deny the place of pain and anger in their motivations while reveling in the marks of pain on their bodies. The specific injury of the World War II incarceration has been the focus of much work in Asian American studies, some of which addresses how it has been carried into later generations. In his memoir, David Mura (1995, 246) records his personal process of coming into political consciousness, noting that "my identity, the most intimate of feelings about my own sexuality, were directly tied to what had happened nearly fifty years ago—the signing of Executive Order No. 9066 and the internment of the Japanese American community." He ponders his deepseated anger and abjection:

> How does the rage latent in any shame break the surface? When the sources of the rage aren't identified, the person directs the rage at any number of objects—intimate relationships, chance encounters on the street, daily life. The destruction such unexamined rage can wreak is enormous. . . .
>
> I do not think my parents could admit their rage: it was stamped down in the camps, in the Japanese concept of *gaman*—enduring, preserving; it was muted by their belief that by fitting in, by forgetting their cultural past, by becoming the model minority, they could assimilate. Their rage would have destroyed this belief. . . .
>
> Yet I know the rage was there, shaping their lives, the world of my childhood. (252–53)

Near the end of this memoir, Mura puts the pieces together in a dramatic act of making: he connects his Nisei parents' experience of incarceration, their denial of rage and abjection, and its impact on his understanding of masculinity and the right to belong. He calls this complex "the internalized internment camp," unacknowledged by the Nisei father and understood only belatedly, at great cost, by the Sansei son (261).

My teacher Rev. Tom Kurai came to taiko in the mid-1970s, at the same time when he began to identify with Sansei rage over the incarceration; he was an early member of the Manzanar Committee. A photograph of him and his friend Kenny Endo, both later leading Japanese American taiko teachers, documents their participation in the 1975 Manzanar Pilgrimage (see figure 27, Tom Kurai and Kenny Endo playing taiko at the 1975 Manzanar Pilgrimage, at *http://wonglouderand-faster.com*). This photo captures a turning point in both their lives, when they each turned to taiko as a performative means to simultaneously explore heritage and define themselves as Japanese American. Neither of them had yet "become" a taiko player, but this performance transformed them into just that. Tom was twenty-eight. He and Kenny wanted to contribute something to the pilgrimage, so they pulled out one of the taiko used in Zen Buddhist ritual at Tom's father's temple in Los Angeles (in front of Tom on the left) and borrowed a tiny American-made taiko from a friend; the latter didn't have a stand, so they propped it up on a box (played by Kenny, on the right). They didn't know how to play any taiko pieces, so they just jammed, and the participants loved it. Bon-odori was by then already reestablished in California Japanese American Buddhist communities, and it was incorporated into the Manzanar Pilgrimage ritual. Taiko and dance were thus central to the rituals of memory and politicization self-consciously created by postwar Japanese Americans, and Rev. Tom's motivation to learn taiko was inextricably bound up with his political awakening.

As I wrote in the previous chapter, Asian American women articulate, define, explore, and rechannel their anger through taiko, and Japanese American men move between macho display and playfully ironic spectacles of their bodies through taiko. Anger, denial, and the continued effects of racist injury are part of the Asian American experience and are acted out in ways that range from vitriolic performance art to the docility of obedient model minorities. The transpacific circulation of these ideas shapes Asian American taiko players' attitudes toward the body as a memorial to pain. This body does its work at a crossroads where the panopticon of a racialized society offers certain conditions for spectacularized visibility and presence. From the outside, taiko looks and sounds good: its celebratory color offers a feel-good thrill to any multicultural gathering, where the aim is usually to do nothing more or less than that—to feel good. From within, a good taiko group is generated by the willingness to give oneself over to the group and to play through pain by drawing on nostalgic ideas about selfless bodily denial and wordless suffering. The framing gesture of *gaman*—the key Issei and Nisei value and strategy that enabled survival in the camps—folds into Sansei and Yonsei willingness to play through coordinated pain to assert a joyful presence. Gaman, enduring the seemingly unbearable with patience and dignity, allows the taiko player to assert *Shikata ga nai,* it can't be helped.

But that gaman is grounded in a dogged insistence on an apolitical taiko, in which heritage is safely celebrated but any explicit reference to anger is rare. The generative anger over the incarceration has given way to a middle-class content-ment, and the core pain of taiko is refashioned as romanticized authenticity rather than a historically specific injury.[11] Susan Leigh Foster (2003, 410) reminds us to attend to "the amount and kind of physical labor that goes in to establishing the connection among bodies," and in this case a huge amount of dedicated work goes into bypassing the pain and citing not it but instead a preincarceration, preimmi-gration body as a way to reconstitute history.

Must Japanese Americans and other Asian Americans endlessly perform their own degradation? The question is whether the site of trauma can be recuperated by revisiting it in a way that changes how it is remembered and known. The pho-tographer Andrew Freeman documents buildings in the desert towns around Manzanar that are constructed out of barracks removed and recycled from the incarceration camp after it closed in 1946. Some of the contemporary owners—none of them Japanese American—are proud to own a piece of history, to reoc-cupy history.[12] The repeated thing becomes merely a piece of history.

I go to taiko for its joy. But that joy will not be a form of Asian American cul-tural production unless we acknowledge that taiko performs a rearticulated body. Scarry argues that the survivor must remake the world shattered by pain, but that pain itself is then one of the first things referenced through language—or as I would say, through performance.[13] Butler (2004, 18) calls for "hearing beyond what we are able to hear." We bring the pain back by insisting it's our strength. Maybe it is. But if the body is "articulate matter" (Foster 2003, 395), then it is discursively able to state only what we are willing to hear, no matter how loud.

7

Cruising the Pac Rim

Driven to Thrill

I would like to get a whole DVD full of the Mitsubishi Girl's music, and an autographed picture too..of course..they are sooo cool..and so is the commercial :-)

—MICHAEL, JULY 30, 2005

Taiko was featured in a 2005 TV ad for a car. In this chapter, I triangulate cars, taiko, Asian Americans, the Pacific Rim, mobile culture, globalization, and transnationalism. I work through three sites here, each defined in different ways and subject to different interpretive issues. The first is the TV commercial, the second is the transnational movement of musics through globalized economies, and the third is an ethnographic encounter in which I participated.

Asian American studies scholars have productively engaged with Asian popular culture as part of Asian America. Japanese popular culture in particular—anime, Hello Kitty paraphernalia made "hip" via ironic consumption, and so on—is omnipresent in West Coast Asian American youth culture. The circulation of material goods between "Asia" and the US reflects new global economies and the inheritance of high orientalism, which combine to create odd new Asian–North American encounters that are sometimes deliberately deracinated and positioned as an apolitical, postmodernist aesthetic. Taiko is a potential response to such postindustrial constructions of a world beyond race and class, even though it too is the result of Pacific flows. If its loud, sweaty, and folkloric gestures seem hopelessly out of step to some young Asian Americans (Gen Y Asian Americans), then it bears asking how the Asian or Asian American body now operates in a new Pacific theater of economic and cultural exchange. Paul Gilroy's (1993) powerful conceptualization of the Black Atlantic forced a new way of thinking about the historical movements of people and/as goods and a necessary understanding of culture and difference as interconstitutive. The Asian and Asian American Pacific

173

likewise repoliticizes the region, making visible the links between corporate and liberal humanist constructions of an open Pacific Rim.

The political economies of musical transnationalism drive virtually all musical practices in the twenty-first century. Few musics are beyond these forces: most popular, art, and folk musics are mediated and mobile. As Timothy D. Taylor (2016, 82) writes, "Perhaps the main symptom of globalization in the cultural industries has been their growing internationalization as parts of multinational corporations," and he traces the music industry in neoliberal capitalism as a cultural form with pervasive effects. The movement of musics through globalized economies and across national borders shapes how ideologies of difference are constructed and maintained. Race and gender are always more than a reflection of the local.

Thick interpretive work on specific places, practices, peoples, and moments is important and necessary but should reveal the movement between the local and the global. Taylor (2016, 182) urges us to "study down" and attend to the experiences of musicians making choices in globalized neoliberal capitalism. Ideally, our critical work will circle back and activate gendered and raced understandings of theory and methodology. In this chapter, I offer several kinds of interpretive work, including reading a fixed object, reading the actions of participants, reading what participants say about their own actions, reading my own experience, reading theory, and reading associatively between spheres. This chapter is meant to be like anti-illusionist theater in the Brechtian sense, in which the seams show and you aren't swept up by theoretical, commodified, or ethnographic spectacle. The ethnography of mediated international encounter is hard work but necessary for anyone living in a borderlands or on the Pacific Rim. Finally, I hope you are left with a sense of movement and the feeling that your own identifications or commitments—as a consumer, performer, or cultural worker—can land at more than one point.

I begin with an object. The sixty-second TV commercial for the 2006 Mitsubishi Eclipse was filmed in April 2005. This ad offers rich evidence of taiko as a globalized (oriental) (erotic) commodity that is the result of Pacific Rim capitalism. It opens with three dark silhouettes against a cloudy gray sky: a large odaiko in the center with a figure before it, arms down, framed by two figures on either side. We hear a drum stroke—*DON*—and two fiery flares shoot up at each end of the stage, briefly illuminating the drummers' red costumes. We hear a solo flute—perhaps a *fue*—play a melancholy rising minor third, and the camera cuts to a red Eclipse seen from the rear driver's side. The driver's door is open. The camera jumps to a view from the front driver's side, and the driver's door shuts. As the camera cuts from behind to in front, we see and hear the door shut twice, with taiko strokes— *don DON*—layered over the sound. The camera pans across a close-up of "GT V6" on the car, and then we see the front headlights come on as the taiko begin a sustained riff: *don DON don-DON* (rest), *don DON don-DON* (rest) . . . Over those eight beats, we see the entire taiko group, now lit but still fairly far away: eight young women in red dresses, with seven chudaiko and the one large odaiko, on tiered risers. The flames flare up again, synchronized with the *DON* on beat two of the measure (*don DON*). In fast-cut shots of less than a second each, we see a hand in the dark interior of the car shift gears, a black boot hit the accelerator, and the needle on the accelerometer go up. The car whooshes by in a blur, and the camera cuts to a close-up of the odaiko player. The odaiko fills most of the frame, and we see the young woman from the waist up, bare backed, reach back and strike the drumhead with both huge bachi at once, on beat two of the pattern: *don DON don-DON*. The camera cuts to one of the car's hubcaps, which spins blurrily as we hear a gong stroke—*crrrrrrrasssssssh*—that seems to emerge from its shaky movement. We see the car swoosh by and then three taiko players, their legs spread wide, play *don-DON*. Over the next four beats—*don DON don-DON* (rest)—we see the car on a dark, wet road; we see all the taiko players; we see the flames shoot up, once again on beat two (*DON*), with another gong stroke underneath. We see two taiko players from the side—odaiko and chudaiko—raise their arms and strike their drums. We see the car on the dark, wet road as if we were looking down from a bridge; the road is lined with fluorescent white lights, and the words "Professional driver on closed course. Do not attempt" appear briefly across it. The car comes toward us and blurs out. Is it drifting? We see taiko players' hands, drumheads, and bachi for less than a second, and then the same two taiko players as before, from the side, but this time the odaiko player is out of focus and our eyes are drawn to the chudaiko player in the foreground as she strikes and shouts "YAH!" This is the first time we have heard any of the musicians' voices: it is halfway through the ad, at the twenty-eight-second mark. Inside the car, we see the driver's hand shift gears. As the car surges forward, we hear a second kakegoe (shout)—the same woman?—"Waaah!" We see the accelerometer needle shoot up toward sixty, and then the camera pans across a row of three young women furiously playing upright okedo on stands. The sound of taiko is now filled in: we hear sixteenth notes echoing the busy hand work of the bachi, even though the sound and image don't align. For a split second, we see round interior car parts—probably pistons—moving in time with the shime's sixteenth notes. We see three taiko players for less than a second before they are drowned out by a rising wall of flame and another sustained kakegoe— "WAAAAH!"—car-women-car-women-car-women, the camera shuttling back and forth as the flute plays a frantic, high-pitched riff. The odaiko player is seen again from the side, but she blurs into a silhouette as she plays. The car is driving toward a huge ball of flame. The odaiko player is now playing sixteenth notes, don-dondondon, the car is rocketing along, and we suddenly see a taiko player's face in close-up, for the first time: her eyes and eyebrows, unmistakably Asian. The flute is wailing, the car surges toward us, and we see a chudaiko head from above as a drummer's hands and bachi come down on it, *dondondondon DON!* The drums abruptly stop at the forty-three-second mark, and the car flies by: a tail of smoke and a shuddery gong stroke mark the silence. At the forty-four-second mark, we see a chudaiko player in silhouette from the side—her face and shoulders—as she inhales, then exhales, and we hear her breathe. The sonic intimacy of her breath makes it clear what's happened: climax → release. Suddenly it all starts up again— car-women-car-women-car-women, the drums and flute both wild, the car drift- ing—and at the fifty-second mark a woman screams as the car spin-drifts almost 180 degrees. The camera cuts back to a proscenium-stage shot of the taiko players as they play one last *dondondondon DON* and then stop. They don't freeze: after their last drum stroke they relax slightly, and that split-second sense of release is erotic. A man's voice says, "Introducing the all-new 2006 Mitsubishi Eclipse." The screen fades to black and we see the words "The all-new 2006 Eclipse." The camera cuts to a full-body shot of the car in repose as the narrator continues, "Available six-speed, two-hundred-and-sixty-three-horse MIVEC V6."[1] The Mitsubishi logo, three red diamonds, spins across the screen, and its impact—*splat!*—is marked by a . . . single door slam? shime strike? followed by the narrator saying, "Driven to thrill."

This commercial was shot on April 26–27, 2005, at a studio named the Stages at Playa Vista, in Southern California. It was directed by Samuel Bayer, best known for helming Nirvana's music video for "Smells like Teen Spirit" and videos for Green Day. The music is by Stewart Copeland, formerly the drummer for the Police and now a well-established composer. The taiko performers were drawn from three Southern California groups: TAIKOPROJECT, UCLA's Kyodo Taiko, and Venice Koshin Taiko. Most of the commercial's visual tropes are well estab- lished and familiar: it's assumed that the car's driver is a man, although he is never seen, and the car is a woman—indeed, it is a powerful and powerfully erotic Asian woman in a skintight red dress. If you drive the car, you drive her. The sound engineering of the commercial is intensely effective and brilliantly coordinated with visual cues.

I'm reluctant to address this Mitsubishi Eclipse commercial, because naming the endlessly repeated tropes of commercialized orientalism reiterates them. In my past writing, I have addressed the use of taiko in the 1993 film *Rising Sun* (Wong 2004, 209–14),[2] but other examples abound. Taiko players love to talk about taiko scenes in film and television because we know who the performers are: they are *known*—they usually aren't faceless generic stand-ins. In the first *Charlie's Angels* film (2000), for example, Zenshuji Zendeko Taiko is in the background playing the hell out of their drums while Bill Murray and Tim Curry as the villain go at it in sumo suits.[3] The Mitsubishi Eclipse ad is thus an almost banal place to look, because mediated racist representation is the norm. There are no pure spaces. Rather than simply offer a close reading of this ad and thereby treat it and myself as the interrogator as contained, unitary subjects and objects, respectively, I instead locate my reading as an exercise in antiracist and anti-imperialist work, with atten- tion to the experiences of those most closely involved.

One of my long-term concerns is the absence, ephemerality, and vulnerability of something that might be called an Asian American public sphere. Silence and invisibility are the twin demons of being Asian American. I search for an Asian American public sphere not out of cultural nationalism but because the visibility and audibility of communities are predicated on democracy, however defined. Minoritarian communities live their own discursive realities, which may or may not be known in the macro systems of majority culture. If there is an Asian American public sphere—and I think there is, sometimes, in some places—it is both necessary and impure. Constructing "an" Asian American public sphere or diverse Asian American public spheres creates presence, and presence creates the possibility of a tipping point. This entire project, however, is complicated by the powerfully troubling perception of Asian Americans as eternal foreigners and unassimilable Others, with one foot out the door. The new Pacific Rim generated new kinds of global distribution, but it also reactivated some very old ideas about Asian and American incongruities.

TRANSNATIONALISM AND GLOBALIZATION

Taylor (2001, 135) warns that "the term *globalization* can hide old forms of exploitation dressed up in contemporary business language." Lawrence Grossberg (2005, 147) argues that globalization goes hand in hand with the partner forces of modernization, industrialization, and late corporate capitalism. It serves the needs of a specific kind of international finance market, which emerged with postindustrial information technologies. As Grossberg puts it, "The interests of this highly mobile finance capital were not always well served by the nationally organized systems of industrial capitalism. Newly empowered neo-liberal and neo-conservative regimes in the advanced capitalist world championed a new discourse of free trade, deregulation, marketization, and privatization." Market globalization ideology was most broadly operationalized during the administrations of Ronald Reagan in the US and Margaret Thatcher in the UK. Its principles—downplayed spatial relationships, free trade, outsourcing, supply chains—drove flat-world international arrangements like the North American Free Trade Agreement and institutions like the World Trade Organization, the World Bank, and the International Monetary Fund (Friedman 2005). Grossberg (2005, 148) points to the concomitant glorification of information technology as a utopian means of democratization and its roots in older kinds of technological superiority and determinism. He suggests that two things—the movement of popular culture and the migration of "former colonial populations . . . to the centers of colonial power"—have led to a celebration of commodified hybridity largely replacing earlier fears about the homogenizing and imperialist effects of American popular culture (149). He also warns that old asymmetries have been replaced by new ones—that the "intensification" of movement and information creates new kinds of borders, despite the prevalence of public and academic discourse about porous boundaries (150).

Some of the most critically adept scholarship on transnational popular music has focused on the Pacific Rim. Shūhei Hosokawa (1997, 1999), Andrew F. Jones (2001), Tony Mitchell (2001, 2008), Christine Reiko Yano (2002), and Ian Condry (2006, 2012) have generated work that assumes interconstitutive relationships among music, multisited communities, and ideological formations. They show how these circulations are always defined by imperatives in the Asian-Western encounter. Writing about hip-hop in Japan, Condry (2006, 224n7) pushes against any assumption that it isn't "Japanese" by arguing that popular music can potentially mobilize principled globalized processes: "As Cornel West (2004, 22) says, globalization is inescapable; the question is whether it will be an American-led corporate globalization or a democratic globalization. The answer, of course, is that globalization is and will be both corporate-led and potentially democratic. This points us toward what is perhaps the more important question, namely, what kinds of social structures and motivations can drive democratic globalization? What kinds of organizing principles besides corporate capitalism can encourage transnational cultural movements? The early years of hip-hop in Japan offers some lessons." Using the Japanese word for "a place, a site where something happened," Condry offers "*genba* globalization" as a hip-hop-driven model for addressing how particular moments can "actualize . . . the global and the local simultaneously." As he puts it, genba globalization "reorients our attention away from culture flows from place to place toward questions of how global culture gains its force from the ways performances energize people in particular locations" (90).

Christopher L. Connery's (1994, 31) powerful overview of "Pacific Rim discourse," or the discursive construction of US multinational capitalism and the American right to expansionist trade, is essential to my understanding of taiko. He historicizes this practice as follows: "My argument, simply, is that the idea of the Pacific Rim came into being in the mid-1970s, that it was dominant in the U.S. geo-imaginary until the end of the 1980s, and that this dominance was determined by the particular stage of late capitalism marked by that period and by the economic and political situation of the United States in the late Cold War years." Connery argues that Pacific Rim discourse is distinctively different from earlier forms of orientalism because it is "a non-othering discourse" dedicated to rendering centers of power invisible (32). Shifting the discourse from nation-states to an ocean space meant that "the Pacific would be at its essence a noncolonial space where a pure capital would be free to operate" (40). When Japan became not only a regional but a global power, it was necessary for the US to think about the "transformative miracles" of capitalism in new ways (34). I add that Pacific Rim discourse also depends on a discursive deracination of exchange: as the center vanished, its racializing logic was also compromised and had to be reworked. As Rob Wilson and Arif Dirlik (1994, 5) observe, "The promise is always there for a new, soft, more supple form of Orientalist knowledge and transnational control rephrased as a postmodern co-prosperity sphere."

The literary theorist Rachel C. Lee (1999, 251) asserts that Pacific Rim discourse is class based. She also notes "the reluctance of Asian Americanists to be framed as experts or apologists for the new 'model minority'—the transnational Asian capitalist." As she puts it, "Asian American critics do not simply resist globalization but decry a particular form of global-Pacific studies—one that triumphantly heralds the entrepreneurial Asian transnational class" and flattens the Pacific Rim into a deracinated, classless region of "exchange" (250). Connery (1994, 43) suggests that the celebration of this Asian transnational class addressed yellow-peril fears by constructing California and especially Los Angeles as emblematic of all that was good about Pacific trade, "flush with Asian capital influx and enlivened by the 'new immigrants,' largely from Asia (read: 'good' immigrants who have money and work hard)." Note that "the futurology of Pacific Rim Discourse" could be seen as a means of taking "conceptual possession of the entire region" (Wilson and Dirlik 1994, 5, 6).

In short, the models I find most useful for thinking about Pacific Rim exchange are not celebratory. Rather than broadcast a triumphant present-future of exchange unburdened by class, race, or nation, I ask who is served by the end of difference.

FIRST PASS: RACE, GENDER, AND SEX

The Mitsubishi commercial depends on some well-established if not tired tropes in car ads. Images of women are used to sell cars, though it is in no way obvious why sex should sell cars or why the images of these women should convince consumers to buy the Eclipse. REAL! (OBJECTIFICATION & DEHUMANIZATION)

This ad was part of a broader Mitsubishi campaign, titled Driven to Thrill, which relied on a tangled mess of interrelated ideas about gender and race. The taiko commercial was the first of three focused on the release of two models, the 2006 Eclipse and the new Raider.[4] It was meant to appeal to both men and women. One of the other ads (sometimes run back to back with the taiko ad) featured no human beings but rather images of non-Mitsubishi cars "bowing" in a Japanese manner to the Eclipse while parts of the taiko ad's soundtrack were heard. The Raider ad riffed on filmic references to samurai wisdom, all drawn from stereotypical representations of "traditional" Japanese culture: images of Zen-like calligraphy and the claims that driving this car offers "the inner peace that comes from brute strength" and that "you must promise to use it only for good."

The taiko players in the first Eclipse commercial are sexy and powerful, but how exactly does that come across, and what might sexy power mean to different viewer-consumers? If the web is any indication, the sounds and images of the women playing taiko made a big impression. Between 2005 and 2007, I did several searches for the words "Mitsubishi" and "taiko" and found site after site where wildly different virtual communities discussed the commercial. Most taiko players loved it; car aficionados thought it was stylish; TV-commercial fans were enthused. The producer-curator of Estrogenius, an internet radio station devoted to women musicians, loved the ad's female strength and power.[5] These diverse taste communities were oddly (though indirectly) connected.

Carla Freeman (2001, 1007n) has argued for "an integrated feminist approach" to globalization theory and has pointed out that both globalization as a process and globalization theory as a body of work have been gendered masculine. Women are "inserted" into globalized industries and processes as laborers, and studies of their participation in those industries become a kind of localized, ground-level, feminized theoretical work in marked contrast to macro theory. Mitsubishi inserted the female taiko players into the Eclipse ad in an astonishingly literal manner. The organizing structure of the commercial is quick cuts back and forth between images of the car and images of the taiko players.[6] Two-thirds of the way into the sixty-second spot, the car and the taiko players are visually and sonically conjoined. The viewer can understand this in several ways: if you drive the Eclipse, you are therefore "like" those gorgeous and powerful women, or perhaps driving the car is "like" driving one of those gorgeous and powerful women. The ad thus works for both male and female viewers, straight or queer. The heterosexist male viewer can conflate the car and the women; the female viewer, whether straight or gay, can identify with the strong and sexy women/car. In this sense, the ad is clever, because it worked well for multiple viewers. Good for that time

Sound and visuals are intensely interrelated in the ad. Easily understood, the minute linkages of what's seen and heard are technically accomplished. Sound engineering makes the car into a shouting, thrashing Asian woman. In addressing the problem of reiteration in great depth, the critical theorist Sheng-mei Ma (2000, xi–xii) argues that evocation is necessary in order to do away with orientalist stereotypes. He describes orientalism and Asian American identity as "symbiotic." An autonomous or authentic Asian American identity is thus outside the conditions of possibility because it is already defined by racist representation. The articulation between orientalism and Asian American identity is not predetermined, though familiar patterns may be followed. The Mitsubishi ad deployed established patterns. The commercial is technically breathtaking but dreadfully predictable. The taiko players invite being understood as submissive geisha or dragon ladies, the two stereotypes available to Asian and Asian American women.[7] Butterfly and the dragon lady are both exotic and sexy, but in different ways. Butterfly is subservient, compliant, industrious, eager to please, and fragile, whereas the dragon lady is threatening, perverse, scheming, untrustworthy, and back stabbing—an exciting but untrustworthy dominatrix. The taiko players are no butterflies, and their assertiveness is not in question, so they must be dragon women. Besides, they're wearing red and are surrounded by torches that flare when they strike their drums.

The car and the musicians are not in the same place: the car has no visible human being in it besides a hand that shifts gears and a black shoe that presses the accelerator, and the taiko players are in a cavernous, dark hall lit by torches.

They're all young and incredibly fit. The "sound" of their playing links up with visual images at several key points—the opening torch flare, the closing of the car door, the doublehanded strike on the odaiko—but the audio track is heavily mixed down. The car drives along nighttime streets. A subtle but significant buildup extends over the sixty seconds: adding on musical parts creates a sense of increasing activity and excitement. At about the twenty-six-second mark, the sounds gel as Japanese festival music: they become *matsuri-bayashi* when an (unseen) *kane* and *shinobue* are added. The flute plays long sustained notes for the first twenty-five to thirty seconds and cranks into a busier and almost frantic mode after that. At the forty-two-second mark, the music stops for four crucial seconds: you hear the swish of wind as the car whooshes by, and then you see and hear one of the taiko players inhale and exhale through pursed lips, in profile, like an athlete. At that moment, you "know" that the taiko players *are* the car, because the sound of air (the sound of her body) has told you so. You barely have time to make that connection before the music starts right back up.

The taiko players' kakegoe are a key sonic element. The sound of their voices is first heard at the twenty-eight-second mark and is constant after that. Kakegoe are part of any taiko performance but in this case tie in with the long-established practice of using women's voices to eroticize commercials. Images of naked women were once woven subliminally into photographs of ice cubes in liquor ads, and the sounds of women moaning and gasping were similarly woven into the sound design of ads and film scores to create an (often subliminal) erotic effect. At the forty-eight-second mark, the car goes into a skid—a practice known as dragging or drifting in street car racing—and one woman's long, drawn-out scream picks it up sonically, reinforcing the overlaid identities (car-is-taiko-is-woman-is-car).

The images of the taiko women—or "taiko girls" or "Mitsubishi girls," as internet bloggers almost invariably called them—conflate tried and true images. The thigh- and (actually) ass-baring red costumes cite the cheongsam, the Chinese dress made famous by the actress Nancy Kwan in *The World of Suzy Wong* (1960), always skintight and slit up the thigh. I was told that the ad's costume designer also did the costumes for the film *Chicago* (2002).[8] Whereas Honō Daiko's costumes are designed to reveal the performers' upper-body musculature, these costumes deliberately evoke a predictable exotic erotics, effective because it is so familiar.

One could say that much of this is the stuff of generic sexist representation, but the Japaneseness of the car is not an afterthought—it's the core reinvention of the Driven to Thrill campaign. At one level, Asianness is visually and sonically evident everywhere in the taiko footage, but one shot makes it unmistakable. At the forty-second mark, a taiko player's eyes appear in close-up, and that image is a key visual trope, endlessly replayed in popular culture: the objectified Asian eye, usually shown as a body part unto itself, the iconic marker of Asian difference, the site/sight of Asian exoticism, inscrutability, and mystery. Once that split-second image appears, the ad is racialized beyond all discussion.

Gorgeously produced, the ad is a tour de force of its kind and depressingly easy to critique. I now step back to consider the car and taiko as exemplars of Pacific movement.

THE MITSUBISHI ECLIPSE

The anthropologist Sarah Lochlann Jain (2004, 71) argues that cars changed the American sense of self, writing that "the promise of a technology that would act entirely as a human prosthetic was crucial in consolidating a rational underpinning to a hegemonic kinematic social fantasy." She shows how a series of twentieth-century tort law decisions situated cars as benign objects and bystanders as "random parts of the environment" (61). Her work illustrates how attitudes about the automobile have structured US social life, from the rise of the suburbs to the death of public transportation. Following Jain, I view the car as a distinctively ethnicized (White American or Japanese) prosthetic that creates the terms of possibility for "culturalized" value mobilized in a circuit of desire via a particular set of links across the Pacific Rim. I do not describe this movement as open ended, because I think the so-called Mitsubushi girls are compelling precisely because of the specific histories of (Japanese) cars in the US—from Detroit to war to occupation to economic miracle to globalized industry. The car makes the taiko players sexy and powerful rather than vice versa, through a specific series of mobile fantasies.

The movement of Japanese cars into the US began in the 1970s and expanded in the 1980s. The American auto industry declined in the 1970s because of rising gasoline costs and more stringent federal emissions regulations. "Buy American" had specific meaning in the 1980s, and driving a Japanese car in certain parts of the US was asking for trouble then. Japanese-owned US-based manufacturing plants created tensions in the Midwest, especially around Detroit, where local economies were heavily dependent on the auto industry. Honda was the first Japanese company to assemble cars in the US when it opened a plant in 1982 in Ohio. That same year, twenty-seven-year-old Vincent Chin was beaten to death with a baseball bat outside a Detroit bar by two unemployed White auto plant workers who assumed he was Japanese. Tensions between Japanese plant managerial staff and American workers was reflected in films like *Gung Ho* (1986).

Most of the leading Japanese automobile manufacturers now have US-based production, and Mitsubishi is no different. However, Mitsubishi Motors North America was in serious financial trouble in 2004–5: according to various sources, it had been losing money steadily, and it was described as Japan's only unprofitable automaker. US managers and executives started leaving the company in fall 2004, and by February 2005 it was close to a decision to seek a buyer for its US operations (though its management denied this). In a somewhat desperate move, Mitsubishi hired a veteran executive named David Schembri to lead its US marketing operations. The company was widely regarded as "Japan's only unprofitable automaker," having lost an estimated $470 million during the final three months of 2004 (Szczesny 2005). In May 2005—right in the middle of production for the Driven to Thrill ads—the two head executives of marketing and strategic planning resigned over differing opinions about how to market the 2006 Eclipse.[9] Twenty-five million dollars was budgeted for its campaign—not regarded as very much when the car was supposed to create a comeback for the company.

The Driven to Thrill advertising campaign for the Eclipse and the Raider was American in multiple ways: the cars were designed for US consumers and manufactured in the US, and the campaign was created by BBDO, a New York City–based ad agency. As the journalist Paul A. Eisenstein (2005) writes,

> In an unusual move, Mitsubishi launched the new Eclipse three weeks earlier than originally planned. The debut was backed by an aggressive ad campaign during "finale week" on network television, when most series wrap up for the summer. The catchy Eclipse spots marched to the drumbeat of a 2000-year-old musical form called Taiko, which some liken to "rolling thunder." Whether the car will connect with consumers is unclear, but the ads have been among the most highly ranked in recent months, AdCritic.com declaring [them] among TV's most popular.
>
> Ironically, there's more than a little irony to the Mitsubishi campaign. It's designed to underscore the Japanese heritage of the Eclipse, but the coupe was actually designed in California, is being built at Mitsubishi's assembly plant in Normal, Illinois, and won't even be sold in Japan.

The logic of globalized marketing is such that this isn't ironic at all but rather the status quo in a denationalized free market designed for First World exchange. In fact, automobiles have long been hybrid material objects, with different parts made in different nations and assembly done somewhere else. Yet this ad campaign played up Mitsubishi's Japanese character, which raises the question of where that Japaneseness is located. The distinction between deterritorialized international markets and soft-power cultural exchange is less clear than some scholarship would suggest, and the roles that Japan inhabits as a First World economic and financial center *and* the source of a massively exported popular culture create odd conflations (as the second paragraph of Eisenstein's review suggests). The Japaneseness of the Eclipse is based on a set of carefully maintained (and sometimes carefully denied) associations. Nonetheless, Japan was frequently if not automatically cited as the most important signifier in the Driven to Thrill campaign.

By contrast, the muscle cars of the 1960s were self-consciously American and were created by putting big engines into (relatively) small cars, at a price that a working-class man could afford, and almost always in American-made models. One can certainly read big American gas guzzlers against the small, efficient Japanese imports in gendered and racialized terms, but I am more interested here in considering the Driven to Thrill ad campaign as an exercise in racialized transnational movement. Mitsubishi was struggling against falling sales and was in dire need of a new concept. It had long been at pains to downplay its Japanese associations, but the Driven to Thrill campaign did the exact opposite. A *Detroit News* article—and note the paper's location, in the heart of Motor City—addressed the implicit American-Japanese tensions embedded in the campaign:

> Struggling Mitsubishi Motors Corp. is hoping to win back lost ground in the American market by turning its Japanese roots into a selling point.
>
> "While our competitors are kind of hiding from the fact that they are Japanese (we want) to celebrate the Japanese-ness of our brand," said Dave Schembri, head of sales and marketing for Mitsubishi Motors North America Inc. "If you want the American story, we have that as well."
>
> Speaking at a press event in Romulus marking the launch of its new Raider pickup—which will be built in Warren—Schembri said Mitsubishi's marketing research shows that most Americans associate Japanese products with quality and value. So, while other Asian automakers try to hide their overseas origins by promoting their made-in-America products, Mitsubishi is peppering its advertisements with sumi brushstrokes and taiko drums. It is all part of an effort to ride the wave of "J-cool"—a love affair with all things Japanese, notably comics, video games, and animation—that Schembri compares to the British invasion of the 1960s.
>
> Not everyone is convinced it is a good idea.
>
> "It's controversial," said Jim Sanfilippo, senior industry analyst with AMCI Inc. in Bloomfield Hills. "I'm not sure what value that has with the American consumer." (Hoffman 2005)

In the first week of October 2005, the next part of the Driven to Thrill campaign focused on the Raider and also drew on Japanese pop culture themes, though more subtly than the Eclipse ad. An article on *Brandweek.com* described the Raider TV commercial:

> Dave Schembri, [executive vice president of] sales and marketing, said the campaign for the truck will follow a theme established by the spring launch of the Mitsubishi Eclipse sport coupe. That campaign, which juxtaposed female Taiko musicians pounding drums with shots of the car, was meant to invoke the spirit of Japanese popular culture.
>
> Schembri said the new effort, via BBDO West, will posit the truck as a samurai-type good guy with the truck facing off against another truck in the desert. He said the drummers wouldn't be visible, but that the drumming will provide the soundtrack. "After the Raider does maneuvers in the sand," said Schembri, "another truck on a hill faces off with it." (Greenberg 2005)

Print ads used the text "You must promise to only use it for good," as if the truck were a magic weapon given to a hero. A review of the Raider on Autobytel.com questioned its Japaneseness, arguing,

> The new Mitsubishi truck is about history. . . . As this Japanese automaker tries to get its sales wheels spinning again and rebuild its brand in America, the

Raider—Mitsubishi's first truck in more than a decade—joins an upgraded stable of models being advertised with the trendy, urban imagery of "J-Cool" (Japanese-cool), tribal graphics and *Taiko* music, an ancient and powerful form of Japanese drumming. Developing a new ad campaign—Driven to Thrill—that will run across its car, sport-utility vehicle and new truck lines, this Asian manufacturer wants to call forth its Japanese DNA and create a cohesive new image of its full product line that will appeal to more adventuresome buyers who set themselves apart from the crowd.

We came to beautiful northwestern Oregon to look beyond the pretty scenery, however, and to see beyond the urban hip of J-Cool and *Taiko* drums. We came to drive this new truck and assess whether Mitsubishi has forged an identity of its own with its rebadged Dodge Dakota. What we found was a sculpted truck designed to attract young buyers and fun-seekers. The 2006 Mitsubishi Raider brings to market notable features, such as a V8 engine and the ability to carry six, making it an appealing offering in a competitive and still-growing market.

On sale in late September, prices for the 2006 Mitsubishi Raider will range from below $20,000 to around $30,000. Mitsubishi expects that 65 percent of sales will be 2WD, 35 percent part-time 4WD and 10 percent full-time 4WD. As for its success, exact pricing and probable incentives will likely carry more weight than tribal graphics and *Taiko* drums. But, as much as Mitsubishi has high hopes for its new truck, this three-diamond marque has higher hopes to trump with its new product line theme—Driven to Thrill. (Mead 2005)

The Raider ads were unmistakably directed toward men (aired during sports programming and in any number of men's magazines), whereas the Eclipse ads were run for a crossover male and female market, for instance during reruns of *Sex and the City* on TBS and *The West Wing* on Bravo. The ad campaign adroitly managed the two key valences—and the two potential sources of tension—that any Japanese-associated auto company must negotiate. While its Asianness could easily be read as feminine and passive, its ads work on an odd assortment of heterosexist associations: the gruff masculinity of filmic samurai, the power of women playing drums, the world of good old boys who buy pickups, and the crossover eroticism of sports cars.

The Raider and Eclipse effort rode on yet another feature of the global economy at a turn of the historical moment: the control of the oil industry. Whereas the gasoline crisis of the 1970s was front-page news, the 2005 crisis-that-was-not-a-crisis, driven by the US occupation of Iraq (2003–11), got relatively little attention, due to a White House administration seated in the oil industry and centralized media control. A chilling, key component of the Driven to Thrill campaign was the "Gas comes standard" offer: a year's worth of gas for buyers of the new Mitsubishi models. In other words, the campaign effectively addressed two radically different aspects of the global economy: the rising gas prices resulting from the US military-industrial complex, and US corporate assertion of control over mass culture from Japan.

RACING CARS AND RACIALIZATION

Let's take the Mitsubishi Eclipse out for a spin in another direction: the West Coast import and compact street racing scene, where it is one of the most popular cars. Street racing exploded among Generation Y Asian Americans in the early 1990s.[10] Asian American youth, viewed as wealthy, upwardly mobile, and aspiring to Whiteness, are immediately subject to accusations of privileged materialism. Asian American car culture is then racialized in ways parallel to how the African American emphasis on large fancy cars is racialized, which in turn activates tropes of big Black cars and small Asian American compact racing cars, both the objects of elaborate accessorizing and display.[11] The cars made by such Japanese companies as Honda, Mitsubishi, Nissan, Toyota, Mazda, and Subaru were the archetype of late twentieth-century Pac Rim movement. The First World success of Japanese cars has long been racialized, and their doubled role as sleekly accessorized prostheses for Asian American youths is thus striking and risky. These cars have strong associations: they are at once affordable, economical, and well made, and are often described as an "influx" (i.e., an infestation) into the Fordian dream of American automobiles.

Oliver Wang (2018) has explored Nikkei car clubs of the 1950s and 1960s, and the journalist C. N. Le (2005) notes that customizing cars has a long history in California. In the 1980s, Asian American youths in California started accessorizing and modifying compact imports for higher performance. The cars were part of a new public presence for young Asian American men that prompted anxieties. Informal nighttime gatherings in relatively deserted urban and suburban areas mushroomed into illegal street racing events that sometimes drew thousands of spectators and participants. Although the phenomenon attracted non-Asians as well, it is widely acknowledged that young Asian American men started the trend and continue to lead it (Namkung 2004). The size of the gatherings, some spectacular deaths, and suburban uneasiness led to massive police crackdowns that raised new fears about profiling young Asian men in general (compare Black men in accessorized cars).[12] In other quarters, the street racing trend activated old American worries about Asians as dishonest and undeservedly affluent: the accessorizing was often extremely expensive, and chop shops specializing in Japanese imports led to a rise in targeted car thefts.

Susan Kwon (1999) describes the import racing scene as uniquely Asian American and part of the long US history of ethnic-specific youth car cultures, such as White Americans with their hot rods and muscle cars and Latinos with their lowriders. Tracing the import scene back to Japanese American youths in Gardena in the 1980s, she argues that its subsequent pan–Asian American explosion was not a coincidence: "There are explicit ways in which Asianness is asserted in the Import scene. Most evident is the conscious choice to purchase and soup up Japanese cars. The act of owning and buying a Japanese car is an act against the dominant white American ideology and patriotism. The slogans 'Buy American' and 'Made in America' are still strong today. Furthermore, buying a Japanese car [in the 1980s] was considered downright unpatriotic by those sympathetic to the American auto industry." She notes that many L.A. and Bay Area street teams chose names that were Asian or Asian sounding. Some teams were ethnic specific (e.g., Filipino, Chinese, Vietnamese), but most were pan–Asian American. Importantly, the scene explicitly constructed Asian American men as tough, streetwise, defiant, hip, and out in front of American popular culture rather than as model minority members or nerds.

The series of films that started with *The Fast and the Furious* in 2001 marked the move of drag racing into mainstream popular culture, and some Asian American youths saw it as an appropriation of their scene, not least because Asian Americans have minimal roles in the films despite their significant presence on the street.[13] The journalist Kimberly Chun (2001) noted that *The Fast and the Furious* makes Asians and Asian Americans into the villains and wondered whether this decision was "some kind of holdover from the American vs. Japanese auto industry wars." Interestingly, the White hero (Paul Walker) drives a 1995 Eclipse in his first street race. The first two films revolve around urban environments with markedly multiethnic street racing communities. The Los Angeles streets in the first film are depicted as heavily Black and Latino and give way to Asian American space only when the protagonists follow the Vietnamese villains into Little Saigon in Orange County. Rick Yune plays the lead bad guy, Johnny Tran, but is actually Korean American. The second film is set in Miami, and only two Asian Americans spend any time on the screen: MC Jin, who has a supporting role as a mechanic, and Devon Aoki, as the sole female driver (and eye candy for the audience). *2 Fast 2 Furious* (2003) features another emcee, Ludacris (also in a supporting role), and the third film features Bow Wow: hip-hop artists of color were inserted to create a sense of street authenticity. The issue of Asian American presence took an interesting turn with the third film, *The Fast and the Furious: Tokyo Drift* (2006). This was the introduction to blockbuster action franchises of Justin Lin, a young Asian American director previously known for indie films (e.g., *Better Luck Tomorrow*, 2002). Despite Lin's declared commitment to nonstereotypical Asian characters, the plot involves Yakuza links and the Tokyo underworld. During the casting period, Asian American Film's website posted this summary:

> The film is about an obsessive street racer named SHAUN who is exiled to Tokyo after annoying the local police once too often.
>
> SHAUN is treated like an outsider and mocked for being a gai-jin. He is drawn to the subculture of drift racing, a dangerous and sometimes deadly sport that he masters with startling speed. In the process, Shaun makes a deadly enemy and meets the love of his life, Tani.

TANI is a stunning Japanese girl who attends the same school as Shaun in Tokyo. When they interact at first, she dismisses him until she realizes that he is an obsessive street racer as well. Chaos arises when Shaun finds out that she is in fact D.K.'s girl-friend (the "Drift King" of Tokyo). Shaun enrages D.K. by challenging him to a drift race, while at the same time forming a friendship with Tani, which eventually evolves into a forbidden romance.

REEVISE (A.K.A. TWINKIE) is a fellow classmate of Shaun, who is the first to befriend him in Tokyo. He too is car-crazy and drives a Nissan S15 Silvia. Initially Shaun is rude to Reevise, claiming "he doesn't need friends", but soon they develop a friendship as Reevise tutors Shaun on Japanese culture as well drift racing.[14]

The protagonist, as in the series's other seven films to date, is a young White American man, despite the call for a lead with no specific ethnicity: "SEEKING MALE ACTORS (any ethnicity) and JAPANESE FEMALE ACTRESSES: both must be able to play High School role." Asian American Film jumped on the possibility of actual color-blind casting: "FAST AND FURIOUS 3: TOKYO is casting lead roles 'color blind' and is looking for Asian/Asian American/Hapa male and females to apply for these lead roles. The process to submit is easy and involves a video tape. How cool would it be if FF3 was all Asian American!!! Damn!!!" But these hopes weren't real-ized: the lead role went to Lucas Black. To summarize, the first three films reflect a mainstream fascination with a phenomenon largely created and maintained by Asian American youths. Although they depict Los Angeles—the originating site of street racing—Miami, and then Tokyo, they pass over repeated opportunities to accurately represent deep Asian American involvement in the scene.

Coming back to the Mitsubishi Eclipse ad, those seconds right at the end when the car drags/drifts into a sideways skid and the taiko player's sustained kakegoe carries it further are thick with evocative association if you care to hear it and see it. Of course, it's part of a crass effort to appeal to the street racers who were already drawn to the Eclipse, yet it also summarizes (deliberately or not) the pow-erfully wrought social and material aesthetics of import cars and their authority in the hands of youths who take them past cookie-cutter factory extras and speed limits. The kakegoe re–Asian Americanizes that brief, brief second . . . even if it is wrapped in the deathly embrace of orientalist representation (Ma 2000). In yet another way, that second of Asian American sonic and visual representation is made hip through the mediation of J-cool, to which I now turn.

J-COOL

Somewhere along the way, both taiko and the transpacific circulation of cars became J-cool. Street racing is cool even if no Asian Americans are in sight. More than a few journalists have opined that Japan has become a cultural powerhouse in ways that evoke its former strength as an economic powerhouse in the 1980s (e.g., Hoskin 2015). J-pop, anime, manga, Pokémon, and Hello Kitty are all major exports; American films from the 2000s like *The Last Samurai* (2003), *Lost in Translation* (2003), and *Kill Bill* (*Volume 1*, 2003; *Volume 2*, 2004) drew on the trendiness of Japanese popular culture; and the ubiquity of sushi and ramen restaurants in major cities are part of the phenomenon of Japanese hip, J-culture, or J-cool.

The writer Douglas McGray (2002) coined the phrase "gross national cool" in a *Foreign Affairs* article, suggesting that pop culture could become Japan's next global industry. Describing Japan as a "cultural superpower," he argues that "cultural accuracy is not the point. What matters is the whiff of Japanese cool": J-cool is thus a Western-Asian mix of elements that reemerge as uniquely Japanese—and cool. McGray also suggests that the Japanese economic recession in the 1990s helped to generate the conditions for J-cool: as major corporations failed, some of the social hierarchies of the business world loosened up, allowing youthful entrepreneurs to rise quickly. He also argues for a political economy of mass culture (though he doesn't call it that), which very few "globalization nations" have achieved: "In cultural terms at least, Japan has become one of a handful of perfect globalization nations (along with the United States). It has succeeded not only in balancing a flexible, absorptive, crowd-pleasing, shared culture with a more private, domestic one but also in taking advantage of that balance to build an increasingly powerful global commercial force. In other words, Japan's growing cultural presence has created a mighty engine of national cool." McGray posits that J-cool works because it speaks both to and beyond Japanese consumers, and in so doing creates new terms for conjoined economic and cultural success. However, he also attributes "soft power," "the nontraditional ways a country can influence another country's wants, or its public's values," to the success of McDonald's, jeans, *and* Pokémon. Soft power like J-cool succeeds because it is attractive and pleasurable. The feminized force of soft power is such that it creeps into ideology and can be terrifically effective if it is exerted in tandem with the "hard" stuff of economics and military might. Joseph S. Nye Jr. (2004), who coined the term in the 1980s, writes that "soft power—getting others to want the outcomes you want—co-opts people rather than coerces them. Soft power rests on the ability to shape the preferences of others. At the personal level, we are all familiar with the power of attraction and seduction. In a relationship or marriage, power does not necessarily reside with the larger partner, but in the mysterious chemistry of attraction." As a former assistant secretary of defense for international security affairs in the Clinton administration, Nye is not offering a metaphorical means for thinking about power relations; he discusses soft power as a strategy used in US foreign relations to address everything from terrorism to the occupation of Iraq.

J-cool and Asian hip are pervasive in West Coast Asian American youth culture. While this demographic valorizes and consumes Asian-produced commodities, something more than that is going on. A generation-specific exploration of Asian American identity is self-consciously, centrally part of it. The success of the Los Angeles–based Giant Robot is a case in point. With a long run, from 1994 to 2011, *Giant Robot* was a magazine that expanded into a store and a website. Its owner-editors (Eric Nakamura and Martin Wong) explained the magazine's purpose in terms that lay out a very particular Asian–Asian American relationship:

> From movie stars, musicians, and skateboarders to toys, technology, and history, *Giant Robot* magazine covers cool aspects of Asian and Asian-American pop culture. Paving the way for less knowledgeable media outlets, *Giant Robot* put the spotlight on Chow Yun Fat, Jackie Chan, and Jet Li years before they were in mainstream America's vocabulary.
>
> But *Giant Robot* is much more than idol worship. *GR*'s spirited reviews of canned coffee drinks, instant ramen packs, Japanese candies, Asian frozen desserts, and marinated bugs have spawned numerous copycat articles in other publications. *GR*'s historical pieces on the Yellow Power Movement, footbinding, Asian-American gangsters, and other savory topics have been cited by both academics and journalists. Other regular features include travel journals, art and design studies, and sex.[15]

While Nakamura and Wong offer no specific cultural or political rationale for their hip (rather than fraught) attention to both Asian and Asian American pop culture, Asiaphilia haunts that glamorous intersection. After a certain point, the subscribers to *Giant Robot* magazine were about 50-50 Asian American and non–Asian American, suggesting something we already know: non–Asian American youths assiduously consume Asian pop culture. Anime and manga have a huge White American youth fan base, largely of boys and young men.

The merging of US and Japanese cultural economies is especially evident in Gwen Stefani's brilliant, two-pronged efforts as a singer and the creator of a fashion line. In 2003 she began working on a solo album titled *Love. Angel. Music. Baby.* (released in 2004) and founded L.A.M.B.—an acronym taken from the album title—a line of clothing. One of the album's songs celebrates the whimsical fashion sense of teenage girls in Tokyo's Harajuku area. This look draws together cuteness and ironic references to gothic, Lolita (rococo little girl clothes), and punk fashions, usually realized through layers and colors. In "Harajuku Girls," Stefani expresses admiration for this style and the girls who wear it, while simultaneously, in a perhaps inevitable elision of style, advertising, and content, promoting her own line of clothing, which isn't an accurate representation of the Harajuku style as much as it is an appropriation of its social aesthetics:

> You're looking so distinctive like D.N.A., like nothing I've ever seen in the U.S.A.
> Your underground culture, visual grammar
> The language of your clothing is something to encounter
> A Ping-Pong match between eastern and western
> Did you see your inspiration in my latest collection?

Just wait 'til you get your little hands on L.A.M.B.,
'Cause it's (super kawaii), that means (super cute in Japanese)
The streets of Harajuku are your catwalk (bishoujo you're so vogue)
That's what you drop

Although the song is narratively set up so that Stefani addresses Harajuku girls and expresses admiration for their clothes sense (and they "answer" at intervals in Japanese slang), it's really about Stefani's collection and *her* style sense in the end.

Further, Stefani accessorized herself with four "Harajuku girls" who performed on the 2005 Harajuku Lovers Tour in support of the album, as seen in countless promo shots. These four performers (three Japanese-born women and one Japanese American woman from L.A.) are positioned in much the same way in every photograph—arranged around and/or behind Stefani, who is always front and center—often wearing identical clothing and usually with impassive or pouting expressions. Groups of interchangeable, nonspecific, unnamed Asians is a very, very old trope (*The Five Chinese Brothers,* Jay Leno's Dancing Itos). Margaret Cho blogged that these women were just another minstrel show; she sarcastically flagged the problem of Asian American invisibility by adding, "I am so sick of not existing, that I would settle for following any white person around with an umbrella just so I could say I was there."[16] The Harajuku girls were stand-ins or mannequins for L.A.M.B., but in another way they are pure J-cool, pure style. They were Stefani's accessories. Her Harajuku Lovers fashion line, part of L.A.M.B., was sold through Urban Outfitters and online. In Stefani's hands, "Harajuku" became less a Tokyo neighborhood or a particular community of young Japanese stylistas than a conveniently floating signifier reclaimed as "her" line of clothing.

Stefani is a telling example of how Americans consume J-cool. Objects, people, ideas, and practices—including taiko—are imbued with J-cool and then put up for grabs; I question the processes through which they *become* unmoored and appropriable. All aspects of Asian culture are then subject to mediation through the lens of Asian hip. Cultural authenticity has always been a retreating horizon, and anything Japanese or Asian can be made hip. The aura of J-cool touches even "traditional" Japanese culture: the martial arts and taiko thus become J-cool when Uma Thurman kills Bill and when the Mitsubishi girls play the hell out of those drums.

The Mitsubishi girls' traditionality morphs into orientalism in the service of J-cool. But their traditionality had to be revamped for this to happen: their costuming and hairstyles in the ad were significantly different from what most of the TAIKOPROJECT performers usually wore, and were evidently meant to evoke anime, with the multisectioned, spiky updos and skintight, revealing, sci-fi, superwoman clothing of a certain type of heroine. A makeup and hairstyling team created this distinctive look for the taiko performers. In short, their costumes were reconfigured to evoke the cool of anime rather than to accommodate the more prosaic need to move and sweat.

PARTICIPATION, ACCOUNTABILITY, DISCLOSURES, FORECLOSURES, INTERVENTIONS, GUILT

How can Asian Americans participate in the North American production and consumption of Pac Rim commodified culture without being cast in a minstrel show? Bryan Yamami was in the middle of the Eclipse commercial's staging, so his perspective is essential: he helped curate the taiko performers' participation and choreography. Yamami is one of the most energetic and visionary young taiko players in North America. He rose to a position of authority in the taiko world in the early 2000s, when he was in his twenties. In 2000 he was one of the founders of TAIKOPROJECT, a superbly skilled group of players mostly recruited from the collegiate taiko scene and thus young (in their midtwenties) and impressively skilled. Because he is a leader in the North American taiko community, Yamami's work and vision for taiko are important, and he has a strong sense of how taiko is tied to Asian American history and community.

Yamami told me that all the music for the ad was written by Stewart Copeland and prerecorded in the studio.[17] In other words, none of the sounds heard in the ad's soundtrack were made by the taiko players seen in the ad, or perhaps even any taiko players at all—it's possible that they were all electronically generated. The magic of the studio means that we "hear" taiko but that those sounds have been radically modified or simply invented elsewhere. Taiko is notoriously difficult to record; if you remix the levels, the drums can end up sounding like tin cans. Yamami described the music as "fake taiko," and his job was to make sure that it looked like the performers were actually playing it. He felt that "the costumes were tastefully sexy but not overdone (no chopsticks in the hair or fake Japanese writing on them)." Some years later (in 2014), he told me that the ad was originally "scripted for all men in fundoshi" and the TAIKOPROJECT women were "bitter" about it. When the ad concept was changed to all women, he knew they were chosen for looks and not skill: though most were taiko players, some had been playing for only a few months. He was clear about his role in the ad: he was "a consultant," whereas a firm did the casting, used TAIKOPROJECT drums for the shoot, and asked Yamami "to teach hot Asian women actors to play taiko." He admitted that he had asked himself at different moments during the shoot what a "passable" level of taiko playing was, given the circumstances.

Yamami also told me that TAIKOPROJECT now frequently plays "high-end corporate gigs" and gets more recognition from theater presenters and festival producers thanks to its exposure from the Mitsubishi ad. I asked him what he thought of the ad's final version and how he felt about having been involved with it. He answered,

> I think it turned out very well, and I am proud that I was a part of it. I think one of the things I'm most proud of is that the group looked very, very strong, when in reality only a few of the girls were really experienced taiko players. Many of them

were UCLA students who were "good-looking" but had little taiko experience and not-so-solid basics. Most of the girls stepped up and took direction well, and with the shortness of each taiko clip it all looked strong and powerful. I think the girls are happy with how it turned out.

While two of the performers were quite advanced, most of the musicians were inexperienced, but this isn't evident in the ad, since each shot is no longer than a second or two.

I will now circle in even more closely toward the ethnographic center of Asian and Asian American hip. I obviously have grave doubts about whether it's a good idea to go in up to your elbows, but refusing to participate isn't the only possible response either. I can't demand spaces of unsullied political will and representational control, because no such spaces exist. The political economy of Pacific Rim mobility makes accountability a moving target.

What I haven't yet revealed is that I played my own small part in the Mitsubishi commercial. No, I'm not in it; rather, I had a walk-on role in the early stages of casting and conception. Here's what happened. On Saturday, April 2, 2005, two weeks away from the big annual taiko concert at my home campus, the University of California, Riverside, Satori Daiko had an extra rehearsal at Sozenji Buddhist Temple, Rev. Tom Kurai's temple in Montebello, California. I was deeply and intensely involved in Satori Daiko at that point, and hosting the full-length evening taiko concert at UCR was one of my contributions. UCR's collegiate group Senryu Taiko had agreed to meet with us that day to go over the program and to show us their pieces, to be followed by a potluck so the two groups—one primarily from the Japanese American community and the other from a university—could spend some downtime together. About twenty-five of us were there. Rev. Tom announced that two members of a local production company would visit that afternoon to audition anyone willing for a car commercial that would soon be shot in Los Angeles.

When they arrived, we all sat in the temple pews to hear them explain what they were looking for. They both appeared to be White, a man and a woman, both very confident, both enthusiastic but slightly condescending in the way that Hollywood industry workers often are with outsiders. They explained that the commercial was for the Mitsubishi Eclipse and that the concept involved taiko. The man had brought a series of charcoal storyboards, and he walked us through the plan for the commercial with great satisfaction; it was clear that he expected us to be thrilled and excited. He provided a dramatic narrative as he went through the storyboards one by one. The first showed a series of men playing odaiko in V-formation, all nearly nude except for fundoshi and hachimaki, all seen from the back. In the center was a very large odaiko with another man in front of it, arms raised. These men were from either Ondekoza or Kodo: the costuming and the emphasis on odaiko are emblematic of these groups in taiko circles. The man from the production company didn't acknowledge the players as members of group, and as he went on, it was clear that he regarded the taiko in the ad as generic rather than a specific piece by a specific group. The next storyboard showed part of the Eclipse—a headlight and part of the hood, I think—and then "shot of taiko," as he said, then (next storyboard) "shot of car" (a tire), then "shot of taiko" (a muscled back), then "shot of car" (pistons or some other engine part), then "shot of taiko" (hands holding bachi), and so forth. He explained that taiko would be heard throughout all this, working up to a thunderous crescendo. He enacted this with a flourish, flipping through to the final images and ending with a satisfied "Boom!" We applauded on cue. The woman then explained that they wanted to audition "Japanese men" for the commercial, that they wanted to video-tape the auditions, and that getting paid would involve signing away rights to the material. Both gave every indication that they were doing us a huge favor. I had been simmering from the moment when I realized they had no idea that they were ripping off Ondekoza's or Kodo's work, and I went into a silent rolling boil when they announced that they were interested in auditioning only "Japanese men." You simply don't want to get on the wrong side of me when it comes to the old confusion between Asians and Asian Americans.

I was also in high gear because members of Senryu Taiko were present. I would have been irritated had only the members of my own taiko group been there, but the presence of the undergraduates raised the stakes for me: as their faculty adviser and an educator, I didn't want them to learn that compliance is the only possible response to the racism of the entertainment industry or, indeed, the world. I was also aware that Rev. Tom might be interested in the gig as a professional opportunity, so I didn't want to estrange the visitors either. I raised my hand feeling quite conflicted—annoyed but determined to be diplomatic, reminding myself to try to work toward constructive change. I told the production team that their concept was drawn directly from a Kodo composition and asked whether they had approached Kodo to be in the commercial. They looked confused and said no, that it would be too expensive to hire a Japanese group or to shoot in Japan, since the commercial was for Mitsubishi's US branch. I pressed on and asked whether they would consider auditioning women. Knowing where I was headed, Rev. Tom told them (mildly, not confrontationally) that about 75 percent of all taiko players in the US are women. The team looked surprised and a little interested. I said not only that they should audition women but that they needed to rethink their decision to consider only "Japanese" performers, because there were only a few Japanese taiko players in Southern California but tons of Japanese Americans and Asian Americans. The team started to look defensive. They could tell that I was on to race, and they didn't want to go there. Furthermore, I said, some of the best players around were of mixed ethnicity or even not Asian at all, and using American taiko players should result in a more accurate picture of the US taiko scene.

By then I couldn't hide the fact that I was pissed off, and this was definitely not the right way to go about making an intervention, because the woman from the ad agency came back with exactly the kind of defensive answers that infuriate me: they had gotten their instructions from above, they thought we *wanted* to audition, and besides (wait for it), she herself had some Native American ancestry, so she was totally sensitive to these issues and had no problem with this ad, which was going to be "very respectful." I said that surely they knew they might need to adjust to the situation and surely it wouldn't be the first time that concepts shifted during production? She looked at Rev. Tom and told him that they were under some time constraints and that they had come because they thought people were there to audition. Rev. Tom handled this nicely: he asked whether we could have a few minutes to discuss the matter among ourselves, and he invited the two of them to wait in the foyer.

I wish I could tell you that we rallied and presented a united front, but we didn't. We had a good discussion that lasted about half an hour (long enough that the woman from casting stuck her head in the door at one point to ask whether we could move it along). One member of my group, a Japanese American man who wanted to audition, asked whether it could just be a matter of individual choice whether anyone auditioned or not, and Rev. Tom said yes, but that it was still worth talking about. Two Asian American guys from the student club childishly asked if they could just go audition because they were hungry and were eager to start the potluck. (Other members of the club shushed them.) A multiethnic teenage girl in my group voiced her displeasure that they were auditioning only men, because she really wanted to audition. One of the codirectors of the student club, a multiethnic Japanese American woman, said that she had doubts about the commercial because the casting team didn't seem to know anything at all about taiko. Another student—a young White American woman who had been listening to everything intently—said that the concept for the commercial seemed centered on an idea of Japan that had nothing to do with US-based taiko, and she felt the most appropriate solution would be for them to show a group of American performers who were both men and women of different ethnic backgrounds.

To my own discredit, I didn't moderate the discussion in the way that I'm trained to do and in fact am reasonably good at (at least in a classroom setting). I may have started the whole conversation, but I had a failure of nerve, due partly to the lines of authority in our group: I wasn't sure whether I was ruining an opportunity that Rev. Tom was still hoping to get. Conversely, I was dismayed by the willingness of so many of the taiko players to simply accept the terms as given. Having to take on *both* the representational might of the entertainment industry *and* the apparent eagerness of some of my colleagues to participate in it sent me into a tailspin. The casting team came back in without being invited, saying that they were running out of time, and they ended up getting their way: they auditioned only men who appeared to be Asian, and the rest of us—women; non-Asians; hybrid, inauthentic mongrels—started the potluck.

Of course, you already know that the final version of the commercial features only women, and all of them California-based women of Asian descent. So what happened? Did our conflicted intervention make a difference? Somewhere along the way, the production team started thinking about gender. Most likely, they noticed that they were encountering some fabulously good-looking Asian American women taiko players and went with them. I don't know exactly what happened, but I have access to the outer ends of the story—from audition to finished product—and I turn now to an analytical through line for both the production and the reception of the Mitsubishi ad, and indeed for this entire book.

TAIKO IN THE PACIFIC RIM THEATER

Taiko is not exempt from late capitalism. I have moved through three ways of looking at and understanding the Mitsubishi commercial. I began with the ad itself—its sounds and images—and then reflected on the globalized economies that led to the concept of the Pacific Rim and the critical response from cultural theorists to its late capitalist formation. I then unpacked the associations that Japanese import cars have for Asian Americans, focusing on economies of violence and reclamation for which cars are quite literally the vehicles. Finally, I addressed the ground-level participation of taiko players in peopling the ad with stand-ins for Pacific Rim exchange. I chose to start with the spectacularized object and then read the most particular and the most ethnographic, ground-level details of what happened.

I'm circling around my own disquiet about the ad, which has had an astonishingly long afterlife on the internet. At the World Taiko Gathering in Los Angeles in July 2014, Bryan Yamami spoke on a panel about collaboration in taiko that focused in large part on what it means to appear in entertainment industry productions. Looking back on his role in the Mitsubishi commercial of nine years earlier, he admitted that he had "gotten a lot of flak" about it from taiko players over the years, but he was still inclined to take the call if and when the phone rang.[18] An audience member asked Yamami whether he had had second thoughts when TAIKOPROJECT members were told to wear ski masks in the 2012 music video for "Up in the Air" by Thirty Seconds to Mars. He responded, "[That video] got eleven million views! We'll never get that many on our own. If we have less control but lots of exposure, it still makes people get interested in taiko. If I have to put on a ski mask, to me, that's great. There will always be criticism—the taiko community will always do taiko in its own way. Exposure has other benefits." I understand the glamour, allure, and power of the long-lived tropes in the Mitsubishi ad as well as any other twenty-first-century American. Yet the critical effort of progressive understanding can create another set of responses. Still, learning new critical tools for antiracist, antisexist, antisubordination interpretation doesn't necessarily free you from the other interpretive tools that you absorb as a member of US culture.

I experience the thrill of watching those sexy women play, and I am seduced into wanting to look like them, to be desired like them, and to be powerful like them. Such enculturated responses kick in, inevitably, like well-oiled machinery, but my other habits of watching with critical awareness start up at the same time and then keep running, like overlapping newsreels. It's noisy inside my head.

Any Asian American practice is subject to instant commodification, and any Asian American practice is imbricated with globalized orientalism. When Asians are racialized through global corporate capitalism, any Asian American space is rendered inauthentic. The entertainment industry ensures that any kind of critical accountability is diverted and obscured; everyone is complicit, or *made* complicit. Interventions are folded back into the master system of representation. Neither Yamami nor the taiko performers in the ad were sellouts or unwitting victims, and obviously I am dissatisfied with my own inadequate role in the whole business.

For me, the final blow was learning that *we don't actually hear those musicians in the ad*—they literally move to someone else's beat, someone else's idea.[19] In this book, I have argued repeatedly that the tumultuous, intrusive sound of taiko is central to its power—literally, metaphorically, and politically. But some of our choreographies are driven by music not our own. Transnational movement means that sites of cultural production are more complicated than ever. Whatever might be "our own" must be constructed in mindful and critically informed ways. Any oppositional stance will be already compromised unless we build in dialogical awareness that that is unacceptable. Our strategies for participation must be as mobile as the ideologies that move us into position as performers. I have argued elsewhere that consumption is a kind of cultural production (Wong 2004, 257–97), but I am now less certain that it is a game-changing response to the absence of an Asian American public sphere. We will need better critical tools for thinking about how to live in a society that valorizes unfettered mobility and consumption.

The Pacific Rim was named and defined by legislators and representatives of transnational postindustrial corporations who wanted to ensure easy access to new markets. It is evidence of the desire for a market as unencumbered as possible and exemplifies the neoliberal logic of unrestrained capitalism. North American taiko moves around the Pacific Rim in nonarbitrary ways. Taiko sometimes does radically performative cultural work, but since the 1980s the cultural space of the Pacific Rim has created terms for troubled Asian and Asian American encounters. Asian American taiko players are continually positioned to reiterate old ideas in hip new ways.

Transition

How to Leave a Taiko Group

You're thinking about moving on from your taiko group, for any number of reasons. Perhaps you no longer like its personality or character, or you feel undervalued, or you've had a falling out with someone, or you just need something different—you need to grow.

This is a primer of best practices. I didn't do any of these things.

You should to try to fix what's wrong before taking the extreme measure of leaving, because building up all the rewards of belonging to any taiko group takes time. The longer you are in a group, the better you will know its repertoire, will appreciate the nuances of its teaching and learning style, and will earn the trust and respect of your colleagues. Most important, it takes time to create the bonds of affection that make good taiko groups great: ideally, a taiko group feels like a family.

Most likely, *you* are the thing that has changed. Ideally, you still value and respect what your group has given you, but you want to develop in ways that aren't possible in this group. You have longings, or the opportunity to join another group has appeared. How can you exit without burning bridges? How can you seize the chance to grow with another group but not leave behind strained feelings and a circle of people who suddenly feel discarded?

I hope it is possible for any North American taiko player to experience the joys of playing with more than one group in their lifetime, to see how different each group is . . . but also to see how "the taiko spirit," that ineffable thing, manifests in different groups. I imagine all taiko players would want to maintain good, respectful, and productive relationships with every group and teacher they have ever worked with. Ideally, each experience will lead to more ways that you are part of the taiko community and more ways that you are one node through which others connect. Community is accumulative. You should try to maintain relationships even after you have moved on.

So you need a change. First, you should start by speaking one-on-one with the leader(s). Explain your situation. Don't revisit grievances. Emphasize how much you have learned and how your respect for the group has only grown over time. Explain that your need for new kinds of personal growth motivates you at this point. Ask if there is anything you can do to ease the transition (e.g., delaying your departure).

Second, there are several ways to change your status in the group:

Make a clean exit—that is, say your good-byes and remove yourself from the roster, stop paying dues, and so forth.

Take a leave of absence, ideally with agreed-upon dates of departure and return.

Agree to be in two groups at once: stay with the original group and begin working with another one. This should be done only with the explicit agreement of both groups and an open understanding among all parties.

Whatever you choose, let the rest of the group know, both in person and in writing. Tell everyone at once if you can, in a group meeting, so no one feels outside the circle. Emphasize how much you value them and desire to maintain ties. Follow up with a letter given to all members of the group, reiterating these things and thanking them for the good times and friendship you experienced with them.

Leaving should be about the importance of continued good relations with the original group and making this a priority no matter what the circumstances. If things have been unhappy, rise above it. Focus on what's been right. Set the stage for a different relationship by making sure your old one is sound.

I didn't leave Satori Daiko. I simply got caught up in burgeoning midcareer responsibilities and told everyone I needed a leave of absence for the three years I would be a department chair at my university. Somehow, I never went back after those three years. During the time I was off, other Satori members drifted away. The teenage members went to college and the family groups at the heart of Satori dissipated; without their daughters at practice, the mothers stopped coming. Others wanted new opportunities. A major break occurred when the Taiko Center of Los Angeles's other performing group, then called Shinzen Daiko, formally separated from TCLA and regrouped independently as Yuujou Daiko. At the time of this writing, Satori Daiko still exists but is much smaller, and most of the members I spent so much time with from 1997 to 2009 are no longer in it. I went back to the group once, for an epic performance with the Yellow Magic Orchestra and Yoko Ono at the Hollywood Bowl in 2011. It was one of those all-hands-on-deck moments, and I played Rev. Tom's piece "Aranami" with about fifty other TCLA members.

I was longing for something. I was deep into writing this book, and I could no longer avoid my need for a kind of taiko that addressed my most urgent hopes. I wanted to play taiko or simply be with other Asian American community-based performers who had already come to consciousness—who were woke, in Black radical terms. I sought out those kinds of taiko players and Japanese American community workers. I attended PJ Hirabayashi's TaikoPeace workshop at Senshin Buddhist Temple in L.A. I went to the East Coast Taiko Conference and followed around the members of Raging Asian Women—an all-woman feminist Asian American taiko group—like the star-struck fan I am. I had long, intimate, and inspiring conversations with Karen Young, who founded the Genki Spark, another all-woman feminist Asian American taiko group, in 2010. In 2013 I began to follow Nobuko Miyamoto's community-building project called FandangObon, and I am now deeply involved in it. I gradually got quite serious about bon-odori, realizing that it exemplifies a lot of the things I valued most about kumi-daiko.

I'm ready, willing, and eager. I left but I haven't left. In the summer of 2017, Beverly Murata and I went to the twenty-third annual Taiko Gathering in the JACCC Plaza, where we enjoyed three hours of kumi-daiko performances, including a terrific thirty-minute set by Senryu Taiko, and then hurried over to East First Street, where we danced for two hours straight in the closing ceremonies for Nisei Week, the official end of Obon season in SoCal. As I danced to Nobuko, Martha Gonzalez, and Quetzal Flores's song "Bambutsu no Tsunagari," I was suddenly pierced with sadness—the season was ending, so I wouldn't get to dance this for another ten months, an eternity—and then I remembered that Nobuko would hold her fourth FandangObon Encuentro in October, in conjunction with the explosion of SoCal Día de Muertos events. And I was happy because I knew I would dance again, soon.

Conclusion

Core Values

There's a joke at the end of the recording of "Bambutsu no Tsunagari" by Nobuko Miyamoto's longtime band of Japanese American and Chicanx musicians and Rev. Mas Kodani, with whom Miyamoto has written quite a few new bon-odori songs and dances.[1] As the song builds to a joyous conclusion, the dancers take three steps inward so we're all looking at one another, arms upraised, and the recorded singers hit the final chord, "FandangObooonnnnn . . ." It's a perfect ending. Then, after it seems like the song is done, you hear a little vocal tag. It's Rev. Mas. He's using his Issei farmer's voice—it's not his everyday Sansei voice but is gruff, in his chest. It's a memory, an evocation, an homage. He says, "Wha'? You wan' mo'?"[2]

What, you want more? You want to keep dancing? The North American kumi-daiko scene is changing so rapidly that I can't possibly bring this book to any tidy conclusion. This book reflects my love for and impatience with the taiko community. We tend to refer to "the taiko community," as if it were a collectivity with shared values. That moment passed around 2000, when taiko expanded rapidly and uncontrollably in North America and Western Europe. Like any community, it has always contained multiple, competing perspectives, but it has fractured further since 2010 or so. And yet—and yet. This far-flung "community" also has compelling values and ethical principles that are discussed, disseminated, and sustained in powerfully connected ways across the globe; they are explicitly articulated. For instance, in 2013, along with fifty other taiko teachers and practitioners representing a broad spectrum of age, ethnicity, gender, and region, I participated in three days of intensive planning for the new Taiko Community Alliance (TCA), including an entire day spent in a carefully democratic process to generate core values for the organization. With virtually no disagreement, the resulting list was "respect," "heritage and evolution," "empowerment," "inclusivity," and "transparency."[3]

I have encountered these core values many times before and since: they are constantly discussed, whether within or between taiko groups, and certainly at the huge convenings that have marked North American taiko since 1997, when the first North America Taiko Conference was held. Naturally, the core values are discussed when disrupted or challenged, and such fissures are constant; still, no substantive change ever results. North American taiko has relied on established practices for creating collectivities of Japanese Americans and allied Asian American communities . . . until recently.

My personal disappointments are real enough. The taiko community doesn't like to talk about its own gender inequities. The majority of taiko groups are led by men, despite the fact that the majority of players are women . . . though this might be changing—we'll see. The acceptance of heterosexist hierarchy sometimes means that older men are automatically elevated to positions of authority and leadership. Deep habits of silence—despite the noisiness of our work—mean that we rarely call out orientalist practices even when confronted by them.

Rather than approach taiko as a quaintly folkloristic practice transplanted from Japan to the US, I have written about it as a deeply mediated bundle of representational fields that were (and are) constructed by war, global capitalism, struggles over First World ownership, fraught race relations, and so forth. These conflicts are particularly marked in Southern California. I love taiko, but my purpose lies in showing, again and again, how the ethnography of performance offers essential tools for living in a mediated environment of shifting authority defined by corporate centralization and community invention. I hope my approaches speak beyond my materials. I think ethnography-based methodologies could open up the political economy of any twenty-first-century music. This means attending to the political economy of the form, and this dimension has been missing from a lot of my previous work.[4]

This book is situated in the broader project of antiracist scholarship.[5] It is not about race, ethnicity, and gender "in" taiko. My questions centrally concern these matters, but I hope that my critical emphasis on difference is so fundamentally attentive to them that they cannot isolate or contain my work. As Purnima Mankekar and Louisa Schein (2012, 3) state, "Prevailing conceptions of Asia conjure an eroticized space formed through desires and anxieties embedded in 'the Western gaze.'" That was necessarily my starting point rather than where I have arrived. I paraphrase George Lipsitz (2014, 9), who paraphrases Ruth Wilson Gilmore, to say that this book is about "the fatal couplings of power and difference" that shape lives and slingshot drums across oceans, wars, and time. Ethnomusicology is overdue to focus its gaze routinely and unapologetically on such matters, in ways that would put us into more direct conversation with the best work in the humanities. I have not offered a comprehensive history of taiko, whether in the US, greater North America, Japan, or the world. This book provides a partial view of a huge phenomenon. I can no longer comfortably refer to taiko as "a" tradition, given its explosive expansion, multiple locations, and intensely mediated character. I finished this book at a point when the relationship between taiko and Japanese

American identity was/is no longer the dominant narrative. I am deeply uneasy about this change. Within the taiko community, I hear Japanese American and other Asian American practitioners declaring that taiko is "for everyone," instantiating a radically open-door policy for this cultural practice.[6] The traditional and the folkloric are deceptively available to anyone because their intermediation is concealed. As Masumi Izumi (personal communication, April 30, 2018) suggested to me, many Generation Y and even Generation Z Asian Americans in greater Los Angeles have diverse, transnational identities and comfortable class positions, making it difficult to generalize about the politics of the "taiko spirit," because fewer are committed to taiko as an Asian American practice. North American taiko is unsettled, contradictory, pleasurable, frustrating, and slippery.[7]

Obviously, this worries me. As an ethnomusicologist, I have no desire to hold any music tradition in place or demand that it stop changing. Musics change and change again; never do they *not* change. But I wonder whether, over time, North American kumi-daiko will have fewer Asian American practitioners, and fewer students of any ethnicity who choose to regard it as an Asian American tradition. Such forgetting would be a triumph of the most predictable neoliberal multiculturalism. But I also see how kumi-daiko could be, and perhaps already is, a site where the growing White body politic can learn not just about personal empathy and feel-good encounters but about Asian American histories. As Angela Ahlgren (2018, 139) writes, "Taiko is deeply enmeshed with Asian American politics, consciousness, and identity," right here and now, not in some distant past. The joy of playing taiko is a real start, but that feeling must be channeled into the struggle that antiracist work always is. Intra–Asian American kumi-daiko offers powerful strategies for antiracist coalition work, to which non–Asian American taiko players should commit.

This book is less celebratory than it would have been had I written it after one year or three years or five years of passionate involvement with taiko. I am both frustrated and inspired by taiko. I sometimes sound skeptical and even cynical in this book, because my hopes are so high. In some places, taiko does urgently important things for some Japanese Americans and other Asian Americans, both performers and audience members. Certainly it shows how community-based expressive culture complicates the "continuum between the poles of victimization and resistance," as Lon Kurashige (2001, 389) puts it. But as the ethnomusicologist Louise Meintjes (2004, 193) warns, "A dance about power can become a source of power." Having seen, heard, and felt how taiko can become a source of power, I feel an extreme alarm over some of its redirections. I am continually surprised and dismayed by what Thuy Linh Nguyen Tu (2010, 3) calls "the popular appetite for Asianness," which taiko players feed and satisfy even as they do progressive cultural work.

I write at a historical moment of political disaster, when the progressive Left is demoralized yet regrouping and many wonder what new and old violence, hate, and hurt are coming our way. Immigrants both legal and less than legal are terribly vulnerable. White men march in the streets with torches. Nativism drowns out other voices. The pain and injuries of US history are not metaphorical right now, and the loudness of Asian American taiko speaks in a context of xenophobic noise. The insistent volume of Japanese American and other Asian American drumming is absolutely needed in this environment of real and present danger. This is no retreat to ethnic nationalism. Rather, I have shown in this book that taiko is an example of how racial projects appear from sometimes unexpected places and sources.

Lest it be thought that I overstate the power of Japanese American politicization, I note that the Japanese American Citizens League came out the gate loud and fast immediately after 9/11 and hasn't slowed down for a moment since then. As anti-Muslim (and anti-Sikh) violence followed hard on the heels of terrorism, the JACL defended civil liberties and stood as a moral reminder of where fear and nativism can lead. Since 2001, the organizers of the Manzanar Pilgrimage have annually included members of the Council on American-Islamic Relations in the program, ensuring that connections are made across history, memory, difference, and experience. In 2017 alone, the JACL issued numerous press releases and provided amicus briefs to the US Supreme Court opposing the Muslim-country travel ban, the end of the Deferred Action for Childhood Arrivals (DACA) policy, and the presidential pardon of former Maricopa County sheriff Joe Arpaio, an unapologetic anti-immigrant racist. Japanese Americans know how it goes down.

Taiko players too know the history and carry the memories. In 2016, Portland Taiko strategically revived an original musical-narrative piece titled "A Place Called Home," which depicts the Japanese American community before, during, and after the incarceration, highlighting the means to stand with and for vulnerable communities and building it into their public performances since then. Portland Taiko members have also rewritten their online bios to emphasize their personal immigrant histories.[8] For the historic Women's March held on January 21, 2017, the Genki Spark director Karen Young worked with the taiko players Elise Fujimoto and Tiffany Tamaribuchi and generated the slogan "We Play for Unity. See Us Hear Us Join Us," meant to compel other taiko players to action (see figure 28, Karen Young wearing a "We Play for Unity" T-shirt, 2017, at *http://wonglouderandfaster.com*). Young (personal communication, October 28, 2018) said, "My activism and my commitment to community and empowerment have more than doubled since the election. I feel like I've just gotten started."[9] Taiko tells a story about immigration, violence, resistance, and politicization. Taiko teaches skills that have urgent new relevance.

Taiko thus floods any space with news the world needs to hear.[10] Community making that calls new collectivities into being is what taiko offers, right here, right now, at a moment when the Republic of California is organizing the resistance. Taiko is fatally part of commodity capitalism and all too susceptible to neoliberal strategies of racialized containment, but it also provides the means to create a body politic that overruns attempts to fold it back into obedience and colonial fantasy. Its exuberance and discipline do not mask the pain. I have seen and heard its coordinated and improvised grace sweep through Asian American audiences, prompting tears, joy, memory, and determination. The North American taiko community articulates its core values in precisely the ways that the most powerful and effective political movements have articulated and mobilized new collectivities. Respect, heritage, empowerment, inclusivity, and transparency are exactly what's needed right now, and are exactly what taiko teaches.

I finish this book at a time when I have not actively studied taiko for some years yet still consider myself a taiko player. Performance is never only about performing. I have stayed closely in touch with the taiko world; I seek out taiko performances; I shout kakegoe when I listen to other people playing taiko; I dance bon-odori and think of summertime as a series of Obon festivals. Kumi-daiko has carried a formation of ideas, values, beliefs, hopes, movements, and sounds across Asian America, and they grow louder and faster all the time, pounding together the pain and the joy.

NOTES

INTRODUCTION

1. I am indebted to George Lipsitz for this phrasing . . . and much more, of course.

2. In fact, many friends and acquaintances were there, including Martha Gonzalez and Quetzal Flores, to perform "Bambutsu no Tsunagari—FandangObon" with Nobuko Miyamoto; Rev. Mas Kodani; George Abe; Johnny Mori; a fleet of musicians who play the jarana (a small guitar-like fretted stringed instrument from Veracruz, Mexico); Atomic Nancy (Nancy Sekizawa, whose family ran the Atomic Café, a punk hangout in Los Angeles's Little Tokyo in the 1970s and 1980s); the *sonero* (master *son jarocho* singer and improviser) and luthier César Castro; the shamisen player Sean Miura; and Rip Rense and Annie Chuck.

3. Rev. Masao Kodani, interviewed in the documentary *Obon: Gathering of Joy* (Seligman 1985). The full quotation, beginning at 8:01, is as follows: "One way of explaining *bon-odori* is to [*pause*] dance—to consciously dance unconsciously. [*He smiles.*] Or to unconsciously dance consciously. Whichever way you want to put it. It's a very [*pause*] delicate moment in which you're fully involved in what you are doing but you don't—you're not watching yourself do it. There's no sense of *look at me, I'm doing well*. Because when that moment comes, you lose it."

4. Following current critical practice in Asian American Studies, I use the term *incarceration* rather than *internment* or *relocation*. See Hirabayashi 2015; Daniels 2008.

5. My thinking on these matters is fundamentally unformed by Elinson and Yogi 2009; Johnson 2013; Kun 2005; and Pulido 2006.

6. I am paraphrasing Martha Gonzalez (personal communication, April 26, 2014). We were reflecting on the FandangObon project, and she said she felt that the Chican@ musicians had been "invited into the living room" of the Japanese American Buddhist community.

7. There were three collegiate taiko groups in 1992, and at the time of this writing there are more than thirty (at least thirteen on the West Coast and at least seventeen east of the

Mississippi). The North American Taiko Conference, formerly held every two years, has routinely attracted more than five hundred participants from all over North America, and the East Coast Taiko Conference has been held annually since 2011, attended by about three hundred people.

8. The Discover Nikkei database was started in 2005 as part of the Japanese American National Museum's groundbreaking exhibit *Big Drum: Taiko in the United States.* The website (*http://www.discovernikkei.org/en/*) is maintained by JANM and is a major online resource for Japanese diasporic history and culture.

9. These reports are available at *https://taikocommunityalliance.org/events/census/*. See Walker 2016 for empirical data and interpretation.

10. Quote from Joe Schloss's website (*http://josephschloss.com*), floated on Facebook on August 3, 2014; quoted with permission.

11. Nobuko Miyamoto (personal communication, August 27, 2018) notes that enough members of the Southern California Japanese American community have expressed discomfort with the phrase that she will likely remove it from her song.

12. I deliberately refer here to the work of Alton L. (Pete) Becker (1995, 3): citing Ernest Becker and José Ortega y Gasset—his two favorite philosophers of language—he asks, "What are the boundaries, the limits, of our languaging, our inner language . . . ? . . . Where does languaging stop and another kind of 'thinking' begin in my own 'inoneselfness'?" The limits to translation and thus to the translatability of subjectivity was Becker's lifelong question.

13. Shawn Bender's 2012 book is the authoritative English-language source on this important history.

14. About ten US-based scholars, most in their thirties, currently conduct research on taiko; most rely on "performing identity" paradigms from the 1990s.

15. E.g., Ahlgren 2011; Carle 2008; Endo 1999; Itoh 1999; Kobayashi 2006; Konagaya 2007; Lorenz 2007; Pachter 2013; Panalaks 2001; Powell 2003; Tusler 1995, 2003; Viviano 2013; Vogel 2009; Williams 2013; Yoon 1998. Benjamin Pachter has made his bibliography "Taiko Resources: A Listing of Books, Articles, and Other Publications about Taiko" available on Scribd (*https://www.scribd.com/document/87602918/Taiko-Resources*) and at his website, *https://taikosource.com/*.

16. *http://ondekoza.com/aboutus.html.*

17. Wynn Kiyama, personal communication, May 5, 2017.

18. *http://www.kodoarts.org/sample-page/.*

19. In general, the NATC has been dominated by community-based performers and the ECTC by collegiate performers, though both gatherings draw a rich mixture of each. There are more collegiate than community taiko groups on the East Coast, which is why collegiate groups have hosted the ECTC to date: Yamatai at Cornell in 2011, 2015, and 2019; Kaze at Wesleyan University in 2012; Gendo at Brown University in 2013, 2016, and 2017; SkiDaiko at Skidmore College in 2014; and Taiko Tides at Stony Brook University in 2018.

20. "Imagine otherwise" is an homage to Kandace Chuh (2003).

21. See Titon 1995; Baily 2001; Rasmussen 2004 for good discussions of bimusicality in post-1990s ethnomusicology.

22. See Codetta Raiteri 2016 for a careful consideration of Southern California taiko as labor.

23. In July 2014, for example, the Seattle-based taiko teacher Stanley Shikuma's cover photo on Facebook was a beautiful, desolate, wind-swept image of Abalone Mountain seen from the Tule Lake "Segregation Center," taken when he attended the annual pilgrimage earlier that month.

24. Katherine In-Young Lee's (2018) wonderful work on Korean *samulnori* addresses similar questions.

25. Examples include *Echo: A Music-Centered Journal, Critical Studies in Improvisation / Études critiques en improvisation, Trans: Revista Transcultural de Música / Transcultural Music Review, Resonance: An Interdisciplinary Music Journal,* and *Radical Musicology.*

26. Errington, "What *is* multi-media ethnography?" (audio clip), at *https://people.ucsc. edu/~sherring/migrated/mediaethno/class/#.*

TRANSITION: DON

1. I am indebted to the following friends and colleagues who responded quickly and energetically to my Facebook query about the syllable *don* on August 10–12, 2015: Marië Abe, Kenny Endo, Robert Garfias, Shawn Higgins, Minoru Kanda, Nana Kaneko, Tom Kurai, Edmundo Luna, Noriko Manabe, Richard Miller, David Novak, Satomi Oshio, Josh Pilzer, Stephen Sano, Shzr Ee Tan, Nanako Taki Terada, and Larry Witzleben. Manabe and Pilzer noted that manga contains numerous onomatopoetic syllables (often to depict violence) and that the children's author Gomi Taro has written a bilingual English-Japanese illustrated dictionary of onomatopoetic and mimetic words.

2. Satomi Oshio, personal communication, August 11, 2015.

3. Noriko Manabe, personal communication, August 11, 2015.

1. LOOKING, LISTENING, AND MOVING

1. I stop using quotation marks around "music" from here, but the reader should consider that frame present, simultaneously ironic, irritated, and resentful.

2. Ethnomusicologists' energies have been much drawn off by the necessity of explaining how and why our discipline is different from historical musicology, but it seems a moot point to me. Our debt to anthropology is obvious, even if the study of performance is still a secondary area within that discipline. It is far more useful to see how we might fit into the field of performance studies, and I have argued for this elsewhere (Wong 1998). Performance studies emerged in the 1970s from the confluence of theater studies and anthropology; it was the result of a friendship and intellectual partnership between the actor, director, critic, and theorist Richard Schechner and the anthropologist Victor Turner. Together they set in motion a new approach to "performance" as a broad range of behaviors that had the simultaneous effect of redefining "theater" (with all its Western bias) and blurring the lines between the proscenium stage and the performance of everyday life (Schechner and Turner 1985; Turner 1986; Schechner and Appel 1990). Three lively doctoral programs in performance studies dominate the young discipline in the US. The Department of Performance Studies at New York University was the first of its kind, created by Schechner; it is decidedly interdisciplinary, and its faculty contains folklorists, anthropologists, literary theorists, and theater studies scholars. At Northwestern University, the Department of Performance Studies has a more anthropological

bent. At UCLA, the Department of World Arts and Cultures has a somewhat stronger tie to intercultural performance praxis (especially in dance), and its faculty is made up of dance scholars, folklorists, ethnomusicologists, and theater studies specialists. Each doctoral program has a distinctive character and produces markedly different kinds of students.

3. Music as an object and music analysis as a historically specific set of practices are each based in certain ideologies of music. René T. A. Lysloff (2003) has argued that the field of music theory and analysis relies on the overdetermined role of notation in the Western art music tradition: "More often than not theorists analyze scores rather than real acoustical phenomena" and rely on an epistemological elision that makes the score into "the music." As Maus (2003) put it, music theorists have generally treated compositions as "self-sufficient" enactments of abstract principles. A "common technical vocabulary" creates flattening theoretical exemplars (e.g., "the dominant seventh typically leads to a tonic triad") that pull away from the particularities of any given "piece" of music. Similar language is deployed to arrive at "a non-contextual generality" about any piece. Rather than force music analysis to "work" for non-Western musics (the problem that sidetracks too many ethnomusicologists), Maus imagined a music analysis that would open up other aspects of the Western art music tradition: one that could reverse the naturalized hierarchy of "composition versus performance, music itself versus experience, structure versus embodiment."

4. David Novak (2013) addresses noise as "a subject of scholarly attention" and noise as a specific Japanese genre, and his work is of course authoritative in this area. He writes that noise is "an essential reference for the incalculable effects of globalization and technological fragmentation on the human condition. The rise of noise has become the new grand narrative of transnational circulation, but at the same time is recognized as an essential object of cultural relativism" (228). I am particularly drawn to scholarly work on Japanese urban soundscapes (e.g., Novak 2010). Jeffrey Hanes (2013) examines how the extreme noisiness of the interwar Osaka soundscape famously caused hearing loss and sleep deprivation for the city's residents. He notes that Osaka remains "notorious for its noise" (29), but in the early twentieth century its industrialized cacophony was heard as the sounds of progress and modernity (30–31). At the same time, noise abatement emerged as a critical need, as Hanes describes in vivid terms. He writes that "the anxiety over noise stemmed from the suspicion that it was already uncontrollable" (35).

5. The drum circles at the Occupy Wall Street protests are an example of how the sound of drumming was perceived by some as music and by others as noise and thus a problem. Gina Arnold (2011) wrote, "Community organizers both inside and outside OWS said they were distressed by the continuous noise that these protesters are making," and she held White men predominantly responsible for the "overabundance of snares," resentments over their ability to drown out the human microphone, and a White hippie aesthetic assumption that drum circles are automatically countercultural.

6. Rev. Tom also taught "Aranami" to Chikara Daiko of Centenary Methodist Church, Little Tokyo, Los Angeles; Yoki Daiko of Tenrikyo (Shinto) Church, Los Angeles; the University of California, Riverside, Taiko Ensemble class; and, in a fascinating case of Japanese American–Japanese exchange, Yamanari Daiko of Tsubetsu Town, Hokkaido, Japan.

7. See my discussion of the piece and dance "Korekara" in chapter 3.

8. These ideologies run deep. Art music composers are created, sustained, rewarded, discouraged, and excluded along fraught lines defined by gender, sexual orientation,

ethnicity, geography (e.g., North and South Hemisphere distinctions), and more. These boundaries are long lived. One journalist argues, for instance, that "black composers remain on the outskirts of classical music" (Robin 2014).

9. Ki and its Chinese counterpart, chi, are centuries-old concepts of vital energy but continue to change through contemporary thinkers and practitioners. Ki is sometimes presented as a Buddhist concept, but its origins go beyond Buddhism, and, more important, contemporary thinkers explore it through a mixture of intercultural and transhistorical influences. An example is the Japanese philosopher of religion Yasuo Yuasa (1925–2005), who wrote extensively about ki, drawing from an exceptionally broad range of ideas (Yuasa 1993). North American taiko teachers approach ki through similar kinds of cultural mediation, though their students may sometimes prefer to absorb it as a timeless concept.

10. Junko Ihrke, a student codirector of Senryu Taiko from 2002 to 2004, told me that their arrangement of "Aranami" was created by the former codirectors Mieko Moody and Reina Fujii, who had already graduated by the time she learned it from other students.

11. Marking important events with large numbers of performers isn't unusual, but the massing of taiko performers has its own history, and the JANM opening was meant to evoke the huge taiko group of two thousand drummers put together for the opening ceremony of the 1998 Winter Olympics in Nagano, which is now infamous in taiko circles.

12. My thanks to Jeff Packman for bringing up participatory discrepancies and for information on American studio drummers' attitudes toward flamming, which provided a comparative perspective.

13. Chin was a Chinese American beaten to death in 1982 outside a bar in Detroit by two White American men who had been laid off work at an auto plant. Thinking that Chin was Japanese and thus linked to the demise of the US auto industry—and the loss of their jobs—the two men killed him with a baseball bat. They were charged with and pleaded guilty to manslaughter, and each received a sentence of three years' probation and a three-thousand-dollar fine; neither served any jail time. The case was memorialized in the documentary *Who Killed Vincent Chin?* (1988) and is seen as emblematic of anti-Asian violence in the US.

14. Michelle Kisliuk (1995, 79) takes issue with Keil's terminology and the phantasm of "science" looming behind it: "I agree with Charles Keil's call for a focus on 'groove.' . . . But the term 'participatory discrepancies' puts Keil in a bind. It has a distancing, scientist flavor, and implies that syncopation and drive relationships are somehow 'discrepant,' that is, abnormal. The term itself is un-groovy, foreshadowing the contradictions embedded in Keil's rhetoric ('participation theory and funism' are what Keil says he is after, but measuring the groove does not sound like much fun to me)."

15. The search for homologous relationships between music and culture was one of the major contributions of ethnomusicology during the 1980s, when anthropologists of music—particularly Feld, Judith and Alton Becker, and Marina Roseman—looked closely at the iconic relationships between the formal characteristics of music and the societies containing them. Becker and Becker (1981) demonstrated how the cyclic time structures of Javanese gamelan music are related to Javanese conceptions of calendrical time; Roseman (1984) showed how Temiar conceptions of song as a pathway are both metaphorical and literal, opening up channels between the sacred and human worlds.

2. INVENTORIES

Epigraphs. Frank H. Watase Media Arts Center 2005; Miller 2009, 5.

1. See Tusler 2003 for very well wrought chapters that provide an orderly introduction of this kind.

2. Inventories are a time-honored method in folklore and anthropology, deployed to get past predisposed ideas about importance and significance by attending to everything in a given unit of analysis. Visual anthropologists may inventory an entire room (e.g., Collier and Collier 1992). I offer my inventories in this chapter as a window onto material practice and a way to draw value-intense accumulations of objects into view. For instance, the artist Ulrike Müller used an inventory list of feminist T-shirts she found in the Lesbian Herstory Archives to generate an art project focused on retranslating feminist imagery (Schröder, Kelly, and Müller 2014).

3. North American taiko ensembles tend to emphasize the identicality of their costuming and make great efforts to ensure it. Western symphonic orchestras offer a counterexample: while their musicians are all expected to wear "concert black," male musicians aren't all told to buy the same jacket from a selected designer, for instance, and female musicians have a broad range of clothing options.

4. In a more literal way, some composers argue that the physicality of musical instruments creates the terms for musical language. Luciano Berio (quoted in Mosch 2012) has said that his *Sequenza* compositions for solo instruments rely on dialogues with the entire history of a given instrument—the instrument is not "just" a sound-producing object.

5. See Montagu 2003 for a phenomenological model for the importance of organology.

6. Such museums are legion, but Orhan Pamuk's *Museum of Innocence* (the novel and its interconstitutive physical site in Istanbul) and Chile's Museum of Memory and Human Rights are two examples.

7. Morgan (1926–2010) was the first non-Japanese to form a taiko group, called Morgan Taiko, in Los Angeles in 1976. (See the photo gallery of the Japanese American National Museum *Big Drum* website, *http://www.janm.org/exhibits/bigdrum/,* for a photograph of Morgan Taiko.) Morgan continued to make taiko until 2000 or so and also led a group called MoGan Daiko in Tucson, Arizona (no longer active).

8. David Leong's (1999) account and overview of the issues on his blog *Rolling Thunder* remains authoritative. He wrote it in the months when the controversy emerged, and his "FAQ" addresses the issues from Sukeroku's perspective. Although the post is titled Version 1.02 and states that it was last updated on March 1, 1999, the text refers at one point to events from 2000. Leong stopped updating *Rolling Thunder* in 2010, and the links in the "FAQ" to the Japanese patent office and to Sukeroku's patents for two stands are unfortunately no longer active. In an earlier publication (Wong 2004, 223–26), I quoted extensively from Leong's blog post, which at that time included an English translation of Sukeroku's letter to the North American taiko community outlining the permissions process.

9. See Terada 2008 and 2010 for an article and an extraordinary documentary, respectively, about Ikari Taiko and its relationship to the Buraku human rights movement in Japan. The anthropologist Joseph Hankins (2014, xvii) argues that Buraku labor is embedded in both global capitalism and emergent Japanese ideas about multiculturalism.

10. See Miyoshi's website (*http://miyoshidaiko.com/*) for pictures and price lists.

11. See *http://www.stanford.edu/group/stanfordtaiko/manual/index.html.*

12. The Stanford Taiko website (*https://web.stanford.edu/group/stanfordtaiko/cgi-bin/ about.html*) offers this account of the group's origin: "The seeds for Stanford Taiko were planted in 1991 in a class taught by Susan Hayase, a former member of San Jose Taiko, as part of a special program of Stanford Workshops on Political and Social Issues (SWOPSI). The class contextualized the art of taiko by discussing its link to the Japanese American experience and inspired Ann Ishimaru ('93, A.M. '94) and Valerie Mih ('92) to apply for an Undergraduate Research Opportunity grant to research and build a taiko. Stanford Taiko took root in the winter of 1992 after Ishimaru, Mih, and fellow students completed the first drum and invited fellow SWOPSI course graduates and other interested people to form a taiko ensemble at Stanford University. The original 13 charter members were taught basic taiko form in a workshop with San Jose Taiko. They also learned basics from workshops with Susan Hayase, Gary Tsujimoto, and Nancy Ozaki from One World Taiko."

13. In an article titled "Why Your Yoga Class Is So White," Rosalie Murphy (2014) leafs through a stack of glossy American yoga magazines and muses, "Nearly every spread features a thin woman, usually in slim yoga pants and a tight tank, stretching her arms toward the sky or closing her eyes in meditation. Nearly all of these women are white."

14. Jessica Knapp (2015, 16) writes, "In 1965, plastisol ink for fabrics was patented, allowing screen printing. T-shirts were no longer expected to remain a blank canvas." Lynn Neal (2014, 186, 187) argues that the T-shirt "helps monitor the boundaries and norms of American society" by offering a platform for "American individualism," whether progressive or xenophobic. Colin Symes (1989, 88) declares that "the t-shirt is a garment like no other, one in which the language of clothing meets the language of statement, in which textile becomes textuality."

15. My thanks to Anthea Kraut for recommending this book.

TRANSITION: SHE DANCES ON A TAIKO

1. The oldest extant version is in the *Kojiki,* an eighth-century collection of myths focusing on kami, later absorbed into Shinto practice.

2. Kagura are also enjoyed as entertainment. They are regarded as containing traces of very old shamanic practices, and their masked performance at Shinto shrines both depicts kami and activates their presence. Gerald Groemer (2010) argues that they have undergone considerable transformation over the centuries. Once danced only by Shinto priests, kagura are now maintained as a folkloric practice while still regarded as sacred (Sōhei 2011). Terence Lancashire's (1997, 2001, 2004a, 2004b) extensive work on kagura addresses their history and contemporary practice. Irit Averbuch (1998, 295, 315) writes that "this myth describes a shamanic rite in which the goddess Ame-no-uzume . . . performs a frenzied dance of possession," and she explains how Hayachine kagura depicts Uzume's dance as the first shamanic possession. Drawing from Donald L. Philippi's (1969, 81–85) translated edition of the *Kojiki*, Averbuch writes, "The *Kojiki* version can be summarized thus: When the sun goddess Amaterasu . . . hid herself in the Heavenly Cave, the whole world plunged into darkness. The myriads of kami gathered to perform a rite to lure out the sun. At the climax of the rite, the goddess Ame-no-uzume bound up her sleeves with a sacred cord, held bamboo leaves in her hands, overturned a bucket upon which she started stamping

and dancing. She then became possessed . . . and took off all her clothes. Then the heavens shook as the eight-hundred myriad deities laughed, arousing the curiosity of Amaterasu, who opened the door a crack to inquire. She was then pulled out of the cave, and light and life returned to the world" (321n4). Hugh De Ferranti (2000, 25, 26) writes that "the sounds of instruments appropriately played could harness and deliver *kami*" and that the *Kojiki* version of Uzume's dance describes her rhythms as a means "to induce a trance (a state of reception to *kami*)."

3. DANCING THE BODY POLITIC

1. Rev. Patti Usuki, "What Is Obon?," http://westlosangelesbuddhisttemple.org/activities/obonfestival.

2. There are several Japanese words for "dance," including *odori, buyo,* and *ondo. Odori* suggests lively dance, especially folk dance. *Buyo,* as in *nihon buyo,* is classical staged dance that requires extensive training. *Ondo* has come to mean a secularized form of unison group odori set to a distinctive rhythm (2/2 with a swing) and is often referred to as "street" dancing.

3. Writing in 1938, Katsumi Onishi noted that this practice was already well established in Hawai`i. She described the Bon season in Hawai`i as extending from "late June to early September" and remarked, "In an effort to make the *Bon-odori* a success, the sponsors try to choose a weekend relatively free of *Bon* dances in the neighboring communities. Except for Honolulu, rarely does a community witness two sponsors attempting *Bon-odori* on the same weekend" (50). The development of Japanese bon-odori was quite different in Hawai`i than in California, and I will not address it to any significant extent here, since other scholars have done so in depth and detail (see also Combs 1979; Smith 1962; Van Zile 1982).

4. The S. K. Uyeda Department Store specialized in Japanese clothing and home goods. It was founded in 1945, after the Uyeda family left Manzanar, and closed in 2016. It was regarded as "a pillar of Little Tokyo" (Kaplan-Reyes 2009).

5. Van Zile (1982, 4) and Rev. Kodani (1999, 9) write that bon-odori in Hawai`i predate bon-odori on the mainland by at last two decades and that the first mention of them was in a 1905 issue of a Japanese American newspaper, which noted that they were already popular. See also Smith 1962; Yano 1984, 1985. Jo Anne Combs (1979, 57) interviewed two Issei who remembered bon-odori performed on Central Avenue in Los Angeles in 1925, but that was almost certainly unusual for the time.

6. "Yuiyo Bon-odori" (1984), "Tampopo Ondo" (1994; rev. 1998), "Gardener's Song / Gardena Bushi" (1998), "Manzanar Bushi" (2002), "Mottainai" (2011), "Bambutsu No Tsunagari" (2013), and "Sembazuru" (2015).

7. Van Zile (1982, 22) notes that the ethnomusicologist Barbara Smith researched bon daiko in Hawai`i and took lessons: "She became the first female drummer in Hawai`i and continues to participate in several dances each summer. . . . Following her lead, a female member of the Yamada Bon Dance Club now drums with the Iwakuni Bon Dance Club."

8. While a live bon drummer is the norm in Southern California, few groups play live for bon-odori. One of the most well known is the Matsutoyo-kai ensemble, a minyo group of adult students led by their teacher, Matsutoyo Sato. Sato-sensei's daughter Marisa Kosugi leads Minyo Station, also often seen performing at Obon festivals. Both ensembles are

sometimes invited or hired to accompany bon-odori, but even then, recorded music is used for certain songs that a minyo group can't perform.

9. Few of the recordings carry any of their original attributions (e.g., names of singers or composers). In some cases, I found that bon-odori participants simply knew who the singer was. I am certain that the recording of "Tokyo Ondo" (composed by Shinpei Nakayama) used for bon-odori is not the 1933 original sung by Katsutaro Kouta and Issei Mishima, but I don't know anything else about the version now used.

10. The BCA Bookstore can be accessed at *http://bcabookstore.mybigcommerce.com/*.

11. Personal communications, June 30 and July 2, 2015.

12. Recordings of both these songs were recently rediscovered and are documented in Kiyama, Kodani, and Miyamoto 2016, 15, 19.

13. For example, the camp newsletter *Poston Press Bulletin*, vol. 20, no. 1 (August 3, 1944), contains a notice about the Hatsubon service and an invitation to join the "Obon odori," which was evidently held on Sunday evening, August 27 (see *http://www.bookmice.net/darkchilde/japan/poston108.html*). In vol. 20, no. 15 (August 26, 1944), a brief announcement notes that the "YBA"—the Young Buddhist Association, a lay youth group under the BCA—was "grateful for the obon success" (*http://www.bookmice.net/darkchilde/japan/poston110.html*). Neither notice states that Rev. Iwanaga led the bon-odori, but chances are that he did. At least one bon-odori was held at Amache (see *https://northbaydigital.sonoma.edu/digital/collection/nbedc/id/795/rec/1* for a slide of Amache Obon dancers; *http://www.discovernikkei.org/en/nikkeialbum/albums/544/slide/?page=67* for a photo by Jack Muro, "the underground photographer of Amache," of young women in kimonos dancing around Block 6H). A series of twenty-seven photographs taken by George Hirahara and his son Frank document bon-odori at the Heart Mountain Relocation Center in Wyoming in August 1943 (*http://content.libraries.wsu.edu/digital/collection/hiraharag/search/searchterm/obon*).

Van Zile (1982, 6–7) notes that "it is extremely likely" bon-odori in Hawai'i stopped during the war years. After Pearl Harbor and the US engagement in the war, Japanese Buddhist priests were taken into custody, and many were interned on the mainland. Temples were closed, and Japanese were prohibited from gathering publicly. Displays of pride in Japanese cultural heritage were simply too risky. Bon-odori was revived by Japanese in Hawai'i in 1948.

14. This quintessentially Buddhist performative gesture is meaningful far beyond Jodo Shinshu. This book is in many ways an extended gassho, connecting my research across many years in several Buddhist lifeways, from Theravada Buddhism in Bangkok to Jodo Shinshu and Zen Buddhism in Japanese America. This gassho—or *wai* in Thai—began in 1986 with my study of Thai performers' rituals. See Wong 2001, 74–76, for my thoughts on the importance of the wai for Thai epistemologies of performance.

15. Akiyama 1989, 126, cites Onishi 1938, 56, for this information.

16. Victor of Japan, MV-1 (JES-1041), originally recorded on 78 rpm as Victor V-41543, according to Van Zile 1982, 52.

17. "How to Dance Tankobushi," Must Love Japan: Video Travel Guide of Japan, *http://www.mustlovejapan.com/category/hwt/dbo/*. This website is bottomless and claims to "cover every aspect of tourism in Japan," which it very nearly seems to do, from gardens, *onsen* (public bath houses), and festivals to cities and regions. It is in English and is directed at foreign tourists. Twenty bon-odori dances are featured, complete with textual instructions

and videos, in which the "dance team" of Minato Waodorinokai and Ran no Kai joins Ike-mura Sensei.

18. During World War II, African Americans moved into the neighborhood, which was then briefly known as Bronzeville, when the internment emptied it, demonstrating how US communities of color are all too often forced to benefit from one another's dislocation. Only one-third of its Japanese American residents returned, slowly, after 1945, but it was no longer a thriving retail area. The neighborhood was redeveloped over three periods between the 1970s and the present. As Kelly Simpson (2012) puts it, postwar Little Tokyo illustrates "a complicated relationship between urban renewal and Japanese American identity."

19. The JACCC facilities—a set of buildings, plaza, and Japanese garden—were constructed between 1978 and 1983 after a capital campaign and a long, considered process of planning. The creation of "a permanent center for the community where arts and culture come alive and can flourish for future generations" was part of the 1970s redevelopment of Little Tokyo (*http://www.jaccc.org/history/*). In 1978 the Friends of Little Tokyo Arts commissioned Noguchi to create a plaza with an anchoring work of public art, and the JACCC Plaza was dedicated in 1983 with *To the Issei,* two basalt boulders on a mountain-like brick pedestal, at its center.

20. The project is described in detail at *http://www.publicartinla.com/Downtown/Little_Tokyo/home_little_tokyo.html.*

21. Miyamoto has created new songs and dances to explore environmental issues (e.g., "Mottainai," about recycling and avoiding waste) and to model interethnic, community-based collaboration. Her FandangObon project is a long-term series of *encuentros* between her band of Japanese American singers and musicians and the band Quetzal, along with African drummers from South Central Los Angeles. Putting *son jarocho* music and dance together with Japanese American bon-odori, sometimes with the infusion of West African drumming, is driven by a careful, strategic series of community workshops every year, leading up to a "convening" in October at the JACCC Plaza just before Día de Muertos. This ongoing project is so rich that I hope to write about it at length elsewhere. Miyamoto's friendships and collaborative efforts with dance teachers, especially Elaine Fukumoto, have led to the incorporation of her dances into the annual set performed during Obon season. Her dance and song "Sembazuru," about Sadako Sasaki, her origami cranes, and Hiroshima, was featured in the summer of 2015; "Bambutsu no Tsunagari," a song and dance from the FandangObon project, was featured in the summer of 2015; and some of her other pieces ("Mottainai," "Yuiyo Bon-Odori," "Tampopo Ondo," "The Gardener's Song") are still performed.

22. In 1994, Hirabayashi wrote a kumi-daiko part and choreographed an accompanying dance, and she frequently teaches both in three-hour workshops. As a result, thousands of taiko players know "Ei Ja Nai Ka" and are familiar with the explicitly Asian American labor histories acted out through its dance moves, including railroad work and fishing with nets. See Hirabayashi's website, *http://pjhirabayashi.com/,* for information about her ongoing "Ei Ja Nai Ka" workshops. As Angela Ahlgren (2016; 2018, 25–47) has discussed in detail, Hirabayashi designed "Ei Ja Nai Ka" as an open-source work. It is always attributed to her and is now regarded as canonic in the bon-odori repertoire; I am told it is always danced at the San Jose Obon and can attest that it is frequently featured in Southern California bon-odori circles.

23. This was on the On Ensemble blog (accessed on August 14, 2015), but it is no longer available as of 2018.

24. By Mark Ronson, featuring Bruno Mars, a huge hit in 2014.

4. GOOD GIGS, BAD GIGS

1. See Palumbo-Liu 1999 for more on this.

2. I am indebted to Emily Roxworthy's (2008) scholarship on performance in the Japanese American incarceration camps and on the key role of spectacle in the US government's internment strategies. She writes that spectacle has a "propensity to disengage its audience—to render even its participants as passive spectators" and that "the structural trauma of the internment [was] located in the spectacularization imposed upon Japanese Americans by the U.S. government and mass media" (8, 3). See also Colborn-Roxworthy 2006, 2007; Roxworthy 2013, 2014. In short, just as the incarceration camps were a kind of spectacle, the Manzanar National Historic Site—run by the US National Park Service—is another.

3. The boycott has a long and honorable history in the Asian American Movement, including

- 1994: a boycott of Denny's restaurants nationwide, in response to waitstaff refusals to serve Asian and Asian American customers in Syracuse, New York
- 2000: the Yellow Fist Campaign, boycotting the hip-hop crew the Bloodhound Gang and its song "Yellow Fever"
- 2001: a boycott of Forever 21, a national multimillion-dollar retailer based in Los Angeles, in support of garment workers' rights
- 2002: a boycott of Abercrombie & Fitch for its apparel featuring racist depictions of Chinese laundrymen.
- 2002: a national boycott movement initiated by Professor Ling Chi Wang with the help of two Asian American national organizations—Asian Pacific Americans in Higher Education (APAHE) and the Association of Asian American Studies (AAAS)—against the national laboratories funded by the US Department of Energy, when Wen Ho Lee was accused of spying

Asian Americans have also boycotted many films and theatrical productions, including Clint Eastwood's *Absolute Power* (1997), *Rising Sun* (1993), *Miss Saigon* on Broadway (1991), and *The Mikado* at Pomona College (1990).

An Asian American boycott activates different anxieties than African American boycotts. In a detailed consideration of Black participation in the public sphere through consumption, Regina Austin (1994, 226) argues that the everyday practices of Black consumerism are often treated as deviant (marked by bad if not insulting service, refusals of service, or assumptions that the Black consumer is a potential shoplifter). Black consumerism is suspect before it even takes place, whereas Asian American consumerism is seen as "natural," albeit grudging, money-grubbing, and self-serving. Asian Americans are viewed as having too much money, so they are not potential shoplifters but rather privileged participants in American capitalism. When Asian Americans activate a boycott, they are not necessarily seen as questioning the terms of capitalist production but instead are viewed as poor sports and untrustworthy (unpatriotic) foreigners. Whereas "Buy Black" campaigns have deep affective and political weight for African American communities, with an emotive political force that strikes straight at the heart of capitalism's contradictions, a "Buy Asian" campaign would probably prompt an all-too-predictable backlash (because the Asian American is the eternal foreigner), and a "Buy Asian American" campaign is a bit of an oxymoron. Austin further argues that Black critiques of conspicuous consumption within the African American community have addressed the reinscription of class differentials and the very terms of a racialized socioeconomic system (232–34). In addition, she notes that an overly close focus on consumption is less useful than a broader consideration of the production and distribution of commodities: "Consumption is more disruptive, however, when its linkages to production and distribution are acknowledged, and consumption practices are altered in a way that attacks the discriminatory and oppressive manner in which goods are made and sold as well as bought" (240).

4. See Visweswaran 1994; Rice 2008; Titon 2008; Newton and Stacey 1995, 296–97.

5. A parallel is instructive here. Theodore S. Gonzalves (2010) critiques the Pilipino Culture Night (PCN) as reinscribing and valorizing the Philippine nation-state, its assimilation of ethnic others, and certain celebratory narratives about the Filipino American immigrant experience. He looks closely at the loaded processes of folkloricization that frame the PCN's obligatory dances (e.g., *tinikling*). Both the process of interviewing PCN organizers and participants in several locations and Gonzalves's ethnographic and experiential base as a longtime PCN organizer and participant in his own right are central to his critique. Still, it is complicated by the fact that Filipinx American students at UC Irvine now read his book (and Christi-Anne Castro's [2011], also on the cultural politics of Filipino American and Philippine performance) and are self-consciously addressing their own processes of representation as part of their creative efforts to stage PCNs (personal communication from Filipinx American students at UCI, April 2003). One student described Gonzalves's and Castro's dissertations as "my bibles."

5. TAIKO, EROTICS, AND ANGER

1. This is not his real name.

2. The anthropologist Jeffrey Tobin (2000) has considered working-class Argentine soccer fans' pleasures and their risky interface with the homoerotic; Sharon Mazer (1990, 1998) offers a close look at the visceral pleasures of WCW wrestling and its fans' delight in its gendered, racialized morality plays.

3. The interviews with Harriet Mizuno-Moyer and Taylor Moyer and with Beverly Murata took place at Sozenji Buddhist Temple in Montebello, California, on June 19, 2001.

4. Hill Collins (1998, 85) observes, "Those victimized by hate speech often choose not to fight back. . . . Although fear, rage, and shock may characterize the victim's reaction, she or he may not think of an appropriate response until much later. Moreover, the effect of dehumanizing language is often flight rather than fight." Hill Collins thus argues that fighting words are more likely to prompt silence than to incite a violent response.

5. Many thanks to Yayoi Uno Everett for giving me the poster. It can be seen in Bender 2012, 160. I was amused to learn years later that Ahlgren (2011, 199) also had a Honō Daiko poster on her wall.

6. My thanks to George Lipsitz for this point.

7. Most all-women taiko groups were formed in response to gender inequity in existing taiko groups or as proactive efforts to explore alternative kinds of kumi-daiko. Sawagi Taiko in Vancouver is one such group, described on its website (*http://sawagitaiko.com/*) as follows: "Sawagi Taiko is the first all-women's taiko group in Canada, formed in 1990. In Sawagi Taiko, we pool our common and unique experiences as East Asian women living in Canada and focus our creative energy and ideas into a powerful expression that is always heard and can't be ignored. As a performing group, we're looking to smash hierarchies and create an environment where all our members can initiate and explore their artistic visions."

Around the same time, in 1988, Tiffany Tamaribuchi created the all-women and mostly queer-identified performing ensemble Jodaiko; see Ahlgren 2018, 111–35, for a detailed examination of this group. Since then, Raging Asian Women (RAW) was founded in Toronto in 1998, Inner Truth Taiko Dojo was founded in Toronto in 2004, and the Genki Spark was founded in Boston in 2010.

8. A few North American taiko groups have gone on tour in Japan, but most would agree that this takes considerable chutzpah. I acknowledge that I may have overstated the unidirectionality of this relationship. The American Studies scholar Masumi Izumi (personal communication, April 30, 2018) told me that some female members of Kodo have been much inspired by San Jose Taiko and Katari Taiko in Vancouver and greatly influenced by North American taiko particularly, because the majority of taiko players have been women in North America from the beginning. The relationship between North American and Japanese taiko might be more reciprocal than what I argue, though Izumi's observations suggest that that reciprocity is gendered.

9. Bushido encompassed sobriety, simple living, duty and loyalty to one's lord, obedience to parents, the willingness to face death, the dedicated practice of the martial arts to discipline the mind and body, good manners, compassion for others, and more. It was both feudal and Buddhist in its values and is still deeply part of any Japanese martial arts training. Bushido is rarely explicitly named as integral to taiko praxis; rather, it is present in unarticulated forms via the relationship between taiko and martial arts.

10. Unless otherwise noted, all comments and quotations from Akemi Jige and Ayano Yamamoto are from the workshop they conducted for Satori Daiko at the Asano Taiko Company studio on August 22, 2001, in Matto, Ishikawa, Japan. Jige speaks only Japanese, so Rev. Tom served as translator, and I suspect he translated only about 50 percent of what she said, due to time constraints.

11. The documentary *Paris Is Burning* (Livingston 1990) amply demonstrates how the sartorial becomes a performative embodiment that provides imagined access to class and privilege. Few scholars of performance have offered extended critical analyses of costuming, but the ethnomusicologist Veit Erlmann's (1996, 197–203) close consideration of South African *isicathimiya* groups' concert dress connects the racialized body, labor, colonial pathologies, and performance in a radically historicized reading of dress as embodiment. Without resorting to easy dichotomies of resistance and reinscription, he maps how choirs' different uniforms signify and explore Black migrant workers' possible social spaces, from enactments of social advancement (e.g., by wearing suits and white gloves) to expressions of pan-African protest (e.g., by wearing dashikis). He treats dress as symbolic narratives that tack between production and consumption, here telling stories about the laboring Black body's history.

12. Men and women generally wear the same costumes, except in two instances. When women dance, they usually wear a kimono or a yukata (an informal cotton robe shaped much like a kimono), and sometimes they even play taiko in yukata. I have never seen a man play taiko wearing a yukata, though men may wear them when relaxing at home.

13. The fact that Honō Daiko has personal designers is noteworthy because it connects them to the Japanese fashion industry. Dorinne Kondo (1997, 56) treats the products of the fashion industry as performance, closing the link between clothes and costuming. By closely "reading" design, she argues that the fashion industry as a whole is "quintessentially transnational in its dispersal and reach, [even as] it is simultaneously rife with essentializing gestures that refabricate national boundaries." She notes the discomfort that some designers feel in being designated "Japanese," which is a particular aesthetic marketing niche in the fashion industry that all too quickly slides into japonaiserie (60). Japanese designers thus struggle with expectations of kimono evocations or Zen simplicity, and Kondo suggests that the field of sartorial play "articulate[s] complex forms of Japanese autoexoticism [and] counter-Orientalisms" (72). She presents the work of certain avant-garde Japanese designers and their symbolic attempts to reconfigure key fashion concepts such as "prettiness" and "decoration" in what she calls "an implicit critique of Eurocentrism" that is necessarily racialized and gendered (120, 122). A key Japanese design gesture has been making clothing that does not follow the lines of the woman's body but rather creates a new kind of space around/for the body, thus disrupting "the presumed relationship between clothing and bodies" (123) and the very construction of gender. "Shapeless," or non-gender-specific, clothes address the linkages between race, nation, gender, and the global market (124). Finally, Kondo does not shy away from the close relationship between the fashion industry and global capitalism (145), noting that the critiques and rebellions implicit in design are in instant, interconstitutive dialogue with the shaping force of the market.

14. Hakama are usually but not always worn by men. Samurai are frequently seen wearing hakama over a kimono, and Shinto priestesses always wear plain red hakama over a white kimono.

15. Tiffany Tamaribuchi, the director of Sacramento Taiko Dan, is widely known among North American taiko players for taking first place in the odaiko contest at the annual O-Taiko Festival in Fukui, Japan. In an interview (Barakan 1995), the Honō Daiko member Miyuki Ikeda stated that she viewed the odaiko specifically and taiko generally as masculine (also discussed in Carle 2008, 60–61).

16. Bender (2012, 146–50) offers an excellent overview of the gendered theatrical norms and absence and presence of women on the Japanese stage.

17. At this point, Rev. Tom (who was translating) added, "My teacher, Sudo-sensei, says the same thing."

18. The literal dictionary translations of these terms are "straight line" (*chokusen*) and "curved line" (*kyokusen*), but Jige seemed to be using them more metaphorically.

19. Ahlgren (2011, 184–93) echoes Jige's comments in her exegesis of Tiffany Tamaribuchi's performances of "Odaiko" and the production of queer spectatorship. Ahlgren argues that binaries of masculine-feminine and butch-femme are not the most salient distinctions in Tamaribuchi's all-women, mostly queer taiko group, Jo-Daiko.

20. Again, my thanks to George Lipsitz for this phrasing.

21. On *M. Butterfly*, see Kondo 1990; Morris 1994; Eng 2001.

22. Bender (2012, 78–91) offers a detailed history of the film and its influence on Den Tagayasu and Ondekoza's elevation of the odaiko solo to "the ultimate display of physical power in taiko performance" (91).

23. This email and the responses were sent from March 10 to 12, 2004.

24. All biographical information on Tanaka Seiichi was taken from the old San Francisco Taiko Dojo website (www.taikodojo.org), accessed March 14, 2004. This site is no longer extant and has been replaced by *https://www.sftaiko.com/*, which also has a biography of Tanaka.

25. I haven't interviewed Tanaka-sensei, though many other scholars have. I am not part of his lineage. I acknowledge and respect his founding authority and his pervasive influence on the kumi-daiko "tradition." In 2001 I attended the celebration in San Francisco after the National Endowment for the Arts named him a National Heritage Fellow, recognizing his achievement as a US-based culture bearer, and it was deeply moving to see two generations of students turn out in his honor.

26. *http://www.sftaiko.com/essence-2017/*. See also Varian 2013, 83–95, for a detailed discussion of Tanaka-sensei's "four main elements of taiko."

27. The version of "Tsunami" I describe here is seen on *Frontier Spirit: Seiichi Tanaka and San Francisco Taiko Dojo* (1998, produced by San Francisco Taiko Dojo, videocassette [VHS]).

28. The Imperial Rescript on Education was a fixture of Japanese classrooms from the late nineteenth century until the end of World War II. Students were required to memorize this text, which demanded filial piety and undying loyalty to the emperor.

29. *Naked Festival* showcases a gorgeous "photo-essay" of black-and-white photographs taken by Tamotsu Yato at a number of festivals, framed by several written essays. The photographs are undated but are presumably from the 1960s. In a review of the book, the anthropologist David Plath (1970) is impatient with its reliance on a Japan-versus-West binary. He notes that the book's "object is to get middle-aged urban sophisticates to become 'true and unchanging men of Japan' (p. 151) by shucking their polluted Western shorts and cinching up once more in undefiled *fundoshi*. . . . The authors blame Western Imperialism for dragging Japanese manhood out of Eden and making it ashamed of nakedness, but they admit that the case is weak."

30. *http://www.Kodo.or.jp/member/yoshikazu_en.html*.

31. *Kodo* (Sony Music Entertainment, 1992, videocassette [VHS]).

32. Karen Kelsky's (1999, 245) research suggests that this is also true for Japanese men in the US: "Matsui Machiko, in her study of Japanese study abroad students in the United States, celebrates Japanese women's advantage over their 'Oriental' male counterparts based on women's exclusive ability to assimilate into the white mainstream through marriage with Americans, an opportunity, she implies, out of reach for Japanese men (1994:137-138). Likewise, my informant Ishizaki Reiko, a 24-year-old woman who had studied for two years at the University of California at Santa Barbara, explained to me, 'Japanese guys feel more inferiority than girls do that they are racially despised by the world. With Japanese girls, you are popular just for being a Japanese girl. For us, it's almost an advantage. But Japanese men have no standing [*tachiba ga nai*]. Race becomes a problem for Japanese men, but for women race is "excused" [*yurusareru*].' It seems, however, that in Japanese women's case race is not so much excused as fetishized. Japanese men, by contrast, like the Asian American men

described by Ebron and Tsing in a recent article, are seen as representatives of too much tradition in a regime of modernity that defines the traditional as 'outside, ineffective, and already having lost the game' (1995:397)."

33. Feng (1996) reports on a conversation he had with the director Steven Okazaki, who said that he decided to use actors in a fiction film rather than make a documentary specifically to bypass Asian conflict avoidance: "You know, I did that film on Hiroshima [*Survivors* (1982)], and someone says, 'I saw my mother and father burned alive,' and then they giggle and cover their mouth and apologize for saying that—I did not want anyone to do that, and I think in many ways most Asian Americans would do that in some way, 'This bad thing happened to me, but I still like white people.' And I just wanted actors to say, 'This is what happened,' and then hold it there, not start backing away from it. I normally love and believe in documentaries, but I felt stronger about the subject than I did about the medium on this."

6. PAIN AND THE BODY POLITIC

1. I ask the same questions that Susan Leigh Foster (2003, 397) approaches quite evocatively in her study of mass social protest: "What are these bodies doing?; what and how do their motions signify?; what choreography, whether spontaneous or pre-determined, do they enact?; what kind of significance and impact does the collection of bodies make in the midst of its social surround?; how does the choreography theorize corporeal, individual, and social identity?; how does it construct ethnicity, gender, class, and sexuality?; how have these bodies been trained, and how has that training mastered, cultivated, or facilitated their impulses?; what do they share that allows them to move with one another?; what kind of relationship do they establish with those who are watching their actions?; what kinds of connections can be traced between their daily routines and the special moments of their protest?; how is it possible to reconstruct and translate into words these bodies' vanished actions?; how is the body of the researcher/writer implicated in the investigation?"

2. I am acutely aware that many, many North American taiko players will disagree with this. Certainly, some of the leading North American taiko teachers and performers are well respected in Japan. But that isn't my point, which is that the ideology of Japanese authenticity and authority is maintained by *both* Japanese and North American taiko players, for different reasons. The first World Taiko Gathering, in Los Angeles in July 2014, was a self-conscious attempt to break down the binary between Japan and everywhere else by positioning taiko as a global phenomenon, with Japanese performers holding pride of place but nonetheless sharing the stage with ensembles from the US, Australia, the UK, Italy, and elsewhere.

3. DeFrantz (2005, 660) writes, "As conceived by literary theorist Houston Baker, the term 'mastery of form' suggests discursive strategies that allow for articulations of African American subjectivity through the appropriation and reshaping of stereotypical representations, while 'deformation of mastery' proposes methods that allow black people to reveal themselves to themselves through manipulation of established representational tropes."

4. The documentary covers Hernández's time in Los Angeles as a member of Rev. Tom Kurai's group Sozenji Taiko, his years in Japan with Ondekoza, and then his postamputation recovery in Los Angeles and his determination to keep running marathons.

5. *Sogakuron* is a compound word invented by Ondekoza: *so (u),* running + *gaku,* music (*ongaku*) + *ron,* theory, doctrine. My thanks to Dr. Takako Iwasawa for explaining this.

6. *http://www.ondekoza.com/aboutus.html.*

7. See my article on Aoki for his thoughts on how the meanings associated with taiko have changed with its movement into North America (Wong 2006).

8. This taped conversation took place on February 28, 2007. I thank Beverly Murata, Shirley Gutierrez, and Rev. Tom Kurai for allowing me to share their comments here.

9. The flip side of this ideology is the use of music as torture by the twentieth- and twentieth-first-century American military, as detailed in Cusick 2006.

10. See T. Yamamoto 1999, 133–34, for more on Japanese American femininity and abjection.

11. In contrast, progressive and even radical Japanese American organizations such as Nikkei for Civil Rights and Redress, the Little Tokyo Service Center, Sustainable Little Tokyo, and Great Leap do social justice work and name the problems, and I remain inspired by their ongoing efforts.

12. A feature on Freeman's work describes his project as follows:

[It] deals with historical erasure, one that occurred when almost all buildings were removed from the Manzanar internment camp after World War II.

Andrew Freeman tracked down and photographed scores of these structures, which the government first sold for $333.13 each to veterans, and then to anyone who would cart them away. The purpose was to clear the site, and then the historical slate, of the imprisonment of Japanese Americans that Manzanar represented. Don Becker is proud of how he's upgraded these two examples, relocated to the property long before he bought it. He's also pleased by the link they now provide between his home and a national historic site.

You can't blame him for the bitter irony the internees and their descendants might find in his embrace of their history. Nor was it Freeman's purpose to find fault with the current owners. He only wanted to connect the historical dots. The pretty picture he made of Becker's yard reflects Freeman's desire to show the buildings as they're valued now. In America, one man's misery has often been turned into another man's luxury. (Westerbeck 2007, 9)

13. Put another way, "Strangely enough, beyond the history of the methods developed to block or erase pain, a history of pain must include the products of our efforts to bring it back" (Holmes and Chambers 2005, 135).

7. CRUISING THE PAC RIM

I no longer have the URL for this post from a TV-commercial fan site, and it no longer appears online (I found nothing after extensive searching in August 2014). I copied the series of posts in 2005 as follows:

Kathy Moore (27-Jun-2005 10:27), How can I get a copy of this music??? My dad really likes it.

Luke Machac (05-Jul-2005 04:42), HI Can you please tell me where I could purchase the music from your commercial? I really love it. Great advertisement, great video, great car. Luke.

Wayne Corteville (15-Jul-2005 01:56), Yes, I too would like to know where I can buy a copy for this wonderfull music. I would even like a copy of the execellent video.

Tony Feiza (21-Jul-2005 13:32), I also would like to buy a CD of this music. How can I do that??? Tony.

michael (30-Jul-2005 14:40), I would like to get a whole DVD full of the Mitsubishi Girl's music, and an autographed picture too..of course..they are sooo cool..and so is the commercial :-)

1. MIVEC, for "Mitsubishi Innovative Valve timing Electronic Control system," is the brand name of a variable-valve-timing engine technology developed by Mitsubishi Motors.

2. Yoon (2009, 114–16) addresses the *Rising Sun* scene featuring Tanaka-sensei in very similar terms (see n. 6 below).

3. There are other examples. San Francisco Taiko Dojo is featured on the soundtracks for *Return of the Jedi* and *The Right Stuff* (both 1983). Kinnara Taiko performed Nobuko Miyamoto's song and bon-odori "Yuiyo" in the Obon scene in *The Karate Kid Part II* (1986); indeed, taiko is the very first sound heard in the film, before any images appear.

4. It debuted in late May 2005, during the season finales of three popular shows, *Desperate Housewives, 24,* and *Two and a Half Men.*

5. Now discontinued, the station and its blog were available at *http://arhythmius.com/* in 2005.

6. Intercutting footage of taiko and something completely unrelated to it creates a predetermined relationship between them. Exactly the same editing and allusional technique was used in the scene from *Rising Sun* that intercuts Tanaka-sensei playing odaiko with sex and a murder (see Wong 2004, 209–14).

7. See Shah 1997, xiv–xv, for "a brief political history" of the dragon lady.

8. This is unsubstantiated, but if true it would indicate Mitsubishi's investment in the ad campaign, because Colleen Atwood, who won an Oscar for her work on *Chicago,* also designed the costumes for other top-end films, including *Philadelphia* (1993), *Beloved* (1998), the remake of *Planet of the Apes* (2001), and *Memoirs of a Geisha* (2005)—which, not coincidentally, came out the same year as the Mitsubishi ad.

9. This was discussed in a post, no longer available, on Autoblog, *http://www.autoblog. com/entry/1234000630042227/* (accessed October 13, 2005).

10. Le (2005) writes, "Cars and specifically modifying and customizing cars have always been popular with American youth, especially in California. First there was the hot rod and muscle car days in the 1950s and 1960s. In the mid and late 1980s there was the mini-truck scene. Then starting in the early 1990s, following the lead of a small group of young enthusiasts in Japan, kids in southern California turned their attention to modifying compact imports in droves."

11. Again, Le (2005) offers useful context: "Further adding 'fuel to the fire,' some in the auto insurance industry have even claimed that a large portion of the [Asian American] import scene is financed through auto theft and insurance fraud, although the insurance industry has yet to offer much proof to substantiate their allegations. Unfortunately, these particular criticisms again play off the stereotype that all Asians are affluent, or the 'Fu Manchu' or 'Ming the Merciless' stereotype of Asians as somehow being inherently devious or immoral."

12. The California Highway Patrol has had a webpage (*https://www.chp.ca.gov/programs-services/programs/asian-pacific-islander-outreach-program*) directed toward Asian American street racing prevention since at least the mid-2000s.

13. *Furious 7* was released in 2015 and *The Fate of the Furious* in 2017. In 2019, the producers announced that the ninth and tenth films in the franchise would be released in 2020 and 2021 and that the tenth film would be the last.

14. Though its website (*http://www.asianamericanfilm.com/*)—and probably the organization—no longer exists, the collective called Asian American Film explicitly attempted to create a broader base for Asian American involvement in film as both audiences and actors; its manifesto stated, "The purpose of AsianAmericanFilm.com is to build an engaged, involved, active, and excited audience for Asian American films." Posting this casting call was thus a proactive effort to involve Asian American actors in the film.

15. From the Giant Robot website, accessed August 7, 2014. The current info page (*https://www.giantrobot.com/pages/about-us*) has less detail about the defunct magazine and arguably places less emphasis on Asian American contexts.

16. "Harajuku Girls," from Margaret Cho's blog, October 31, 2005, *http://margaretcho. com/2005/10/31/harajuku-girls/*.

17. Except where otherwise noted, Yamami's comments in this section are from an email exchange we had on October 17, 2005, following an in-person conversation a week earlier. I am grateful for his willingness to share his thoughts and experiences.

18. The quotes in this paragraph are from extensive notes I took while sitting in the audience. My thanks to Wynn Yamami Kiyama, the panel organizer, for his thoughtful role as both organizer and moderator, including asking his brother Bryan some tough questions.

19. Responding to this point, Shawn Bender (personal communication, March 19, 2018) wrote to me, "In the Japanese film *Rickshaw Man* [also discussed in chapter 5], . . . the actor (Mifune), who is not a taiko player, plays the drum, [but] the style in which he drums has no empirical connection to the style of festival drumming in the location where the film is set (Kokura Gion Daiko). And the drum rhythms that he plays also bear no relation to the rhythms of Kokura Gion Daiko (they were composed specifically for the film). That is to say, perhaps there is a longer transnational 'tradition' of altering taiko for visual media (film/commercials) that extends from *Rickshaw Man* through to the making of the Mitsubishi commercial?" Bender makes a good point: the sound of taiko is often removed or replaced in films and television. Its acoustic invasiveness may be a practical reason, but in any case, the filmic practice of disregarding musicians' sounds and overwriting them with sometimes outrageously different if not inappropriate sounds is well established. Diegetic musical sound is the exception rather than the norm, which makes it that much easier to map sonic ideologies onto the silent bodies of musicians.

CONCLUSION

1. Sometimes referred to as "the Mottainai band." *Mottainai* is an expression of regret over waste and is the title of one of Miyamoto's most well-known Obon song-dances. See Asai 2016 for more on Miyamoto's contemporary Obon songs and dances.

2. Rev. Mas can be heard saying this in (literally) the last two seconds of the video *Fandango Obon 2014*, at *https://youtu.be/S1QVkjELRvU*.

3. "Core Values and Guiding Principles," *http://taikocommunityalliance.org/about-tca/ core-values-and-guiding-principles/*.

4. To date, I have relied on straightforward thick interpretive work out of the Geertzian school, and while I think it has served me well, the questions I now pursue can't be answered using only culturalist models.

5. I note with pleasure that two non–Asian American scholars—Angela Ahlgren (2008, 2011, 2016, 2018) and Kimberly Powell (2003, 2004, 2005, 2008, 2012a, 2012b, 2012c)—explicitly position their work within Asian American political effort. Powell's (2005, 291–92) ethnographic research with San Jose Taiko is nicely informed by that group's sustained attention to Asian American cultural production. As she puts it, the members are "preoccupied with" and dedicated to exploring "the borders of a recognizable Asian American experience and identity."

6. Millie Creighton (2008, 42) has written apolitically about this rhetorical shift, noting that it offers evidence for different kinds of political change all at once: "Just as *taiko* within Japan began to be embraced as a statement of universal human identity, rather than just Japanese cultural identity, *taiko* outside Japan began to embrace and address such issues. In areas where *taiko* groups arose to express a positive identity of Japanese heritage, there were initial tensions when people without any Japanese or Asian descent became interested in performing *taiko*, not just listening to it. in other cases, long-term foreign residents of Japan who had learned *taiko* in Japan wished to join *taiko* groups when they returned to their home countries, raising questions about whether the suggested boundaries of *taiko* as a percussion form associated with a particular cultural heritage—and the corresponding expectation that only Japanese or those of Japanese descent could perform *taiko*—should be shifted. After years of such discussion, the percussion did shift, allowing *taiko* to be re-staged as a drumming event that could speak to the connections between human beings more generally. *Taiko* came to be seen as performing Japan, but also as performing a particular variety of music produced by humanity, that anyone with training, practice and preferably a good sense of rhythm could participate in."

I have learned much from Creighton's intelligent ethnographic work on Japanese taiko, but in this case her reliance on universalist tropes erases the specific ways that taiko addressed Sansei needs to reclaim and refashion traumatic Japanese American experiences.

7. My thanks to one of the anonymous readers for the University of California Press for this phrase.

8. See *https://portlandtaiko.org/category/performers/*. Wynn Kiyama (Portland Taiko executive director), personal communication, May 5, 2017.

9. She also noted, "I spearheaded [the T-shirt], but Elise Fujimoto took charge of the design after many conversations about our hopes and intent for the shirt."

10. I am indebted to George Lipsitz (personal communication, May 5, 2017) for this phrase and many others in this section.

ACKNOWLEDGEMENTS

I spent many years researching and writing this book, and I received abundant help, support, and advice along the way.

Many friends and colleagues responded to early versions of these chapters when I presented them in colloquium settings, mostly in Departments of Music. It was a gift to share my work at Appalachian State University; Ehwa Woman's University; Emory University; New York University; Union College; the University of California, San Diego; the University of California, Santa Barbara; the University of Chicago; the University of Michigan; the University of North Carolina, Chapel Hill; the University of Pittsburgh; the University of Virginia; and the University of Wisconsin, Madison.

Conferences are the heartbeat of the academic world, and I am grateful to have had the chance to present parts of this book at meetings of the Association for Asian American Studies, the Association for Theatre in Higher Education (ATHE), Feminist Theory and Music VI, Gesellschaft für Musikforschung (German Musicological Society), the International Council for Traditional Music, and—of course—the Society for Ethnomusicology, my scholarly home. Presenting my research at two conferences in Japan, at the National Museum of Ethnology in Osaka and at Seijo University in Tokyo, was also extremely valuable.

Three havens stand out. The gift of extended time at the Center for Ideas and Society at the University of California, Riverside; the University of California Humanities Research Institute; and the National Humanities Center has left a deep mark on these pages.

Over the years, many colleagues provided feedback (even if they didn't always know they were doing so): Anthea Kraut, Dana Simmons, Erica Edwards, Jacqueline Shea-Murphy, Jayna Brown, Jennifer Hughes, Mary Gauvain, Michelle

Raheja, and Tiffany Ana López; Cheng-Chieh Yu, Chiou-Ling Yeh, Dorinne Kondo, Donatella Galella, Grace Wang, Karen Shimakawa, Kevin Fellezs, Lin Shen, Mitsuya Mori, Rachel Lee, and Tamara Ho; Bell Yung, Gabriel Solís, Ian Condry, Josh Pilzer, Michelle Kisliuk, Phil Bohlman, Robert Garfias, Ron Radano, Shuhei Hosokawa, Tim Taylor, and Yayoi Uno Everett; Ajay Heble, Daniel Fischlin, Ellen Waterman, Eric Lewis, Frédérique Arroyas, Gillian Siddall, and the dynamic team at the International Institute for Critical Studies in Improvisation; Ellen Koskoff, Liz Tolbert, Tomie Hahn, and the Society for Ethnomusicology's Section on the Status of Women; Michelle Habell-Pallán, Sherrie Tucker, Sonnet Retman, and the vital circle of Women Who Rock in Seattle.

At UCR, I thank my department chair, Leonora Saavedra, and the two deans of the College of Humanities, Arts, and Social Sciences—Steve Cullenberg and Milagros Peña—who granted me sabbaticals. I am grateful that the faculty and staff of the UCR Department of Music have supported the taiko class and the taiko club since 1998. The UCR Academic Senate provided grants that supported interview transcriptions and more. A warm thanks to my closest colleagues, Jonathan Ritter, Liz Przybylski, René T. A. Lysloff, and Xóchitl Chávez, for having my back. UCR Multimedia Technologies and Muhammad "Siddiq" Siddiqui-Ali generously helped me prepare my rich media materials.

The circle of ethnomusicologists who write about taiko has made all the difference: a big thanks to Angela Ahlgren, Jennifer Milioto Matsue, Lei Ouyang Bryant, Mark Tusler, Paul Yoon, Shawn Bender, and Yoshitaka Terada for years of wonderful conversations and shared experiences.

My deep gratitude to Kokyo Taiko in Chicago and Triangle Taiko in Raleigh, North Carolina, especially Rocky and Yoko Iwashima, for welcoming me as a guest. Asian American arts comrades who showed me the way include Francis Wong, Jon Jang, Melody Takata, Hafez Modirzadeh, and Tatsu Aoki; Bryan Yamami, PJ Hirabayashi, Roy Hirabayashi, and Kenny Endo; the members of Senryu Taiko; Nobuko Miyamoto, Donna Ebata, Martha Gonzalez, Quetzal Flores, and Dan Kwong; Sojin Kim; Terry Nguyen, Junko Ihrke, and Shih-wei (Willie) Wu. Women and Taiko is my newest taiko family, especially Karen Young, Sarah Ayako, and Pat Calvelo. I have taken workshops with extraordinary teachers, including Kenny Endo, PJ Hirabayashi, Roy Hirabayashi, Kaoru Watanabe, Karen Young, Raging Asian Women, Linda Uyehara Hoffman, and Tiffany Tamaribuchi. Steve Sano's and Linda Uyechi's warmth, wisdom, and generosity stand out. (See figure 29, the author editing with colleagues at her elbow, at *http://wonglouderandfaster.com*.)

Many thanks to my mother, Jean Carol Huffman Wong, who came along for the ride and understood why I loved the Taiko Center of Los Angeles.

Niels Hooper and the University of California Press got this book out into the world, and I couldn't be more grateful. The copy editor Juliana Froggatt smoothed out every sentence. Four scholars assessed my manuscript near the end and provided invaluable feedback: I thank the two anonymous readers as well as Shawn

Bender and Masumi Izumi, who offered vital, detailed suggestions. George Lipsitz, Wynn Kiyama, and Angela Ahlgren workshopped my manuscript at the finish line, and their comments made a world of difference. I am especially grateful to George for guiding me toward the American Crossroads series, and for the collegial model he offers to so many of us in American Studies and Ethnic Studies.

I offer my heartfelt thanks to the members of Satori Daiko, who are all over these pages. You can't know how much you've given me. Or perhaps you can, because I sometimes think that the feelings generated by playing taiko are collective all the way down. Much love to Amy Shimamoto, Antoine Gautier, Beverly Murata, Brian Grannan, Chester Hashizume, Denise Donovan, Gary St. Germain, Glen Shimamoto, Glenn Watanabe, Grace Shimamoto, Judi Kaminishi, LizAnn Shimamoto, Harriet Mizuno-Moyer, Lani Nakasone, Maceo Hernandez, Mike Penny, Miki Dun, Ray Nagami, Shirley Gutierrez, Stan Moyer, Suzanne Nagami, Taylor Moyer, and Yukiko Matsuyama. I send a special thanks to Audrey Nakasone and Elaine Fukumoto for talking with me over many years about our taiko experiences.

My deepest debt is to Rev. Shuichi (Tom) Kurai (1947–2018), for teaching me, for introducing more than one thousand UCR students to the magic of taiko, and for sharing your life with me and the members of Satori Daiko. *Otsukaresama deshita.*

GLOSSARY

amanojaku	A supernatural being associated with Japanese folklore and the Shinto cosmos. This small member of the subclass of demons called *oni* plays on a person's darkest desires and thus pulls him or her into doing bad things.
Asano Taiko Company, Ltd (*http:// www.asano.jp/en/*).	One of the two best taiko manufacturers in Japan (along with Miyamoto Taiko). This family business was founded in 1609, and its factory, showroom, and small museum are in Matto, Ishikawa Prefecture. It opened Asano Taiko U.S., its California-based showroom and the home of the Los Angeles Taiko Institute, in 2013.
atarigane	Also called *kane*. A small handheld bronze gong, struck with a thin bamboo beater that has a head of deer antler. Often used to keep time because its sound cuts through that of a taiko ensemble; generally plays the *ji*.
bachi	A drumstick. Also refers more generically to any oblong object used to create sound, e.g., the plectrum for a shamisen.
bon daiko	The solo taiko playing that accompanies *bon-odori*, often quite spare and simple because it accents and supports the rhythms of the song and the dancing. The taiko player stands in the *yagura*, the tall tower at the center of the *bon-odori* circle.
bon-odori	The large participatory group dances that are a highlight of the Japanese and Japanese American Buddhist Obon celebrations held at temples in July and August to honor the ancestors. *Bon-odori* are both traditional and contemporary; Japanese Americans have created new repertoire and choreography over the past hundred years.

Buraku	A minority group at the lowest level of the Japanese social system, segregated by occupation, marriage, and locality. These communities traditionally worked as butchers, undertakers, and leatherworkers, in constant contact with "unclean" materials. Taiko makers were also traditionally from this class. Since the 1970s, the Buraku rights movement has gathered momentum, but Buraku still experience pervasive structural and everyday discrimination.
chindoya	A raucous form of hybrid Western-and-Japanese street music performed by groups of three to four musicians and a singer who carry sandwich boards to advertise the businesses that hire them. They are gaudily made up and usually costumed in *yukata* (traditional cotton robes). One performer generally wears a *chindon,* a frame supporting three percussion instruments: a *shime,* a two-sided tacked drum (*ōdō*), and a small metal gong called *kane.* Others play clarinet, shamisen, or electric guitar. They perform songs and short skits in between busking, with lots of slapstick and boisterous behavior. See Abe 2018 for much more.
chudaiko	A midsized, barrel-shaped taiko with two heads tacked onto a hollow wooden body. It is placed either vertically or diagonally on one of a variety of different stands so that a single musician can play it, usually with sixteen-inch drumsticks.
collegiate taiko	A recent American extension of taiko, based on college campuses and regarded as distinct from community taiko. The first collegiate taiko group was Stanford Taiko, founded in 1990; there are now more than twenty collegiate groups. Most write most of their own repertoire, run their own rehearsals without an adult sensei, and make their own taiko.
Dharma school	The Dharma is the Buddha's teachings, and most Jodo Shinshu Japanese American Buddhist temples offer Dharma school for children and youth. The topics are broad, ranging from Buddhist etiquette in the temple to sutras, the Four Noble Truths, the Eightfold Path, Buddhist ethics and values, Buddhist heritage and history, etc.
dojo	(*Do,* "way"; *jo,* "place.") A traditional Japanese school (for martial arts, music, etc.), always led by a particular teacher.
enka	A Japanese popular music genre that emerged in the early twentieth century and was regarded as nostalgic by the late twentieth century even though still very popular. It has strong associations with traditionality, in both musical style and cultural values.
fandango	A Mexican or Mexican American community gathering featuring *son jarocho* music and dancing on a *tarima* (a raised platform that amplifies the percussive footwork of the dance), with a social aesthetic of participation and *convivencia,* a social value that emphasizes community building and the spirit of making and living life together.

FandangObon | A project drawing together Japanese American *bon-odori* with the transnational *son jarocho* tradition (see also "fandango"), founded in 2013 in Los Angeles and sustained as an annual gathering. The original collaborators were Nobuko Miyamoto, Rev. Mas Kodani, Martha Gonzalez, Quetzal Flores, César Castro, Elaine Fukumoto, and many other musicians and dancers. Together they created a song and dance titled "Bambutsu no Tsunagari—Fandango Obon," which was first performed at Senshin and Nishi Hongwanji Buddhist Temples in July 2014; subsequently, all the other Jodo Shinshu Buddhist temples in Southern California performed the dance to a recording of the song that summer.

fundoshi | A Japanese loincloth worn only by men. It is a long piece of cloth, usually white cotton, about fourteen inches wide and approximately eight feet long, twisted and tied so that the genitals are concealed but the buttocks revealed. A twisted section of the cloth runs between the buttocks.

gaman | A Japanese social value that became extremely important in the Japanese American internment camps: enduring the seemingly unbearable with patience and dignity.

gassho | An important expression of belief in Japanese and Japanese American Jodo Shinshu Buddhism, both a physical gesture and a spoken prayer. The believer places the hands midchest, with palms together, fingers straight and pointed at a 45 degree angle upward, and wrists close to the chest, and then recites the Nembutsu, "Namu Amida Butsu." The pose symbolizes the Dharma (the teachings of the Buddha) as well as readiness to receive it. In a ritual context, when a priest or lay leader simply says "Gassho," everyone brings their hands together.

hachimaki | A headband, often a rectangular piece of cotton that is twisted and then circled around the head, crossing the forehead, and tied in a large knot on the side of the head. Although the *hachimaki* has a practical function as a sweatband, it is also symbolic, indicating a readiness to work hard with others and to persevere.

happi coat | (*Han*, "half"; *pi*, "to wear.") A traditional Japanese cotton jacket. Worn originally by shopkeepers and now by Japanese and Japanese Americans for festivals, they are deeply associated with festive occasions. These jackets are typically hip length, open in front, and brightly colored. Contemporary Japanese American *happi* coats are often a distinctive mixture of traditional shape and contemporary graphic design. In North America, most Japanese American Buddhist temples have *happi* coats with the temple name (often in both English/*romanji* and kanji) and crest (mon) on the back. During Obon season, *bon-odori* dancers usually wear *happi* coats over informal clothing (e.g., T-shirts and shorts or slacks), so when groups from different temples attend Obon festivals to participate in *bon-odori,* they are easily identified by their jackets.

hara	Abdomen, belly, stomach, mind, heart. In the human body, the *hara* is the physical location of ki, energy. This concept is central to taiko, classical Japanese dance (*nihon buyo*), and the Japanese martial arts. As the ethnomusicologist and dance ethnographer Tomie Hahn (2007, 164) writes, "The *hara* is where *ki* energy, or power, resides. . . . In *nihon buyo*, movement must originate from the *hara* center and ripple up the torso, out the arms, legs, head, and even the gaze of the eyes."
hayashi	A general term for the music ensembles that accompany Noh and Kabuki, usually featuring different kinds of drums, flutes, or shamisen.
ikebana	The Japanese tradition of flower arranging, which has a deep base in philosophy and spiritual practice as well as aesthetics.
Issei	"First generation," members of the first generation of Japanese who emigrated. In the US, changing immigration legislation meant that Issei arrived there between 1880 and 1924; their children, the second-generation (Nisei) Japanese Americans, were mostly born between 1910 and 1930.
ji	A traditional Japanese ostinato rhythmic pattern maintained by one or more instruments, often the *shime* or *atarigane*. Three basic *ji* are used in almost all *kumi-daiko* pieces: continuous eighth notes (doko doko doko doko), eighth notes with a swing feel (don-zu don-zu don-zu, don-zu), and *matsuri* ("festival"; don doko don don).
Jodo Shinshu Buddhism	Also known as Shin Buddhism or True Pure Land Buddhism. Founded in Japan in the early thirteenth century, it is now the most popular form of Buddhism there and among Japanese Americans. In the United States, the Buddhist Churches of America serves as its administrative institution, with ties to the head temple, Nishi Hongwanji, in Japan. Most Jodo Shinshu temples in North America serve as Japanese American cultural centers as well, offering classes in Japanese language, music, calligraphy, and more.
Kabuki	A form of Japanese staged drama that emerged in the seventeenth century, combining music, dance, and stories drawn from legends and historical events. It has been all male for most of its history, and performers specialize in either male or female roles.
kachi kachi	A handheld percussion instrument made from wood or bamboo, similar to the bones or castanets. The curved clappers are held loosely, one pair in each hand, and clicked against each other. They are most commonly played by dancers, in time with the music.
kakegoe	Also called *kiyai*. Shouted syllables (e.g., "Ho!" "Yo!" "Sore!") that are sonic realizations of ki, used in taiko and the Japanese martial arts. They can be part of a musical line or can be uttered spontaneously as an expression of ki or as a means of encouraging other participants.

kane	See *atarigane*.
kanji	Chinese ideographs that are part of the written Japanese language.
kata	"Stance," the proper bodily form used in taiko and the Japanese martial arts.
ki	An essential form of energy that is both physical and spiritual in nature. It is located in the solar plexus (*hara*) but can be channeled throughout the body.
Kibei	American-born Japanese who are educated in Japan. Kibei are usually bicultural and bilingual in ways that Japanese Americans are not.
Kodo	Arguably the most famous Japanese *kumi-daiko* group. Its founding members were originally in Za Ondekoza but broke away to form Kodo in 1981. Its repertoire consists of pieces built from folk music materials as well as newly composed works. Its school is on Sado Island, where the group hosts the annual Earth Celebration, featuring musicians from all over the world in concerts and workshops. In 1997 the Kodo Cultural Foundation was created, to administer Kodo's apprenticeship program and to support research on traditional Japanese culture from the region (see Bender 2012, 94–104).
kuchi shōga	(*Kuchi*, "mouth"; *shōga*, "song.") Mnemonics for Japanese drum strokes, indicating speed, pitch, strike point (drumhead vs. rim), etc.
kumi-daiko	(*Kumi*, "group"; *daiko*, "drum.") "Group taiko," the relatively recent tradition of ensembles of drums and performers.
Kurai, Rev. Shuichi Thomas (Rev. Tom; 1947–2018)	A seventh-generation Soto Zen Buddhist priest and the abbot of Sozenji Buddhist Temple in Montebello, California. He was born in Japan and emigrated to Southern California at age five. Active as a taiko player and teacher from the mid-1970s; the founder and director of the Taiko Center of Los Angeles. My teacher from 1997 to 2009.
kyahan	Leggings.
Los Angeles Taiko Institute (LATI; *https://taiko.la/*)	Founded in July 2013 and based in Torrance, California, this taiko instruction school is housed in Asano Taiko U.S., the US storefront of one of the two leading Japanese taiko makers and a self-described "full-service taiko facility" (*https://asano.us/*). At the time of this writing, LATI classes are taught by leading young taiko performers under the guidance of Head Instructor Kris Bergstrom and Principal Instructor Yuta Kato.
ludic	(From Latin *ludos*, "play.") In performance, describes behaviors that playfully-seriously construct new identities and/or social realities, often through inversions, masquerade, tricksterism, etc. Performance studies posits the ludic as central to the social power of performance.

ma

The Japanese aesthetic principle of using emptiness to create dynamic movement or activity. Emptiness creates potential. Space or silence is inserted into paintings, landscapes, music, and dance to create dynamic tension.

Manzanar

One of ten concentration camps for Japanese Americans created in the wake of Executive Order 9066 in 1942. Located at the western edge of Death Valley in eastern California, it was in operation from 1942 to 1945. Originally called the Manzanar War Relocation Center; now the Manzanar National Historic Site, overseen by the National Park Service. Groundbreaking for its NPS interpretive center and headquarters began in 2002.

Manzanar Pilgrimage

The annual gathering at the site of Manzanar War Relocation Center, organized by the Manzanar Committee, first held in December 1969. It now occurs on the last Saturday of April and features a long morning that begins with an interfaith memorial service followed by music, speeches, the roll call of the camps, and a *bon-odori* circle. The daytime program attracts one thousand to two thousand attendees, with a large non–Japanese American presence including, since 2001, a significant number of Muslim Americans. Manzanar at Dusk is an evening program of intergenerational conversations about the internment and civil liberties. The Manzanar Committee was also centrally involved in the Japanese American redress movement of the 1960s–1980s and in the site's designation as a California State Landmark in 1972, a National Historic Landmark in 1985, and a National Historic Site in 1992.

matsuri

A Japanese festival. Every region of Japan has *matsuri* traditions, including unique music and dance. Most focus on a local shrine, and a statue or altar for a place spirit may be borne through the local streets in procession on a *mikoshi* carried by many people and accompanied by music. *Matsuri* include rituals focused on the spirit, at the shrine, but are also joyous and raucous events that fill an entire community.

mikoshi

A portable shrine central to Shinto festivals. Each one symbolizes a local deity and features an ornate gilded and lacquered altar on a palanquin supported by two poles. Pole bearers—usually large numbers of men—run *mikoshi* through the streets during *matsuri* (festivals), which often feature elaborate choreography, lots of *kakegoe,* and drunkenness. *Mikoshi* come in many sizes; an ordinary one weighs half a ton and is carried by thirty to fifty men. The *mikoshi* of Tomioka Hachimangu Shrine in Fukagawa, Tokyo, is the largest, weighing 4.5 tons and requiring three hundred people to carry it; it cost ten million dollars to build in 1991.

minyo

A generic term for Japanese folk song.

Miyamoto Taiko (Miyamoto Un-osuke Co., Ltd.; *http://www. miyamoto-unosuke. co.jp/english/*)	One of the two best taiko manufacturers in Japan (along with Asano). Founded in 1861, the company specializes in festival-related crafts, especially taiko and *mikoshi*. Its main showroom is in Tokyo's Asakusa neighborhood.
momohiki	(*Momo*, "thigh"; *hiki*, "to pull back.") Indigo work pants of heavy cotton, originally worn by farmers and other workers and now understood as festival (*matsuri*) clothing. The legs are narrow, but the waist is wide and tied to fit closely: the fabric around the waist is held in place with the long ties that extend from the waistband. It takes at least a yard and a half of fabric to make a *momohiki*. They can be knee or ankle length and are worn by both men and women.
Namu Amida Butsu	The Japanese version of the Sanskrit *Namo Amitabha Buddhaya*, which means "I take refuge in the Buddha of Immeasurable Life and Light." It is called the Nembutsu in Jodo Shinshu Buddhism and is recited three times with the hands in *gassho*, as a profession of intent.
nihon buyo	Classical Japanese dance that originated in the seventeenth century; performed as a stand-alone stage dance tradition and featured in Kabuki and Noh. It is done by both men and women and requires serious long-term training. Numerous lineages (*iemoto*) of dance teachers oversee the transmission of the tradition.
Nikkei	Japanese in diaspora.
Nisei	Second-generation *Nikkei*. The generation that was in their teens or twenties during internment.
Obon	The Japanese Buddhist summer ritual honoring the ancestors. In Hawai`i and on the US West Coast, Japanese American communities expanded Obon into a temple festival featuring Japanese cultural performances, games, food booths, and more, culminating in participatory *bon-odori* at dusk. The network of Jodo Shinshu temples in Southern California (the Southern District Buddhist Churches of America) organize their Obon gatherings so that no more than two are held on any given weekend between late June and early August, enabling easy attendance at multiple temples. Between San Luis Obispo and San Diego, each Obon festival is attended by hundreds of community members. Obon in Japan is mostly regarded as an opportunity for family gatherings and ritual remembrance, whereas it has a more all-encompassing importance for Japanese American communities as a set of place-making activities that sustain and support ethnic identity.

odaiko	A large barrel-shaped taiko with two heads, placed horizontally and high on a wooden stand so that two musicians can play it at the same time, one on each head. Any gender can play this largest drum in the *kumi-daiko* ensemble, though it is associated with masculine prowess. The male soloists who play *odaiko* may wear *fundoshi* to display their strength and form.
okedo	A two-headed laced drum that has a strap, so the player can wear it over the shoulder and thus move around or even dance while playing.
ondo	The broad category of Japanese traditional folk music. Many *ondo* songs have associated dances (also called *ondo*) that are distinct from classical Japanese dance (*nihon buyo*) and Buddhist ritual group dances (*bon-odori*). Many *ondo* dances are from specific regions and have had that association from the beginning; newer ones are often created to accompany a song that may be popular, traditional, or both.
oni	Japanese demons, devils, ogres, and trolls who feature prominently in folklore and traditional narratives. Some are clever but many are not, and all create trouble wherever they are found. *Amanojaku* are a kind of *oni*.
onnagata	Male Kabuki performers specializing in female roles.
otokoyaku	Female Takarazuka performers specializing in male lead roles.
Rafu Shimpo	A bilingual Japanese American Los Angeles newspaper, founded in 1903 and still based in Little Tokyo.
romanji	The use of the Roman alphabet to transcribe Japanese words.
Sansei	Third-generation *Nikkei*.
sashiko	Traditional Japanese embroidery that is both decorative and functional, because it can reinforce areas of clothing that receive wear. Geometric patterns sewn with white cotton thread in a running stitch on indigo cotton clothing or fabric are the most common.
Satori Daiko	The performing group of the Taiko Center of Los Angeles, led by Rev. Tom Kurai from 1999 to 2018. *Satori* means "enlightenment."
Senryu Taiko (*http://2010.sen-ryutaiko.com/*)	The collegiate taiko group at the University of California, Riverside, founded in 1998.
sensei	"Teacher," an honorific title; e.g., Rev. Tom Kurai was sometimes referred to as Kurai-sensei.
shamisen	A three-stringed traditional Japanese fretless lute, played with a heavy wooden or ivory plectrum. Used by both men and women in a variety of contexts, including songs called *kouta* (played by geisha) and the theater (e.g., Kabuki and puppet drama).

shikata ga nai	A Japanese social value that became extremely important in the Japanese American internment camps: it can't be helped, that's the way it is.
shime or *shime-daiko*	Small, high-pitched two-headed drum with heavy rope laces. Played either sitting or standing.
Shin Issei	The "new" Issei, postwar Japanese immigrants to the US.
shinobue	A traditional Japanese side-blown transverse flute played in festival (*matsuri*) contexts and in ensembles (*hayashi*) accompanying Noh or Kabuki. They come in three sizes, with different pitch centers. Most are made from bamboo and covered with lacquer.
son jarocho	A traditional folk music from southern Veracruz, Mexico, that features as many stringed instruments as possible, including guitars and jaranas (small rhythm guitars), accompanying singers who exchange improvised verses called *décimas*. *Son jarocho* is generally performed in informal gatherings called fandangos, at which the musicians play around a raised platform (*tarima*) where participants take turns dancing in pairs, and now appears widely in Mexican diasporic communities north of the border, often in a spirit of post–Civil Rights Movement community building and identity work.
Soto Zen Buddhism	A Japanese school of Zen Buddhism founded by Dogen in the thirteenth century; the sect in which Rev. Tom Kurai was ordained.
tabi	Fabric footwear, traditional in preindustrial Japan, with a thick sole of either rubber or padded fabric and a separated big toe (like a mitten). They may be ankle length or extend all the way to the knees and are fastened with hooks and eyes. *Tabi* come in many colors and fabric weights; many taiko players wear thick indigo ones.
taiko	"Large drum," the generic term for any of the drums used in *kumi-daiko*.
Taiko Center of Los Angeles (TCLA; *https://taikocentero-fla.com/*)	Taiko school founded by Rev. Tom Kurai in Los Angeles in 1996. Its performing group was Satori Daiko.
Takarazuka	An all-female revue founded in 1913 as a counterpart to the all-male Kabuki. A popular culture form, it is strongly influenced by Broadway, and its fan base is primarily women.
Tanaka, Seiichi	The director of San Francisco Taiko Dojo, who emigrated to the US from Japan in 1968. Widely regarded as the founder of North American *kumi-daiko*.

tekko	Stiff fabric wristbands about five inches wide, fastened with either Velcro or hooks and eyes. They support and stabilize the wrists and were originally worn by farmers and samurai as protection.
tenugui	Long rectangular cotton towels, originally used by laborers. Women often fold them lengthwise and wear them around the neck to outline the collar of their *yukata* (traditional cotton robe) or kimono. Men may tie them around the forehead as *hachimaki*. Some *bon-odori* choreography includes *tenugui*, e.g., waving them, stretching them tight between the hands, taking them off and putting them on in unison. Temples may print the names of sponsors or donors on *tenugui* and sell them to raise funds.
tsuzumi	A two-headed drum laced to an hourglass-shaped wooden body with thick rope. It is held on the right shoulder when played and is prominently featured in the music for Noh and Kabuki.
uchiwa	A generic word for "fan." It can refer to the fans held by dancers, usually flat paper ovals with short handles of either bamboo or plastic, or to a paddle-like frame drum, held in the left hand and struck with a *bachi* in the right hand.
wadaiko	The wide range of Japanese percussion instruments that includes taiko and the ensembles of the postwar *kumi-daiko*. While most regions and prefectures in Japan have unique taiko traditions, *wadaiko* also usually refers to the shared, transregional category of tradition-based percussion music.
wedgie	A joking and/or humiliating procedure, often practiced by bullies, usually boys. A group will surround the victim, grab the elasticized waistband of his underwear, and yank it up, bunching or "wedging" the underpants between the victim's buttocks in an uncomfortable or even painful way.
yagura	In the context of Obon and *bon-odori,* a temporary wooden tower about fifteen feet high that places the musicians above the dancers. Its stage platform is usually quite small, with room for no more than three or four musicians crowded around a *chudaiko* or *odaiko*. More generically, *yagura* were watchtowers in rural Japan.
Yonsei	Fourth-generation *Nikkei*.
yukata	Traditional cotton robe.
Za Ondekoza	One of the early *kumi-daiko* groups, founded in 1969 by Den Tagayasu. Its members all moved to Sado Island to live communally and rehearse daily. Their philosophy of running has attracted much attention. Several members eventually broke off and formed the famous group Kodo in 1981.

REFERENCES

Abe, Marié. 2018. *Resonances of Chindon-ya: Sounding Space and Sociality in Contemporary Japan*. Middletown, CT: Wesleyan University Press.

Abra, Jock. 1987. "The Dancer as Masochist." *Dance Research Journal* 19 (2): 33–39.

Adriaansz, Willem. 1973. *The Kumiuta and Danmono Traditions of Japanese Koto Music*. Berkeley: University of California Press.

Ahlgren, Angela. 2008. "'In Search of Something Else': Tiffany Tamaribuchi, Taiko Drumming, and Queer Spectatorship." In *Dance Studies and Global Feminisms: 41st Annual Conference, November 14–16, 2008, Hollins University, Roanoke, VA*, edited by Teresa Randall, 1–7. Birmingham, Ala.: Congress on Research in Dance.

———. 2011. "Drumming Asian America: Performing Race, Gender, and Sexuality in North American Taiko." PhD diss., University of Texas at Austin.

———. 2016. "A New Taiko Folk Dance: San Jose Taiko and Asian American Movements." In *Contemporary Directions in Asian American Dance*, edited by Yutian Wong, 29–61. Madison: University of Wisconsin Press.

———. 2018. *Drumming Asian America: Taiko, Performance, and Cultural Politics*. Oxford: Oxford University Press.

Ahmed, Sara. 2004. *The Cultural Politics of Emotion*. New York: Routledge.

Akiyama, Linda Cummings. 1989. "Reverend Yoshio Iwanaga and the Early History of Doyo Buyo and Bon Odori in California." MA thesis, University of California, Los Angeles.

Alinder, Jasmine. 2012. "Camera in Camp: Bill Manbo's Vernacular Scenes of Heart Mountain." In *Colors of Confinement: Rare Kodachrome Photographs of Japanese American Incarceration in World War II*, 81–101. Chapel Hill: University of North Carolina Press, in association with the Center for Documentary Studies at Duke University.

Arnold, Gina. 2011. "The Sound of Hippiesomething; or, Drum Circles at #OccupyWall-Street." *Sounding Out! The Sound Studies Blog*. November 7, 2011. https://soundstudiesblog.com/2011/11/07/the-sound-of-hippiesomething-or-drum-circles-at-occupywallstreet/.

Asai, Susan Miyo. 2016. "Sansei Voices in the Community: Japanese American Musicians in California." In *Musics of Multicultural America: A Study of Twelve Musical Communities,* edited by Anne K. Rasmussen and Kip Lornell, 2nd ed., 368–94. Jackson: University Press of Mississippi.

Austin, Regina. 1994. "'A Nation of Thieves': Consumption, Commerce, and the Black Public Sphere." *Public Culture* 7 (1): 225–48.

Averbuch, Irit. 1998. "Shamanic Dance in Japan." *Asian Folklore Studies* 57 (2): 293–329.

Baily, John. 2001. "Learning to Perform as a Research Technique in Ethnomusicology." *British Journal of Ethnomusicology* 10 (2): 85–98.

Balkin, Jack M., and Reva B. Siegel. 2003. "The American Civil Rights Tradition: Anticlassification or Antisubordination?" *Issues in Legal Scholarship* 2 (1): 1–23.

Barakan, Peter. 1995. "Discussion: A Woman Playing Japanese Drums." In *Wadaiko,* edited by Koichi Ikanoshi, 124–35. Tokyo: Kawade Shobō Shinsha.

Bartleet, Brydie-Leigh, and Carolyn Ellis. 2009. "Making Autoethnography Sing / Making Music Personal." In *Music Autoethnographies: Making Autoethnography Sing / Making Music Personal,* edited by Bartleet and Ellis, 1–20. Bowen Hills, Queensland: Australian Academic Press.

Becker, Alton L. 1995. *Beyond Translation: Essays toward a Modern Philology.* Ann Arbor: University of Michigan Press.

Becker, Judith, and Alton Becker. 1981. "A Musical Icon: Power and Meaning in Javanese Gamelan Music." In *The Sign in Music and Literature,* edited by Wendy Steiner, 169–83. Austin: University of Texas Press.

Behar, Ruth. 2013. *Traveling Heavy: A Memoir in between Journeys.* Durham, N.C.: Duke University Press.

Bender, Shawn. 2003. "Drumming between Tradition and Modernity: Taiko and Neo-folk Performance in Contemporary Japan." PhD diss., University of California, San Diego.

———. 2005. "Of Roots and Race: Discourses of Body and Place in Japanese Taiko Drumming." *Social Science Japan Journal* 8 (2): 197–212.

———. 2012. *Taiko Boom: Japanese Drumming in Place and Motion.* Berkeley: University of California Press.

Bendix, Regina. 1997. *In Search of Authenticity: The Formation of Folklore Studies.* Madison: University of Wisconsin Press.

Bergstrom, Kris. 2008. "Free Art License 1.3." *On Ensemble Essays* (blog). December 7, 2008. http://k--b.org/articles/philosophy/free-art-license-13/.

———. 2011. "Copyleft and the Future of Taiko." *On Ensemble Essays* (blog). September 8, 2011. https://taiko.la/sites/default/files/copyleft_future_of_taiko.pdf.

Bohlman, Philip V. 1996. "Pilgrimage, Politics, and the Musical Remapping of the New Europe." *Ethnomusicology* 40 (3): 375–412.

Bolt, Barbara. 2013. "Introduction: Toward a 'New Materialism' through the Arts." In *Carnal Knowledge: Towards a "New Materialism" through the Arts,* edited by Estelle Barrett and Bolt, 1–13. London: I. B. Tauris.

Brown, Bill. 2001. "Thing Theory." *Critical Inquiry* 28 (1): 1–22.

Butler, Judith. 2004. *Precarious Life: The Powers of Mourning and Violence.* London: Verso.

Carle, Sarah. 2008. "Bodies in Motion: Gender, Identity, and the Politics of Representation in the American Taiko Movement." MA thesis, University of Hawai`i at Manoa.

Castro, Christi-Anne. 2011. *Musical Renderings of the Philippine Nation*. New York: Oxford University Press.

Chan, Erin. 2002. "They're Beating the Drum for Female Empowerment." *Los Angeles Times*, July 15, 2002. http://articles.latimes.com/2002/jul/15/local/me-taiko15.

Chow, Kat. 2014. "Roundtable: The Past and Present of 'Yellowface.'" *Code Switch: Frontiers of Race, Culture and Ethnicity* (blog), NPR. August 14, 2014. http://www.npr.org/blogs/codeswitch/2014/08/14/339559520/roundtable-the-past-and-present-of-yellowface.

Chow, Rey. 1993. *Writing Diaspora: Tactics of Intervention in Contemporary Cultural Studies*. Bloomington: Indiana University Press.

Chuh, Kandice. 2002. "Imaginary Borders." In *Orientations: Mapping Studies in the Asian Diaspora*, edited by Chuh and Karen Shimakawa, 277–95. Durham, N.C.: Duke University Press.

———. 2003. *Imagine Otherwise: On Asian Americanist Critique*. Durham, N.C.: Duke University Press.

Chun, Kimberly. 2001. "Where Are the Protestors Now? Playing Fast and Loose with Asian American Car Culture in *The Fast and the Furious*." *AsianWeek*, July 13, 2001. http://www.asianweek.com/2001_07_13/arts3_carculture.htm (site discontinued).

Codetta Raiteri, Chiara. 2016. "Taiko: Cultural and Social Uses of a Performance Practice. Ethnography of the Taiko Center of Los Angeles." MA thesis, Universita degli Studi di Milano-Bicocca, Italy.

Colborn-Roxworthy, Emily. 2006. "Trading 'Earnest Drama' for Prophecy: Performing Japanese American Internment after 9/11." *Journal of Dramatic Theory and Criticism* 20 (2): 27–49.

———. 2007. "'Manzanar, the Eyes of the World Are upon You': Performance and Archival Ambivalence at a Japanese American Internment Camp." *Theatre Journal* 59 (2): 189–214.

Collier, John, Jr., and Malcolm Collier. 1992. *Visual Anthropology: Photography as Research Method*. Rev. ed. Albuquerque: University of New Mexico Press.

Combs, Jo Anne. 1979. "The Japanese O-Bon Festival and Bon Odori: Symbols in Flux." MA thesis, University of California, Los Angeles.

———. 1985. "Japanese-American Music and Dance in Los Angeles, 1930–1942." *Selected Reports in Ethnomusicology* 6: 121–49.

Condry, Ian. 2006. *Hip-Hop Japan: Rap and the Paths of Cultural Globalization*. Durham, N.C.: Duke University Press.

———. 2012. *The Soul of Anime: Collaborative Creativity and Japan's Media Success Story*. Durham, N.C.: Duke University Press.

Connery, Christopher L. 1994. "Pacific Rim Discourse: The U.S. Global Imaginary in the Late Cold War Years." *Boundary 2* 21 (1): 30–56. https://doi.org/10.2307/303396.

Crafts, Susan D., Daniel Cavicchi, Charles Keil, and the Music in Daily Life Project. 1993. *My Music*. Music/Culture. Middletown, Conn.: University Press of New England.

Creef, Elena Tajima. 2004. *Imaging Japanese America: The Visual Construction of Citizenship, Nation, and the Body*. New York: New York University Press.

Creighton, Millie. 2004. "Changing (Heart) Beats: From Japanese National Identity and Nostalgia to the Taiko Rhythms of Citizens of the Earth." Paper presented at the Association for Asian Studies Annual Meeting, San Diego, March 4–7, 2004.

———. 2008. "Taiko Today: Performing Soundscapes, Landscapes and Identities." In *Performing Japan: Contemporary Expressions of Cultural Identity*, edited by Henry M. Johnson and Jerry C. Jaffe, 34–67. Folkestone, UK: Global Oriental.

Csikszentmihalyi, Mihaly. 1990. *Flow: The Psychology of Optimal Experience.* New York: Harper and Row.

Cusick, Suzanne G. 2006. "Music as Torture / Music as Weapon." *Trans—Revista Transcultural de Música / Transcultural Music Review* 10. http://www.sibetrans.com/trans/a152/music-as-torture-music-as-weapon.

Daniels, Roger. 2008. "Words Do Matter: A Note on Inappropriate Terminology and the Incarceration of the Japanese Americans—Part 1 of 5." *Discover Nikkei: Japanese Migrants and Their Descendants* (blog). February 1, 2008. http://www.discovernikkei.org/en/journal/2008/2/1/words-do-matter/.

Dave, Shilpa, Leilani Nishime, Tasha G. Oren, and Robert G. Lee, eds. 2005. *East Main Street: Asian American Popular Culture.* New York: New York University Press.

Davidson, Michael. 2008. "On the Outskirts of Form: Cosmopoetics in the Shadow of NAFTA." *Textual Practice* 22 (4): 733–56. https://doi.org/10.1080/09502360802457475.

De Ferranti, Hugh. 2000. *Japanese Musical Instruments.* Images of Asia. New York: Oxford University Press.

DeFrantz, Thomas. 2005. "Composite Bodies of Dance: The Repertory of the Alvin Ailey American Dance Theater." *Theatre Journal* 57 (4): 659–78.

Deleuze, Gilles, and Félix Guattari. 1987. *A Thousand Plateaus: Capitalism and Schizophrenia.* Translated by Brian Massumi. Minneapolis: University of Minnesota Press.

Denzin, Norman K. 2003. *Performance Ethnography: Critical Pedagogy and the Politics of Culture.* Thousand Oaks, Calif.: Sage.

Dicks, Bella, and Bruce Mason. 1998. "Hypermedia and Ethnography: Reflections on the Construction of a Research Approach." *Sociological Research Online* 3 (3). https://doi.org/10.5153/sro.179.

Doi, Joanne. 2003. "Tule Lake Pilgrimage: Dissonant Memories, Sacred Journey." In *Revealing the Sacred in Asian and Pacific America,* edited by Jane Iwamura and Paul Spickard, 273–89. New York: Routledge.

Dong, Arthur E., dir. 2002. *Forbidden City U.S.A.* [Ho-Ho-Kus, N.J.]: DeepFocus Productions. DVD, 56 min.

———. 2008. *Hollywood Chinese: The Chinese in American Feature Films.* Harriman, N.Y.: DeepFocus Productions.

———. 2014. *Forbidden City U.S.A.: Chinese American Nightclubs, 1936–1970.* Los Angeles, Calif.: DeepFocus Productions.

Dunbar-Hall, Peter. 2009. "Studying Music, Studying the Self: Reflections on Learning Music in Bali." In *Music Autoethnographies: Making Autoethnography Sing / Making Music Personal,* edited by Brydie-Leigh Bartleet and Carolyn Ellis, 153–66. Bowen Hills, Queensland: Australian Academic Press.

Eisenstein, Paul A. 2005. "Mitsu Tries to Eclipse Its Past: Troubled Maker Depending on New Product to Reverse Downfall." *TheCarConnection.Com* (blog). June 20, 2005. Reposted by Swallow Doretti, June 27, 2005, in "The Car Lounge" forum, *VW Vortex: The Volkswagen Enthusiast Website,* https://forums.vwvortex.com/showthread.php?2060480-Mitsu-Tries-to-Eclipse-its-Past&p=21780968.

Elinson, Elaine, and Stan Yogi. 2009. *Wherever There's a Fight: How Runaway Slaves, Suffragists, Immigrants, Strikers, and Poets Shaped Civil Liberties in California.* Berkeley, Calif.: Heyday Books.

Endo, Kenny. 1999. "Yodan Uchi: A Contemporary Composition for Taiko." MA thesis, University of Hawai`i at Manoa.

Eng, David L. 2001. *Racial Castration: Managing Masculinity in Asian America*. Durham, N.C.: Duke University Press.

Erlmann, Veit. 1996. *Nightsong: Performance, Power, and Practice in South Africa*. Chicago: University of Chicago Press.

Esaki, John, dir. 1993. *Maceo: Demon Drummer from East L.A.* San Francisco: National Asian American Telecommunications Association [distributor]. Videocassette (VHS), 44 min.

Feld, Steven. 1982. *Sound and Sentiment: Birds, Weeping, Poetics, and Song in Kaluli Expression*. Philadelphia: University of Pennsylvania Press.

Feng, Peter. 1996. "Redefining Asian American Masculinity: Steven Okazaki's 'American Sons.'" *Cineaste* 22 (3): 27–29.

Fiske, John. 1993. *Power Plays, Power Works*. London: Verso.

Flavin, Philip. 2008. "Sokyoku-Jiuta: Edo-Period Chamber Music." In *The Ashgate Research Companion to Japanese Music*, edited by Alison McQueen Tokita and David W. Hughes, 169–95. Farnham, Surrey: Ashgate.

Foster, Susan Leigh. 2003. "Choreographies of Protest." *Theatre Journal* 55 (3): 395–412.

Frank H. Watase Media Arts Center. 2005. *Big Drum: Taiko in the United States*. Los Angeles: Japanese American National Museum. DVD, approx. 2 hrs.

Freeman, Carla. 2001. "Is Local: Global as Feminine: Masculine? Rethinking the Gender of Globalization." *Signs* 26 (4): 1007–37. https://www.jstor.org/stable/3175355.

Friedman, Thomas L. 2005. *The World Is Flat: A Brief History of the Twenty-First Century*. New York: Farrar, Straus and Giroux.

Fujie, Linda. 2001. "Japanese Taiko Drumming in International Performance: Converging Musical Ideas in the Search for Success on Stage." *World of Music* 43 (2–3): 93–101.

Gamlen, Alan. 2003. "Japanese *Taiko*: Where Does Taiko Come From? Makers in the History of Japanese Drumming." NZASIA Newsletter no. 14, New Zealand Asian Studies Society, August 2003, 2–4.

García Canclini, Néstor. 2014. *Imagined Globalization*. Durham, N.C.: Duke University Press.

Gilroy, Paul. 1993. *The Black Atlantic: Modernity and Double Consciousness*. Cambridge, Mass.: Harvard University Press.

Gonzalves, Theodore S. 2010. *The Day the Dancers Stayed: Performing in the Filipino/American Diaspora*. Philadelphia: Temple University Press.

Gotanda, Philip Kan. 1991. *Yankee Dawg You Die*. New York: Dramatists Play Service.

Greenberg, Karl. 2005. "Mitsubishi Boosts Profile with Gasoline Incentive, New Truck." *Brandweek.com* (blog). 2005. http://www.brandweek.com/bw/news/recent_display.jsp?vnu_content_id=1001219708 (site discontinued).

Greene, Paul D. 2003. "Ordering a Sacred Terrain: Melodic Pathways of Himalayan Flute Pilgrimage." *Ethnomusicology* 47 (2): 205–27.

Groemer, Gerald. 2010. "Sacred Dance at Sensōji." *Asian Ethnology* 69 (2): 265–92.

Grossberg, Lawrence. 2005. "Globalization." In *New Keywords: A Revised Vocabulary of Culture and Society*, edited by Tony Bennett, Grossberg, and Meghan Morris, 146–50. Hoboken, N.J.: Blackwell Publishing.

Hahn, Tomie. 2007. *Sensational Knowledge: Embodying Culture through Japanese Dance.* Music/Culture. Middletown, Conn.: Wesleyan University Press.

Hamera, Judith. 2002. "An Answerability of Memory: 'Saving' Khmer Classical Dance." *TDR / The Drama Review* 46 (4): 65–85.

Hanes, Jeffrey E. 2013. "Aural Osaka: Listening to the Modern City." In *Music, Modernity, and Locality in Pre-war Japan: Osaka and Beyond,* edited by Hugh De Ferranti and Alison Tokita, 27–50. Burlington, Vt.: Ashgate.

Hankins, Joseph D. 2014. *Working Skin: Making Leather, Making a Multicultural Japan.* Berkeley: University of California Press.

Heyman, Stephen. 2010. "Tee Time." *New York Times Magazine,* March 2010, 48.

Hill Collins, Patricia. 1998. *Fighting Words: Black Women and the Search for Justice.* Minneapolis: University of Minnesota Press.

Hirabayashi, Lane Ryo. 2015. "Incarceration." In *Keywords in Asian American Studies,* edited by Cathy J. Schlund-Vials, Linda Trinh Võ, and Kevin Scott Wong, 133–38. New York: New York University Press.

Hoffman, Bryce G. 2005. "Mitsubishi Touts Its Japanese Heritage." *Detroit News,* September 27, 2005.

Hollander, Anne. 1978. *Seeing through Clothes.* New York: Viking.

Holmes, Martha Stoddard, and Tod Chambers. 2005. "Thinking through Pain." *Literature and Medicine* 24 (1): 127–41.

Hongo, Garrett. 2004. "The Mirror Diary." *Georgia Review* 58 (2): 458–70. https://www.jstor.org/stable/41402468.

hooks, bell. 1996. *Bone Black: Memories of Girlhood.* New York: Henry Holt.

Hornbostel, Erich Moritz von, and Curt Sachs. 1961. "Classification of Musical Instruments." Translated by Anthony Baines and Klaus P. Wachsmann. *Galpin Society* 14: 3–29.

Hoskin, Peter. 2015. "How Japan Became a Pop Culture Superpower." *The Spectator,* January 31, 2015. https://www.spectator.co.uk/2015/01/how-japan-became-a-pop-culture-superpower/.

Hosokawa, Shūhei. 1997. "Salsa no tiene frontera: Orquesta de la Luz or the Globalization and Japanization of Afro-Caribbean Music." *Trans—Revista Transcultural de Música / Transcultural Music Review* 3. https://www.sibetrans.com/trans/articulo/266/salsa-no-tiene-frontera-orquesta-de-la-luz-or-the-globalization-and-japanization-of-afro-caribbean-music.

———. 1999. "Strictly Ballroom: The Rumba in Pre–World War Two Japan." *Perfect Beat: The Pacific Journal of Research into Contemporary Music and Popular Culture* 4 (3): 3.

Hu-DeHart, Evelyn. 1999. "Introduction: Asian American Formations in the Age of Globalization." In *Across the Pacific: Asian Americans and Globalization,* edited by Hu-DeHart, 1–28. Philadelphia: Temple University Press.

Igarashi, Kenneth. 1997. "A Post-modern Analysis of Noise: A Musical Genre Incorporating Improvisation and Eclecticism." PhD diss., University of California, Los Angeles.

Itoh, Keiko. 1999. "A Journey to Be a Japanese Drama Therapist: An Exploration of Taiko Drumming as a Therapeutic Resource for Drama Therapy." MA thesis, California Institute of Integral Studies.

Ivy, Marilyn. 1995. *Discourses of the Vanishing: Modernity, Phantasm, Japan.* Chicago: University of Chicago Press.

Izumi, Masumi. 2001. "Reconsidering Ethnic Culture and Community: A Case Study on Japanese Canadian Taiko Drumming." *Journal of Asian American Studies* 4 (1): 35. http://dx.doi.org/10.1353/jaas.2001.0004.

Jain, Sarah Lochlann. 2004. "'Dangerous Instrumentality': The Bystander as Subject in Automobility." *Cultural Anthropology* 19 (1): 61–94. https://doi.org/10.1525/can.2004.19.1.61.

Jeon, Joseph Jonghyun. 2012. *Racial Things, Racial Forms: Objecthood in Avant-Garde Asian American Poetry*. Contemporary North American Poetry Series. Iowa City: University of Iowa Press.

Johnson, Gaye Theresa. 2013. *Spaces of Conflict, Sounds of Solidarity: Music, Race, and Spatial Entitlement in Los Angeles*. Berkeley: University of California Press.

Jones, Andrew F. 2001. *Yellow Music: Media Culture and Colonial Modernity in the Chinese Jazz Age*. Durham, N.C.: Duke University Press.

Jordan, June. 1992. *Technical Difficulties: African-American Notes on the State of the Union*. New York: Pantheon.

Kaplan-Reyes, Alexander. 2009. "A Pillar of Little Tokyo: Uyeda Department Store." *Discover Nikkei: Japanese Migrants and Their Descendants* (blog). May 12, 2009. http://www.discovernikkei.org/en/journal/2009/5/12/lt-community-profiles/.

Kawakami, Barbara F. 1993. *Japanese Immigrant Clothing in Hawaii, 1885–1941*. Honolulu: University of Hawai'i Press.

Keil, Charles. 1994. *Music Grooves: Essays and Dialogues*. Chicago: University of Chicago Press.

Keil, Charles, and Angeliki V. Keil. 1992. *Polka Happiness*. Philadelphia: Temple University Press.

———. 2002. *Bright Balkan Morning: Romani Lives and the Power of Music in Greek Macedonia*. Middletown, Conn.: Wesleyan University Press.

Kelsky, Karen. 1999. "Gender, Modernity, and Eroticized Internationalism in Japan." *Cultural Anthropology* 14 (2): 229–55.

Kim, Sojin. 2014. "Just Dance: Connecting Life, Death, Traditions, and Communities in L.A." *Folklife*, magazine of the Smithsonian Center for Folklife and Cultural Heritage, August 25, 2014. https://folklife.si.edu/talkstory/2014/just-dance-connecting-life-death-traditions-and-communities-in-l-a.

Kim, Sojin, Akira Boch, and Masaki Miyagawa. 2005. *Making American Taiko: Innovating Tradition*. In *Big Drum: Taiko in the United States*. Los Angeles: Japanese American National Museum. DVD, approx. 120 min.

Kinsella, Sharon. 1995. "Cuties in Japan." In *Women, Media, and Consumption in Japan*, edited by Lise Skov and Brian Moeran, 220–54. Honolulu: University of Hawai'i Press.

Kirshenblatt-Gimblett, Barbara. 1998. *Destination Culture: Tourism, Museums, and Heritage*. Berkeley: University of California Press.

———. 2001. "Reflections." In *The Empire of Things: Regimes of Value and Material Culture*, edited by Fred R. Myers, 257–68. Santa Fe, N.M.: School of American Research Press.

Kisliuk, Michelle. 1995. "Response." *Ethnomusicology* 39 (1): 79–80.

Kiyama, Wynn, Masao Kodani, and Nobuko Miyamoto. 2016. *Joy, Remembrance, Death: Obon Music for North America*. Los Angeles: Southern District Dharma School Teachers League.

Knapp, Jessica. 2015. "The T-Shirt." *Canada's History* 95 (3): 16. Available at https://www.canadashistory.ca/explore/arts,-culture-society/the-history-of-the-t-shirt.

Kobayashi, Kim Noriko. 2006. "Tracing the Development of Kumi-Daiko in Canada." MA thesis, University of British Columbia. https://open.library.ubc.ca/cIRcle/collections/ubctheses/831/items/1.0092539.

Kodani, Masao Kakuryu. 1999. *Gathering of Joy: A History of Bon Odori in Mainland America.* Los Angeles: Senshin Buddhist Temple.

———. 2004. Life history interview, by Art Hansen, Sojin Kim, and Yoko Nishimura, December 3, 2004, Senshin Buddhist Temple, Los Angeles. Transcript, Manabi and Sumi Hirasaki National Resource Center, Japanese American National Museum, Los Angeles.

———. 2009. "Lecture Note—Bon Odori and Taiko Tradition in the Japanese American Community by Rev. Mas Kodani." *Cultural News* (Los Angeles), August 18, 2009. https://www.culturalnews.com/?p=5030.

———. 2010a. "Hatsubon and Bon Odori." *Prajna Senshin-ji*, August 2010. http://www.senshintemple.org/prajna/Aug10Prajna.pdf.

———. 2010b. "The Jodo Shinshu Sangha." *Prajna Senshin-ji*, February 2010. http://www.senshintemple.org/prajna/Feb10Prajna.pdf.

———. 2012. "What Bon Odori in America Is Not." *Prajna Senshin-ji*, June 2012. http://www.senshintemple.org/prajna/Jun12Prajna.pdf.

Koestenbaum, Wayne. 1993. *The Queen's Throat: Opera, Homosexuality, and the Mystery of Desire.* New York: Poseidon.

Konagaya, Hideyo. 2007. "Performing the Okinawan Woman in Taiko: Gender, Folklore, and Identity Politics in Modern Japan." PhD diss., University of Pennsylvania.

Kondo, Dorinne. 1990. "'M. Butterfly': Orientalism, Gender, and a Critique of Essentialist Identity." *Cultural Critique* 16: 5–29.

———. 1997. *About Face: Performing Race in Fashion and Theater.* New York: Routledge.

Kun, Josh. 2005. *Audiotopia: Music, Race, and America.* Berkeley: University of California Press.

Kurashige, Lon. 2001. "Resistance, Collaboration, and Manzanar Protest." *Pacific Historical Review* 70 (3): 387–417. https://doi.org/10.1525/phr.2001.70.3.387.

———. 2002. *Japanese American Celebration and Conflict: A History of Ethnic Identity and Festival, 1934–1990.* Berkeley: University of California Press.

Kwon, Susan. 1999. "What's the Story behind All Those Asians in the Import Scene? The Import Racing Phenomenon in the Epicenter of California, USA." *Racing Mix*, January 13, 1999. http://www.racingmix.com/word/import_racing.htm.

Kymlicka, Will. 2013. "Neoliberal Multiculturalism?" In *Social Resilience in the Neoliberal Era*, edited by Peter A. Hall and Michèle Lamont, 99–128. New York: Cambridge University Press.

Lancashire, Terence. 1997. "Music for the Gods: Musical Transmission and Change in Iwami 'Kagura.'" *Asian Music* 29 (1): 87–123. https://doi.org/10.2307/834412.

———. 2001. "'Kagura'—A 'Shinto' Dance? Or Perhaps Not." *Asian Music* 33 (1): 25–59. https://doi.org/10.2307/834231.

———. 2004a. "From Spirit Possession to Ritual Theatre: A Potential Scenario for the Development of Japanese Kagura." *Yearbook for Traditional Music* 36 (January): 90–108.

———. 2004b. "The Kagura Dance: Variation and the Problem of Representation in Iwami Kagura." *World of Music* 46 (2): 47–78.

———. 2011. *An Introduction to Japanese Folk Performing Arts.* SOAS Musicology Series. Farnham, Surrey: Ashgate. http://lib.myilibrary.com/detail.asp?ID=331539.

Le, C. N. 2005. "Import/Sport Compact Racing Scene." *Asian-Nation.* http://www.asian-nation.org/import-racing.shtml.

Lee, Katherine In-Young. 2018. *Dynamic Korea and Rhythmic Form.* Middletown, Conn.: Wesleyan University Press.

Lee, Rachel C. 1999. "Asian American Cultural Production in Asian-Pacific Perspective." *Boundary 2* 26 (2): 231–54.

Lee, Robert G. 1999. *Orientals: Asian Americans in Popular Culture.* Asian American History and Culture. Philadelphia: Temple University Press.

Leong, David. 1999. "Oedo Sukeroku Daiko FAQ." *Rolling Thunder: Your Total Taiko Resource* (blog). March 1, 1999. http://www.taiko.com/taiko_resource/history/oedo_faq.html.

Ling, L. H. M. 1999. "Sex Machine: Global Hypermasculinity and Images of the Asian Woman in Modernity." *Positions: East Asia Critique* 7 (2): 277–306.

Lipsitz, George. 2014. "A New Beginning." *Kalfou: A Journal of Comparative and Relational Ethnic Studies* 1 (1): 7–14. https://doi.org/10.15367/kf.v1i1.7.

Livingston, Jennie, dir. 1990. *Paris Is Burning.* Burbank, Calif.: Miramax Home Entertainment; distributed by Buena Vista Home Entertainment.

Lord, Albert Bates. 1960. *The Singer of Tales.* Cambridge, Mass.: Harvard University Press.

Lorenz, Shanna. 2007. "'Japanese in the Samba': Japanese Brazilian Musical Citizenship, Racial Consciousness, and Transnational Migration." PhD diss., University of Pittsburgh.

Luvaas, Brent Adam. 2012. *DIY Style: Fashion, Music and Global Digital Cultures.* London: Berg.

Lysloff, René T. A. 2003. "Worlding Music Theory." Paper presented at the 48th Annual Meeting of the Society for Ethnomusicology, Miami, October 1–5, 2003.

Ma, Sheng-mei. 2000. *The Deathly Embrace: Orientalism and Asian American Identity.* Minneapolis: University of Minnesota Press.

Magowan, Fiona. 2005. "Playing with Meaning: Perspectives on Culture, Commodification and Contestation around the Didjeridu." *Yearbook for Traditional Music* 37: 80–102.

Malm, William P. 2000. *Traditional Japanese Music and Musical Instruments.* New ed. Tokyo: Kodansha International.

Manbo, Bill T., and Eric L. Muller. 2012. *Colors of Confinement: Rare Kodachrome Photographs of Japanese American Incarceration in World War II.* Chapel Hill: University of North Carolina Press, in association with the Center for Documentary Studies at Duke University.

Mankekar, Purnima, and Louisa Schein. 2012. "Mediations and Transmediations: Erotics, Sociality, and 'Asia.'" In *Media, Erotics, and Transnational Asia,* edited by Mankekar and Schein, 1–31. Durham, N.C.: Duke University Press.

Marcus, George E. 2009. "Notes toward an Ethnographic Memoir of Supervising Graduate Research through Anthropology's Decades of Transformation." In *Fieldwork Is Not What It Used to Be: Learning Anthropology's Method in a Time of Transition,* edited by James D. Faubion and Marcus, 1–34. Ithaca, N.Y.: Cornell University Press.

Mason, Bruce, and Bella Dicks. 2001. "Going Beyond the Code: The Production of Hypermedia Ethnography." *Social Science Computer Review* 19 (4): 445–57. https://doi.org/10.1177/089443930101900404.

Maus, Fred E. 2003. "Using and Delimiting Music Theory." Paper presented at the 48th Annual Meeting of the Society for Ethnomusicology, Miami, October 1–5, 2003.

Mazer, Sharon. 1990. "The Doggie Doggie World of Professional Wrestling." *TDR / The Drama Review* 34 (4): 96–122. https://doi.org/10.2307/1146046.

———. 1998. *Professional Wrestling: Sport and Spectacle.* Jackson: University Press of Mississippi.

McCoy, Karen Kawamoto, and Carolina Yao. 1999. *Bon Odori Dancer.* Chicago: Polychrome.

McGray, Douglas. 2002. "Japan's Gross National Cool." *Foreign Policy,* May 2002.

Mead, Sue. 2005. "2006 Mitsubishi Raider First Drive: The Three-Diamond Marque Hopes to Trump with Its New Truck." Autobytel.com. https://www.autobytel.com/mitsubishi/raider/2006/reviews/2006-mitsubishi-raider-first-drive-748/.

Meintjes, Louise. 2004. "Shoot the Sergeant, Shatter the Mountain: The Production of Masculinity in Zulu Ngoma Song and Dance in Post-apartheid South Africa." *Ethnomusicology Forum* 13 (2): 173–201.

Meizel, Katherine L. 2009. "Making the Dream a Reality (Show): The Celebration of Failure in *American Idol.*" *Popular Music and Society* 32 (4): 475–88. http://dx.doi.org/10.1080/03007760802217725.

Melamed, Jodi. 2006. "The Spirit of Neoliberalism: From Racial Liberalism to Neoliberal Multiculturalism." *Social Text* 24 (4) [89]: 1–24. https://doi.org/10.1215/01642472-2006-009.

Miller, Monica L. 2009. *Slaves to Fashion: Black Dandyism and the Styling of Black Diasporic Identity.* Durham, N.C.: Duke University Press.

Mishima, Yukio. 1968. "Introduction: On Nakedness and Shame." In *Naked Festival: A Photo-Essay,* by Tamotsu Yato, translated by Meredith Weatherby and Sachiko Teshima, 7–15. New York: Walker/Weatherhill.

Mitchell, Tony, ed. 2001. *Global Noise: Rap and Hip-Hop outside the USA.* Music/Culture. Hanover, N.H.: University Press of New England.

———. 2008. "2nd Generation Migrant Expression in Australian Hip Hop." In *Post-colonial Distances: The Study of Popular Music in Canada and Australia,* edited by Beverley Diamond, Denis Crowdy, and Daniel Downes, 47–66. Newcastle: Cambridge Scholars.

Montagu, Jeremy. 2003. "Why Ethno-organology?" *European Meetings in Ethnomusicology* 10 (January): 33–44.

Morinaga, Maki Isaka. 2002. "The Gender of *Onnagata* as the Imitating Imitated: Its Historicity, Performativity, and Involvement in the Circulation of Femininity." *Positions: East Asia Cultures Critique* 10 (2): 245–84.

Morris, Rosalind C. 1994. "*M. Butterfly:* Transvestism and Cultural Cross-dressing in the Critique of Empire." In *Gender and Culture in Literature and Film East and West: Issues of Perception and Interpretation,* edited by Nitaya Masavisut, George Simson, and Larry E. Smith, 40–59. Honolulu: University of Hawai'i Press.

Mosch, Ulrich. 2012. "'I Have Never Tried to Alter the Nature of the Instrument . . .': Luciano Berio's Concept of Musical Instrument in the *Sequenzas.*" Translated by Bradford J. Robinson. In *Luciano Berio: Nuove Prospettive / New Perspectives,* edited by Angela Ida de Benedictis, 65–83. Florence: Olschki.

Moy, James S. 1993. *Marginal Sights: Staging the Chinese in America*. Studies in Theatre History and Culture. Iowa City: University of Iowa.

Mura, David. 1995. *Where the Body Meets Memory: An Odyssey of Race, Sexuality, and Identity*. New York: Anchor.

Murphy, Rosalie. 2014. "Why Your Yoga Class Is So White." *Atlantic*, July 8, 2014. http://www.theatlantic.com/national/archive/2014/07/why-your-yoga-class-is-so-white/374002/.

Nakamura, Tadashi, dir. 2006. *Pilgrimage*. Los Angeles: Center for EthnoCommunications of the UCLA Asian American Studies Center. DVD, 22 min. Available at http://www.tadashinakamura.com/Tadashi_Nakamura/Pilgrimage.html.

Namkung, Victoria. 2004. "Reinventing the Wheel: Import Car Racing in Southern California." In *Asian American Youth: Culture, Identity, and Ethnicity*, edited by Jennifer Lee and Min Zhou, 159–76. New York: Routledge.

Nandy, Ashis. 1988. *The Intimate Enemy: Loss and Recovery of Self under Colonialism*. Delhi: Oxford University Press.

Nash, Pamela, and Kevin Malone. 2000. "One Man's Noise Is Another Man's Music: The Demise of Pitch in Kevin Malone's *Noise Reduction*." *Contemporary Music Review* 19 (4): 105–13.

Neal, Lynn S. 2014. "The Ideal Democratic Apparel: T-shirts, Religious Intolerance, and the Clothing of Democracy." *Material Religion* 10 (2): 182–207. https://doi.org/10.2752/17518 3414X13990269049400.

Newton, Judith, and Judith Stacey. 1995. "Ms. Representations: Reflections on Studying Academic Men." In *Women Writing Culture*, edited by Ruth Behar and Deborah A. Gordon, 287–305. Berkeley: University of California Press.

Niessen, S. A., Ann Marie Leshkowich, and Carla Jones, eds. 2003. *Re-Orienting Fashion: The Globalization of Asian Dress*. Oxford: Berg.

Novak, David. 2010. "Listening to Kamagasaki." *Anthropology News* 51 (9): 5.

———. 2013. *Japanoise: Music at the Edge of Circulation*. Durham, N.C.: Duke University Press.

Nye, Joseph S., Jr. 2004. *Soft Power: The Means to Success in World Politics*. New York: Public Affairs.

Ochoa Gautier, Ana María. 2014. *Aurality: Listening and Knowledge in Nineteenth-Century Colombia*. Durham, N.C.: Duke University Press.

O'Meara, Caroline Polk. 2013. "Clarity and Order in Sonic Youth's Early Noise Rock." *Journal of Popular Music Studies* 25 (1): 13–30. https://doi.org/10.1111/jpms.12012.

Ongiri, Amy Abugo. 2002. "'He Wanted to Be Just like Bruce Lee': African Americans, Kung Fu Theater and Cultural Exchange at the Margins." *Journal of Asian American Studies* 5 (1): 31–40. https://doi.org/10.1353/jaas.2002.0009.

Onishi, Katsumi. 1938. "'Bon' and 'Bon-Odori' in Hawai'i." *Social Process in Hawai'i* 4: 49–57.

Otsuka, Chie. 1997. "Learning Taiko in America." MA thesis, University of Tsukuba.

Pachter, Benjamin. 2013. "*Wadaiko* in Japan and the United States: The Intercultural History of a Musical Genre." PhD diss., University of Pittsburgh.

Palumbo-Liu, David. 1999. *Asian/American: Historical Crossings of a Racial Frontier*. Stanford: Stanford University Press.

Panalaks, Miyako Saito. 2001. "The Ma of Taiko." MA thesis, Dalhousie University.

Philippi, Donald L., trans. 1969. *Kojiki*. Princeton: Princeton University Press; Tokyo: University of Tokyo Press.

Pink, Sarah. 2013. *Doing Visual Ethnography*. 3rd ed. London: Sage.

Plath, David W. 1970. Review of *Naked Festival: A Photo-Essay*, by Tamotsu Yato. *American Anthropologist*, n.s., 72 (2): 396.

Powell, Kimberly. 2003. "Learning Together: Practice, Pleasure and Identity in a Taiko Drumming World." PhD diss., Stanford University.

——. 2004. "The Apprenticeship of Embodied Knowledge in a Taiko Drumming Ensemble." In *Knowing Bodies, Moving Minds: Towards Embodied Teaching and Learning*, edited by Liora Bresler, 183–95. Dordrecht: Kluwer Academic.

——. 2005. "The Ensemble Art of the Solo: The Social and Cultural Construction of Artistic Practice and Identity in a Japanese Taiko Ensemble." *Arts and Learning Research* 21 (1): 273–95.

——. 2008. "Drumming against the Quiet: The Sounds of Asian American Identity in an Amorphous Landscape." *Qualitative Inquiry* 14 (6): 901–25.

——. 2012a. "Composing Sound Identity in Taiko Drumming." *Anthropology and Education Quarterly* 43 (1): 101–19. https://doi.org/10.1111/j.1548-1492.2011.01159.x.

——. 2012b. "The Drum in the Dojo: Re-sounding Embodied Experience in Taiko Drumming." In *Thinking Comprehensively about Education: Spaces of Educative Possibility and Their Implications for Public Policy*, edited by E. Dixon-Roman and E. Gordon, 123–40. New York: Routledge.

——. 2012c. "A Pedagogy of Embodiment: The Aesthetic Practice of Holistic Education in a Taiko Drumming Ensemble." In *The Heart of Art Education: Holistic Approaches to Creativity, Integration, and Transformation*, edited by Laurel H. Campbell and Seymour Simmons III, 113–23. Reston, Va.: National Art Education Association.

Prashad, Vijay. 2001. *Everybody Was Kung Fu Fighting: Afro-Asian Connections and the Myth of Cultural Purity*. Boston: Beacon.

Pulido, Laura. 2006. *Black, Brown, Yellow and Left: Radical Activism in Los Angeles*. Berkeley: University of California Press.

Rahaim, Matthew. 2012. *Musicking Bodies: Gesture and Voice in Hindustani Music*. Middletown, Conn.: Wesleyan University Press.

Rasmussen, Anne K. 2004. "Bilateral Negotiations in Bimusicality: Insiders, Outsiders, and the 'Real Version' in Middle Eastern Music Performance." In *Performing Ethnomusicology: Teaching and Representation in World Music Ensembles*, edited by Ted Solis, 215–28. Berkeley: University of California Press.

Reily, Suzel Ana. 2003. "Ethnomusicology and the Internet." *Yearbook for Traditional Music* 35: 187–92. https://doi.org/10.2307/4149330.

Rense, Rip, and Annie Chuck. 2006. "Why We Dance at Obon." West Los Angeles Buddhist Temple. http://westlosangelesbuddhisttemple.org/activities/obonfestival.

Rice, Timothy. 2008. "Toward a Mediation of Field Methods and Field Experience in Ethnomusicology." In *Shadows in the Field: New Perspectives for Fieldwork in Ethnomusicology*, edited by Gregory F. Barz and Timothy J. Cooley, 2nd ed., 42–61. New York: Oxford University Press.

Rinder, Irwin D. 1965. "A Note on Humor as an Index of Minority Group Morale." *Phylon* 26 (2): 117–21.

Rivoli, Pietra. 2005. *The Travels of a T-shirt in the Global Economy: An Economist Examines the Markets, Power and Politics of World Trade.* Hoboken, N.J.: John Wiley and Sons.

Robertson, Jennifer. 1998. *Takarazuka: Sexual Politics and Popular Culture in Modern Japan.* Berkeley: University of California Press.

Robin, William. 2014. "Great Divide at the Concert Hall: Black Composers Discuss the Role of Race." *New York Times,* August 8, 2014. http://www.nytimes.com/2014/08/10/arts/music/black-composers-discuss-the-role-of-race.html.

Roseman, Marina. 1984. "The Social Structuring of Sound: The Temiar of Peninsular Malaysia." *Ethnomusicology* 28 (3): 411–45.

Roxworthy, Emily. 2008. *The Spectacle of Japanese American Trauma: Racial Performativity and World War II.* Honolulu: University of Hawai`i Press.

———. 2013. "Blackface behind Barbed Wire: Gender and Racial Triangulation in the Japanese American Internment Camps." *TDR / The Drama Review* 57 (2): 123–42. https://doi.org/10.1162/DRAM_a_00264.

———. 2014. "Revitalizing Japanese American Internment: Critical Empathy and Role-Play in the Musical *Allegiance* and the Video Game *Drama in the Delta.*" *Theatre Journal* 66 (1): 93–115. https://doi.org/10.1353/tj.2014.0015.

San Jose Taiko. 1998. *San Jose Taiko.* San Jose: San Jose Taiko. Videocassette (VHS), 60 min.

Scarry, Elaine. 1985. *The Body in Pain: The Making and Unmaking of the World.* New York: Oxford University Press.

Schechner, Richard, and Willa Appel. 1990. *By Means of Performance: Intercultural Studies of Theatre and Ritual.* Cambridge: Cambridge University Press.

Schechner, Richard, and Victor Turner. 1985. *Between Theater and Anthropology.* Philadelphia: University of Pennsylvania Press.

Schippers, Huib, and Catherine Grant, eds. 2016. *Sustainable Futures for Music Cultures: An Ecological Perspective.* New York: Oxford University Press.

Schnell, Scott. 1999. *The Rousing Drum: Ritual Practice in a Japanese Community.* Honolulu: University of Hawai`i Press.

Schröder, Barbara, Karen Kelly, and Ulrike Müller, eds. 2014. *Herstory Inventory: 100 Feminist Drawings by 100 Artists.* Brooklyn: Dancing Foxes.

Schwenkel, Christina. 2009. *The American War in Contemporary Vietnam: Transnational Remembrance and Representation.* Tracking Globalization. Bloomington: Indiana University Press.

Seligman, James, dir. 1985. *Obon: Gathering of Joy.* Video posted by Booking Manager on YouTube, June 20, 2013. https://www.youtube.com/watch?v=ztLTePLzQ60.

Shah, Sonia. 1997. "Introduction: Slaying the Dragon Lady—Toward an Asian American Feminism." In *Slaying the Dragon: Asian American Feminists Breathe Fire,* edited by Shah, xii–xxi. Boston: South End.

Shimakawa, Karen. 2002. *National Abjection: The Asian American Body Onstage.* Durham, N.C.: Duke University Press.

Shinagawa, Larry Hajime, and Gin Yong Pang. 1996. "Asian American Panethnicity and Intermarriage." *Amerasia Journal* 22 (2): 127–52.

Simpson, Kelly. 2012. "Three Waves of Little Tokyo Redevelopment." *Departures* (blog), KCET. August 1, 2012. http://www.kcet.org/socal/departures/little-tokyo/three-waves-of-little-tokyo-redevelopment.html.

Slobin, Mark. 1993. *Subcultural Sounds: Micromusics of the West.* Hanover, N.H.: University Press of New England.

Small, Christopher. 1998. *Musicking: The Meanings of Performing and Listening.* Hanover, N.H.: University Press of New England.

Smith, Barbara Barnard. 1962. "The Bon-Odori in Hawaii and in Japan." *Journal of the International Folk Music Council* 14: 36–39.

Sōhei, Nagasawa. 2011. "The Deity and the Mountain." *Asian Ethnology* 70 (1): 105–18.

Sontag, Susan. 2003. *Regarding the Pain of Others.* New York: Farrar, Straus and Giroux.

Spielvogel, Laura. 2003. *Working Out in Japan: Shaping the Female Body in Tokyo Fitness Clubs.* Durham, N.C.: Duke University Press.

Sterne, Jonathan. 2012. "Quebec's #Casseroles: On Participation, Percussion and Protest." *Sounding Out! The Sound Studies Blog.* June 4, 2012. http://soundstudiesblog.com/2012/06/04/casseroles/.

Stoller, Paul. 1997. *Sensuous Scholarship.* Philadelphia: University of Pennsylvania Press.

Symes, Colin. 1989. "Keeping Abreast with the Times: Towards an Iconography of T-shirts." *Studies in Popular Culture* 12 (1): 87–100.

Szczesny, Joseph. 2005. "Mitsubishi's Woes Keep Building." The Car Connection. February 21, 2005. https://www.thecarconnection.com/tips-article/1006900_mitsubishis-woes-keep-building.

Takahashi, Mutsuro. 1968. "The Japanese Loincloth." In *Naked Festival: A Photo-Essay,* by Tamotsu Yato, translated by Meredith Weatherby and Sachiko Teshima, 149–51. New York: Walker/Weatherhill.

Taylor, Timothy D. 2001. *Strange Sounds: Music, Technology and Culture.* New York: Routledge.

———. 2007. *Beyond Exoticism: Western Music and the World.* Refiguring American Music. Durham, N.C.: Duke University Press.

———. 2016. *Music and Capitalism: A History of the Present.* Chicago: University of Chicago Press.

Terada, Yoshitaka. 2001. "Shifting Identities of Taiko Music in North America." In *Transcending Boundaries: Asian Musics in North America,* edited by Terada, 37–59. Osaka: National Museum of Ethnology.

———, dir. 2005. *Drumming Out a Message: Eisa and the Okinawan Diaspora in Japan.* Osaka: National Museum of Ethnology. DVD, 75 min.

———. 2008. "Angry Drummers and Buraku Identity: The Ikari Taiko Group in Osaka, Japan." In *The Human World and Musical Diversity: Proceedings from the Fourth Meeting of the ICTM Study Group "Music and Minorities" in Varna, Bulgaria, 2006,* edited by Rosemary Statelova, 309–15. Sofia: Bulgarian Academy of Sciences, Institute of Art Studies.

———, dir. 2010. *Angry Drummers: A Taiko Group from Naniwa, Osaka, Japan.* Osaka: National Museum of Ethnology. DVD, 85 min.

———. 2011a. "Rooted as Banyan Trees: Eisā and the Okinawan Diaspora in Japan." In *Ethnomusicological Encounters with Music and Musicians: Essays in Honor of Robert Garfias,* edited by Timothy Rice, 233–48. Farnham, Surrey: Ashgate.

———, dir. 2011b. *Taiko in North America.* Osaka: National Museum of Ethnology. DVD, 15 min.

Titon, Jeff Todd. 1995. "Bi-musicality as a Metaphor." *Journal of American Folklore* 108 (429): 287–97.

———. 2008. "Knowing Fieldwork." In *Shadows in the Field: New Perspectives for Fieldwork in Ethnomusicology,* edited by Gregory F. Barz and Timothy J. Cooley, 2nd ed., 25–41. New York: Oxford University Press.

Tobin, Jeffrey. 2000. "A Question of Balls: Sexual Politics of Argentine Soccer." In *Decomposition: Post-disciplinary Performance,* edited by Sue-Ellen Case, Philip Brett, and Susan Leigh Foster, 111–34. Bloomington: Indiana University Press.

Tsuda, Takeyuki. 2016. *Japanese American Ethnicity: In Search of Heritage and Homeland across Generations.* New York: New York University Press.

Tu, Thuy Linh Nguyen. 2010. *The Beautiful Generation: Asian Americans and the Cultural Economy of Fashion.* Durham, N.C.: Duke University Press.

Turino, Thomas. 2008. *Music as Social Life: The Politics of Participation.* Chicago: University of Chicago Press.

Turner, Victor W. 1986. *The Anthropology of Performance.* New York: PAJ.

Tusler, Mark. 1995. "The Los Angeles Matsuri Taiko: Performance Aesthetics, Teaching Methods, and Compositional Techniques." MA thesis, University of California, Santa Barbara.

———. 2003. "Sounds and Sights of Power: Ensemble Taiko Drumming (*Kumi Daiko*) Pedagogy in California and the Conceptualization of Power." PhD diss., University of California, Santa Barbara.

Van Zile, Judy. 1982. *The Japanese Bon Dance in Hawaii.* Kalilua, Hawai`i: Pacifica.

Varian, Heidi. 2013. *The Way of Taiko.* 2nd ed. Berkeley: Stone Bridge.

Visweswaran, Kamala. 1994. *Fictions of Feminist Ethnography.* Minneapolis: University of Minnesota Press.

Viviano, Anna Marie. 2013. "Made in Japan: Kumi-Daiko as a New Art Form." DMA thesis, University of South Carolina.

Vogel, Brian. 2009. "Transmission and Performance of Taiko in Edo Bayashi, Hachijo, and Modern Kumi-Daiko Styles." DMA thesis, Rice University.

Walker, Kate. 2016. "Taiko in the USA and Canada: Key Findings from the Taiko Census 2016." Taiko Community Alliance. https://taikocommunityalliance.org/wp-content/uploads/TCA_Census2016_NorthAmerica.pdf.

Wang, Oliver. 2015. Review of *The Making of Asian America: A History,* by Erika Lee. *New York Times Book Review,* September 6, 2015.

———. 2018. "From Internment Camps to Souped-Up Chevys: The Rise of Nikkei Car Clubs." Interview by Sasha Khokha for *The California Report,* KQED. April 17, 2018. https://www.kqed.org/news/11662128/from-internment-camps-to-souped-up-chevys-the-rise-of-nikkei-car-clubs.

Waseda, Minako. 2000. "Japanese American Musical Culture in Southern California: Its Formation and Transformation in the 20th Century." PhD diss., University of California, Santa Barbara.

Wei, William. 1993. *The Asian American Movement.* Asian American History and Literature Series. Philadelphia: Temple University Press.

Westerbeck, Colin. 2007. "Photo Synthesis." *West Magazine,* March 11, 2007. Available at http://www.luminous-lint.com/app/blob/Colin__Westerbeck_01/10/.

Williams, Jay McKay. 2013. "Cultural Performance: The Personal and Collective Negotiation of Ethnic Identity through Powwow and Taiko Drumming in Chicago." PhD diss., University of Chicago.

Wilson, Rob, and Arif Dirlik. 1994. "Introduction: Asia/Pacific as Space of Cultural Production." *Boundary 2* 21 (1): 1–14.

Wissoker, Ken. 2013. "The Future of the Book as a Media Project." *Cinema Journal* 52 (2): 131–37.

Wong, Deborah. 1998. "A Response to Charles Keil." *Ethnomusicology* 42 (2): 317. https://doi.org/10.2307/3113895.

———. 2000. "Taiko and the Asian/American Body: Drums, Rising Sun, and the Question of Gender." *World of Music* 42 (3): 67–78.

———. 2001. *Sounding the Center: History and Aesthetics in Thai Buddhist Performance.* Chicago: University of Chicago Press.

———. 2004. *Speak It Louder: Asian Americans Making Music.* New York: Routledge.

———. 2005. "Noisy Intersection: Ethnicity, Authenticity and Ownership in Asian American Taiko." In *Diasporas and Interculturalism in Asian Performing Arts: Translating Traditions,* edited by Hae-kyung Um, 75–90. London: RoutledgeCurzon.

———. 2006. "Asian American Improvisation in Chicago: Tatsu Aoki and the 'New' Japanese American Taiko." *Critical Studies in Improvisation / Études critiques en improvisation* 1 (3). https://www.criticalimprov.com/index.php/csieci/article/view/50/106.

———. 2008. "Moving: From Performance to Performative Ethnography and Back Again." In *Shadows in the Field: New Perspectives for Fieldwork in Ethnomusicology,* edited by Gregory F. Barz and Timothy J. Cooley, 2nd ed., 76–89. New York: Oxford University Press.

———. 2014. "Sound, Silence, Music: Power." *Ethnomusicology* 58 (2): 347–53. https://doi.org/10.5406/ethnomusicology.58.2.0347.

Yamamoto, Eric K. 2001. *Race, Rights, and Reparation: Law and the Japanese American Internment.* Gaithersburg, Md.: Aspen Law and Business.

Yamamoto, Traise. 1999. *Masking Selves, Making Subjects: Japanese American Women, Identity, and the Body.* Berkeley: University of California Press.

Yano, Christine Reiko. 1984. "Japanese Bon Dance Music in Hawai`i: Continuity, Change, and Variability." MA thesis, University of Hawai`i.

———. 1985. "The Reintegration of Japanese Bon Dance in Hawaii after World War II." *Selected Reports in Ethnomusicology* 6: 151–62.

———. 2002. *Tears of Longing: Nostalgia and the Nation in Japanese Popular Song.* Cambridge, Mass.: Harvard University Asia Center, distributed by Harvard University Press.

Yegenoglu, Meyda. 2003. "Liberal Multiculturalism and the Ethics of Hospitality in the Age of Globalization." *Postmodern Culture* 13 (2). https://muse.jhu.edu/article/41976.

Yoon, Paul Jong-Chul. 1998. "Soh Daiko: Negotiation and Construction of an Asian American Identity." MA thesis, Columbia University.

———. 2009. "Asian Masculinities and Parodic Possibility in Odaiko Solos and Filmic Representations." *Asian Music* 40 (1): 100–130. http://dx.doi.org/10.1353/amu.0.0022.

Yoshida, George. 1997. *Reminiscing in Swingtime: Japanese Americans in American Popular Music, 1925–1960.* San Francisco: National Japanese American Historical Society.

Yuasa, Yasuo. 1993. *The Body, Self-Cultivation, and Ki-Energy.* Translated by Shigenori Nagatomo and Monte S. Hull. Albany: State University of New York Press.

AMERICAN CROSSROADS

Edited by Earl Lewis, George Lipsitz, George Sánchez, Dana Takagi, Laura Briggs, and Nikhil Pal Singh

INDEX

CPSIA information can be obtained
at www.ICGtesting.com
Printed in the USA
LVHW030904160519
617998LV00002B/2